C000213656

The Road To Kabul

The Second Afghan War
1878–1881

THE ROAD
TO KABUL

THE SECOND AFGHAN WAR
1878–1881

by

Brian Robson

SPELLMOUNT
Staplehurst

British Library Cataloguing in Publication Data:
A catalogue record for this book is available
from the British Library

Copyright © Brian Robson 1986, 2003

ISBN 1-86227-196-8

First published in the UK in 1986 by
Arms and Armour Press Limited

This edition published in 2003 by
Spellmount Limited
The Old Rectory
Staplehurst
Kent TN12 0AZ

Tel: 01580 893730
Fax: 01580 893731
E-mail: enquiries@spellmount.com
Website: www.spellmount.com

1 3 5 7 9 8 6 4 2

The right of Brian Robson to be identified
as the author of this work has been asserted by him
in accordance with the Copyright, Designs
and Patents Act 1988

All rights reserved. No part of this publication may be
reproduced, stored in a retrieval system or transmitted in
any form or by any means, electronic, mechanical,
photocopying, recording or otherwise,
without prior permission in writing from
Spellmount Limited, Publishers.

Printed in Great Britain by
T.J. International, Padstow, Cornwall

CONTENTS

MAPS

To my father (France, 1915–1918)
and my brother (Bomber Command, 1942–1945)

' "But what good came of it at last?",
  Quoth Little Peterkin: –
"Why that I cannot tell," said he,
"But 'twas a famous victory." '

Robert Southey, *After Blenheim*

PREFACE

This book owes its origins to Sherlock Holmes.

Re-reading *A Study in Scarlet* some years ago, I came across the reference to Dr Watson's having been wounded at the Battle of Maiwand. I realized that I did not know where Maiwand was or why there had been a battle there, and in an idle moment I decided to find out. The result in due course was an article in the *Army Quarterly* and a growing realization that not only Maiwand but the Second Afghan War as a whole was virtually unknown, even to military historians. There seemed to be a gap to be filled and I decided to fill it.

There were other reasons. I had the honour, as a very young and sadly unperceptive subaltern, to serve in the old Indian Army. The unique quality and ethos of that remarkable institution have been splendidly and lovingly analysed by Philip Mason in *A Matter of Honour*. The present book seeks to illustrate in a small way some of the themes in Mr Mason's book and, incidentally, to repay some of the debt that I owe to the officers and men with whom I served.

Above all, it has seemed curious to me that, while there are books in profusion on such relatively unimportant campaigns as the Zulu War, there is very little indeed on the very much more important subject of the Second Afghan War. Hanna's history is one of the great military histories of our language, but it was written more than seventy years ago and it is in any case somewhat dry and indigestible for modern tastes. Since Hanna, there has been nothing of consequence apart from a very short but able survey by Dr T. A. Heathcote. Even before the Russian invasion of Afghanistan, the time seemed ripe therefore for another attempt at a history of the events of 1878–81.

Inevitably I have amassed a series of debts to people and institutions. I am indebted in the first place to Mr John Andrews, the Chief Librarian, and to his staff, at the Ministry of Defence Central Library, for their unfailing help and interest in locating books and papers; similarly to Mr William Reid, Mr David Smurthwaite and the staff of the National Army Museum for allowing me access to the Roberts and Haines Papers and for supplying most of the photographs. The Indian Office Library provided access to the Lytton Papers and supplied the rest of the photographs. Colonel Russell Anderson, late of the National Defence College, arranged for me to borrow the College's copy of MacGregor's suppressed *Official History*, and the Librarian at the Staff College at Camberley assisted similarly. Mrs Margaret Combe very graciously lent me her family copy of Boyce Albert Combe's letters. Dr T. A. Heathcote, Curator of the Royal Military Academy Collections, brought to my attention the Hogg Papers and kindly arranged for me to borrow them. Lieutenant-General Sir John Chapple lent me his transcript of Eaton Travers' diary. The Council of the Royal United Services Institute has permitted

9

the use of extracts from articles which originally appeared in its Journal, and the Controller of Her Majesty's Stationery Office has given permission to quote from documents which are in the Crown copyright. Among individuals I am grateful for the interest and help of Dr T. A. Heathcote, himself an expert on the period; to Mr William Trousdale of the Smithsonian Institution, Washington, another noted expert; to Mr Anthony Bennell; to the Right Reverend Michael Mann, Dean of Windsor; to Mrs Marilyn Horsfall; Mrs Susan Parton; Miss Jayne Bartlett and to many others too numerous to name.

My wife and daughters have borne with exemplary patience and forebearance the alienation of many hours which I should have spent with them, but which I chose selfishly to spend pursuing an interest which must have seemed to them only slightly less incomprehensible than the medieval preoccupation with the number of angels that could dance on the head of a pin. I hope that they will feel repaid by this book.

At the end of the day, I can only echo the Chorus in Shakespeare's *King Henry V*:

> '. . . I humbly pray them to admit th' excuse
> Of time, of numbers, and due course of things,
> Which cannot in their huge and proper life
> Be here presented.'

Brian Robson,
Hove, 1986

INTRODUCTION

I set out to write a straightforward military history of the old-fashioned kind. Since no campaign can be fully understood except in the context of the political and diplomatic scene in which it is imbedded, it was necessary to sketch, however briefly, the events which led up to, and surrounded, the Second Afghan War. This sketch has turned out rather longer than I had intended, partly because Anglo-Afghan and Anglo-Russian relations in this part of the world are much less familiar to the ordinary reader than events in Europe, and partly because British actions in the war are in many cases literally inexplicable except in terms of the wider political scene. The specialist historians will no doubt find the treatment too simplistic while the average reader may find it too detailed. I can only apologise to both and invite them to skip those parts which disagree with them.

It is easy also to fall into the trap of drawing over-close parallels between the First and Second Afghan Wars. Indeed, it would be foolish to deny that there are some parallels. Both wars were, at one remove, a direct result of the Anglo-Russian rivalry in Central Asia. Both wars had as their immediate object the removal of Russian influence and involved the deposition of an Amir widely, if inaccurately, regarded as anti-British and pro-Russian, and his replacement by a more amenable ally on the throne of Kabul. Both wars may be regarded as the product of a vast miscalculation, the result of which was to produce, paradoxically, the right result from the British point of view. Both resulted in peace for forty years. At a more superficial level, the murder of Cavagnari at Kabul in 1879 parallels that of Burnes and Macnaghten in 1841 – and indeed there is more than a superficial resemblance in character between Burnes and Cavagnari. Both wars were in a military sense old-fashioned wars. As I have suggested elsewhere in this book, the armies which marched into Afghanistan in 1838 and 1878 would not have been entirely unfamiliar to Wellington or to each other, particularly in such things as transport, artillery and supply arrangements.

It is important, however, to grasp the senses in which the two wars were very different. In 1838, the British were not yet masters of India and had no common boundary with Afghanistan. Moreover, the moving edge of the Russian frontier in Asia was still 1,000 miles away from Kabul. For the British, the Sikh power in the Punjab and the still smouldering embers of the Maratha confederacy in Central India were factors which had to be considered at least as anxiously as the growing but still relatively long-range threat of Russian expansion. By 1878, the Sikh Kingdom of the Punjab and the power of the Maratha confederacy were part of history. The British controlled the whole of India which had become the brightest economic jewel of the British Crown. The Mutiny was already twenty years old and although fears of native insurrection were not dead, the British increasingly

11

looked outwards from India for threats to their security. They were concerned to conserve what they owned rather than to expand their possessions. While Russia was still expanding, the British in India were satiated for the time being. Militarily, also, the situation had changed. Despite the superficial backwardness in certain areas, the Anglo-Indian armies were better disciplined, better trained (particularly in frontier warfare), better organized and better equipped than they had been in 1838. The spread of the railway had given them a strategic mobility which they had never before had and the electric telegraph and the heliograph had given them a power of communication hitherto unknown. Colley's oft-quoted remark that with a regiment armed with breech-loaders he could march through Afghanistan was merely a recognition of this increase in military power which was both absolute as well as relative *vis-à-vis* the Afghans. By the late 1870s, the Anglo-Russian rivalry itself was beginning imperceptibly to change. In Europe, some British statesmen had begun to sense that the future enemy might turn out to be the German, rather than the Russian, Empire. In Asia, interest was beginning hesitantly to focus on the northern frontier of India. The Pendjeh crisis of 1885 showed that Afghanistan remained a major area of sensitivity, but only a few years later when British and Russian troops met face to face it was on the Pamirs, not on the Hindu Kush which had preoccupied Lytton and his immediate predecessors.

Some commentators have maintained that what most people call the Second Afghan War was actually two wars, distinguishing between the campaign which ended with the Treaty of Gandamak (1879) and that which started with the massacre of Cavagnari and his colleagues in September 1879. What is now called the Third Afghan War, in 1919, would then presumably become the Fourth Afghan War. I understand the argument but I do not subscribe to it. It seems to me more sensible to regard the period 1878–1881 as a unity, both militarily and politically. Even at the time, people like Roberts and John Lawrence saw that Cavagnari's embassy was likely to be only a step towards a further campaign. The achievement of the ultimate British purpose of installing on the throne of Kabul a ruler dedicated to friendship with the British and willing to accept British direction of his foreign relations was achieved only with the installation of Abdurrahman in August 1880. Most contemporaries regarded it as two campaigns but one war. The Second Afghan War, therefore, it is.

Any book dealing with a subject such as this runs into the problem of the spelling of Oriental names. Even something as apparently simple as the capital of Afghanistan offers a profusion of spellings – Cabool, Caubul, Kabul, Qabul, etc. Much the same difficulty arises with the name of the Prophet – Mahomed, Muhammud, Mahomet, Mohammad; the choice is almost endless. Ignoring the savants, I have used as a working rule those spellings which are the most familiar to English eyes – thus Kandahar rather than Quandahar, and Abdurrahman rather than Abd-ur-Rahman. The only exception is where I have quoted directly from contemporary documents.

A word is necessary about sources. The Victorians were marvellous people for publishing contemporary official documents, at a time when the typewriter was a novelty, type had to be set by hand, and the great majority of letters were still written in manuscript. They put modern governments to shame. The historian of the Second Afghan War is therefore well off in terms of official reports, dispatches, telegraphs and minutes, contained in innumerable Parliamentary papers and in the products of the Government printing presses at Simla and Calcutta. The mass of official material is backed up by a large amount of contemporary newspaper material. Very few newspapers had professional war correspondents in the theatre, but most of them employed officers to act as part-time correspondents with the various field forces. Compared with some lesser campaigns such as the Zulu War, there is, however, a marked shortage of personal accounts by officers and men taking part. Among the private soldiers, the shortage is all but total, and what there is is largely worthless. But the biggest gap of all is on the Afghan side. The invasion of Afghanistan in 1979 has made it virtually impossible to gain access to whatever contemporary Afghan material there may be. I am acutely conscious therefore that my account is inevitably one-sided although I have tried to do justice to the Afghan point of view whenever it has been possible to discover it. I have tried consciously to bear in mind the fact that in war, courage and folly, ineptitude and suffering are the monopolies of neither side. Nor are their effects limited only to the fighting men.

When this book was first published in 1986 the nightmare which had haunted the British throughout the 19th century had become a reality and the Russians were occupying Afghanistan. One newspaper headline summed it up pithily: 'The Great Game is over and the Russians have won'. They held securely the main centres of population and the main lines of communication and it seemed possible that modern technology, notably the helicopter, would enable them to establish a secure protectorate. What was clear was that the object of the invasion was basically the same as that which had set the British columns in motion in November 1878. The motives were pragmatic, not ideological, Tsarist rather than Communist. What perhaps no one foresaw was that, despite the apparent strength of the Soviet Union, it would be forced to withdraw because it could not absorb the pressure of its casualties.

The wheel of Afghan history turns and it is now the turn of the Americans to invade Afghanistan, topple the legitimate government and install one more to its liking. Will they be any more successful than their imperial predecessors? The events of 1878-81 offer some clues.

CHAPTER 1

THE LAND AND THE PEOPLE

'India is like a fortress with a vast moat of the sea on two of her faces and with mountains for her walls on the remainder. But beyond those walls, which are sometimes of by no means insuperable height and admit of being easily penetrable, extends a glacis of varying breadth and dimensions. We do not want to occupy it but we also cannot afford to see it occupied by our foes.'

Curzon

From the huge, tangled knot of the Pamirs two great mountain walls diverge south-east and south-west to provide a vast natural fortification across the base of the Indian peninsula. The eastern wall, formed by the Karakorum and the Himalayas, runs for some 1,900 miles in a curve to the east until it comes to a sudden halt in the great bend of the Brahmaputra. It divides India from Tibet and China and throughout the nineteenth century it provided a totally secure boundary. In consequence, British strategic attention focused almost exclusively on the north-western frontier between India and Afghanistan and on the frontier which began to emerge at the end of the century between India and Russia south of the Pamirs.

The western wall is formed by the tangled ridges of the Hindu Kush,* which run for some 600 miles, gradually descending until they disappear on the Persian border. The Hindu Kush is not a single, narrow chain of mountains but rather a series of ridges sometimes parallel, sometimes diverging and occasionally throwing out spur ranges at almost right angles. The Eastern Hindu Kush includes peaks of over 21,000 feet and passes ranging up to 15,000 feet in height. While not totally inaccessible,† the mountains provide no easy access northwards from Afghanistan into Central Asia. Over the centuries, the valleys nestling under the southern face became the last refuge of ancient tribes displaced by successive waves of Central Asian invaders flooding into Northern India and by the ruthless proselytising of Islam. It is in that remote region, known then as Kafiristan (from 'Kafir', the Arabic word for infidel or unbeliever), but since 1895 as Nuristan ('Land of Enlightenment'), that Kipling chose to set one of the finest of his short stories, *The Man Who Would be King.*‡ In 1878, the majority of the area was totally unexplored by Europeans.

At the Anjuman Pass, the Eastern Hindu Kush merges into the Central Hindu Kush. Although still high by European standards, with peaks of over 16,000 feet,

---

*Hindu Kush means 'dead Hindu'; it may refer to some long-forgotten disaster to a Hindu army attempting to invade Turkestan, or alternatively to the export of Hindu slaves to Central Asia.
†For a highly amusing account of a journey in this area see Eric Newby's *A Short Walk in the Hindu Kush*, London, 1958.
‡The inhabitants were forcibly converted to Islam by Abdurrahman who decreed that the name be changed to Nuristan.

15

the Central Hindu Kush has a number of practicable passes giving access north-wards into Afghan Turkestan. Where the Eastern Hindu Kush is essentially a cold desert highland with little or no vegetation, the mountains of the Central Hindu Kush are forested and contain upland valleys of great fertility. One observer thought that the valleys had a very Scottish look about them, resembling the higher Grampians.

The Central Hindu Kush is continued westwards by the Koh-i-Baba which finally divides into a series of diverging ranges – the Band-i-Turkestan, the Band-i-Baba (or Paropamisus) and the Band-i-Bayan.

The Eastern Hindu Kush also throws out a series of southward trending ridges which are continued southwards by way of the Safed Koh, the hills of Waziristan and the Suleiman range of Baluchistan, finally to die away in the coastal ranges of the Mekran coast. Together these provide a continuous natural barrier between India and Afghanistan. Over most of its length, this north–south barrier is paralleled by the Indus which acts virtually as a moat to the fortress wall beyond. East of the Indus lie the settled areas: to the west, the tribal territories which in the nineteenth century were subject to only a rudimentary form of administrative rule on the British side and to virtually no rule at all on the Afghan side. Indeed, the very boundary between the two countries in this area (the so-called Durand Line) was not defined until 1893.

The Hindu Kush and associated ranges, which occupy some 60 per cent of the area of modern Afghanistan, divide the country into three main regions. North of the mountains, the plains of Afghan Turkestan slope down gradually until they merge imperceptibly into the steppes of Central Asia which in turn extend northwards to Siberia. The eastern half of these plains is bounded on its northern edge by the River Amu Darya, the classical Oxus, which at this point forms the boundary between Afghanistan and Russia. The soil here is fertile apart from a sandy strip along the Amu Darya, and, with water for irrigation abundantly available, this has always been a rich food-producing area. The western half of the northern plains is more sandy, less fertile, a region of rolling downs composed partly of soil washed down from the mountains and partly of sand blown off the Kara Kum desert—covered in grass and flowers in spring and summer, bare and wind-blasted in winter.

South of the Hindu Kush, the third main region, the South West plateau, occupies about one quarter of the whole country. Bounded on the north by the Hindu Kush, on the east by the ranges which divide Afghanistan from India and on the south by the coastal ranges of Baluchistan, this region is essentially a con-tinuation of the great central Iranian plateau. Lying at an average height of some 3,000 feet, it consists of a series of so-called deserts – the Registan, the Dasht-i-Margo, the Khash – open, undulating plains of sand, varied by patches of gravel and intersected at intervals by low ridges and isolated peaks. It is hot and dusty in summer, cold and windy in winter. Throughout the summer months, a north-westerly wind, 'the wind of 120 days', blows, bringing drought and sandstorms, accompanied by great heat. But although often referred to as desert ('dasht'), it is not true desert in the sense that nothing grows there. On the contrary, Holdich says of it that 'there is a fairly constant vegetation of scrub – chiefly wormwood – and the profusion of low-growing plants and flowers which appear after the spring

16

rains in this wind-swept region entirely belie the appellation of desert. The "dasht" is never entirely devoid of vegetation.'[1] In the south-west corner, on the borders of Afghanistan and Persia, lies the Seistan depression, the centre of a rich and flourishing civilization until Timur the Lame destroyed the irrigation system of the River Helmund on which it depended.

Altitude plays a major part in dictating the temperature and the length of the winter. Around Kabul, the snow lies thick for two or three months in the winter – the average temperature in January is only 27° Fahrenheit and temperatures below −20° Fahrenheit have been recorded. Spring comes quickly and by March temperatures can reach over 80° Fahrenheit, accompanied by sharp frosts at night. Summer temperatures are fierce – in the summer of 1880, troops at Jalalabad recorded temperatures of 110° Fahrenheit in the shade. Short, furious dust-storms

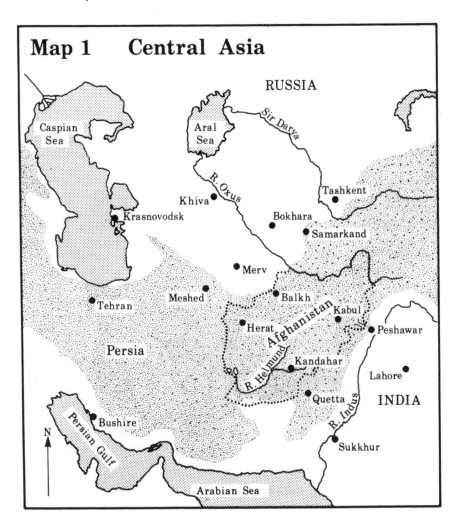

Map 1   Central Asia

are common in the afternoons. Around Kandahar, the winters are milder with snow lying only on the peaks of the hills. In summer, the hot west winds blowing off the surrounding deserts bring frequent dust-storms, and temperatures in June, July and August reach 115° Fahrenheit. Outside the mountain areas, rainfall throughout Afghanistan averages less than ten inches a year – in 1879–80, Kandahar had no rain for ten months.

Although there are areas of fertility in Afghanistan, the country as a whole is harsh and bleak. The approaches from India in particular traverse country which is uniformly dusty and bare, dominated by great rocky hills pierced by narrow defiles in which a handful of determined men might hold up an army and where every convoy invited an ambush. To the ordinary soldier in the nineteenth century, Afghanistan represented heat and dust and stones, varied by piercing winds and snow. In winter, men froze; in summer they died of heat exhaustion. Like Spain, it was a country where large armies starved and small armies got beaten.

The great mass of the Hindu Kush and its associated ranges, cutting diagonally across the country, determines the main approach routes to India from the west. From Central Asia, two obvious routes present themselves. The first crosses the Hindu Kush north of Kabul and then strikes eastwards through the Khyber Pass to Peshawar and the Punjab. The second route passes round the western end of the Hindu Kush via Herat and then strikes south-east across the South West Plateau to Kandahar and then down the Bolan Pass into Sind. This is also the obvious route for an invader from Persia. One or other of these routes has been followed by virtually all of the great invasions of India, from Alexander to Nadir Shah. There are other routes. Alexander himself appears to have avoided the Khyber Pass by following a route north of the River Kabul through Bajaur and Swat.[2] From Kabul another route runs south-eastwards through the Shutagardan Pass and then down the Kurram valley to Thal and Kohat; this was the route followed in reverse by Roberts in 1878–9. From Ghazni an ancient caravan route follows the valley of the Gomal river through the Suleiman Mountains to emerge on the Indus at Dera Ismail Khan. From Persia, invaders could use a third route – that along the Arabian Sea coast, emerging at Karachi. The disadvantage of this route is that it traverses barren, inhospitable country and an army using it needs to be supplied from the sea. Alexander's army attempted this route on its way back from India in 325 BC, and the Arab invader Muhammad Kasim used it *c.*, AD 720, but by the nineteenth century it had ceased to be a serious strategic avenue to India.

In the 1890s, the Indian authorities under Curzon became obsessed by the possibility of a Russian invasion via Seistan and thence along the southern edge of the South West plateau, linking up with the Bolan Pass route south of Quetta. This was a route which had been followed by trading caravans in ancient times, but which had largely fallen into disuse with the decline in prosperity of Seistan. But it was a barren, waterless route and it was clear that large forces could be transported and supplied only by rail. At Army Headquarters in India, vast amounts of energy were expended on calculating the speed with which Russia could extend its railway lines across eastern Persia to Seistan and then to India, and, *per contra*, the relative speed with which the Indian Government could extend its railways to Seistan to block a Russian invading force. In retrospect, it can now

be seen that the threat was illusory. Nevertheless, as part of the general strengthening of frontier defences which took place under Curzon, a single-track railway
along this route was commenced in 1905. By 1914, only some 83 miles of track, as
far as Nushki, had been completed, but British operations in East Persia led to its
being extended as far as the Persian border in 1917. It was then used to supply a
small force, the East Persian Cordon, which throughout the war kept watch
against German and Turkish attempts to infiltrate Afghanistan and India.[3] In
1878, however, the Seistan route was of no significance, fanciful or otherwise.

During the second half of the nineteenth century, fears began to arise in India
about the possibility of a Russian invasion from the north, via the Pamirs.[4] Lytton
stated the case plainly: 'the natural boundary of India is formed by the conver-
gence of the great mountain ranges of the Himalayas and of the Hindu Kush . . . If
a strong, independent and hostile power were established on the north of these
mountains, the passes might become lines of a demonstration . . . which might at
least be useful as a diversion to facilitate and support the flank of more serious
operations in Afghanistan'.[5]

Lytton had put his finger on two important points: first, that the passes into
India from the Pamirs could not be the avenue of approach of a major force but
that, second, they did have a potential value in outflanking and distracting British
forces deployed to meet an invasion via Kabul and the Khyber or involved in a
counter-invasion of Afghanistan. The agitation over the Pamirs route was initially
stimulated by Biddulph's reconnaissance in 1874 which appeared to show that a
relatively easy route existed into Chitral via the Baroghil Pass. It was not until
1886 that Lockhart was able to state, as a result of his exploration, that the
Baroghil did not provide an easy access and that the only pass of strategic importance was the Dora Pass, which provided a route from Turkestan via the Eastern
Hindu Kush into Chitral and thence, via the Malakand Pass, into India north of
Peshawar. Nevertheless, the agitation about the northern passes persisted until
the 1895 Anglo-Russian Agreement on the Pamirs, by which time it had become
abundantly clear that no serious invasion of India was possible that way.

The topography of Afghanistan determines the location and importance of its
three chief cities – Herat, Kabul and Kandahar. The peculiar significance of Herat
lies in its position at the western end of the Hindu Kush, on the border of Persia.*
Lying in a fertile area watered by the Hari Rud, it commanded the main gateway
into Afghanistan from Persia and one of the two main entrances from Central Asia.
By taking the road via Herat, invaders were spared the prospect of crossing the
Hindu Kush, while the city itself and the surrounding district offered abundant
food and fodder. From time immemorial Herat had thus been a major strategic
objective. Its ownership had changed hands on numerous occasions. Its strategic
importance was a matter of profound concern to the Government of India; Persia
and Russia were equally well aware of its potentialities as a means of exerting
pressure on each other and on the British.

Kabul derives its importance from being at the confluence of two major lines of
communication, that across the Hindu Kush into Turkestan and Central Asia, the

---

*Herat is the classical Areia, Alexander's city of Alexandria–Ariana, deriving its name from Aryan
invaders *en route* to India.

second through the mountains to Peshawar and the plains of Northern India. A third route runs south-westward across relatively easy terrain, through Ghazni, to Kandahar which in turn dominates the second main route into India via the Bolan Pass. Apart from its importance as a communications centre, Kabul lies on the edge of an agricultural plain capable of sustaining substantial forces.

In much the same way, Kandahar stands also at the meeting-point of two main strategic routes – from Herat to Kabul and from Herat to the Bolan Pass and

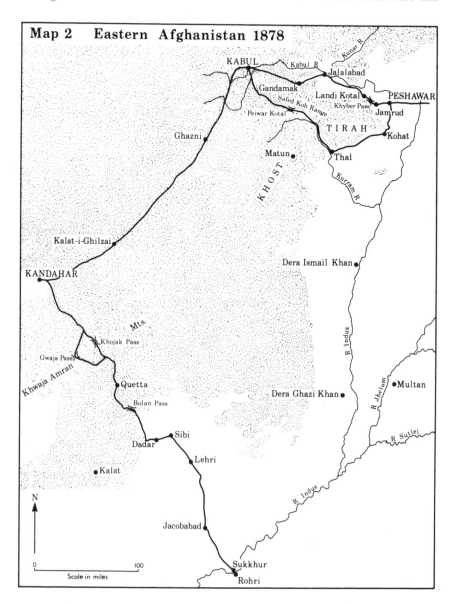

Map 2   Eastern Afghanistan 1878

Sind.* The city itself lies in the fertile valley of the River Argandab, surrounded by orchards.

Kabul, Kandahar and Herat are linked by a road which forms the major communications artery of the country. Beyond Herat the road turns north and then along the north face of the central mountain chain, and finally completes the circle by turning south to Kabul. In 1878, Mazar-i-Sharif had already replaced the very ancient city of Balkh (now Wazirabad) as the chief town of Afghan Turkestan.

Against this general background, it was not difficult for the rulers of nineteenth-century India to conclude that in the north-west the true defence line of India lay along the crest of the Hindu Kush. The further forward the Russian thrusts could be met, the safer India would be. Conversely, if the Russians were allowed to reach Kabul or Kandahar and link up with the frontier tribes, the British hold on India would be seriously at risk. As we shall see, there was a flaw in the reasoning but within it lay the genesis of both the First and Second Afghan Wars.

Afghanistan means literally the land of the Afghans. Their origins are complex and in some respects still uncertain: in consequence, a good deal of mythology remains – for example, their identification with the lost ten tribes of Israel.[6] The actual word 'Afghan' makes its first recognizable appearance in a Sassanian inscription of the third century AD.[7] The use of the term 'Afghanistan' to describe the geographical area is very largely a nineteenth-century development. Strictly speaking, 'Afghan' covers not merely those peoples living within the boundaries of Afghanistan, but also the Pathans of India from Swat to Waziristan. Apart from these tribes the Afghans remain divided between two great confederations of tribes, the Duranis and the Ghilzais. Originally known as the Abdalis, the Duranis rose to power in the middle of the eighteenth century under Ahmad Shah, of the Sadozai line, who seized control of Afghanistan in 1747 on the death of the Persian emperor, Nadir Shah. In the following year, Ahmad Shah took the title Dur-i-Duran (Pearl of Pearls), and the throne name of Ahmad Shah Durani; in consequence, the Abdalis took the name of Durani. The Sadozai line of the Popalzai clan of Duranis ruled in Kabul from 1747 until 1818, but from 1826 the Mohammadzai line of the Barakzai clan ruled. In 1878, as now, the heartland of the Duranis lay in the south-western part of Afghanistan from Kandahar westwards to the Persian border. Substantial pockets existed in and around Kabul, Jalalabad and Herat.

Their great rivals, the Ghilzais, had ruled most of southern Afghanistan and Persia in the late seventeenth and early eighteenth centuries until their power was broken by Nadir Shah in 1732. Their heartland is the eastern part of the country, east of the line Kalat-i-Ghilzai – Kabul.† The Ghilzais were pre-eminently a nomadic people, wintering in the plains and moving in summer to the central highlands. Large numbers moved seasonally through the passes into India, trading and grazing their flocks: these comprised the major element of the so-called 'powindahs' (carriers).

Both the Duranis and Ghilzais are closely linked with the tribes on the north-west frontier of India. All speak the same language, albeit in soft (Pashtu) and

---

*The name Kandahar is almost certainly a version of Iskander, the Persian form of Alexander. It is probably the city he founded under the name of Alexandria–Arachosa.

†The Ghilzais appear to have an admixture of Turkish blood and were regarded by the Duranis as not true Afghans. The distinction is a very fine one and both groups can properly be regarded as Afghans *tout court*.

hard (Paktu) forms, and the tribal genealogies provide a common, mythical ancestor from whom Afghans and Pathans are all descended. Sir Olaf Caroe has shown that these genealogies, mythical as they may be, nevertheless correlate with existing relationships and a consciousness of common origins which persist today. A convenient framework of classification lies in the distinction between those who inhabit the plains and open plateaux and those who inhabit the hills and mountains. The former comprise basically the Duranis and Ghilzais and certain tribes such as the Yusufzais who inhabit the Peshawar plain and the valleys to the north; the latter comprise those tribes who live along the great belt of so-called tribal territory which runs from Swat in the north to Pishin and Sibi in the south, straddling as it goes the border between Afghanistan and present-day Pakistan. These hill tribes include those whose names were written in blood on the records of the British and Indian armies over a period of a hundred years – Mohmands, Afridis, Wazirs, Mahsuds, Orakzais, Utman Khel.

Since the main strategic routes between India and Afghanistan lay through this belt of tribal territory, the importance of the racial links between the hill tribes and the Afghans proper was a military factor of the highest importance. Conflict between Britain and Afghanistan was bound to arouse excitement and, ultimately, hostility among the hill tribes in which no doubt an element of opportunism was mixed. By the same token, it was highly probable that a Russian invasion of India, via Afghanistan, would encounter equally fierce opposition from the tribes, although this factor was often overlooked by those who took the Russian threat seriously.

It was a hard land and it bred hard people, whose character has always exercised a fascination for Englishmen. The qualities which the Afghans prize derive partly from the tough physical environment, partly from the influence of Islam – a passionate love of independence, family loyalty and solidarity, physical courage, a highly developed sense of personal honour and hospitality. It is the over-emphasis of those qualities which provides the darker side of the Afghan character. Loyalty to family and clan takes precedence over loyalties to the state, and, with a love of independence, leads to that unreliability and instability which has been such a marked feature of Afghan history. The developed sense of personal honour has as its corollary, the fierce and bloody pursuit of vengeance when that honour is judged to have been damaged. Physical courage finds its expression in aggressiveness and violence. Even the virtue of hospitality is exercised within strict conventions so that the guest of today may easily be the victim of tomorrow if encountered in different circumstances. All of these contradictions come together in the tribal code of Pashtunwali which is essentially based upon the concepts of blood vengeance (Badal), hospitality (Melmastia), and the right of asylum (Nanawatai). They produce a character which Elphinstone described, with a touch of admiration, thus:

'Their vices are revenge, envy, avarice, rapacity and obstinacy: on the other hand, they are fond of liberty, faithful to their friends, kind to their dependents, hospitable, brave, hardy, frugal, laborious and prudent; they are less disposed than the nations in their neighbourhood to falsehood, intrigue and deceit.'[8]

The Duranis and Ghilzais together provided the major part of the population of Afghanistan which, in 1878, numbered about four million. Next in size, if not in political importance, were the Tajiks, speaking a variant of Persian (Farsi) and descended from the Greco-Bactrian populations established originally by Alexander in the region north of the Hindu Kush. Essentially a sedentary people, mainly farmers, artisans or shopkeepers, they were found in large numbers around Herat and Kabul, and along the whole stretch of Afghan Turkestan north of the central Highlands. The third largest ethnic group was the Hazaras, a Persian-speaking people of Turkish or Mongol origin and appearance, inhabiting the central section of the central Highlands, the Hazarajat, west of Kabul.* They are an agricultural people who remained largely independent of Kabul rule until the 1890s. Unlike the Afghans, who are Sunnis, the majority of Hazaras were Shiite Muslims and this contributed to keeping them apart from the dominant Duranis and Ghilzais.† In consequence, they played little direct part in the Anglo-Afghan conflicts, although they used the British presence to pay off some old scores with the Ghilzais.

The fourth element were the nomadic tribes known collectively as Chahar Aimaks. Of mixed origins, including Mongol, they all spoke Persian and were mainly Sunnis. They were widely scattered over the country and presented no cohesive political force.

In addition to these main racial groups, there were a number of smaller groups – Baluchis, Hindus, Jews, the tribes of Kafiristan, the Turki-speaking Uzbegs of the northern plains and Brahuis from Baluchistan. None exerted any significant political influence with the exception of the Kizzilbash (meaning 'red headed' a reference to their headgear rather than hair colour), a small, Persian-speaking group centred on Kabul. Descended originally from Turkoman troops raised by Nadir Shah, himself a Turkoman, they formed the backbone of the Afghan cavalry; being Shiahs and thus opposed on religious grounds to the dominant Afghan tribes, the Kizzilbash provided the Amirs of Kabul with a body of loyal and highly reliable troops. Dost Mohammed's mother was a Kizzilbash and he owed much of his early success to Kizzilbash support.

The political structure of the country was based in part upon the tribal system and partly upon a system of feudal obligations not unlike that of medieval Europe. The tribe was the basic unit, led by a chief (Sirdar) elected for life from among the leading tribal family. It was to him that the individual tribesman owed loyalty rather than to the distant Amir in Kabul. Where the sirdar led, the tribesmen would follow. Hence the persistent instability of Afghan political life. But in many cases the sirdar had received grants of land (jagirs) from the Amir in return for which he owed the Amir service which was normally in the form of providing levies of men whenever the Amir required them. It was in this way that the Amir could call upon very large numbers of tribesmen to assist him in time of war, quite apart from those tribesmen impelled purely by religious or xenophobic emotions to take up arms against an invader. National unity might not exist, but that did not mean

---

*Between 1904 and 1932 Hazaras were enlisted in to a special regiment of the Indian Army, the 106th (later 4th) Hazara Pioneers. They proved excellent, reliable soldiers.
†The schism between Sunnis and Shiahs arose in the first instance from a dispute over the Prophet's successor. Essentially, the Sunnis believe that his successors were to be temporal leaders, chosen by election from the Quresh tribe: the Shiahs believe that the successors to Mohammed were spiritual leaders and that the first was Ali, the Prophet's cousin and son-in-law. But the schism has, over the centuries, acquired a deeper and more complex doctrinal aspect.

that an invader would not face immense forces of spontaneous resistance. Every rock potentially hid a guerrilla.

The importance of Afghanistan and its peoples to India was political and strategic. In normal times, the country exported fruit, hides, some silk and wool, as well as asafoetida, to India, and received, in return, wool and cotton cloth, tea, sugar, indigo and hardware. In 1878, Anglo-Afghan trade probably totalled less than a million sterling; it played no significant part in Anglo-Afghan relations.

NOTES

1. Holdich, T. H. *India*. London, n.d., p. 57.
2. See Sir Olaf Caroe *The Pathans*. London, 1958, map facing p. 43.
3. See the official history *Operations in Persia 1914–1919* by Brigadier-General F. J. Moberly, published by the Historical Section of the Committee of Imperial Defence (n.d.).
4. For a detailed treatment of this subject, see G. J. Alder, *British India's Northern Frontier 1865–95*. London, 1963. For a fictionalized treatment see John Masters' novel *The Lotus and the Wind*. London, 1953.
5. Alder, op. cit., p. 13.
6. The best modern account of Afghan origins is in Caroe, op. cit.
7. Caroe, op. cit., p. 79.
8. Mountstuart Elphinstone, *An Account of the Kingdom of Caubul*. London, 1815, p. 253.

CHAPTER 2

THE LION AND THE TIGER:
ANGLO-AFGHAN RELATIONS UNTIL 1874

The history of modern Afghanistan effectively dates from 1747. In that year, the Persian Emperor, Nadir Shah, whose empire had included Kabul, Kandahar and Herat, was assassinated by his own bodyguard of Kizzilbash. In the resulting confusion, the leader of Nadir's Abdali contingent, Ahmad Khan, took the opportunity to seize Kandahar and have himself proclaimed Shah of all the Afghan territories. A year later, he took the formal title of *Dur-i-Duran* (Pearl of Pearls) and his clan, the Abdalis, took the name of Duranis.

He took advantage of the confusion in Persia after Nadir's death and of the disintegration of the Mogul Empire in India to carve out a new, independent state. In the course of eight invasions of India, he acquired Peshawar, Lahore, Multan and Kashmir. Simultaneously he was pacifying the Afghan tribes and devising a system of administration. When he died in 1773, a unified state of Afghanistan had begun to emerge.*

His successor, Timur Shah, was of a very different stamp, a man of taste and culture, attracted to Persian rather than Afghan manners. He moved his winter capital to Peshawar and his summer capital from Kandahar to Kabul. The factional quarrels which his father had stifled revived under Timur's weak rule. His death in 1793 ushered in a long period of dynastic strife which effectively dissipated much of the power and possessions accumulated by his father.

Timur was initially succeeded by his eldest son, Zaman Shah, who in 1800 was deposed and blinded by his half-brother, the vicious and degenerate Mahmud. Three years later Mahmud in turn was deposed by Zaman's son, Shuja. Six years later, he was the victim of a counter-coup by Mahmud. The true gainers from all this were the Sikhs. Profiting from the chaos in Afghanistan, they had by 1798 seized Rawalpindi, Multan and most of the Punjab, and forced Zaman to make their leader, Ranjit Singh, his viceroy at Lahore.

It was at this point that the British came into contact with Kabul for the first time. As the Mogul empire had decayed, the British had been forced steadily to expand their influence to fill the power vacuum developing in Northern India. In 1798, when he meditated an invasion of India, Zaman summoned the British to help him: '. . . he should consider our not joining his royal standard, and not assisting him in the restoration of Shah Alam and in the total expulsion of the Mahrattas in the light of an act of disobedience and enmity'.[1] The potential threat to the British possessions in Bengal was too obvious to be ignored. The British would have to erect their own barrier against the threat from the west. In 1801 the

---

*The use of the word Afghanistan is a relatively modern custom of convenience. In the 18th and 19th centuries, native contemporaries would have referred simply to the Amir and his territories, or sometimes to 'The Kingdom of Kabul'.

King of Oudh was forced to cede the territory of Rohilkund and the area between the Ganges and Jumna to the East India Company. Two years later, the Company acquired the overlordship of Delhi and Agra, and became the protector of the Mogul Emperor, who lingered on powerless in Delhi.

But as the British stake in India increased, so the British were compelled increasingly to look beyond India. In 1800, a treaty was negotiated with the Shah of Persia which provided mutual security against attacks by the French or Afghans. It was well timed because in the following year Napoleon and the Tsar concluded an alliance to invade India; a Russian army was to move, via the Caspian and Central Asia, across the Hindu Kush into Afghanistan and India, while a French army was to move via Persia and Afghanistan to link up on the Indus. The project collapsed when the Tsar was murdered, but was revived again at Tilsit in 1807: by then a French Army training mission was at work in Persia under General Gardanne who acted also as French Ambassador to the Shah.

Early in 1808, Lord Minto, the Governor-General in India, was instructed to do all in his power to cultivate good relations with all the states to the west and north-west of India, in order to raise a protective barrier to the British possessions. In the course of 1808, therefore, missions were dispatched to Persia, to the Amirs of Sind, to Ranjit Singh at Lahore and to the Amir Shah Shuja.

The mission to Sind was a failure. The envoy, Seton, exceeded his instructions and his treaty was disavowed. A revised treaty of mutual friendship had to be negotiated the following year. John Malcolm's mission to Persia was also a failure. The Shah refused to see him and a mortified Malcolm returned to India to try to persuade Minto to seize the island of Khargh (or Kharakh) in the Persian Gulf in retaliation. But the situation had already been retrieved by an envoy sent direct from London. Sir Harford Jones, an old rival of Malcolm's, was a remarkable, choleric character, with somewhat curious diplomatic methods.* Equipped with rather stronger material inducements than Malcolm, he succeeded in negotiating a preliminary treaty in March 1809. Persia undertook to prevent forces hostile to Britain entering Persia and to assist the British in the event of an Anglo-Afghan war. In return, the British agreed to assist Persia against any European power invading Persia, provided that the Persians were not the aggressors, and to refrain from interfering in any war between Persia and the Afghans, unless invited to mediate. The treaty was subject to a number of alterations before it was ratified in 1814, but even in its preliminary form it succeeded in neutralizing French and Russian interests in Persia.†

Charles Metcalfe was also successful at Lahore. Ranjit Singh, the ruler of the Punjab, by a masterly display of craft and violence had succeeded in establishing within a very few years a powerful, independent Sikh kingdom; as a contemporary

---

*At one interview with the chief Persian minister, Jones lost his temper with that aged gentleman, threatened to beat out his brains, and, finally, in his own words, 'pushed him with a slight degree of violence against the wall which was behind him, kicked over the candles on the floor, left the room in darkness, and rode home without any of the Persians daring to impede my passage'. He took the surname of Brydges in 1826 and appears thus in the Dictionary of National Biography.

†The preamble to the treaty strikes a poetic note absent alas! from the flat, bureaucratic formulae of today's diplomacy: 'Praise be to God, the All-Perfect and All-Sufficient! These happy leaves are a nosegay plucked from the thornless garden of Concord and tied by the hands of the plenipotentiaries of the two great states in the form of a definitive treaty in which the articles of friendship and amity are blended.'

observer noted, 'The whole Punjaub belongs to Runjeet Sing who in 1805 was but one of many chiefs but who, when we passed, had acquired the sovereignty of all the Sikhs in the Punjaub and was assuming the title of King.' Ranjit was too crafty to accept a specific commitment to help the British, but he was prepared to agree to a treaty of perpetual friendship, together with a pledge to limit his activities south of the Sutlej where it bordered on British territory; the British agreed not to interfere north of the Sutlej.

From our point of view, the most significant of the four missions was that of Mountstuart Elphinstone to Shah Shuja. It was the moment when two adversaries, whose destinies were to be closely linked for 140 years, first came face to face. It was the moment when for the first time the British grappled with the mysteries and splendours of the hitherto largely unknown Kingdom of Kabul. Elphinstone himself went only as far as Peshawar where he spent four months negotiating a defensive alliance against any Franco-Russian attempt to invade India. In the end it all went for nothing because Shah Shuja was toppled by Mahmud and Elphinstone had to withdraw to the Punjab where he watched the blind Zaman Shah trailing into exile with the royal harem and treasure. The real gain of Elphinstone's mission was a close, detailed portrait of the Durani kingdom in the last phase of its splendour when it still embraced Kashmir and Peshawar and before it began to crumble in face of internal strife and Sikh aggrandisement. Elphinstone's account of his mission, published only in 1815, is still today well worth reading for the insight it gives into the Afghan character and the nature of Afghan society.

The seventeen years which followed was a period of confused, vicious and bloody intrigue in Afghanistan. When the dust settled, Mahmud retained Herat, Shah Shuja was an exile in India and the rump of what remained of the Afghan empire was in the hands of Dost Mohammed, brother of Mahmud's former chief minister, Fath Khan, whom Mahmud had had murdered in circumstances of revolting cruelty. Dost Mohammed, a Durani of the Barakhzai clan, ruled over a much reduced kingdom; Kandahar was in the hands of his brothers, the outer territories (Sind, Baluchistan and Afghan Turkestan) had thrown off the Afghan yoke altogether and, worst of all, Peshawar and Kashmir had been annexed by the Sikhs.

From 1826 until 1838, Anglo-Afghan relations were to be dominated by three factors: the struggle between the Afghans and Sikhs for Peshawar; the attempts of Shah Shuja to regain his former throne; and the growing perception of a Russian threat to India. The interplay of these factors was to produce the First Afghan War.

It is not necessary here to trace the tortuous events which linked Dost Mohammed, Shah Shuja and the Sikhs during this period. Suffice it to say that at the end Shah Shuja was still in exile, the Sikhs retained Peshawar and the British had made it clear that if forced to opt between the Afghans and the Sikhs, they would support the latter.

In the meantime the perception of a Russian threat had strengthened. At the beginning of the nineteenth century, the Russo-Persian boundary was still north of the Caucasus, along the River Terek. Russian expansionism and Persian weakness made it an unstable frontier, and fighting in 1801 and again in 1812 brought the boundary for the first time south of the Caucasus. Further fighting in 1827–8 resulted in the Russian frontier reaching the River Araxes, roughly the line today, and in Russian control of the Caspian Sea.

The significance of these events – and the implications for the Anglo-Persian Definitivé Treaty of 1814 – had not escaped the attention of British statesmen. Only by claiming that the fighting which broke out in 1827 was the result of Persian aggression had the British been able to avoid coming to the direct aid of Persia. By offering to pay a proportion of the war indemnity due under the Treaty of Turkmanchai, the British Government was able to secure the abandonment of the awkward clauses in the 1814 Treaty. The gain was illusory. The Persians wanted support rather than money. Otherwise, they could have no prospect of avoiding falling under Russian domination and that could lead only to pressure on Herat, recognized now as the gateway to India. Since the Russians now had two complementary lines of advance available – eastwards from the Caspian into Central Asia and the Hindu Kush, and south-eastwards via Herat – it appeared to some worried British statesmen that India faced the prospect of Russian troops on the Indus. 'That Russia will attempt, by influence of conquest, to secure Persia as a road to the Indus, I have the most intimate conviction' wrote Ellenborough, President of the Board of Control of the East India Company, to Wellington, the Prime Minister.*[4] In his diary, Ellenborough expanded upon his anxieties: 'Upon the subject of the invasion of India, my idea is that the thing is not only practicable but easy, unless we determine to act as an Asiatic Power. On the acquisition of Khiva by the Russians we should occupy Lahore and Cabul. It is not on the Indus that an enemy is to be met. If we do not meet him in Cabul, at the foot of the Hindu Koosh or in its passes, we had better remain on the Sutlege. If the Russians once occupy Cabul they may remain there, with the Indus in their front, till they have organised insurrection in our rear and completely equipped their army . . .'[5] Both Ellenborough and Wellington were powerfully influenced in their views by the appearance in 1829 of a book entitled *On the Practicability of a Russian Invasion of India*, by Colonel de Lacy Evans, who argued that the thing was relatively easy.

Events were to show that it was not so, but in 1829 the British knew little about Central Asian geography. Between them, however, de Lacy Evans and Ellenborough had highlighted certain themes which were to recur constantly in British thinking – the belief that Russian expansion in Central Asia must lead to an invasion of India; that the true defences of India lay accordingly on the Hindu Kush and that control of Afghanistan was therefore essential; the importance of Khiva as a touchstone of Russian intentions; and, finally, the fear that Russian influence in Afghanistan would lead to internal disaffection in India. What was not clearly perceived was the link between events in Central Asia and in Europe. Even Wellington believed that it was possible to treat Anglo-Russian relations in the two areas on quite different bases.

The Russians had been moving eastwards into Siberia since the sixteenth century; it was not until the eighteenth century that they began to move south-wards into Central Asia. By 1830, the Russian frontier ran in a huge, undemar-

---

*Pitt's India Act of 1784 placed control of the political and military policy of the East India Company in the hands of a Board of Control appointed by the Government. The President of the Board was, in effect, the Secretary of State for India and, from 1812 at least, invariably a member of the Cabinet.

cated curve from the mouth of the River Ural through Orenburg to Omsk and Semipalatinsk in the east. British statesmen regarded this Russian expansion as unjustified and malign. The Russians saw it as the inevitable consequence when a civilised state met savage, restless tribes with no culture except plunder. As Gortschakov put it in his famous Circular Memorandum of 1864, Russia must either 'abandon the incessant struggle and deliver its frontier over to disorder which renders property, security and civilisation impossible, or it must plunge into the depths of savage countries, where the difficulties and sacrifices to which it is exposed increase with each step in advance'. Thus the Russian phenomenon was no different from that of 'Manifest Destiny' which was pulling the United States of America ever westwards, or the experience of British expansion in India. Some British statesmen were to see it in the same sympathetic light; writing of the native states in India in the 1870s, Sir John Strachey said, 'This chronic state of turbulence and disorder, destructive of ancient landmarks and boundaries, and producing only weakness and disintegration both provokes and invites annexation . . . it was this state of things in India which forced on the extension of the British Empire to the mountains beyond the Indus. It is this state of things, more than the lust of conquest that has extended, in spite of herself, the dominion of Russia in Asia.'*

In 1830, the British and Russians were roughly equidistant from the cities of Central Asia, and the moving edge of the Russian frontier was still a thousand miles from Kabul. It was this fact which directed British attention to the potentiality of the Indus as a trading artery right into the heart of Central Asia. Little was known in detail of its navigation, but it seemed to offer the possibility of shipping cargoes almost to the foot of the Hindu Kush whence it should be an easy step via Kabul to the markets of Bokhara, Samarkand, Khiva and Tashkent. Russian muskets could be checked by the trade goods of Birmingham and Lancashire.

The time seemed ripe to explore the Indus and the attitudes of the two riverain powers, the Amirs of Sind and the Sikhs. The pretext chosen was a gift of horses to the Sikh ruler, in return for a similar gift which Ranjit had made to George IV when Regent some years before. A young political assistant in Kutch, Alexander Burnes, was chosen to make the trip. He reached Lahore in the summer of 1831 and on his way back visited Shah Shuja at Ludhiana. He was welcomed with calculated warmth: 'Had I but my kingdom, how glad I should be to see an Englishman at Cabool and to open the road between Europe and India.'[6] Late in 1831, the second stage of the British plan was put into effect. The Resident in Kutch was instructed to obtain navigation rights for the British on the Indus from the Amirs of Sind, while Burnes was dispatched to Kabul and Bokhara to assess the political and commercial prospects.

There was one snag. On closer acquaintance the Indus proved to be not very suitable for navigation because of its shallowness, its shifting sandbanks and the lack of fuel for steamboats. The dream persisted, however, and Burnes left in January 1832. He reach Kabul in May 1832 where he was enchanted by the city and impressed by Dost Mohammed. He quickly came to believe that the future lay

---

*It is ironic, however, that Russian expansion coincided with the creation of relatively stable states in the southern part of the Central Asian steppes. The most powerful and longest lasting, the Emirate of Bokhara, was founded in 1753, the Khanate of Kokand in 1798 and that of Khiva in 1804.

in an alliance with the Amir. For his part, Dost Mohammed made it clear that there could be no end to his quarrel with the Sikhs unless and until they gave up Peshawar.

From Kabul, Burnes went on to Bokhara. His observations led him to conclude that the ease of navigation on the Oxus meant that the British could never compete in heavy manufactured goods, but that British textiles could successfully compete via the Indus. At the end of 1833, Burnes was back in England, a made man and the lion of London society. But his proposals for an alliance with Dost Mohammed and the establishment of a Commercial Agency at Kabul were quietly shelved.

Two years later, a new Governor-General, Lord Auckland, sailed for India. The external situation he inherited was complex. In the Punjab, Ranjit Singh was ageing, his health sapped by years of debauchery. His kingdom was buttressed by the alliance with the British, but that alliance was coming under strain over the future of Sind. Dost Mohammed plotted the recovery of Pershawar from the Sikhs, and Herat from Mahmud's son, Kamran Mirza; he dreamed still of reconstituting the empire of Ahmad Shah. Some ground had been gained with Persia but Herat remained a trouble-spot. Beyond Persia lay the Russian menace. Auckland's predecessor had put it thus:

> 'It is the interest of Russia to extend and strengthen the Persian Empire, which occupies a central position between the double lines of operation of the Autocrat to eastward and westward, and as Persia can never be a rival of Russia the augmentation of her strength can only increase the offensive means of Russia . . . What the Russian policy might be after taking possession of Herat it is unnecessary now to consider but it is impossible to deny that she might arrive at that point in legitimate support of her ally, the King of Persia, and it is equally difficult to deny that from that point she may proclaim a crusade against British India, in which she could be joined by all the war-like, restless tribes that formed the overwhelming force of Timur.'[7]

Auckland was not at first persuaded of the immediacy of a Russian threat, either direct or via the medium of a Persian attack on Herat. He was not therefore disposed to seek any direct political involvement with Kabul but rather to continue the not yet discredited policy of commercial penetration. He attached a good deal less importance than did the home government to the warnings from British envoys in Teheran about Russian activities in the direction of Herat. But as the months went by and 1837 succeeded 1836, Auckland was increasingly forced to make a decisive judgement about relations with Kabul. The catalyst was the Sikh Kingdom of the Punjab. Put in its simplest form, the dilemma was this. The best defence against a Russian threat to India might be thought to lie in alliance with a strong, united Afghanistan, but the price of that would be a deal with the Sikhs over Peshawar. Tolerance or even encouragement of a weak, disunited Afghanistan, by contrast, might avoid friction with the Sikhs, but it offered no protection against the Russians and actually increased the possible need to interfere directly in the affairs of Kabul. Forced to choose between Dost Mohammed and Ranjit Singh, Auckland had little difficulty in preferring to stick to the latter. But the dilemma remained. One way out of it was obvious – to replace Dost Mohammed.

In the spring of 1837, the dilemma seemed likely to be resolved in another way. Dost Mohammed defeated the Sikhs at Jamrud in the Khyber Pass and stood poised to take over Peshawar. If he had done so, it is probable that the British would have exerted pressure on Ranjit Singh to accept the *fait accompli*. The opportunity passed and a few weeks later the Shah began his move on Herat, seeking Dost Mohammed's help in the enterprise. Burnes, who was now on a commercial mission to Kabul, was instructed to dissuade Dost Mohammed but he was given no effective cards to play. The most that Auckland was prepared to offer was an intercession with the Sikhs to allow Peshawar to be held by a member of the Barakzai clan as a vassal of Ranjit Singh. Even that was sabotaged by Auckland's envoy at Lahore, Captain Wade, who was violently pro-Sikh and anti-Afghan. The balance tilted permanently against Burnes with the arrival in Kabul of a Russian envoy, Vitkevich. Despairing of British support, the Amir began to turn increasingly to the Persians and Russians. Burnes left Kabul in the spring of 1838, deeply grieving that Auckland had not found it possible to support Dost Mohammed: 'He is a man of undoubted ability and has at heart high opinions of the British nation; and if half you must do for others were done for him, and offers made which he could see conduced to his interests, he would abandon Persia and Russia tomorrow . . . it should not be forgotten that we promised nothing, and Persia and Russia held out a great deal . . .'[8]

Auckland was now clear in his own mind that, with British support and encouragement, Shah Shuja must be put back on the throne of Kabul as the essential step to defeating Russian and Persian intervention in Afghanistan. All now depended upon obtaining Sikh co-operation. Without it, Auckland did not dare to move across the Indus; with it, the chances of success of an expedition to expel Dost Mohammed and replace him by Shah Shuja were enhanced almost to the point of certainty. Ranjit Singh already had a treaty with Shah Shuja to assist him in his attempts on the Kabul throne in return for the abandonment of any claim to Peshawar. When Auckland proposed that the treaty be expanded to include Britain the Sikh ruler was predictably amenable: 'This would be adding sugar to milk.' The revised treaty was signed by Shah Shuja on 16 July 1838 and by Ranjit on the 23rd. The only question left now was to settle a plan of campaign and in particular to decide whether British troops were to be included to stiffen Shah Shuja's forces.

There is no need in this book to retail the melancholy course of the First Afghan War. By a supreme irony, the Russo-Persian attack on Herat, which had furnished the immediate cause for British intervention, had effectively failed a month before the Tripartite Treaty was finally signed. Logically, it could be argued, there was now no need to intervene. But political policies and military preparations acquire an impetus of their own which it is hard to stop even given the will. At the end of 1838, Shah Shuja, accompanied by a British army, began his march on Kabul, via Kandahar. Nine months later, after enormous exertions but little fighting except at Ghazni, the combined forces of Shah Shuja and the British occupied Kabul and installed Shah Shuja on the throne from which Dost Mohammed had fled. It took a year or so to overcome the continued resistance of Dost Mohammed and his supporters, but in November 1840 the former Amir surrendered and was promptly deported to India. Success seemed finally to have rewarded Auckland's policies.

31

The reality was different. Shah Shuja's popularity had proved a myth and his continuing rule depended upon the continuing presence of a British army at Kabul. Even the British were safe only within the range of their guns. They could not stay indefinitely and when the time came for the troops at Kabul to withdraw to India the whole rickety edifice collapsed. In the depths of winter, the British army retreating from Kabul was massacred in the passes between Kabul and Jalalabad, and although contrary to popular mythology Dr Brydon was not the sole survivor, the reality was so close to the mythology as to be not worth arguing about. In the summer of 1842, a fresh British army re-occupied Kabul and destroyed the main bazaar as a symbolic act of retribution. It then withdrew. When it re-crossed the Indus into the Punjab at the end of 1842, the adventure was over. Shah Shuja was murdered outside Kabul and Dost Mohammed re-occupied the throne which he was to hold until his death in 1863.

The war had two long-term consequences of immense importance. The total destruction of Elphistone's army in the winter of 1841 also destroyed for ever the myth of British invincibility which had grown up since Plassey. This was to have repercussions throughout Asia as well as in India itself where it was to be a significant factor in the outbreak of the Mutiny sixteen years later. The war had also created an immense bitterness and distrust of the British among the Afghans. Afghanistan became effectively a closed country to the British for more than thirty years. There was no longer any reason why the Afghans should prefer the British to the Russians – indeed rather the opposite.

The rights and wrongs of Auckland's policy have been endlessly argued. The weight of opinion has hitherto condemned it, but the case for Auckland has been brilliantly argued in recent years by J. A. Norris in what is the best modern treatment of the war.* He has clearly demonstrated that there is more to Auckland's case than most historians have conceded, and that at all significant points he carried his advisers and the home government with him. Nevertheless, in the final analysis, political policies have to be judged by their results, and in this case the judgement of history is unequivocal. That two years after the last British soldier had left Afghanistan the British were at war with the Sikhs is perhaps the most convincing illustration of Auckland's miscalculations.

One thing at least was clear to everyone. There could be no further intervention in Afghanistan for a very long time to come.† There was in any case other work now to be tackled. A short and not very creditable campaign in 1844 finally brought Sind under British rule. Two wars against the Sikhs destroyed their kingdom and brought the British face to face with the Afghans in the Khyber. A lightning campaign in Central India brought the Mahratta wars to a close, while events in Europe and the Middle East dominated Anglo-Russian relations until 1856.

---

*The First Afghan War, 1838–1842. Cambridge, 1967. It is more concerned with the political and diplomatic aspects than the military ones.

†Both Salisbury and Lytton were to complain that all subsequent policy towards Afghanistan had been prejudiced by the disaster of the First Afghan War. Salisbury characterized the Indian opponents of his Quetta policy as men 'who in their youth have seen the Afghan ghost and have never lost the impression'. Lytton told John Morley in 1876 that 'Lord Auckland's unhappy Afghan expedition has been a lasting misfortune to India for it has paralysed the commonsense of all his successors, and bequeathed to the Government of India a perfectly unreasoning panic about everything that concerns our relations with Afghanistan.'

Dost Mohammed had not been able to resist fishing in the troubled waters of the Punjab. In return for aiding the Sikhs with troops in both wars, he had been given back Peshawar. He was to enjoy it for only a short interval. The crowning British victory at Gujerat in 1849 sent his troops fleeing back to Kabul, and Peshawar fell to the British. The episode had no lasting effect on Anglo-Afghan relations and Dost Mohammed turned to his other main preoccupation – unification of the rest of Afghanistan. By 1850 he had reconquered Afghan Turkestan and in 1855 he took over Kandahar when the last of his half-brothers died there. Only Herat now remained outside his control.

At this point, European events impinged on Anglo-Afghan relations once again. The outbreak of the Crimean War led the Russians to exert diversionary pressure on the British by encouraging Persia to attack Herat and by threatening Kandahar.* The British could no longer afford to remain at arm's length from Dost Mohammed. In 1855, a treaty of mutual friendship was signed at Peshawar between the two countries; Dost Mohammed agreed to regard the friends and enemies of the British as his own while the British agreed to respect the independence of Afghanistan. It was only a beginning. When, in the following year, Persia occupied Herat, the British declared war against the Persians and sought Dost Mohammed's military assistance. By the second Anglo-Afghan Treaty, signed at Peshawar in January 1857, the British Government agreed to supply the Afghans with money and arms so long as the war lasted. The money was to be dispensed by British officers sent to Afghanistan for that purpose. The subsidy was to cease with the end of the war when the British officers were to be withdrawn, although the British would be entitled to retain a native agent (the Vakil) at Kabul.

By the time the treaty was signed the war with Persia was over. By the Treaty of Paris of March 1857 the Persians renounced all claims on Herat and the rest of Afghanistan, but Herat remained in the hands of a pro-Persian ruler, Sultan Ahmad Khan. From the British point of view, the end of the war could not have come at a more timely moment because early in May 1857 the Bengal Army broke out in mutiny. When news of the mutiny reached Afghanistan, it was accompanied by a rumour that all the British in India had been killed. At that moment, the Governor of Kandahar found himself with three British officers on his hands. They had come, under the terms of the 1857 Treaty, to superintend the disbursement of the subsidy. The Governor sent a message to Dost Mohammed, suggesting that in the circumstances he should cut their throats. The Amir's reply was revealing: 'It is useless. I know these English well. It may be true that all of those in India have been murdered, but they will come in their thousands from beyond the sea and reconquer the country. Better leave these three alone.'†

The Mutiny absorbed British attention for two years. Dost Mohammed wisely resisted the temptations and pressures of his advisers to take advantage of the British troubles by attempting to regain the territories earlier lost to the Sikhs and now held by the British. At one point, in the high summer of 1857, when British fortunes were at their lowest ebb, John Lawrence, the ruler of the Punjab, advocated the handing over of Peshawar to the temporary keeping of Dost

---

*The Russian initiative was matched by British plans to foment insurrection in the Caucasus – see A. P Thornton. *For the File of Empire*. London, 1965, pp. 137–8.

†One of the three was Lumsden, the founder of the Corps of Guides.

Mohammed, in order to free troops for service elsewhere. He was argued out of that desperate course and thus passed the last chance of the Afghans' regaining their old winter capital, the pearl of the Durani empire.

The Mutiny affected British policy towards Afghanistan in two important ways. First, Dost Mohammed was seen to be entitled to British gratitude for his forbearance when the British were hard pressed. Secondly, the Mutiny precipitated a feeling which had been growing among Indian officials, that the limits of expansion had been reached and that it was time to concentrate on building up the stability and prosperity of British rule within India. The point was made by John Lawrence when he became Governor-General: 'It has been too often the practice in India to be looking beyond our borders and to be making preparation for imaginary dangers, while we neglect the affairs of our own provinces. Do not let us repeat these mistakes. The internecine wars of Afghans and Beloochees . . . are not real sources of danger. If we only take care to manage well at home, we can afford to let our neighbours alone. They will not molest us; and should they do so, they will live to repent such interference. I am fully aware that to be respected abroad we must be strong within British territory; but much strength also lies in the prosperity and contentment of the people which depends on good government and light taxation.'[10]

Thus when Dost Mohammed finally marched against Sultan Ahmad Khan in the spring of 1863, he could be reasonably confident that the British would not react, despite the terms of the Treaty of Paris which had pledged them to protect the independence of Herat. The city was stormed and seized in May 1863. Twelve days after he had completed the re-unification of Afghanistan, Dost Mohammed died.

His death brought yet another long period of dynastic strife. His nominated heir was Sher Ali, the eldest son of his second wife, who thus cut out Mahomed Afzal and Mahomed Azim, the elder sons of Dost Mohammed's first wife. Despite Sher Ali's request for British recognition, the policy followed by John Lawrence, who succeeded Elgin as Governor-General in 1864, was to recognize whoever established himself *de facto* on the throne of Kabul. Thus encouraged, Afzal and Amin contested the succession for nearly six years; at one point Afzal, having succeeded temporarily in occupying Kabul, was recognized as Amir by Lawrence. But Afzal was unable to hold his position. Sher Ali finally triumphed in 1868, driving his rivals into exile. He was promptly recognized as Amir by Lawrence three days before the latter's successor, Mayo, landed at Bombay. Sher Ali was given money and arms, with the promise of more to come in return for his sincerity and goodwill.

The policy which Lawrence had followed, towards events in Afghanistan, logical as it might appear, was nevertheless a mistake. It gave Sher Ali no cause for gratitude or goodwill towards the British; rather the reverse because it had directly stimulated his rivals to wage civil war for six long years – years which had wasted the energies and resources which should have been devoted to consolidating his administration and building up the prosperity of the country he had inherited. Even worse, the policy provided a continuing incentive to others such as his nephew, Abdurrahman, the son of Afzal, to try their hands at seizing the throne.

Mayo was quick to see the need to repair the damage. While the objects of his policy did not differ in essentials from those of Lawrence, he sought to achieve them by stimulating the emergence of a ring of stable, independent, prosperous states around the borders of India which would provide a buffer zone against aggression. He was thus prepared to go further than Lawrence in building up personal relations with Sher Ali and in giving him direct assistance. The foundations were laid at a meeting between Sher Ali and Mayo at Ambala in 1869. Mayo set out to flatter his visitor; so much so that at one point Sher Ali, overcome by the lavishness of his reception, exclaimed 'Now I truly believe myself to be a king!' Mayo was aware that what Sher Ali wanted above all else was a guarantee of defence against external aggression, and British recognition of his heirs against all other claimants. Mayo was keen to give both but could not persuade the home government to go so far. He could go no farther than to promise that the British Government 'will view with severe displeasure any attempt on the part of your rivals to disturb your position as Ruler of Cabul and rekindle civil war, and it will further endeavour, from time to time, by such means as circumstances may require, to strengthen the Government of Your Highness'. With that, and generous gifts of arms and money, Sher Ali had to be content.

Even so, Mayo was conscious that he had exceeded his instructions. He justified himself in a private letter: 'Had I taken the other course and sent him back without a single word that could have been of the least use to him, we should have lost the only opportunity that perhaps will offer for a long time of gaining the friendship of Afghanistan. Our twelve lakhs would have been thrown into the fire, and a fair field opened for foreign intrigue and annoyance.'[11]

Ambala represented the peak of Anglo-Afghan relations. Assured of Mayo's support and friendship, Sher Ali set about reforming Afghanistan. The collection of revenue was put on a fair and efficient basis, the army was re-modelled with the help of ex-Indian Army NCOs and, probably for the first time in its history, was up to date with its pay, and young Afghans were sent to study useful crafts and skills in India.

The assassination of Mayo in 1872 was a tragedy for Sher Ali. It brought in a new Viceroy of a very different and less sympathetic character (Northbrook), at a moment when Sher Ali was becoming increasingly apprehensive of the Russian menace to the north of him, and needed the reassurance of British support.

The Russians had steadily pushed forward in Central Asia throughout the 1840s. They had reached the Aral Sea in 1844 and by 1853 their posts were established at Ak Masjid, 220 miles up the Sir Darya. The end of the Crimean War and of the great rebellion in the Caucasus led by Shamyl initiated the next striking phase of the Russian expansion. Blocked in Europe, Russian energies were diverted eastwards into Central Asia. The great trading centre of Tashkent was stormed and seized in 1865; three years later Samarkand, the golden city of Timur, was occupied and the Khan of Bokhara made a subsidiary ally. In the following year (1869), the Russians occupied Krasnovodsk at the south-east corner of the Caspian and started converting it to a major base for the conquest of the Turkoman tribes to eastwards along the borders of Persia and Afghanistan. In a little over thirty years the frontier had moved a huge step closer to Afghanistan; the Central Asian Khamates were steadily being ground between the Russian advance and the northern frontier of Afghanistan. Small wonder that Sher Ali was anxious about Russia, an anxiety increased when in 1870 he began to receive a stream of official letters from Kauffman, the conquerer of Tashkent and the newly styled 'Governor-General of Turkestan'. The news of the fall of Khiva to a Russian army in June 1873 led Sher Ali to seek an early meeting with Northbrook.

The Russian advance had not escaped British notice either in Calcutta or London. John Lawrence had advocated taking a strong line with Russia: Russia should be told that 'it cannot be permitted to interfere in the affairs of Afghanistan or in those of any state which lies contiguous to our frontier . . . If this failed we might give that Power to understand that an advance towards India beyond a certain point would entail on her war, in all parts of the world, with India.'[12] On the same day that Mayo met Sher Ali at Ambala, the Russian Ambassador in London (Brunow) assured the British Government on behalf of Gortschakov that Russia recognized Afghanistan as lying entirely beyond the Russian sphere of influence. In reply, Clarendon, the Foreign Secretary, proposed the negotiation of a neutral zone in Central Asia designed to keep the Russian and British spheres of influence quite separate.[13]

What Clarendon had in mind was a zone north of the Oxus, effectively preserving the independence of the Khanates. It was an idea strongly supported by John Lawrence and his Council. As the negotiations dragged on, it became clear that the Russian idea was to make Afghanistan the neutral zone. The neutral zone idea gradually foundered but out of the negotiations came the proposal to define the northern frontier of Afghanistan.[14] In these negotiations, which terminated in a slightly flawed agreement in 1873, Indian officials played a prominent part.* It was against this background that Northbrook met Sher Ali's Foreign Minister, the very able Nur Mahomed, at Simla in June 1873. Northbrook had originally proposed to send an envoy to Kabul to tell the Amir about the Anglo-Russian agreement on the Northern Afghanistan boundary, as well as to discuss the results of the British arbitration on the Seistan boundary between Persia and Afghanistan. Antipathetic as always to the idea of British officers entering Afghanistan, Sher Ali had insisted on sending an envoy to India.

Northbrook had never taken the same concerned view of Afghanistan as his predecessor, believing that the greatest danger to British power in India lay in discontent among the native population at taxation to pay for military expeditions. He was therefore against any further expansion. Moreover, he believed that the further the Russians advanced in Central Asia the weaker became their position: 'My view may seem paradoxical but it is that the more Russia extends her possessions in these parts, the more open she is to injury from us, while she has no more power to injure us than she had before . . . the nearer she comes, the less her interposition in India is likely to be looked forward to as a blessing by the Indian Mussalmans who are our most dangerous class.'[15] Nevertheless he was not insensitive to Sher Ali's concern over Russian expansion.

For his part, Sher Ali made it clear through his envoy that while he was bitterly disappointed over the Seistan award, which had given the major part of the disputed area to Persia, he was still anxious for friendship and support from the

---

*The Amir had not been consulted at any stage! It is sometimes forgotten that while the British feared that Russian influence in Afghanistan might stir up trouble in India, the Russians equally feared that British activities in strengthening Afghanistan could lead to Russian difficulties with the Central Asian khanates.

British. What he wanted was an unequivocal guarantee of support against Russian aggression, together with recognition of his son, Abdullah Jan, as his heir to the throne of Kabul.

Like Mayo before him, Northbrook tried and failed to persuade the Cabinet to agree to a form of words which would satisfy Sher Ali. Northbrook was authorized to tell the Amir only that the British Government 'did not share the Ameer's apprehensions, but it would be the duty of the Ameer, in case of actual or threatened aggression, to refer the question to the British Government who would endeavour by negotiation and by every means in their power to settle matters and avert hostilities. Should these endeavours prove fruitless, the British Government are prepared to assure the Ameer that they will afford him assistance in arms and money, and will also in the case of necessity for such aid him with troops.' With that, Sher Ali had to rest content. To sweeten the pill, he was offered 20,000 rifles and a further large sum of money.

Northbrook was conscious that the matter could not sensibly be left there and at the conclusion of the conference wrote to the Amir suggesting that there be further discussions at a suitable opportunity; in the meantime, he proposed that a British military mission survey Afghanistan's northern and western borders to advise on defensive plans.

It has often been claimed that Sher Ali was permanently alienated by the results of the Simla Conference. That has by no means been proved. Nur Mahomed was to deny it rigorously at the Peshawar Conference four years later. Even if the formula for British support was no advance on that provided at Ambala, it had at least been renewed, and very substantial gifts of money and arms had been provided. Finally, Northbrook had been at great pains not to raise the issue of British representation in Afghanistan about which Sher Ali was known to be exceptionally sensitive.*

It is undeniable that after the Simla Conference the graph of Anglo-Afghan relations began to slope downwards. Sher Ali did not take up the offer of a military mission and subsequently refused passage through Afghanistan to a number of British travellers and officials. While taking the arms, he pointedly refused to draw the money placed at his disposal.† Nor was his attitude improved by Northbrook's intervention in 1874 in the quarrel between Sher Ali and his rebellious son, Yakub Khan. Yet Sher Ali was shrewd enough to appreciate that in the last analysis he had more to gain and less to fear from the British than from the Russians. It seems probable, therefore, that given time relations between Sher Ali and the British would have settled down, albeit at a lower level of amity. Time, alas!, was not available. Within months of the conference, a new government was taking office in England dedicated to a renewed forward policy in Afghanistan.

A word needs to be said in conclusion about the so-called policy of 'masterly inactivity' associated with Lawrence, Mayo and Northbrook.‡ It was never

---

*Controversy was to rumble on for many years as to whether Sher Ali had said at Ambala that he was prepared to accept British officers at places other than Kabul. The evidence is by no means clear but on the whole it seems improbable.
†Argyll was later to claim that Sher Ali was afraid that if he accepted all the gifts offered to him it would open the way to renewed British demands for agents to be stationed inside his country. That was certainly a factor not absent from the Amir's calculations.
‡The term was first coined by J. W. S. Wyllie, Lawrence's Foreign Secretary, in an article in the *Edinburgh Review* in January 1867. It is often forgotten that Wyllie wrote a second article in March 1870 entitled significantly 'Mischievous Activity'.

intended to be a total do-nothing policy, as its critics appeared to think. All three Governors-General were prepared to intervene outside India if the need arose, none more so than Lawrence, and all three were prepared to influence Afghan policy by advice to Sher Ali and by calculated gifts of arms and money. Essentially, however, the policy consisted of a refusal to accept specific commitments to defend or interfere in the affairs of countries outside India, coupled with a belief that Indian security was nevertheless best secured by building up the independence and stability of those countries along the Indian border such as Afghanistan. The accent should be on 'masterly' rather than 'inactivity', and one may perhaps conclude that this is one more example of a clever phrase distorting understanding.

NOTES

1. Quoted in Sir John Marriott. *The English in India*. Oxford, 1932.
2. Ephinstone, op. cit.
3. See the texts of the Treaties of Gulistan (1813) and Turkmanchai (1829) in D. C. Boulger. *England and Russia in Central Asia*. London, 1878, vol. II, pp. 375 and 382.
4. Ellenborough to Wellington, 18 October 1829. Wellington *Despatches, Correspondence and Memoranda*. London, 1867–8, vol. II, pp. 238–9.
5. Ellenborough. *Political Diary*, 1828–30, London, 1881, vol. II, pp. 123–4.
6. Alexander Burnes. *Travels to Bokhara*. (3 vols.), London, 1834, vol. I, p. 158.
7. Minute dated 13 March 1835.
8. Burnes to Macnaghten 2 June 1838. *Parliamentary Papers*, 1859 (Session 2), XXV.
9. See Colonel G. B. Malleson. *History of Afghanistan*. London, 1878, p. 420.
10. Minute by Sir John Lawrence, 26 July 1864; *Military Department, Proceedings*, August, 1864.

11. Mayo to Sir Henry Rawlinson, quoted in Sir Henry Rawlinson. *England and Russia in the East*. London, 1875, p. 299.
12. *Correspondence respecting the relations between the British Government and that of Afghanistan since the accession of the Ameer Shar Ali*, C2190, 1878–9, p. 43.
13. Nesselrode, the Russian Chancellor, had proposed the same thing in 1844 – see A. P. Thornton. *For the File of Empire*. London, 1965, p. 134.
14. For a full treatment, see G. J. Alder. *British India's Northern Frontier, 1865–95*. London, 1963.
15. Northbrook to Argyll, 28 March 1873, quoted in E. C. Moulton. *Lord Northbrook's Indian Administration, 1872–1876*. London, 1968.
16. Northbrook to Nur Mahomed, 30 July 1873. IOL. *Political and Secret Letters*, vol. 15, p. 1075.

CHAPTER 3

THE COMING OF WAR:
ANGLO-AFGHAN RELATIONS, 1874–78

A hyena at hand is more to be feared than a lion afar.

Persian Proverb

'Potentates such as the Khan of Khelat or the Ameer of Kabul are mere dummies or counters, which would be of no importance to us were it not for the costly stakes we put on them in the great game of empire we are now playing with Russia.'

Lytton to Sandeman, 1876

In the new Administration, Salisbury took the India Office. He had held the same post briefly in 1866–67 so he was not without experience of Indian affairs, but it would be a mistake to assume that he had at this stage either that close interest in, or mastery of, international affairs which was the hallmark of his subsequent career.

He had at an earlier stage taken a relaxed view of the Russian expansion in Central Asia. 'Several able men appear to regard the advance of Russia with apprehension,' he wrote to John Lawrence in 1866, 'but I cannot bring myself to look on these alarms even seriously. When there is a large room for her to the eastward of Bokhara it would be sheer wantonness on her part to provoke a powerful antagonist by turning to the south, and even if we were less powerful a campaign on the Indus with the Caspian shore for the nearest base could be a very arduous undertaking.'[1] In 1874 he could not ignore the fact that, wanton or not, Russia had turned south a decade before and even now the British Press was agitating over the recent Russian attack on Khiva. It was necessary, therefore, to look urgently to the position of Afghanistan. Four months after taking office he fired the first warning shot in the direction of Northbrook; 'Have you entirely satisfied yourself of the truth of the orthodox doctrine that our interest is to have a strong and independent Afghanistan? I have many misgivings as to the wisdom of making the friendliness of the Ameer the pivot of our policy. If with our help he subdues rebels and accumulates war-like stores and fills his Treasury and drills his people, perhaps one day he may fancy, without our help, adding to these blessings the loot of Hindostan.'[2] A month later he suggested to Northbrook that it might be necessary to send a British envoy to Kabul and be prepared for military moves on Quetta and Herat.[3] These views created apprehension in Calcutta not only because they signalled a radical change in policy, but because in them men could detect a faint reverberation of that earlier, disastrous policy of Auckland's.

Throughout 1874, Salisbury continued to press Northbrook on the question of Afghanistan, becoming steadily more and more impatient at the apparent lack of direct information about Afghan activities and at the reluctance of the Indian Government to pursue the idea of establishing a British agent in Afghanistan. 'I

am getting uneasy as to our lack of information from Afghanistan,' he wrote to
Disraeli in January 1875. 'Almost all we hear of what happens on the Western
frontier comes from St. Petersburg or from Tehran. For it has for many years past
been the policy – the successful policy – of the Ameers to persuade the Calcutta
Government not to send a European representative into the country. We have only
a native Agent who writes exactly what the Ameer tells him . . . I told you of the
anxiety I felt on this subject four months ago. I propose therefore to instruct
Northbrook formally to take measures for placing a resident either at Herat or
Candahar. Cabul is too fanatical to be quite safe . . . But this is a measure of some
little importance; and I should not be right in taking it unless it commends itself to
your judgement.'[4] Disraeli raised no objection and Salisbury wrote formally to the
Government of India instructing it to obtain the agreement of Sher Ali to the
establishment of a British Agency at Herat; once this had been accomplished, it
was the intention to do the same at Kandahar, but not at Kabul which was
accepted as being too dangerous.[5]

The dispatch caused consternation in Calcutta. Not only was existing policy to
be completely reversed, but the basic assumptions on which the new policy
appeared to be founded were not accepted by Indian officials. Salisbury had
largely justified the proposed initiative on the grounds that the Amir had more
than once agreed to accept a British officer at Herat[6] and that the present native
agent in Kabul could not provide adequate information. Those officials whom
Northbrook consulted were unanimous in their view that the native agent was
being falsely criticized and that, whatever the Amir might or might not have hinted
in the past, he would in practice be unwilling to accept a British officer anywhere
within Afghanistan. In any event, it would be impossible for such an officer to
obtain reliable information and the Amir's position *vis-à-vis* his own supporters
would be so weakened that the possibility of serious trouble between the two
countries could not be discounted. These views were formally conveyed to
Salisbury,[7] and Northbrook pressed the same points in private letters to him.

Even in Salisbury's own Council in London there was a deep division of opinion
between those like John Lawrence who supported the status quo and those like
Rawlinson and Bartle Frere who were in favour of forward policy. But Salisbury
did not find Northbrook a sympathetic personality and he had persuaded himself
that recent actions by the Amir, notably Sher Ali's refusal to allow Forsyth to
return from Kashgar via Afghanistan, showed hostility. Sher Ali had actually good
grounds for this action because there was a very real risk of British travellers being
attacked and murdered. But Forsyth was one of the advisers on whom Salisbury
relied at this time for information about Russian activities in Central Asia. In any
case, Salisbury regarded Indian officials as over-influenced by the disasters of the
First Afghan War; men 'who in their youth have seen the Afghan ghost and have
never lost the impression'.

Salisbury agreed with Northbrook that the idea of a Russian advance on India
was a mere chimera, but he was not quite so sure about the possibility of the
Russians inciting the Amir to attack India.[8] In a subsequent letter, he put his
attitude more vividly: 'We cannot leave the keys of the gate in the hands of a
warder of more than doubtful integrity, who insists, as an indispensable condition
of his service, that his movements shall not be observed.'[9] Salisbury was being less

than fair. The British themselves had refused to enter into any sort of alliance with the Amir. Despite this, there was no real evidence to doubt his basic honesty and it was by no means clear that in the circumstances prevailing in Afghanistan a British officer could do more than the native agent already there.

The arguments of the Government of India for letting sleeping dogs lie failed to impress Salisbury. In the summer of 1875 the Eastern Question had reared its head again with the outbreak of revolts in Bosnia and Herzegovina. The possibility of a renewed clash with Russia could be seen on the horizon. He accordingly returned to the charge. In his dispatch dated 19 November 1875 he dissected, and rejected, point by point, the arguments in the Indian Government's dispatch of June 1875. He concluded by instructing Northbrook to find without delay a pretext for sending a temporary mission to Kabul to impress upon the Amir the dangers and disadvantages of refusing to allow British officers to be stationed at points inside Afghanistan.

Northbrook had already warned Salisbury that this policy could lead to war: 'My firm opinion is that to do anything to force him [Sher Ali] to receive Agents of ours in his country against his will is likely to have an opposite effect to that which you desire, and to subject us to the risk of another unnecessary and costly war in Afghanistan before many years are out.'[10] He had made it clear that he would prefer to resign rather than carry out such a policy.[11]

The Indian Government's considered reply was contained in its dispatch of 28 February 1876. It pointed out a number of errors and misrepresentations in Salisbury's dispatch. It went on to raise two questions to which answers were regarded as essential before any sensible discussions could be held with the Amir:

1. Was HMG prepared to give unconditional guarantees of assistance to Afghanistan if it should be attacked by another country?
2. How far was HMG prepared to assist the Amir in fortifying Herat and in improving his army?

It made it clear that the Indian Government did not believe that the Russians had any intention of interfering with the independence of Afghanistan, and that it had no complaint against the Amir in his dealings with other powers. It was firm in its belief that the Amir would resist the temporary deputation of a British envoy to Kabul. It could see no clear advantage in trading guarantees of assistance for reception of a British officer in Afghanistan. It closed with a clear and defiant statement of faith in the policy of 'masterly inactivity': 'We are convinced that a patient adherence to the policy adopted towards Afghanistan by Lord Canning, Lord Lawrence and Lord Mayo, which it has been our earnest endeavour to maintain, presents the greatest promise of the eventual establishment of our relations with the Ameer on a satisfactory footing; and we deprecate, as involving serious danger to the peace of Afghanistan and to the interests of the British Empire in India, the execution, under present circumstances, of the instructions conveyed in your Lordship's dispatch.'[12]

The dispatch was Northbrook's swan-song. There was clearly no possibility of his continuing to work with the policy of the Conservative Administration and his successor, Lytton, had already been appointed. On the same day that Northbrook signed the dispatch in Calcutta, Lytton received his formal instructions in London from Salisbury.[13] The instructions were clear and bold which was not surprising since Lytton had drawn them up.[14] Lytton was to find a pretext to send a temporary mission to Kabul with the object of pressurizing the Amir into accepting the presence of British agents in Afghanistan. In return, the Amir could be promised a subsidy, a more decided recognition of Abdullah Jan as his heir, and a more definite declaration of British support in case of external aggression than that given at Simla in 1873; the British Government would, however, still be the judge of when such aggression had actually occurred. The establishment of an Afghan envoy in India and of a telegraph line to Kabul, via the Kurram Valley, and the reconciliation of Sher Ali with his nephew, Abdurrahman Khan, were also to be canvassed in the discussions. If the discussions proved unsuccessful, 'no time must be lost in reconsidering, from a new point of view, the policy to be pursued in reference to Afghanistan'. The proposed mission to Kabul was to visit Kalat as well in order to re-establish British influence there, thus providing a *point d'appui* from which pressure could, if necessary, be applied to Kandahar and Southern Afghanistan.

The choice of Lytton as Governor-General might appear a curious one. The son of Bulwer Lytton the novelist, and himself a minor poet of some distinction under the pseudonym 'Owen Meredith', Lytton had entered the diplomatic service in 1849. After a succession of junior posts in Europe, he was in 1874 in the relatively minor post of British Minister in Lisbon. From there he was catapulted into what was at that time perhaps the grandest and most powerful post that a British government could offer. Although well-versed in European politics, he had no experience or detailed knowledge of India and Central Asia.

In the latter respect, the choice of Lytton was not strange at all. It was more the exception than the rule for Governors-General to have any background of knowledge or experience of India. Mayo, for example, had been in exactly the same position. Indeed, with his European diplomatic background, Lytton was in some ways better fitted than most. What was remarkable was that he should have been appointed at all, in view of his personality. Perhaps as a result of his childhood, which had been devastated by quarrels between his mother and father, he was extremely highly strung, suffering intensely from migraine when under stress. To a naturally masterful nature he added vanity and intellectual arrogance. No one who has read his correspondence can doubt his ability to disentangle and decide complicated problems. But he tended to trust the judgement of very few and those he chose to trust, like Colley and Cavagnari, tended to share his own faults. Disraeli admitted to the Queen that Lytton would not be a prudent choice in normal circumstances, but that with the prospect of an Anglo-Russian confrontation looming over the Eastern Question, he and Salisbury wanted a Governor-General who could be relied upon to act boldly and imaginatively against the Russians in Central Asia.[15] What is clear is that Lytton's personality and style were congenial to Disraeli (who had been an intimate friend of his father's) and Salisbury in a way which Northbrook's colder, greyer personality was not.

Before he left England, Lytton had had a revealing talk with Schuvalov, the Russian Ambassador in London, who had read out a memorandum from Kauffman, proposing a division of territories in Central Asia (including Afghanistan) between the two Powers. This conversation was to dominate Lytton's thinking. What struck him forcibly was the revelation that while the Russians were apparently in a position to communicate easily with the Amir, the British were unable even to send a temporary mission to Kabul although the Russians held them responsible for exercising control over the Amir in his relations with Bokhara and other Russian satellites: 'I cannot conceive a situation more fundamentally false or more imminently perilous than the one they [these facts] reveal.'[16] The more he brooded over it, the more he became convinced that relations with Afghanistan needed to be put on a new and firm footing: 'The more I think over the geographical facts of our position the stronger becomes my impression that the real key to it is at Kabul . . . from Herat to the north-east extremity of Cashmere one great continuous watershed seems to indicate the natural defensive bulwark of India. I am inclined to think that, if we took our stand along this line, with a sufficient margin north of it to leave us in command of the passes on both sides, our position would be a sufficiently strong one for all defensive purposes.'[17] As regards the state of Afghanistan, he was reluctant at this stage to consider any policy of breaking it up because it still provided the best and cheapest bulwark of defence for India.[18]

By the time he reached India in April 1876, Lytton's views about Afghanistan were clear and precise.[19] He wished to build up Sher Ali and Afghanistan into a strong, stable and peaceful power as the best means of defence against Russian expansion in Central Asia. To achieve this he was prepared to provide money and a guarantee of British aid against external aggression. But in return the Amir would have to agree to British officers being stationed at Herat and Balkh, and a free right of travel in Afghanistan for British subjects.[20] It was a policy with which, as we have seen, John Lawrence would not have violently disagreed. Behind it lay the conviction that there was no such thing as 'the Afghan question'; it was merely an aspect of the much greater 'Russian question'.[21] Lytton was highly critical of certain aspects of Northbrook's policy, notably the Seistan award and Sandeman's current mission to Kalat, because they made more difficult the task of cementing sound relations with the Amir.

Acting on his instructions, Lytton arranged for a message to be sent by the Commissioner at Peshawar to the Amir, announcing the intention of sending a temporary mission to Kabul. The formal purpose was to convey the news of Lytton's arrival as Governor-General and of the Queen's intention to adopt the title of Kaisar-i-Hind (Empress of India). The real purpose was to discuss Anglo-Afghan relations and Sher Ali was shrewd enough to see that the stationing of British officers in Afghanistan would be high on the agenda. His reply was a firm but courteous refusal to accept a mission. He gave three reasons: first, that he could not guarantee its physical safety; second, the fear that the mission would put forward demands which he could not accept; and, third, that if he received a British mission he would be unable to resist a Russian demand to send a similar mission. If a conference was desired, he suggested that his own envoy should wait upon the Viceroy.

By the time that this reply reached Lytton, the Near Eastern crisis had taken a new and dangerous turn with the outbreak of revolts in Bulgaria, the publication of the Berlin Memorandum from Austria, Russia and Germany, insisting on Turkish reforms, and the dispatch of the British Mediterranean Fleet to Besika Bay as an

overt act in support of Turkey. Lytton's reply to the Amir was therefore exceptionally stiff. Rejecting the objections put forward by Sher Ali against receiving a
mission, Lytton did not hesitate to threaten: 'It will, for this reason, cause the
Viceroy sincere regret if your Highness, by hastily rejecting the hand of friendship
now frankly held out to you, should render nugatory the friendly intentions of His
Excellency, and oblige him to regard Afghanistan as a state which has voluntarily
isolated itself from the alliance and support of the British Government.[22] The
Vakil in Kabul was instructed to speak in the same terms.

It may be doubted whether either Lytton or Salisbury were as bold as they
sounded. Lytton was by no means in favour of insisting upon a permanent envoy at
Kabul if Sher Ali was opposed. And Salisbury was in favour of strengthening
British influence in Kalat as an alternative to agents in Afghanistan if the Amir
proved obdurate. Clearly if neither Lytton nor Salisbury was prepared to risk a
confrontation with the Amir over a permanent mission, they could hardly have
been more ready to do so over a temporary mission.[23]

The opportunity to strengthen the British position in Kalat was already available. The Khan of Kalat had been quarrelling with his chieftains for some years
with the result that commercial traffic up the Bolan Pass was completely blocked.
The Deputy Commissioner of Dera Ghazi Khan (Robert Sandeman) had been
dispatched in the early spring to mediate between the warring parties in order to
re-open the Bolan. He was successful and recommended that to keep the situation
in Kalat from deteriorating again, a British agent should be stationed there.
Despite his initial misgivings about Sandeman's mission, the opportunity was now
too good for Lytton to miss. Utilizing a hitherto unused clause in the 1854 Treaty
between Kalat and Britain, which allowed British troops to be stationed anywhere
in Kalat, Quetta was permanently occupied in November 1876. Quetta was in an
area which, historically and ethnically, was closely linked with Afghanistan – in
1839, British troops had actually been employed to attack Kalat and to kill its ruler
in order to bring it under the sovereignty of Shah Shuja. The occupation of Quetta
was almost guaranteed therefore to intensify the Amir's suspiciousness. By this
time, however, Lytton had begun to lose patience with Sher Ali.

In reply to the letter of 8 July 1876, Sher Ali suggested that the British Vakil in
Kabul (Atta Mohammed) should return to Simla in order to explain the Afghan
position. At the ensuing meeting with Lytton in October 1876, Atta Mohammed
reported that the three issues about which Sher Ali continued to feel most strongly
were the stationing of British agents in Afghanistan (and particularly in Kabul),
the recognition of Abdullah Jan as his heir and the guarantee of British support in
money and troops in event of external attack or internal disturbance.*

Atta Mohammed was instructed to tell the Amir that the Indian Government
was ready to start negotiations on these matters, but only on the prior condition
that Sher Ali agreed to British officers being stationed at suitable points in
Afghanistan. (Neither Lytton's Council nor his chosen negotiator, Sir Lewis Pelly,

---

*Lytton was prone to dismiss Sher Ali as an ignorant savage. Some light is shed on this view by Atta
Mohammed's report that the Amir had been particularly upset by a passage in Sir Henry Rawlinson's
book, *England and Russia in the East*, which had appeared to suggest the separation of Herat and Kandahar
from Kabul. Sher Ali was in fact exceptionally well-informed about matters outside Afghanistan and
showed a very shrewd judgement where his interests were concerned.

were entirely happy about this prior condition which they suspected, rightly, would tend to destroy any real hope of negotiation.)[24] Subject to that, the Vakil was told, the Indian Government was ready to negotiate a treaty of alliance.

Coincidentally, Salisbury had enquired of Lytton about the possibility of a campaign in Central Asia against Russia. Colley's plan, which was forwarded to Salisbury, envisaged three large columns moving via the Khyber and the Kurram on to the Oxus, and via Kandahar on Herat. Haines and Norman, the Military Member, were keen to set action in hand to move 5,000 men via the Kurram. Even Lytton could see the folly of that. He was prepared only to start work on improving the approach road from Kohat to Thal, at the entrance of the Kurram, and to sound out the Wazir tribes whose neutrality in event of a move via the Kurram would be essential. Even limited measures such as these, Lytton calculated, would not be lost on the Amir and should bring him to the conference table at Peshawar in a suitably conciliatory frame of mind.[25]

The Amir chose as his representative the very experienced but now mortally ill Nur Mohammed. In the event, the talks, which began at Peshawar at the end of January 1877, were stillborn. Nur Mohammed was not authorized to accept the stationing of British officers in Afghanistan as a prior condition to any negotiations: Pelly had no authority to abandon this prior condition. It was a tragic error of diplomatic judgement on Lytton's part because it became obvious as the talks proceeded that the Amir was, in the last resort, prepared to consider the possibility of British residents in Herat and Kandahar (although not Kabul). What he was not prepared to do was to concede the point in advance. Nur Mahommed took as his starting-point the proposition that Article 6 of the Treaty of 1857 specifically forbade the stationing of British officers in Afghanistan, and that this Article, as well as the Treaty of 1855, was still in force. Lytton, through Pelly, promptly rejected this view although his arguments now seem somewhat sophistical. Pelly tried to get Nur Mahommed to agree that the Amir had been dissatisfied with the results of the 1873 Simla Conference, and that since that time he had become estranged from the British. The Afghan envoy refused to accept this view; it was true that the Amir had been upset by the Seistan award, by Northbrook's intervention on behalf of Yakub Khan, and by a number of minor points of protocol, but he remained the firm friend of the British.

Failing agreement on the 'prior condition', negotiations on the other issues such as a guarantee of British aid against external aggression, and the recognition of Abdullah Jan, never started. In these circumstances, Nur Mahommed argued with great skill that the assurances given at Ambala in 1869 and at Simla in 1873 effectively bound the British to aid the Amir against aggression and that no new treaty was necessary. Lytton, through Pelly, naturally rejected this view, claiming that, on the contrary, the assurances depended upon the Amir's good behaviour and on his maintaining good relations with the British.

Ill and conscious of approaching death, Nur Mahommed took a sombre view of the negotiations. 'It is a very serious business,' he said to a British official, 'and this is the last time that the Ameer will treat with the British Government. God grant that the issue be favourable. But you must not impose upon us a burden which we cannot bear, and if you overload us the responsibility rests with you.'[26] He died at the end of March and Lytton instructed Pelly to close the conference immediately without waiting for Sher Ali's replacement envoy to arrive. If Lytton had been prepared to wait, the indications are that Sher Ali reluctantly would have conceded the issue of British officers in Afghanistan and Lytton knew this.[27] But Lytton had now decided that Sher Ali was not to be trusted and that a new approach was necessary; 'Had I known when I came to India how completely and irreconcilably the confidence of the Ameer had been alienated from the British Government I should have ventured to dissuade Salisbury most strongly from any attempt for its recovery by any overtures on our part.'[28] If Sher Ali repented of his foolishness and sought to re-open negotiations, Lytton was prepared to negotiate again, but the terms would be stiffer – in particular, there would have to be a right to locate British troops at Kandahar and Herat whenever Britain saw fit. In the meantime, Lytton intended to weaken the Amir's position. The course and outcome of the Peshawar Conference were set out in a long and tendentious dispatch. The conclusion revealed Lytton's total confidence in his control of the situation:

'The further course of Cabul politics we cannot foresee and do not attempt to predict. But we await its natural development with increased confidence in the complete freedom and paramount strength of our position. In the meantime, we see no reason to anticipate any act of aggression on the part of the present Ameer, or on our own part any cause for interference with His Highness. Our relations with him are still such as we commonly maintain with the Chiefs of neighbouring and friendly countries.'[29]

Central to this was Lytton's growing belief that the Amir was becoming unpopular in his own country and might, if necessary, be easily toppled and replaced.

The conclusion of the Peshawar Conference marked the beginning of a serious divergence of thinking and policy between Lytton and Salisbury. The latter had never really changed his view of the danger of direct Russian intervention in Afghanistan. In April 1877, he wrote privately to Lytton in words which echo vividly those he had used a decade earlier: 'I cannot go very far with those who dread the Russians. Except the size of the patch they occupy on the map, there is nothing about their history or their actual condition to explain the abject terror which deprives so many Anglo-Indians and so many of our military party here of their natural sleep.'[30]

Moreover, his experience in dealing with the Eastern Question, starting with his attendance at the abortive Constantinople Conference, had led him to take a more relaxed and pragmatic view of Russia generally. By 1878, indeed, he was beginning to feel that Germany might pose a larger potential threat than Russia. As he put it to Lytton, 'The commonest error in politics is sticking to the carcasses of dead policies.'

By contrast, Lytton's anti-Russian stance had grown rather than diminished. He saw the Russian threat to Persia and Afghanistan and thence to India as a real one which had to be combated positively and continuously. Thus in July 1877, in his celebrated 'Merv dispatch', he advocated telling the Russians that further steps towards Herat would be regarded as a cause for war; failing this, he proposed direct military aid to the Turkoman tribes of Merv, as well as to Persia.[31] Not surprisingly this was regarded with incredulity by Ministers in London, including Salisbury who was nevertheless prepared to allow something for Lytton's tendency to paint matters in vivid colours.

Lytton was not slow to perceive this divergence of view. To Sir James Stephen, he grumbled that Salisbury had become anti-Turkish and pro-Russian since his return from Constantinople.[32] As regards Afghanistan, the divergence was perhaps more one of tactics than objectives. Salisbury remained in favour of re-establishing British influence in Afghanistan and to toppling Sher Ali if this could be done without war. But he did not think Afghanistan was worth fighting over; in his judgement, a strong British position in Baluchistan would serve adequately to guard against any Russian move on Herat and to exert pressure on the Amir. He was particularly concerned to ensure that events were not forced without reference to London; 'In the present excited state of the military mind it is of the first importance not to leave the military men the chance of becoming practically the arbiters whether there should be peace or war . . . At all events, I hope you will not stir a soldier beyond the frontier (treating Kalat as within it) without obtaining our view on the matter first.'[33]

Throughout the remainder of 1877 and the first half of 1878, the attention of Ministers in London was focused on the development of the Near Eastern crisis and the outcome of the Berlin Conference. Lytton, temporarily frustrated, concentrated on moves to weaken Sher Ali. Negotiations were opened with the transborder tribes to detach them from the influence of Kabul. Similar negotiations were begun with the rulers of Kashmir, Chitral and Gilgit to form an anti-Afghan front. The base at Quetta was built up and surveys were made of reinforcement routes through what was nominally Afghan territory. If opportunity offered, he was still prepared to negotiate with Sher Ali to establish a dominant British presence at Kabul, but he was increasingly prepared to consider the alternative of breaking up Afghanistan. Provided that Kandahar and the Kurram valley were effectively under British control, the remainder of Afghanistan would present no serious threat. Sher Ali was characterized as a savage, but a savage with a touch of insanity.[34]

The deepening of the Near Eastern crisis in the early months of 1878 could not fail to affect affairs in Central Asia. If Britain could bring pressure to bear on Russia by sending Indian troops to Malta, and the Mediterranean Fleet to Constantinople, Russia could retaliate by moving troops towards India. At the beginning of June, three Russian columns began to move towards Afghanistan and a Russian mission under General Stolietov left Tashkent for Kabul.

Whether these moves were made on instructions from St. Petersburg or were initiated by Kauffman cannot now easily be determined. Several weeks after the mission's departure, the Russian Foreign Office was still denying that it had been planned or sent. According to Rawlinson, however, the British Government had evidence that the matter had been discussed several times in the Russian Council of Ministers.

Rumours of Russian missions to Kabul and the movement of troops had been rife in the bazaars of Central Asia throughout 1877 and the early part of 1878, as the Near Eastern crisis unfolded. The Indian Government had had reliable information of Stolietov's mission and had telegraphed the news of its impending departure on 7 June, a week before it actually left Tashkent. Lytton was initially relaxed about the news, dismissing early reports about the movement of Russian columns as 'moonshine'. By the middle of July, however, he was warning Cranbrook of an approaching crisis and asking whether London wished to treat the matter as an imperial or Indian matter. He had no faith in the remonstrances at St. Petersburg. The reception at Kabul of a Russian envoy,* when contrasted with repeated failure to secure reception of a British envoy, was a situation which neither Lytton personally nor the Indian Government officially could accept. In Lytton's view, the moment had come to resolve the problem of Anglo-Afghan relations once and for all. The essential first step must be to insist upon the Amir receiving a temporary British mission. The aim of this mission should be to get Sher Ali's agreement to:

1. The reception of British missions in Kabul whenever the Indian Government deemed it necessary.
2. The establishment of a permanent British military mission at Herat; and possibly Balkh and Kandahar as well.
3. The need to seek British approval before negotiating with any other country.

In return, the British Government would guarantee Afghanistan against external aggression, recognize as heir-presumptive whoever Sher Ali chose to name, and provide an annual subsidy of up to twelve lakhs of rupees. Lytton believed that political pressure should suffice to secure these demands, but he was ready to contemplate limited military action if necessary. This could take the form of occupying the Kurram valley and making an advance from Quetta in the direction of Kandahar, thus establishing, in Lytton's words, 'two small blisters on the head and foot of the Amir'. In particular, occupation of the Kurram valley presented, in Lytton's view, such a potential threat to Kabul that in future the Amir would not be able to last a week in face of known British hostility. These proposals were telegraphed to London on 2 August.[35] Cranbrook telegraphed back his general approval, subject only to Lytton assuring himself beyond doubt that the Russian mission was still in Kabul. Lytton lost no time in appointing General Sir Neville Chamberlain† to lead the mission and in requesting Sher Ali in peremptory terms to make the necessary arrangements to receive it. At the same time, the Commander-in-Chief in India (Sir Frederick Haines) was asked for his proposals for occupying the Kurram valley and Kandahar.

So far as Sher Ali was concerned, Lytton's request added insult to injury. The Amir had not asked for a Russian mission, he had not wanted to receive one and he

---

*In his published account, Dr Yavorski, a member of the Russian mission, says that it reached Kabul on 11 August 1878. Lytton's printed dispatches indicated 26 or 27 July, but are presumably wrong.

†Commander-in-Chief of the Madras Army. He had served in the First Afghan War; commanded the Peshawar Movable Column in the summer of 1857, with Roberts as his staff officer. He had subsequently been Adjutant-General of the besieging force outside Delhi. After a long period in command of the Punjab Irregular Force, he had commanded the Ambeyla Expedition in 1863. There was no more experienced frontier soldier, but he was now in the closing years of his active career. His son, also called Neville, served on Roberts's staff in 1879, but is better known as the inventor of snooker.

had agreed to receive it only as a result of Russian pressure, including a threat to assist Abdurrahman actively against him. The British were now taking advantage of his difficulties to force him to do something that they knew was against his deepest instincts. By an unfortunate coincidence, Lytton's message reached Sher Ali as he was mourning the death of his favourite son and heir, Abdullah Jan. His reaction was bitter. He resented the timing and the tone of Lytton's request and he was suspicious of the large escort (more than 200 men) which Chamberlain intended to bring. He was prepared in due course to receive a mission, but it would be at his convenience and he would not be hustled or threatened. He therefore made it clear to Lytton, through Chamberlain, that any advance of the mission towards Kabul would if necessary be resisted by force.[36]

In London, Lytton's action was generally approved of by Beaconsfield, Salisbury and Cranbrook save for two points. Lytton had instructed Chamberlain that he was to tell the Amir that negotiations could not start in Kabul until all communication between the Afghan Government and the Russian mission had been broken off; Chamberlain had also been warned to commence his advance on 16 September. The Prime Minister and his colleagues regarded the proposed stipulation about the Russian mission as offering a needless affront to Russia, and Salisbury insisted that the departure of the mission must await receipt and digestion of the Russian reply to the British diplomatic protest about Stolietov, made in St. Petersburg on 19 August. Lytton was told on 13 September that the mission was not to leave without further orders. So much was clear. What the Cabinet had not appreciated was that Lytton intended the mission to go via the Khyber. Preparations on this basis had been going on since the middle of August, and Lytton had made the point quite clear in a letter to Cranbrook on 31 August.[37] Ministers, however, regarded use of the Khyber route as too provocative; they preferred the Kandahar route as giving more time for tension to relax. To cover this point, Cranbrook's telegram of 3 August had included the phrase 'I presume you would not employ force by the Khyber Pass'. To Lytton, the phrase 'employ force' clearly meant the use of violent force which had never been his intention. He therefore assured Cranbrook in good faith that 'no employment of force in the Khyber is contemplated under any circumstances at present foreseen'.[38] But what Cranbrook had really meant was that the mission, i.e., the 'force', should not move via the Khyber.

While Lytton was pushing rapidly ahead with arrangements for the dispatch of the mission, confident that he possessed all the necessary Cabinet approvals save only for the final authority to order the mission forward, a division of opinion was beginning to manifest itself between Beaconsfield and Cranbrook on the one hand and Salisbury on the other. Beaconsfield had returned from Berlin in the middle of July in triumph, claiming 'Peace with Honour'. The continuing Russian presence in Kabul, however, was beginning to make that claim ring somewhat hollow. Peace with Russia might have been secured in Europe, but the threat of a war over Afghanistan persisted all the time that the Russians remained in Kabul and the Amir refused to accept a counter-mission from India. If there proved to be no peace after all, then, as Disraeli himself put it, the public might conclude that there was no honour either. He was therefore entirely in agreement with Lytton's policy and he claimed to detect a strong and rising feeling in the country generally in favour of acting firmly and decisively over Afghanistan. Cranbrook did not dissent. Salisbury, on the other hand, was a good deal less convinced of the need to force matters at Kabul. He distrusted the Prime Minister's bellicosity towards Russia and he feared that Lytton might be being led astray by his military advisers. He did not doubt that a breach with the Amir was inevitable at some stage, but he regarded the present moment as inopportune. He thought that matters should be deferred until a satisfactory situation had been achieved in the Balkans.[39]

Beaconsfield increasingly found himself siding with Cranbrook against Salisbury in this matter, and taking the direction of policy more and more into his own hands. 'There can be no cabinets now, and matters must be settled by myself and the Secretaries of State for Foreign Affairs and India', he wrote to Cranbrook on 22 September. 'Under these circumstances when you and the Viceroy agree I shall, as a general rule, always wish to support you. Salisbury's views, under ordinary circumstances would be prudent; but there are occasions when prudence is not wisdom . . . I am clearly of the opinion that what we want at this present moment is to prove our ascendancy in Afghanistan and to accomplish that we must not stick at trifles.'[40] When Disraeli wrote these words, he did not know that Lytton had already precipitated matters by dispatching the mission. On 21 September, the advance party of the mission under Major Cavagnari reached the Afghan post at Ali Masjid just inside the Khyber Pass. The Afghan commander, Faiz Mohammed, made it clear once again that he had no orders from Kabul to allow the mission to enter Afghanistan and that he would fire on it if necessary. Rebuffed, the mission returned to Peshawar.*

Irritation and frustration over what appeared to be the excessively cautious attitude of Ministers in London had been the basic cause of Lytton taking the bull by the horns. He did not believe that the Russian Government's reply to the British protest would significantly alter the situation at Kabul. If matters were allowed to drift on, British prestige in Central Asia would be diminished and the opportunity, which Lytton had seen from the beginning of the crisis, to resolve the problem of Anglo-Afghan relations would be lost.

Ministers were predictably angry over Lytton's precipitancy and subsequent writers have tended to condemn his action. Whether it actually made much difference in the long run is at least arguable. Neither Disraeli, Salisbury nor Cranbrook had dissented from the proposal to send a mission, nor did any of them expect any significant result from the diplomatic *démarche* in St. Petersburg. It is possible, therefore, – perhaps even probable – that the Cabinet would have authorized Chamberlain's advance in any event and that Lytton anticipated events only by a few days. It is equally possible that given time the Cabinet would have taken a more cautious line; they had had no intention of precipitating a war. Given more time, the Amir would almost certainly have agreed to receive a mission.

Cavagnari's repulse at Ali Masjid added a new dimension to the problem. It had become a matter of Great Power prestige. Lytton and the Cabinet now had to consider whether Sher Ali could be forced by diplomatic pressure alone to accept a British mission and British terms, or whether it would be necessary to employ

---

*It is sometimes overlooked that Lytton and Chamberlain knew several days before that the mission would be turned back.

military force. Lytton himself was more optimistic on this point than Ministers at home. As late as the middle of October 1878, he remained hopeful that the Amir would agree to receive a British mission at Kabul without the need for force. In practice, Lytton was by no means keen to topple Sher Ali whom he regarded as still the best man available and he certainly did not wish to annex Afghanistan which he regarded as an act of the wildest political and military folly. He now found himself in temporary alliance with Salisbury against Beaconsfield, Cranbrook and the Indian military authorities on the question of the extent of the future military operations which would be required. Lytton's strategy was to attempt to detach the tribes in the Khyber and the Kurram valley and the inhabitants of Kandahar from Sher Ali's rule. He was prepared to occupy the Kurram valley (although not necessarily permanently) as well as Kandahar although he was anxious to avoid doing the latter if possible; he was certainly not prepared to attempt to seize Kandahar in face of serious local opposition. He was totally opposed to any advance on Kabul.

Cranbrook and Beaconsfield were for pressing ahead with military action on a scale which would obviate any risk of failure. They were backed in this by the military authorities in India and by the Military Committee at the India Office who regarded the scale of Lytton's military preparations as inadequate. Salisbury had warned Lytton earlier about trusting the experts: 'If you believe the doctors, nothing is wholesome; if you believe the theologians, nothing is innocent; if you believe the soldiers, nothing is safe.' Moreover, it would have been contrary to human nature if, in their desire to make everything safe, the soldiers did not also perceive opportunities for glory and promotion.* The influence of his Military Committee is evident in Cranbrook's reaction to Lytton's proposals for concentrating some 21,000 men on the Khyber, Kurram and Kandahar routes: 'The quarrel may take a shape which will demand large warlike preparations. For an invasion of Afghanistan, I am told that not less than 40,000 men will be needed and a large proportion must consist of British soldiers. If your hopes of defection of tribes – disloyalty of Sirdars – unwillingness (generally) of Afghans to serve be fulfilled, still has not the Ameer an army not small in numbers with arms not of an inferior character and a certain quality of fair artillery? Your troops at the several points named in your telegrams [Peshawar, Kurram, Quetta and on the Indus at Multan] are not very numerous . . .'[41]

Lytton's hopes of achieving his objects by diplomatic pressure were shattered when he received towards the end of October Sher Ali's reply to his letter of 14 August. The Amir complained bitterly of the harsh and threatening tone of the British communications at a time when he was overcome with personal grief. He had no hostility to the British, but if the British Government was hostile to him, then he could only trust in God and let matters take their course. His letter made

---

*Among those desperate for a chance of glory was Wolseley who had just taken over as High Commissioner in Cyprus: 'All through my career I have dreamt of an Afghan war . . . oh, how I would wish to be the lucky man selected to conduct the operation . . . As I lie awake at night, I sometimes imagine I can hear the guns in the Afghan passes, and long to rush to the "sound of the cannon"', he wrote in his journal (see JSAHR, vol. CLV, pp. 10–11, 15). No one in India, however, wanted their glory stolen by Wolseley and he languished in Cyprus until appointed to succeed Chelmsford in Zululand in 1879. It is tempting to speculate on what might have happened if Wolseley had taken command instead of Browne, Stewart or even Roberts.

war virtually certain and Lytton telegraphed home his Council's plan of action. They proposed that, after issuing a manifesto condemning the Amir but professing friendship to the Afghan people,* troops should occupy the Kurram valley and secure the Khyber Pass. Further operations on the Khyber route and an advance from Quetta towards Kandahar would have to wait until the spring of 1879 since it was considered too late to carry them out in 1878 with the winter rapidly approaching.[42]

These proposals were considered at a Cabinet meeting on 25 October which the Prime Minister had been forced to hold by those Ministers led by Lord Cairns, the Lord Chancellor, and Sir Stafford Northcote, the Chancellor of the Exchequer, who were appalled by the sudden prospect of a war for which they could find no good reason. Salisbury joined them in condemning Lytton's precipitancy in ordering forward Chamberlain's mission: '. . . unless curbed, he [Lytton] would bring about some terrible disaster'. Beaconsfield was insistent that there was no alternative now to military action; however he proposed only a limited advance to secure the Kurram valley while making preparations for wider action in 1879 if that proved necessary. It was Cranbrook, surprisingly, who argued forcefully for war 'immediate and complete', primarily because he regarded Lytton's proposals as inadequate. Since Cranbrook himself had hitherto been regarded as Lytton's strongest supporter his attitude, bolstered by the now general distrust of Lytton's judgement, was decisive. The Cabinet agreed to the dispatch of an ultimatum to the Amir. Rejection was to be followed by immediate advances along the Khyber, Kurram and Kandahar routes. The decision was not so much a vote for the Generals as a vote of distrust in Lytton.

The ultimatum was dispatched by Lytton on 31 October. It gave Sher Ali until 20 November to agree to accept a permanent British mission in Afghanistan and to send a suitable emissary to India to tender a full apology for the repulse of Chamberlain's mission, failing which the Amir would be treated as a declared enemy. No answer was received in time and war followed automatically.

Why had it happened? Essentially, the policy of non-interference and discreet support which had characterized British policy between 1842 and 1874 had broken down under the pressure exerted by the Russian expansion in Central Asia. The importance of Afghanistan had increased to the point where the Amir could no longer be given the benefit of any doubt. British policy makers had persuaded themselves that Sher Ali had become basically unfriendly and increasingly susceptible to Russian influence. The acid test had become his willingness to accept British officers in Afghanistan. When he failed that test, it needed only the arrival of Stolietov to tip the balance in favour of the war to which Lytton at least had been unconsciously predisposing himself for more than a year.

---

*A device, it may be observed, similar to that adopted towards Hitler and the German people in 1939.

NOTES

1. Salisbury to John Lawrence, 27 August 1866. Salisbury Papers.
2. Salisbury to Northbrook, 19 June 1874. I.O.L. MSS Eur C. 144/11, pp. 31–2.
3. Salisbury to Northbrook, 17 July 1874. Ibid.
4. Salisbury to Disraeli, 2 January 1875 – quoted in Lady Gwendolen Cecil. *Life of Robert, Marquis of Salisbury*. London, 1921, vol. II, p. 71.
5. Secretary of State to Government of India, 22 January 1875 – No. 2 (Secret). I.O.L. L/P and S/7/320, pp. 3–25.
6. A clear reference to the Ambala Conference – see page 35 above.
7. Government of India to Secretary of State, 7 June 1875. No. 19 (Secret). I.O.L. L/P and S/7/4, pp. 1–8.
8. Salisbury to Northbrook, 19 February 1875. I.O.L. Reel 811/3.
9. Salisbury to Northbrook, 23 April 1875 – Ibid.
10. Northbrook to Salisbury, 30 September 1875. I.O.L. MSS Eur C. 144/12, p. 127.
11. Northbrook to Salisbury, 7 January 1876. Northbrook Papers (NP) vol. 12.
12. No. 10 (Secret) – I.O.L. L/P and S/7/4.
13. Significantly these instructions were not seen by the India Council in London, as was normal, and Lytton was authorized to withhold them from his own Council in Calcutta if he wished.
14. Text in *Causes of the Afghan War*, op. cit., pp. 87–94.
15. See W. F. Moneypenny and G. E. Buckle. *Life of Benjamin Disraeli, Earl of Beaconsfield.* (6 vols.), London, 1910–20), vol. VI, p. 379. For a good sketch of Lytton's character see Ira Klein. 'Who Made the Second Afghan War?' Journal of Asian History, vol. 8 (1974), pp. 100–102. A full-scale biography of Lytton is badly needed.
16. Lytton to Salisbury, 26 February 1876. I.O.L. MSS Eur E.218 (Lytton Papers (LP)) 518/1, p. 8.
17. Lytton to Salisbury, 14 March 1876 – ibid., pp. 27–8.
18. Lytton to Sir Henry Rawlinson, 28 March 1876 – ibid.
19. They owed a good deal to Bartle Frere whom Lytton met in Cairo on his way to India. Lytton found that Frere's views largely coincided with his own. Frere was also close to Salisbury. See J. Martineau. *Life and Correspondence of the Right Honourable Sir Bartle Frere*. (2 vols.), London, 1895.
20. Lytton to Charles Girdlestone, 27 July 1876. LP 518/1, p. 435.

21. Lytton to Salisbury, 2 July 1876 – ibid., p. 262.
22. Sir R. Pollock to Amir of Kabul 1876 – text in *Causes of the Afghan War*. op. cit., p. 99. Three of Lytton's Council, survivors from Northbrook's regime, protested that these words amounted to a totally unjustified threat which could lead to war. Neither Lytton nor Salisbury took any notice except to resolve to route as little through the Council as possible.
23. It should be noted, however, that Salisbury had mooted the possibility of replacing the Amir.
24. The main opponent on the Council was Muir, whom Lytton characteristically dubbed 'a treacherous fool'.
25. For details of this rather odd episode, see Lytton to Salisbury, 30 November 1876 and Lytton to Norman, 27 November 1876, both in LP 518–1. Lytton realized that no Central Asian campaign could be mounted without the Amir's support – see Lytton to Norman, 6 December 1876 – HP, vol. 1, ff. 21–33.
26. *Causes of the Afghan War*, op. cit., p. 116.
27. See Lytton to Salisbury, 25 April 1877 – Salisbury Papers. Also Secret Dispatch No. 13 of 1877, dated 10 May 1877.
28. Lytton to Northbrook, 25 October 1877. LP/518/2, p. 965.
29. See Note 27 above.
30. Salisbury to Lytton, 27 April 1877 – quoted in Cecil, op. cit., vol. II, p. 142.
31. Lytton to Salisbury, 16 July 1877. LP 518/2.
32. Lytton to Stephen, 24 June 1877. LP 518/2, p. 525.
33. Salisbury to Lytton 3 and 10 August 1877 – quoted Cecil, op. cit., vol. II, pp. 157–8.
34. Lytton to Gathorne Hardy (Lord Cranbrook), 8 April 1878 – LP 518/3, p. 226. Cranbrook had succeeded Salisbury when the latter became Foreign Secretary in March 1878; for several weeks Lytton addressed him as Lord Staplehurst under the mistaken impression that he had taken that title instead of Cranbrook, a curious illustration of the problems of communication between London and Calcutta.
35. See also Lytton to Cranbrook, 3 August 1878 – LP 518/3, p. 543.
36. Chamberlain to Lytton on 17, 18 and 19 September 1878. *Causes of the Afghan War*, pp. 175–179.
37. LP 518/3, p. 611. Lytton thought that the Kandahar route would take too long.

38. Lytton to Cranbrook, 5 August 1878.
I.O.L. L/P and S.
39. Salisbury to Beaconsfield, 22 October
1878. Quoted in Cecil, op. cit., vol. II,
pp. 341–342.
40. Disraeli to Cranbrook, 22 September
1878. Text in Moneypenny and Buckle. op.
cit., vol. VI, p. 383.

41. Cranbrook to Lytton, 6 October 1878.
[Lytton Papers].
42. Viceroy to Secretary of State, 19
October 1878. I.O.L. L/P and S/3/222,
pp. 934–5.

CHAPTER 4

THE OPPOSING FORCES

L ong before the ultimatum had expired, the troops had begun to move. It is time, therefore, to look at the opposing armies.

The basic organization of the military forces in India in 1878 was much as it had been before the Mutiny. It was divided into the three Presidency Armies of Madras, Bombay and Bengal, each with its own Commander-in-Chief. Overall operational control was exercized by the Commander-in-Chief of the Bengal Army who was also formally 'Commander-in-Chief in the East Indies'. He was responsible for the planning and conduct of all operations in the event of major hostilities, and for the efficiency, discipline and training of the troops taking part. The supply of men, equipment and stores was, however, the responsibility of the Military Department which was also responsible for pay, allowances and financial matters generally. The head of the Military Department was a serving officer, invariably junior to the Commander-in-Chief, but quite independent of him and sitting in his own right as a full member of the Viceroy's Council, of which the Commander-in-Chief was formally only an Extraordinary Member.

This system of parallel military hierarchies is reminiscent of the organization of the British Army in the first half of the nineteenth century. The friction which inevitably arose from time to time was accentuated by the fact that Army Headquarters was located at Simla for a large part of each year whereas the Military Department resided permanently at Calcutta. The Commanders-in-Chief of the Bombay and Madras Armies had their own separate but smaller head-quarters, and exercized a degree of independence over the organization, manning and training of their own armies, being responsible constitutionally for the efficiency and employment of their forces to their own Governors, rather than to the Commander-in-Chief, India. But it was the Military Department which was responsible for sanctioning all military expenditure and which thus held the ultimate power. Even the most trivial matters shuffled to and fro for months between the Military Department, Army Headquarters, Presidency Army Head-quarters, and frequently provincial and central government civil departments. The evidence put before the Eden Commission in 1879 contains some breathtaking examples of the complexity and slowness of the system. The system was slow and inefficient but not unworkable, although the division of responsibility between Commander-in-Chief and Military Member constantly threatened to paralyse it.*

---

*It was the cause of the titanic quarrel between Kitchener and Curzon in 1904–5. Kitchener won and brought the whole of the Military Department under the direct control of the Commander-in-Chief. But that system in turn collapsed during the First World War under a Commander-in-Chief who did not possess Kitchener's demonic powers of work. The problem was solved only with the introduction of a proper General Staff system.

A good deal of equipment was already made at the various Government arsenals and factories in India, but the remainder, particularly small arms and artillery, was procured in the United Kingdom. In 1878, the Army as a whole cost some £17 million out of a total Indian revenue of £63.25 million.

Each Presidency Army consisted of native Indian troops and of British Army regiments posted to India for a term of duty and paid for, while they were in India, by the Indian Government. While in India, the British troops came under the general operational and administrative control of the Commander-in-Chief, although in matters such as pay, conditions of service and promotion they remained directly under the War Office in London. There were no European regiments raised by the Government of India; those European regiments which had existed under the old East India Company having been absorbed, not without a minor mutiny, into the British Army after the Great Mutiny. The introduction of the short-service system in 1870 meant a greatly increased outflow of time-expired men each year so that the regiments in India were generally under-strength for a significant proportion of time and contained higher proportions of inexperienced and unacclimatized men.*

The largest and most important, although not the oldest, of the three Armies was the Bengal Army. The Great Mutiny had been essentially a mutiny of the Bengal Army; of the 74 regiments of regular native infantry and 28 regiments of cavalry, only the equivalent of eleven infantry and two cavalry regiments survived to be incorporated in the post-Mutiny Army. The regiments which had disappeared had been replaced by units raised during the Mutiny and overwhelmingly recruited from the Punjab. The new Bengal Army differed from its predecessor in three other important respects: virtually all artillery was now in British hands, the proportion of British troops was greatly increased, and all the native cavalry regiments were now recruited on the silladar system.

The transfer of artillery to British hands was a safety measure designed to reduce the fighting power of the native troops in the event of another mutiny. For the same reason, the ratio of British to native troops in the Bengal Army, which had stood at just over 1:5 in May 1857, had been reduced by 1878 to 1:1.7. (Overall there were now 65,000 British and 130,000 regular native troops in India.) Under the silladar system, the regiment was run virtually as a joint-stock company. The trooper purchased his place in the regiment and provided his own horse and equipment, in return for a higher rate of pay. When he retired or was invalided he sold his place in the regiment, the proceeds in effect providing a pension. As in the British Army of the eighteenth century, much of the equipment was purchased regimentally and to special regimental patterns. In peacetime the system had obvious advantages for the government in ease of administration and supply and in producing good-quality recruits with a vested interest in the Army. In theory, it was guaranteed to produce loyalty and discipline since the trooper had always at risk his financial stake. On active service, particularly if prolonged or arduous, the

---

*The British regiments usually remained in India for a considerable number of years, being replenished each winter by fresh drafts from the United Kingdom to replace casualties and time-expired men. In 1878, the longest-serving infantry regiments in India were the 1st (Royal Scots) and the 1st Battalion of the 2nd (Queen's), which had both been in India since 1866. Among the cavalry regiments, the 4th Hussars had been in India since 1867.

system produced serious problems in making up losses of men, horses and equipment.*

Two other post-Mutiny changes were significant. After 1861, British officers of native regiments were posted to a single Presidency Staff Corps, from which regimental, staff and political posts were filled.† Compared to the pre-Mutiny system under which all officers were appointed to specific regiments, whose establishments then had to bear the weight of subsequent postings to staff and other posts, the Staff Corps system represented a step forward. It ensured that regiments on active service could be kept up to strength in officers irrespective of casualties, and it helped to prevent the situation, common under the old system, where the officers serving with the regiments were merely those who were too stupid or too lazy or too lacking in drive to obtain extra-regimental appointments. But the Staff Corps system had one major defect; promotion in it was by time. In consequence, by 1879, all three Staff Corps were overburdened with senior officers for whom there were no posts commensurate with their rank. Thus lieutenant-colonels could be found commanding wings and majors acting as wing officers, with consequent effects on the morale and employment of junior officers.

The second change was in the class composition of the regiments. Pre-Mutiny, the different classes were normally mixed within each regiment – Muslim stood next to Hindu, Jat stood next to Rajput, Punjabi stood next to Pathan. In the post-Mutiny reconstruction of the Bengal Army, regiments were increasingly structured on a class basis. A minority of regiments were wholly one-class regiments; for example, the 14th Bengal Cavalry (Jats), the 23rd and 32nd Bengal Infantry (Mazbi Sikhs) and the 1st, 2nd, 3rd and 4th Gurkha Infantry. The majority of regiments were, however, composed of class companies; as an example, the 5th Bengal Infantry in 1861 had two companies of Brahmans and Rajputs, one company of Hindustani Muslims, one company of Jats, one company of Gurkhas and similar hill tribes, one company of Bundelas, one company of Sikhs and one company of lower-caste Hindus. As time went on and the theory of the so-called 'martial races' became dominant in the minds of men such as Stewart and Roberts, regiments were recruited from a narrower range of classes. By 1884, the class composition of the 5th Bengal Infantry had become three companies of Brahmans and Rajputs, two companies of Hindustani Muslims, two companies of Jats and one company of lower-caste Hindus. Since each regiment remained a wholly separate entity, responsible for its own recruiting and training, replacing casualties during a campaign was difficult.

In 1878, the Bengal Army was composed of 50 native and 32 British infantry regiments, nineteen native and six British cavalry regiments. While individual regiments had seen service since the Mutiny and in the numerous minor expeditions on the Frontier, in China, Bhutan and elsewhere, the reconstituted Bengal Army had not taken part in a major campaign and its fighting quality, equipment and organization was, to that extent, untried and untested.

---

*In March 1880 a fire which destroyed the equipment of three troops of the 13th Bengal Lancers crippled the regiment operationally for several months.
†The three Presidency Staff Corps were amalgamated into a single Indian Staff Corps in 1891, but this was abolished in 1903 when all officers were simply appointed to 'the Indian Army'. Some officers elected in 1861 to stay on their regimental cadre rather than join the Staff Corps.

The same was even more true of the Madras Army, the old Coast Army, the senior of the three Presidency Armies. Its great days had been in the second half of the eighteenth and the first two decades of the nineteenth centuries. Then, under commanders such as Arthur Wellesley, it had played a major part in the extension of British power, and Madras regiments had acquired a high reputation for discipline and courage. Since 1820, the military centre of gravity in India had moved to the north. The Madras Army had been wholly untouched by the Mutiny and some of its regiments had played a useful role in its suppression in Central India. Apart from that, its last major campaign had been the Second Burmese War in 1852. Since then the lot of the Madras Army had been that of garrison and police duty in Southern and Central India and Burma. Faced with the prospect of long years of enervating routine in remote stations, with virtually no chance of active service, officers shunned the Madras Army in favour of the Bengal Army or the irregular forces such as the Punjab Frontier Force. The Madras Army had become a backwater and its men, mainly recruited from the smaller, darker races of Southern India, were increasingly contrasted unfavourably with the more virile-looking 'martial races' of Northern India. The exception was the Madras Sapper and Miners which had a magnificent reputation for skill, hard work and efficiency. Writing in 1871, the Commander-in-Chief of the Madras Army recognized the problem; the Army 'had been so shut out, of late, from all participation of Field Service and Expeditions, that the officers and men are in danger of falling into the delusion that they have nothing but police duties to perform . . . This view of the functions of an army must tend to lower the military spirit in all its members.'*. Mayo, in particular, had had a low opinion of the Madras Army and, since its size was grossly disproportionate to the actual needs of the Presidency, had wanted to abolish one of its cavalry regiments and eight of its infantry regiments. But arguments about its value as a reserve and as a counterweight to the Bengal Army had prevailed. It remained, in 1878, of substantial size, composed of forty native and nine British infantry regiments, and four native and two British cavalry regiments. The native cavalry regiments were unique among the Presidency Armies in being recruited on a normal, non-silladar, basis.

The last of the three Presidency Armies, that of Bombay, was the smallest and showed some of the characteristics of the Madras Army. It too had played a major role in the expansion of British power in Central and Southern India during the period before 1820. It had been very largely unaffected by the Mutiny and had played a useful part in its suppression, but since the Mutiny its only major expedition had been that to Abyssinia in 1867–8. Some of its regiments had never been involved in a major campaign. Even before the Mutiny, a high proportion of its men were recruited from Northern India and this tendency was increasing. Like the Madras Army, its regiments were organized on a mixed, not a class basis. In 1878 it consisted of thirty native and nine British infantry regiments, seven native and one British cavalry regiments and, unique among the three Armies, two native batteries of mountain artillery. Like the other two Armies, it had its own distinguished corps of sappers and miners.

---

*Sir Charles Trevelyan described the Madras Army in 1873 as 'a very peaceable, unmilitary, respectable sort of body'.

In addition to the three Presidency Armies, the Governor of India had at his disposal in 1878 a number of other military forces of which the most important was the Punjab Frontier Force. Created originally in 1846 to police the newly acquired Punjab border against the Pathan Hill tribes, it became the Punjab Irregular Force in 1851 and the Punjab Frontier Force in 1865. In peacetime it did not come under the Commander-in-Chief, India, but under the direct control of the Lieutenant-Governor of the Punjab;* in war, it became available for service in exactly the same way as the other troops in India. Composed almost exclusively of Sikhs, Punjabis and Pathans, it numbered four regiments of Sikh Infantry, six of Punjab Infantry, five regiments of cavalry, together with five batteries of mountain artillery (including a garrison battery) and the Corps of Guides which comprised both infantry and cavalry. (The 5th Gurkhas were in practice brigaded with the Force, although technically part of the Bengal Army.) Trained in a hundred border expeditions, and equipped with its own transport, the Punjab Frontier Force was the most experienced body of fighting troops in India.

Second in size and importance to the Punjab Frontier Force was the Hyderabad Contingent. Formed in 1813 from troops provided by the Nizam of Hyderabad for the Third Mysore War, against Tipu Sultan, it had spent most of its career policing the Nizam's dominions in Central Southern India. It had played a useful role in the suppression of the Mutiny and it had retained its special status thereafter. It consisted of six native infantry and four cavalry regiments, together with four batteries of field artillery.

Finally, there were four irregular battalions of infantry (the Mhairwarra and Bhopal Battalions and the Malwa Bhil and Meywar Bhil Corps), two irregular forces of cavalry and infantry (the Deoli and Erinpura Irregular Forces) and two regiments of cavalry employed on local service. These two cavalry regiments made up the Central India Horse, formed originally from units of irregular cavalry raised during the Mutiny, and located since then in two remote cantonments in Central India where they patrolled the main trunk road between Bombay and Delhi. Minor actions against bands of robbers were frequent and, after the Punjab Frontier Force, they were probably the most efficient fighting units in India.

The forces of the various princely states such as Jodhpur, Kashmir, Mysore and Patiala, offered a further possible source of troops. Many of these state forces were no more than feudal levies, costumed and equipped as in the days of the Mogul Emperors. None of them could compare in efficiency with a regular native battalion but a small number were of sufficient quality to be used to guard lines of communications and, as we shall see, on occasion fought stoutly during the coming war.†

Both British and native infantry regiments were organized into eight companies (two wings of four), total establishments being thirty officers (excluding doctors) and 886 other ranks for British battalions and seven officers and 712 other ranks for native battalions. For cavalry regiments, the corresponding establishments

---

*In 1878 the Punjab included all of what was to become in 1901 the separate North-West Frontier Province.

†After the Second Afghan War, these state forces were taken in hand and a number were re-modelled, with the active assistance of the Government of India, on the lines of regular Indian army units. These 'Imperial Service Troops' performed most useful service in both World Wars, and after 1947 some of them were taken into the regular Indian Army.

were (British) 24 and 455 and (native) seven and 457. Native regiments were normally close to establishment in peacetime, but in the trooping season British regiments were often substantially below. For both British and native regiments, actual fighting strength was always below both establishment and normal strength. Two examples will suffice to show the diminution which occurred. The 29th Bengal Native Infantry had a peace establishment of 712 other ranks and a nominal strength on 1 October 1878 of 711. When it left its peace station for active service in October 1878, it numbered 659 and when it reached the Peiwar Kotal it was down to 556. The 2/8th Foot, with an establishment of 886 other ranks and a nominal strength at the beginning of November 1878 of approximately 900, left Rawalpindi for active service 690 strong. By the time it reached Thal, one-third of the regiment was sick and it actually went into action at the Peiwar Katal 454 strong. For practical planning purposes, Army HQ assumed the following strengths for regiments:

British cavalry	350	Native cavalry	350
British infantry	700	Native infantry	550

The small number of British oficers in the native regiments assumed particular significance on active service. The nominal establishment for both cavalry and infantry regiments was seven, excluding doctors and veterinary surgeons. In addition, the majority of native regiments would have attached to them one or more Staff Probationers – officers from British regiments who wished ultimately to join one of the Indian Staff Corps and were required to spend a period on attachment to a native regiment before being accepted into the Staff Corps.

Against this at least one officer was likely always to be on furlough in the United Kingdom. Under the Indian Military Furlough Rules of 1868, officers were entitled to two years' furlough after eight years' service in India, and thereafter to one year's furlough every six years, up to a maximum of eight years altogether. Revised rules introduced in 1875 provided for one year's furlough every five years, but officers who had joined the Staff Corps before 31 December 1875 could stick to the 1868 rules. Sickness and secondment to other duties were other constant factors in reducing the number of officers actually present.

An official return of officers actually present on 1 September 1878 with those Bengal regiments which would be engaged in the first campaign, showed that only one of the cavalry regiments had its full complement of officers present: the remainder had four and five, with one regiment (13th Bengal Lancers) having only three. In the Bengal infantry regiments destined for the campaign, only one (2nd Gurkhas, then in Cyprus) had all seven officers present; the remainder had on average between four and five, with one regiment (the 2nd Bengal Native Infantry) having only two. The three Madras infantry regiments involved were better off, averaging six officers each; the six Bombay regiments averaged five officers apiece. The situation was no better in the Punjab Frontier Force regiments, and in the irregular regiments which had a lower establishment to start with, the situation was almost farcical, the Bhopal Battalion having only two officers present and the Mhairwarra Battalion one. Once it was known that a regiment was proceeding on service, there were always officers in other, not so fortunate, regiments keen to transfer for a chance of excitement and glory; and if the campaign seemed likely to be prolonged, officers on furlough could be expected to hasten back, especially now that India, via the Suez Canal, was only a month or so distant from the United Kingdom. Thus by June 1879, even the Mhairwarra Battalion had five officers present and many of the regiments had their full seven, with two regiments (2nd Punjab Cavalry and 5th Punjab Infantry) having nine.

Even so, the situation in the native armies contrasted sharply with that in the British regiments. In the summer of 1878, the British cavalry regiments in India had on average 23 officers present and the British infantry regiments 28. The complement of British officers in the native regiments was manifestly too low. One hard-fought action or an outbreak of disease could leave a regiment with virtually no officers at all, and the system of single-battalion regiments with no regimental depots meant that replacements were almost certain to be strangers to the regiment and to the men.[1] A heavy burden of responsibility thus fell on the native officers, of whom there might be sixteen or seventeen present in each regiment, commanding the individual companies and troops. Many were first-class leaders and the Second Afghan War was to produce many examples of initiative and courage. But the slow pace of promotion meant that many were not up to the mental and physical rigours of prolonged active service. By common consent, Indians aged more rapidly than Europeans, yet 52-year-old infantry company commanders were quite common. Brigadier-General Burrows of the Bombay Army expressed what was almost certainly a commonly held view before the Eden Commission in 1879:

'I have a great respect for the Native Officer, and have occasionally met with exceptionally good men, but, as a rule, they are not fit for command and disaster might assuredly be anticipated if, in a case of difficulty, troops are left without the supervision of a European officer.'[2]

The native regiments were recruited on a long-service basis. Full pension was payable only after 32 years' service, but a reduced pension was payable on invaliding after fifteen years. A man could claim his discharge in peacetime after three years, but thereafter the majority sought invaliding after fifteen years. In 1879, some 42 per cent of the Bombay and 30 per cent of the Bengal Army had more than ten years' service.

By contrast, the British Army had begun to change over to short-service engagements in 1870. The regiments which had been longest in India naturally contained higher proportions of long-service men − the 1st (Royal Scots), for example, still contained in 1878 some 80 per cent of men on long-service engagements. The proportions in the more recently arrived units such as the 2nd/4th, 2nd/8th and 2nd/13th were almost exactly reversed.

The changeover to short-service engagements had not been welcomed by the Indian authorities. Drafts coming out to India were increasingly composed of young soldiers with very little service who needed a long period of acclimatization before they could stand up to the heat and the disease. It was widely believed as a result that short-service regiments were less effective on active service than those with a preponderance of long-service men. The truth is difficult to ascertain. Some short-service regiments in the Second Afghan War, such as the 2nd/8th, certainly suffered severely from sickness and their efficiency was correspondingly impaired.

Some long-service regiments, such as the 92nd and 1st/17th, performed extremely reliably.* There were other regiments with a high proportion of men on long-service engagements which did less well – the 81st Foot, for example, which had to be withdrawn in January 1879 after only six weeks in the field, because of sickness. Given the primitive state of prophylactic medicine and the unenlightened official attitude towards the feeding and housing of the private soldier, it seems probable that the law of the survival of the fittest ensured that long-service men as a class were in fact more effective campaigners. This was the conclusion reached by the authorities themselves: 'As far as susceptibility to climatic disease on the one hand and inefficiency in the field from lack of power to withstand fatigue and hardship on the other, the young and unacclimatized corps and soldiers of the present day contrast unfavourably with the older and acclimatized corps and men of the past or present time.'[3] But a great deal depended upon circumstances and upon the quality of the officers.

In the British infantry regiments, the men were equipped with the Martini-Henry rifle which had replaced the Snider in 1871. A single-shot, breech-loader of .45in calibre, the Martini-Henry was perhaps the best military rifle of its time and regarded with great trust and affection by its users. Very accurate and firing a heavy, man-stopping bullet, its defects were the powerful kick and a marked tendency to jam in sandy conditions. The Indian infantry were equipped with Snider rifles thrown out by the British Army when it re-equipped with the Martini-Henry. The Snider was a single-shot, breech-loader of .577in calibre, but it was very much a makeshift being the result of a competition to find the most effective and economical method of converting the 1853 pattern Enfield muzzle-loading rifle to a breech-loader. It was an effective weapon, but longer, heavier and slightly less accurate than the Martini-Henry. It had been introduced into service in the native regiments only in 1874 and not all of them were experienced in its use. In the cavalry regiments, the situation was similar. The primary weapons here remained the sword and lance, and the differences between the British and Indian regiments were marginal. But the Martini-Henry breech-loading carbine used by the British regiments was a better weapon than the Snider carbine used in the native cavalry and mountain artillery.† These differences in equipment reflected the principle that the native troops should not have the same up-to-date weapons as the British soldier.

The Anglo-Indian forces appeared least well-equipped in the field of artillery. The six mobile batteries of native mountain artillery were equipped with a rifled, muzzle-loading gun which threw a 7lb shell to a maximum range of 3,000 yards. Easily broken down for carriage on animals or by porters, and weighing only 200lb, it was a highly mobile piece, but its short range and small projectile were serious disadvantages.‡ The four field batteries of the Hyderabad Contingent were

---

*Surgeon-General Evatt wrote of the 1st/17th 'It was about the last of the long-service battalions of that army which was just then disappearing before the short-service system, and better specimens of that old regime could not be seen than the men of the 17th who, for weight and space occupied per man, were probably 30 per cent heavier and broader than the young soldiers of today.'

†The 9th Lancers received its Martini-Henry carbines in December 1878 during its march to join the Peshawar Valley Field Force. The 12th Bengal Cavalry had been in Afghanistan for six months when it received its final batch of Snider carbines.

‡This was not the famous 'screw gun' of Kipling's, which appeared in native mountain batteries only in 1889, although used by British mountain batteries as early as 1879.

each equipped with two 12-pounder howitzers and two 6-pounder guns. These were muzzle-loading weapons of short range and small projectile, and virtually obsolete. The remainder of the artillery was in British hands and consisted of fifteen horse, 43 field, four heavy, three mountain and 21 garrison batteries. Fifty of the horse and field artillery batteries were equipped with 9-pounder rifled, muzzle-loading guns; eight had 9-pounder or 12-pounder breech-loading Armstrong guns. The heavy batteries deployed a mixture of rifled, muzzle- or breech-loading 40-pounders, and 6.3in or 8in smooth-bore, muzzle-loading howitzers. Each battery normally had four 40-pounders and two 6.3in or 8in howitzers. These batteries were either bullock-, camel- or elephant-drawn. The garrison artillery batteries were static units manning a wide variety of obsolescent fortress guns. Rangefinders were only gradually coming into use and most batteries did not have them.*

In terms of equipment, the artillery in India was the most obsolete arm of the service and there were to be occasions – most notably at Maiwand – where it was patently outmatched by the Afghans. The situation is the more remarkable in that steel breech-loading guns of high accuracy and longer range were already common in Europe.

The geographical boundaries between the three Presidency Armies (in theory at least) should have been reasonably clear-cut, and to some extent they were. Thus the Madras Army was responsible for south-east India, most of the east coast and Burma; the Bombay Army for the west coast, the Deccan, Kutch, Rajputana, Aden and Sind; while the Bengal Army was responsible for Assam and Northern India, including Bengal, Bihar, Orissa, Oudh, Rohilkund, and the Punjab. But the Presidency boundaries had not been adjusted over the years to match the acquisition of new territory. By 1878 more than half of the Madras Army was serving outside the boundaries of the Madras Presidency. In Baluchistan and Central India, the armies were mingled in a confusing and haphazard way. At Nowgong, the 20th Madras Infantry shared the station with the 5th Bengal Cavalry. At Dera Ghazi Khan in the Punjab, three regiments of the Punjab Frontier Force shared the station with the 29th Bombay Native Infantry.

Behind the intermingling of the Armies lay a greater problem – that of sheer dispersion. In 1878, only a handful of stations – Peshawar, Rawalpindi, Lahore, Secunderabad, Lucknow, Bangalore, Calcutta – boasted a large concentration of troops. The majority of the troops were scattered through the length and breadth of the sub-continent, in one- or two-regiment stations. Higher operational formations in the form of brigades, divisions and corps, did not exist in peacetime, and higher formation training was virtually unknown.† In wartime, brigades and divisions had to be organized hastily from regiments which might never have seen one another before. The staffs were formed by denuding regiments and static headquarters.

Just as there were no higher operational formation staffs in peacetime, so there was no General Staff at Army Headquarters to draw up campaign plans.

---

*I have come across only two instances of rangefinders being used in action, both in April 1880. In static positions, ranges were sometimes plotted by theodolite or even sextant.
†Geographical areas called brigades and divisions existed for administrative purposes, but had no operational significance.

Operational planning was the responsibility of the Quartermaster-General, as was Intelligence. In practice, plans were often drawn up *ad hoc* by the Commander-in-Chief or by a designated staff officer. Either way, there was no properly organized Intelligence Branch to provide full and accurate information about the enemy or his intentions. The absence of a proper Intelligence Branch is curious since Roberts, who was QMG from 1874 to 1878, was keenly aware of developments in the British Army in the United Kingdom and had pressed for an Intelligence Branch at Army Headquarters in India. Moreover, Northbrook, both at the War Office and the Admiralty, had played an important role in getting Intelligence on to a proper footing there. There is some evidence that in 1878 the concentration on preparing plans for operations against Russia had diverted effort from obtaining information about the Amir's plans and forces.

If the armies in India lacked a brain, they also lacked in-built mobility. By 1878 there was a network of more than 8,000 miles of railway which facilitated strategic movement within India itself. In the north-west, this network effectively stopped at the Indus which was not crossed by a railway bridge until 1881. In the south, the railhead for Quetta for troops from Bombay was on the west bank of the Indus at Sukkhur; for troops coming from the Punjab or Bengal, however, the railhead was at Rohri. Between Rohri and Sukkhur, only a steam ferry operated. Beyond the railheads the troops had to rely upon animal transport – primarily bullock-carts and camels, supplemented where practicable by horses, ponies and mules as well as more exotic creatures such as elephants and, on occasion, even yaks. Since 1861, the Government had maintained a small amount of transport at a considerable number of stations, sufficient to enable movable columns of all arms to take the field at short notice. In theory, this transport was sufficient in total for 45,000 troops; in practice, because it was dispersed all over India, because some of it was suitable only for certain types of country and because some of it had in any circumstances to be retained for internal security duties, only a fraction was available for an expeditionary force. The Punjab Frontier Force had its own regimental transport and the silladar cavalry regiments maintained a form of regimental transport in the shape of ponies to carry baggage, but generally the situation was such that the Commander-in-Chief of the Bombay Army could say in 1879 that 'I am not aware that there is any organized system of transport in the Bombay army.'[4] So little was the transport system regarded that a quantity of animals and carts was actually sold off in the summer of 1878. Not only was all this animal-drawn transport painfully slow, but because a high proportion of its carrying capacity was needed to carry forage for the animals themselves, the net carrying capacity was low.* The result was that an enormous number of animals had to be hired, requisitioned or purchased at the beginning of each campaign, and because the animals invariably died in vast numbers through neglect and poor management, transport officers were perpetually at their wits' end.† Operations

---

*The speed of a bullock-cart on a reasonable, level road was roughly 1½ miles an hour, that of a camel or mule-cart perhaps 2–2½ miles an hour. A camel could carry about 300 pounds, a mule about 160 and a donkey only 100 pounds.

†In July 1880, the 1st Madras Light Cavalry was issued with 350 untrained baggage bullocks for its march from Sibi to Quetta: only 80 survived the first day's march. The Eden Commission (q.v.) recorded after the opening campaign that 60,000 camels had died and operations had been brought to a halt after four months because of lack of transport.

had frequently to be delayed or abandoned because sufficient animals could not be found in time. The problem had continually exercised the minds of the more able soldiers in India and in April 1878, the Commander-in-Chief had proposed the formation of a Committee to inquire into the problem with a view to setting up the nucleus of a permanent transport force for service abroad. But the proposal was overtaken by the outbreak of war.

Medical facilities were still relatively primitive. British regiments had an establishment of three doctors and native regiments one. They would be assisted in British regiments by a number of trained medical orderlies, while in an Indian regiment the medical officer might be assisted by two or three native apothecaries or dressers. Hospital facilities were normally organized on a regimental basis, but as the war progressed and the numbers of casualties and sick mounted, separate field and base hospitals began to be organized. Opinion as to their relative value remained sharply divided throughout the war. In action, casualties would be carried or assisted back to the regimental dressing station where the regimental doctor would dress their wounds and put them into the regimental hospital. If they had to be sent back to a field hospital or otherwise carried for a long distance, they were transported on camels or mules or in litters, called doolies or dandies, carried by non-combatant bearers; wheeled ambulances were unknown in India. As far as medical treatment was concerned, surgery had progressed notably as a result of the Crimean War, and antiseptics and anaesthetics such as chloroform were in normal use. But there were no antibiotics or blood transfusion. Gangrene following wounds or amputation remained an insoluble problem, and penetrating wounds in the chest and abdomen gave only an even chance of survival. Camp sanitation was better understood and practised and malaria could at least be kept in check with quinine, although not eliminated. But there was no prophylactic against deadly diseases such as cholera, pneumonia or typhoid fever because their causes were not known. When they broke out, they were likely to sweep through a regiment, decimating it in a matter of days.* In peacetime, the only remedy practiced for cholera was to segregate the regiment and to keep it on the move until the disease died out; that was not feasible in war.

The final striking feature of the Anglo-Indian armies was that there were no reserves of any kind for the native regiments. In an emergency, numbers could only be made up by intensified recruiting or by inter-regiment transfers. Recruiting and training took time: thus very few of the recruits authorized in the summer of 1878 (page 70) reached their regiments in Afghanistan before the end of the first campaign in May 1879. By March 1880, the Government was reduced to offering a bounty of 50 rupees (a considerable sum in those days) for every native recruit prepared to serve for three years in regiments on active service.

The Anglo-Indian army which went to war with Afghanistan in 1878 was, nevertheless, essentially an old-fashioned army by European standards. It was an army basically organized for peacetime functions. Its defects were not serious so long as it was engaged on frontier expeditions of short duration. They became serious when faced with an extended campaign on a large scale. It would have been sur-

---

*In 1869, the Royal Munster Fusiliers lost 27 men from cholera in a single night. Between 1870 and 1879, more than 11,000 British soldiers died of disease in India. In the native regiments, the toll was even higher.

prising if amidst the traditional excitement of officers' messes facing the prospect of active service there had not lurked also a certain anxious curiosity as to how the post-Mutiny armies would fare in their first extended test.

Nevertheless, since 1849, the army had had extensive campaigning in the mountainous terrain of the North-West frontier. By trial and error, and with some bitter experiences, it had evolved a reliable code of tactics for mountain warfare. This, plus the possession of superior rifles and the extensive use of the heliograph, meant that tactically at least the troops were well-equipped for their task.

In the absence of an Intelligence Department, Army Headquarters India was forced to rely upon police reports provided by the Foreign Department for detailed information about its opponents. These reports put the strength of the regular Afghan Army at some 52,000 of which roughly half were located in and around Kabul, Kandahar and Kurram; the remainder were at Herat and in Afghan Turkestan. There were 62 regiments of regular infantry, 16 regiments of cavalry and 49 batteries of artillery. Sher Ali had made great improvements in the drill, discipline and equipment of his troops, but it was believed that military service was still unpopular and the troops badly paid so that they were highly likely to desert or disperse in the event of a war with the British. There was also a high degree of jealousy between the individual regiments. The artillery was the élite force and in terms of size and equipment presented a potentially serious threat. It consisted of two elephant-drawn heavy batteries, 22 horse artillery batteries, eighteen mountain batteries using mule transport and seven bullock-drawn field batteries. The police reports greatly under-estimated the number of breech-loaders available, and since most of the British guns were muzzle-loading there was in fact little to choose between the two sides in terms of equipment. In the fighting to come, the Afghan artillery showed itself not to be despised and indeed played a decisive part in the British defeat at Maiwand. As far as small arms were concerned, the Afghan Army possessed some 7,000 Snider breech-loaders, mainly given by the British; the remainder of its weapons were muzzle-loaders, chiefly Enfields. The Afghans had ample stocks of ammunition and both rifles and ammunition could be manufactured at Kabul without difficulty. The Afghan army had no serious equipment deficiencies and Roberts in particular was impressed by the quantity and quality of the equipment he found at the Peiwar Kotal and at Kabul.

In addition to his regular troops, the Amir could call upon substantial numbers of irregular levies. He actually paid for 24,000 such levies to be maintained by his sirdars in peacetime, but in the event of hostilities he could in practice call upon very large numbers of peasants all of whom were accustomed to carrying arms. In any war with the British, he could count also upon help from the formidable transborder tribes who acknowledged neither Afghan nor British rule, but whose ethnic and religious ties drew them strongly towards Kabul. The police reports warned that the Amir could assemble 100,000 armed men at Kabul without serious difficulty and the events of December 1879 showed the accuracy of this assessment.

What they lacked in discipline, the Afghans made up for in mobility. Time and again they showed a remarkable ability to concentrate and move large forces very quickly. Accustomed to living frugally, they had no need of the cumbersome logistics of their Anglo-Indian opponents. Although overshadowed by the legend of Roberts's march from Kabul to Kandahar, Ayub Khan's march from Herat to Maiwand in June–July 1880 was in some ways an even more remarkable achievement since he was accompanied by a large quantity of wheeled artillery of which Roberts had none.

While on paper the discipline and trooping of the British armies gave them a clear advantage, the difficulties of the terrain and the reputation of the Afghans as tough and aggressive fighters meant that the campaign was not necessarily going to be easy or short or the result predetermined.

NOTES

1. K. M. L. Saxena in *The Military System of India, 1850–1900*. New Delhi, 1974, has argued (pp. 214–15) that this was not so. But the collapse of the 30th Bombay Native Infantry which precipitated the rout of Maiwand was clearly due to a shortage of officers (see below). The officer establishment of British regiments was probably unnecessarily large.

2. Eden Commission Report, Appendices, vol. II, p. 258.
3. *Army Medical Department Report for the year 1880, Appendix III – Special Report on the Hospital Organisation, Sanitation and Medical History of the War in Afghanistan, 1878–79–80*, London, 1880, p. 280.
4. Eden Commission, Appendices, vol. I, p. 175.

CHAPTER 5

THE OPENING ROUND: NOVEMBER 1878–JUNE 1879

The possibility of a second Afghan War had been apparent since 1876. In 1877, both Roberts, as QMG, and Haines, as Commander-in-Chief, had submitted notes to Lytton on the mounting of a campaign against Russia via Afghanistan. Both had pointed out serious deficiencies in organization, equipment and communications which would have to be rectified before the Indian Army could expect to campaign successfully. Virtually nothing had been done. Nor is there much evidence that any real, detailed thought had been devoted to a plan of campaign. The two obvious routes into Afghanistan – via the Bolan Pass on Kandahar, and via the Khyber on Kabul – were known in considerable detail as a result of the First Afghan War. Army Headquarters had, however, neglected to assemble and issue this material or to provide maps. Commanders found themselves having to read published histories and volumes of memoirs to get information about the country over which they would have to operate. The information available related only to the area east of a line joining Kabul and Kandahar; Central Afghanistan, Herat and Afghan Turkestan were, for campaigning purposes, virtually *terrae incognitae* as far as Army Headquarters was concerned.

What little information there was about the Afghan army came from the Indian civil police reports – the Quartermaster-General's office had no sources of its own.

For the British, a war against the Amir presented peculiarly difficult military problems. The country was harsh and bleak, and while some supplies should be procurable, much would have to be supplied from India.* The traditional invasion routes passed through mountainous country and narrow defiles where a handful of determined men might delay an army. The distances were great – Herat, for example, was 800 miles from the Indus and Kabul was nearly 200 miles from Peshawar and more than 300 miles from Kandahar. The supply lines would be long and would pass through the territory of fierce, predatory, independent tribes, whose prowess the British knew from thirty years of border fighting. There were no metalled roads in Afghanistan and hence little wheeled transport. Above all, the planners faced the problem of a suitable strategic objective. The regular Afghan army was widely dispersed and did not in any case constitute the ultimate military strength of the country. There were only three cities of any size and one of them, Herat, could, for practical purposes, be ruled out as an object of attack. Given the rudimentary administration and economy of the country, even the occupation of Kabul and Kandahar could not be guaranteed to bring the Afghans to heel.

---

*Large supplies of wheat, barley, vegetables, meat in the form of mutton, and forage proved to be procurable at Kabul and Kandahar, the latter area also producing quantities of rice. Even so, huge quantities of these and other foodstuffs had to be imported from India.

Occupation of the whole country was clearly impossible in view of the military resources which would be required. Even the occupation of the eastern area of the country was likely to require a very considerable force against the prospect of large-scale guerrilla fighting in a country where every man habitually went armed.

Faced with these problems, Lytton opted for a war of strictly limited objectives. The occupation of Kandahar and the Kurram valley would by this calculation bring the Amir to heel quickly and cheaply because he would see that their loss and the consequent damage to his prestige was too high a price to pay for denying the British an envoy.

Sher Ali regarded the prospect of war fatalistically. He had made no plans to resist a British invasion and no attempt to concentrate troops from Herat and Afghan Turkestan. His only positive action was belatedly to reinforce the garrisons guarding the Khyber and the Kurram – but the decision was taken so late that not all the reinforcements had arrived when the British invaded.

It was not until the beginning of August 1878 that the Commander-in-Chief was asked for his views about a campaign in Afghanistan. He was asked specifically to advise upon the forces and organization required to occupy the Kurram valley and form a cantonment near its head, and to occupy and hold Kandahar from Quetta. It was to be assumed that there would be no advance beyond the Helmund or Kalat-i-Ghilzai, or through the Khyber. For planning purposes, the Afghan army was reckoned at 60,000, of whom 15,000 could be assembled at Kandahar.

Haines considered it unwise to strip the frontier of its existing garrisons. In particular, the Punjab Frontier Force should remain in its existing locations in order to keep the transborder tribes quiet. He was concerned that in a war with Afghanistan, Muslim, and particularly Pathan, troops might be subjected to religious and racial pressures from their Afghan brethren; it would be wise to use only British, Sikh or Gurkha troops as far as possible in the Kurram Valley force. Finally, he was in favour of a limited demonstration along the Khyber route to deceive the Afghans as to the real objectives. He recommended that the first priority be to reinforce the Quetta garrison against a surprise Afghan move. The existing force there of some 1,800 men should be reinforced by a field battery, eight squadrons of native cavalry, one British and four native infantry regiments, bringing the garrison at Quetta up to some 5,400 men. The force to occupy and hold Kandahar should be deployed in two divisions, consisting of two regiments of British and four regiments of native cavalry, eight batteries of artillery, four British and twelve native infantry regiments, together with eight companies of sappers and miners, totalling in all nearly 13,000 men and 45 guns, including a siege train. In addition, it would be necessary to muster a reserve division of some 6,000 men with eighteen guns for garrison and lines of communications duties. The troops should concentrate at Sukkhur, Jacobabad, Multan and Dera Ghazi Khan; Sukkhur would be the main supply base for Bombay and Madras troops and Dera Ghazi Khan the base for Bengal troops. Arrangements would have to be made to improve bridges and ferries across the Chenab and Indus, and animal transport collected to move men and supplies from Sukkhur to Quetta.

For the Kurram valley, Haines specified a force of four squadrons of cavalry, one regiment of British and five of native infantry, two batteries of artillery and a company of sappers and miners, totalling 4,030 men and twelve guns. (The strength of both British and native cavalry regiments was assumed for practical purposes to be 350 men, while British and native infantry regiments were calculated at 700 and 500 respectively.) For the Khyber demonstration some of the existing Peshawar garrison should encamp near the mouth of the Pass, and to deceive the Afghans negotiations to purchase provisions for 20,000 troops should be put in hand.

The repulse of Chamberlain's mission transformed the military situation. War was now imminent, but no action had actually been taken to assemble the necessary forces. Two days after the momentous meeting at Ali Masjid, Lytton approved the immediate formation of a field force for action in the Kurram and the assembly of the first division of the Kandahar force. He also approved the immediate dispatch of the reinforcements for Quetta which was now dangerously exposed to an Afghan attack from Kandahar. To remedy the weakness of the existing native regiments, orders were given at the beginning of October to increase the strength of all native regiments north of the River Narbada by 96 (cavalry) and 200 (infantry).

No decision was taken about the formation of a second or a reserve division for the Kandahar force, nor about operations through the Khyber, although it was clear to most military men that these were going to be essential. This situation reflected a serious division of opinion between the Viceroy and the Commander-in-Chief. Lytton, despite his flamboyant words, was anxious to avoid anything in the nature of a 'regular invasion of Afghanistan'. His aim remained, as it had been in August, to exert pressure on the Amir by occupying the Kurram valley and threatening Kandahar. He was prepared to extend the pressure to the Khyber, but he had no intention of marching on Kabul. He was confident that this pressure taken in conjunction with what he believed to be the worthlessness of the Afghan army would produce the necessary results. In this he leaned heavily upon the military advice of his Private Secretary and friend, Colonel Colley. Colley was Lytton's *éminence grise* and one of Wolseley's famous 'Ring' of brilliant, intellectual officers. Between him and Lytton had sprung up a friendship of almost feminine intensity. Wilfred Blunt, observing them at close quarters, wrote of Colley that he was: 'A man of extreme self-confidence and one who had acquired so great an influence over Lytton that he had persuaded the Viceroy that between them they could direct the whole detail of the plan of campaign from Simla.'[1] Sir Neville Chamberlain, speaking of Lytton's conferences with his military advisers, made the same point: 'Colonel Colley is always present but sits away and says nothing. I feel all the time that he has given the Viceroy the key to the discourse and is his real military mentor.'[2] Colley was reputed to have said that with a regiment armed with breech-loaders he could march through Afghanistan. He was to be killed at Majuba in 1881 in circumstances which throw some doubt on his real talents as a general.

Haines and his colleagues regarded Lytton's limited measures as insufficient. If the Viceroy's political judgement proved wrong, the Indian army would be involved in full-scale war, and the Afghan army, and especially its artillery, might not prove to be as inconsiderable as Lytton and Colley seemed to think. Very large forces would then be required; Haines and his senior colleagues, notably Sam Browne, the Military Member, and Neville Chamberlain, believed that these forces should in prudence be assembled immediately.

The first units of the Quetta Reinforcement (70th Foot, E/4 RA and one company of Bengal Sappers and Miners) left Multan on 25 September, only two days after Lytton's authorization. Their march illustrates the problems caused by lack of timely preparation. The source of stores and equipment was the arsenal at Ferozepur, 200 miles away. But there was no direct rail link between Ferozepur and Multan and time was at a premium. The troops marched, therefore, in thin summer dress and without engineer stores. Their transport had been hastily assembled from civilian sources and the animals were ill-fitted for the rigours ahead. The troops were under the direct command of Major-General Michael Biddulph, commander of the Reinforcement. He had had no experience of active service in India but he had drive and determination, qualities which he was to need in abundance.

The urgency of the potential threat to Quetta determined the route. Floods along the Indus prevented use of the obvious route by rail and ferry to Sukkhur. The Multan troops were to move instead via Rajanpur on the Indus and thence through the Bugti country to Lehri and Dadar at the mouth of the Bolan. This route had never been traversed by a large force; only two years before it had been reported impassable for wheeled artillery, and lacking water.

Even before the force reached Rajanpur, large numbers had had to be sent back sick to Multan. From Rajanpur onwards, the march developed into a race against disaster. Three days' of ploughing through heavy sand, in intense heat, accompanied by sandstorms, brought the troops exhausted to Bandowali.* There they faced a 23-mile march across waterless desert to Kabradani. Biddulph took the bold decision to leave all surplus supplies, equipment and wagons under the care of the local Baluch chief and to use the animals to reinforce the gun teams and to carry the sick and footsore. Beyond Kabradani, the sand gave way to rocky ridges which bruised the feet of men and animals and entailed endless labour in man-handling the guns and remaining wagons. By the time the force reached Dadar, it resembled a sick convoy. There was no respite, however, at Dadar, one of the hottest places on earth. Beyond it the route through the Bolan, precipitous, shingly and treeless, ascended to the valley in which Quetta lay, at a height of 5,000 feet above Dadar. Overworked, under-nourished, ill-conditioned to the cold of the mountains, the transport animals lay down and died in their hundreds. Similarly under-fed and without proper winter clothing, the native followers succumbed to exhaustion, frost-bite and pneumonia.[3] Biddulph finally reached Quetta with the remnants of his force on 9 November.

The regiments for the Kurram Valley Field Force had been earmarked even before the repulse of Chamberlain's mission and they were now ordered to assemble as rapidly as possible at Thal at the entrance to the valley. Their commander, Major-General Frederick Roberts, VC, arrived at Kohat, the force's

---

*Hanna, who accompanied Biddulph, wrote of this stage of the journey: 'With the sun came a curious phenomenon; hundreds of fickle little winds flickered about in every direction, carrying up with them, high in the air, slender columns of hot sand which waltzed and whirled, and rose and sank as if invisible spirits were engaged in a great top-spinning contest. After a while, these died away, to be succeeded by dense clouds of sand which completely enveloped the moving mass of men and animals, filling mouth and nostrils, eyes and ears with fine, sharp dust. Through rents in these clouds, the figures of the camels, viewed at a distance, grew strangely elongated, broken and spectral; and on the far horizon, great reaches of calm water mocked the thirst of man and beast.' Hanna, op. cit., vol. 1, pp. 304–5.

main base, 63 miles east of Thal, on 9 October and immediately set to work to assemble stores and transport. To expel the Afghans and occupy the valley, which was roughly 73 miles in length, he had been allotted a force of one and one-half regiments of cavalry, seven infantry battalions and three batteries of artillery. The Commander-in-Chief thought this ample for the task; unlike Lytton, he regarded the Kurram as essentially a diversionary theatre. Roberts saw greater opportunities and had Lytton's ear; he managed to get a further three battalions added to his force.

The military commitment was beginning to escalate and yet no clear plans had been made for operating through the Khyber. At the beginning of October, the Commander-in-Chief was asked about the formation of a reserve division of 5,000 men at Hasan Abdul. Five days later, he was asked to submit proposals for the formation of a corps of two divisions at Peshawar for operations through the Khyber. By 16 October, however, all that had actually been approved was the reserve division, together with a substantial reinforcement of the Peshawar garrison.

In the meantime, Cavagnari had put forward a bold plan for seizing the Afghan fort at Ali Masjid, the key to the Khyber, by a *coup de main*. Lytton gave it his enthusiastic support and Ross, the commander of the Peshawar garrison, was persuaded to give his unwilling support. The plan was nipped in the bud by the arrival at Ali Masjid of strong Afghan reinforcements.[4] Cavagnari then busied himself with negotiating Shinwari and Afridi agreement to unobstructed use of the pass in return for substantial cash subsidies.

At the beginning of November, Lytton finally accepted plans for an advance through the Khyber as far as Dakka. For this purpose, the size of the reserve division was to be increased from 6,000 to 10,000 men and its commander was to be Major-General Frederick Maude, VC. Within weeks, the plans changed again. Two divisions were now to be employed, one to conduct operations through the pass, and the second to guard the lines of communication. Maude assumed that he would get the 1st Division but it was given to Sam Browne. There was no more experienced frontier soldier than Browne and his appointment was fully justified on military grounds. As Military Member he had clashed with Lytton on a number of issues, notably the size of the forces required for the war. By replacing Browne with Neville Chamberlain, Lytton hoped to get a more amenable colleague. In this he was to be mistaken but Browne, whose forte was clearly fighting rather than writing, was happy to take command in the field.[5] Unusually, the two divisions retained their independence. This could easily have led to friction and confusion, but to Maude's credit he voluntarily accepted the lesser role and acted for practical purposes as if he were under Browne's command. Cavagnari was appointed Political Officer, responsible directly to the Government of India.

When the ultimatum expired, nearly 40,000 men were on the move towards the frontier,* and repercussions were being felt throughout India. At French Rocks,

*Peshawar Valley Field Force	16,200 men	48 guns
Kurram Valley Field Force	6,650 men	18 guns
Quetta Reinforcement	5,500 men	18 guns
Kandahar Column	7,300 men	60 guns
Kandahar Reserve Division (formally sanctioned 27 November 1878)	3,900 men	24 guns
Totals	39,550	168

near Mysore, 1,500 miles south of Peshawar, the 30th Madras Native Infantry had been warned for service; 1,200 miles to the east, the 3rd Bengal Native Infantry at Dinapore had been ordered to reinforce Kohat. From its remote cantonment in Rajputana, the Mhairwarra Battalion had been summoned to join Maude at Peshawar. In messes and barrackrooms all over India, men were eagerly speculating about the coming campaign and their chances of taking part.

Problems of supplies and transport had surfaced immediately. Because the Peshawar Valley Force had not been established until November, the depots at Peshawar had already been drained by Roberts's Kurram Valley column. There was thus an acute shortage of tents, transport and supplies of every kind. Roberts, in turn, complained that his column was short of transport and some necessary supplies because his main base at Rawalpindi had been drained by the needs of the Peshawar troops. Three years of famine in the Punjab had in any case greatly reduced the number of animals available for purchase or hire. Those that remained were young or weakened. If the troops started the campaign ill-equipped and clothed, the condition of the followers, on whom the troops heavily depended, was even worse. Without winter clothing, they were to succumb in their hundreds to the cold of the mountains.

Sam Browne's task was to expel the Afghan garrisons from the Khyber and occupy Dakka or some other position which would guard the western exit of the pass. The bulk of his force was then to be withdrawn to British territory. Roberts was to occupy the Kurram valley and Khost but not to go beyond the Shutagardan and Zurmat Passes. Stewart was to occupy Kandahar and to venture no further in any circumstances than the Helmund and Kalat-i-Ghilzai. Understandably, and prudently, the Indian Government did not wish to become involved in an occupation of Kabul. The maintenance of a force at Kabul involved a line of communication of at least 190 miles through difficult mountain country and even more difficult tribesmen. Once at Kabul, it would be necessary to establish there a substantial force capable of maintaining itself in face of popular insurrection as well as deploying large numbers of troops to keep open the lines of communication. Since the political strategy was to fasten responsibility for the war firmly on Sher Ali alone and, by showing that Britain meant business, force his submission or replacement, a military strategy of strictly limited objectives was entirely logical. Whether it would prove practicable and effective was another question.

Despite the fact that the Peshawar Valley Field Force was the last of the three main forces to be established, it was the first to come into action. The key to the Khyber was the fort of Ali Masjid, nine miles from Jamrud, on the west bank of the River Kabul. The fort occupied the top of a steep detached hill rising some 500 feet above the floor of the pass which at this point runs roughly north-north-west along the bed of the river and is very narrow. It had been carefully reconnoitred by Lieutenant-Colonel Jenkins and the Guides on 23 October: Browne himself examined it on 16 November; when orders were given by the Indian Government on 20 November to commence hostilities on the following day, his plans were already prepared.

South of the fort, a line of entrenchments and sangars (breastworks of piled stones) ran roughly east and west, connected at its western end to lofty hills to the north and north-west of the fort (map 3). These entrenchments rested on three peaks each of which commanded the fort, the easternmost peak being about 500 yards from it. Across the river from the fort, on the east bank, another line of entrenchments ran along a ridge eastwards from cliffs above the river and merged into the lofty hills around the Rhotas peak (5,460 feet above sea level). The fort and entrenchments were held by an Afghan regular force estimated at 3,700 with 24 guns.

The Afghan position was a formidable one, but like most mountain positions it could be turned. Reconnaissance had shown that this could be achieved by using the Lashora valley, some four miles to the east, which ran roughly parallel to the Khyber.

Browne planned to put in a frontal, holding attack while sending two brigades up the Lashora valley to get behind the Afghan position. The 1st and 2nd Infantry Brigades would move from Jamrud, via Lashora, to Sapri, north-east of Ali Masjid, a distance of nearly five miles as the crow flies. From there, a small flank guard would be detached to hold the peak of Multani Sir, north-west of Sapri. The 1st Infantry Brigade was then to move roughly south-south-westwards to occupy positions from which direct fire could be brought to bear on the rear of the Afghan position. The 2nd Infantry Brigade would move westwards from Sapri to occupy Kata Khushtia thus blocking any escape through the pass. The main column,

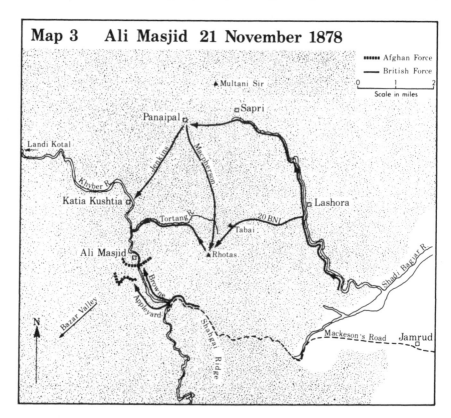

Map 3   Ali Masjid 21 November 1878

consisting of the 3rd and 4th Infantry Brigades under Brigadier-Generals Appleyard and W. B. Browne, with the cavalry brigade and most of the artillery, was to advance through the Khyber to demonstrate against the Afghan positions frontally. Once they had been taken, the cavalry was to push through the pass and seize Landi Khana.

Detailed orders were issued on 19 November. The 1st and 2nd Brigades were to start on the evening of the 20th in order to be in position to open their attack on the morning of the 21st with the expiry of the ultimatum. En route to Sapri, the 1st Brigade was to detach 240 rifles to move via Tabai to seize the ridge leading to the Rhotas peak in order to prevent the enemy from doing so. The two brigade commanders were given discretion as to what to do after they had reached their primary objectives at Kata Khushtia and Rhotas. They could either descend into the pass itself to aid directly the main column, or continue along the heights on the eastern side of the pass towards Landi Khana, in effect picketing the route of the main body. The main column, having established its guns on the Shahgai ridge, was to move forward, as opportunity offered, on both sides of the river in order to fix the Afghans in their positions while the turning movement developed. For maximum effectiveness, the plan required communication between the turning columns and the main body and for this purpose a signal party would accompany the detachment moving via Tabai. The main body would start its attack at 13.00 hours on the 21st when it was expected that the 1st and 2nd Brigades would be in position.

The success of the whole operation depended upon the speed with which the turning columns reached their objectives. The route via Lashora and Sapri had been reconnoitred as far as Panaipal by Colonel Jenkins who reported that the distance from Jamrud to Panaipal was between twelve and thirteen miles, and that the Guides could cover it in three hours. Acting on this advice, the final orders provided for the 2nd Brigade to move from Jamrud in the early evening of the 20th, giving it eighteen hours to reach Kata Khushtia. The 1st Brigade was to move in the early hours of the morning of the 21st, thus having some ten hours to get into position on Rhotas. On the face of it, the timing was generous.

The 2nd Brigade (Brigadier-General J. A. Tytler, VC) moved out of Jamrud at 17.20 hours on 20 January 1878, thus inaugurating the Second Afghan War. It was led by the Guides Infantry, followed by the 1st Battalion 17th Foot, 1st Sikh Infantry PFF (minus one company) and the supply animals, with one company of 1st Sikhs acting as escort to the supplies and as rearguard – in all about 1,740 men. Almost immediately, the column ran into trouble. It was a dark night and the going was exceptionally difficult. On two occasions the native guide lost the route and the column had to retrace its steps. It proved difficult to maintain touch and by the time the column reached Lashora, it had taken five hours to cover seven miles and the troops were cold and wet from tramping through the Lashora stream. At Lashora the brigade halted but no fires were allowed, and the cold night allowed no proper rest. The brigade moved off again at 06.15 hours on the 21st, just as the 1st Brigade arrived. Beyond Lashora the going became worse, being narrow and very steep so that the troops had to move in single file. The morning heat was intense and there was no water to be obtained until Panaipal was reached at 13.30 hours after a march of sixteen miles. By this time, the British troops in particular were exhausted, the supply animals with the next two days' rations were far behind, and the column was already hopelessly late. In these circumstances Tytler decided to send on Jenkins with the Guides and 1st Sikhs while he himself remained at Panaipal with the 1/17th awaiting the supply animals. It was his intention to move on as soon as the 1/17th had been fed, but by nightfall the bullocks had still not arrived and Tytler camped where he was.

Jenkins reached Kata Khushtia at about 16.00 hours, just in time to intercept Afghan cavalry coming from Ali Masjid. At this point the pass was only 600 yards wide and Jenkins' troops were able to close in with their rifle fire. The Afghan troops at Ali Masjid, who had by this time been under frontal attack from the main column for several hours, now knew that their direct line of retreat through the pass was blocked. A further large body of cavalry and infantry fleeing from Ali Masjid was intercepted by Jenkins' force at dusk.

The 1st Brigade (Brigadier-General H. T. Macpherson, VC) left Jamrud nine hours after Tytler. It consisted of 4th Gurkhas, 20th Bengal Native Infantry (BNI), 4th Battalion Rifle Brigade and No. 4 (Hazara) Mountain Battery – in all, just under 2,000 men with four guns. It reached Lashora in about four hours. En route, four companies of 20th BNI were detached to occupy the ridge leading from Tabai to Rhotas and, if possible, Rhotas peak itself.

Macpherson was forced to wait at Lashora to allow Tytler's 2nd Brigade to get clear. When he moved on at 07.30 hours, his column was impeded by the lagging supply animals of 2nd Brigade. The head of the 1st Brigade column reached Sapri at 11.30, but the rear did not get in until 13.00 hours. Like 2nd Brigade, the 1st was now well behind its schedule, but it pushed on until 15.00 hours towards Rhotas. At that point Macpherson decided to halt for the night. He was far short of his objective, but his troops were tired, their rations had not arrived and the going ahead was very steep. To cap it all, the officer in charge of the signal party had attached himself by mistake to Tytler's 2nd Brigade and Macpherson was unable to communicate with Sam Browne at Jamrud.

Browne was blissfully ignorant of this state of affairs when the main body moved out from Jamrud at 07.00 hours on the 21st. An advance party of engineers had already been at work improving the road at the entrance to the pass, and signallers had occupied the peak at Surkhai to provide a link between Jamrud and the Shahgai heights. The main body moved in three columns:

1. The advance guard, consisting of 14th BNI, half of 81st Foot, I/C Royal Horse Artillery (RHA), 11/9 (Mountain) RA, a troop of 10th Hussars and two companies of Bengal Sappers and Miners;
2. The main body consisting of the remainder of the 81st Foot, 51st Foot, 27th, 6th and 45th BNI, E/3 (Field) and 13/9 (Heavy) RA;
3. The Cavalry Brigade, under Brigadier-General C. J. S. Gough, VC, consisting of two squadrons of the Guides Cavalry, two squadrons of 10th Hussars and two squadrons of 11th Bengal Lancers.

The first shots of the war were fired shortly after 10.00 hours by men of the 81st Foot against a patrol of Afghan cavalry which had been watching the entrance to the Khyber. Shortly after 11.00 hours the advance guard began to occupy the Shahgai ridge and a detachment was pushed out along the ridge to the north-west to provide a flank guard against attack from Afghan forces seen now to be holding the Rhotas position in strength. As soon as the Shahgai ridge was occupied, the artillery – first I/C, then E/3 and 13/9 – were brought forward to open fire on Ali Masjid at a range of roughly 2,500 yards. The Afghan guns replied and an artillery duel began which was to last until dusk. The Afghan gunnery was good, but the damage relatively slight since the Afghans were using round shot rather than shells; the effect of the British gunnery on the Afghan positions around Ali Masjid seems to have been equally ineffective.

By 14.30 hours, nothing had been heard or seen of the turning movement by the 1st and 2nd Brigades, but Sam Browne decided that the time had come to launch his frontal attack. The major part of Appleyard's 3rd Brigade, consisting of 14th and 27th BNI and a wing of the 81st Foot, was directed to move forward across the River Khyber at Lala China and endeavour to work its way into the Afghan entrenchments south of the fort, with the ultimate object of seizing the three hills on which the entrenchments rested. Brigadier-General Browne's 4th Brigade was to move forward on the eastern side of the pass to occupy a ridge a mile or so ahead of the Shahgai ridge and roughly midway between Ali Masjid and Rhotas peak.

Appleyard's attack was fiercely contested but, supported by 4 guns of I/C which moved forward up the pass to within 1,200 yards of the fort, 14th BNI had by late afternoon reached the easternmost of the three hills, on which the mountain guns of 11/9 now also began to play.

On the other side of the valley, the advance of Browne's 4th Brigade was equally sharply contested. He was supported initially by two guns of I/C and by 11/9 firing shrapnel and common shell. By about 16.00 hours, the brigade was stalled with no prospect of getting further. 11/9 was withdrawn to a ridge in rear and commenced to fire in support of Appleyard's attack across the valley.

By 17.00 hours the efforts of the main column had come to a halt. The attack on the right could go no farther against a virtually impregnable position. I/C was out of action because its ammunition was temporarily expended, and Appleyard's attack was facing fierce resistance which showed no signs of diminishing. There was still no sign of the turning movement by the 1st and 2nd Brigades. Sam Browne decided to call it a day. The attacking troops of 4th Brigade on the right were able to withdraw without difficulty, but the retirement of the advanced troops of 3rd Brigade was fiercely followed up. Reinforcements from 81st and 51st Foot had to be brought forward to effect the withdrawal.

Despite the formidable nature of the Afghan position and the fierce resistance, British casualties had not been heavy (two officers and fourteen men killed; one officer and 33 men wounded) and Browne issued orders for the attack on the fort to be renewed the next day. At daybreak on the 22nd, 11/9 moved forward across the river at the same point as I/C had crossed the previous day, and opened fire on the Afghan positions. There was no reply and it quickly became apparent that the enemy had gone. Some 300 of the enemy had been intercepted and made prisoner by Jenkins at Kata Khushtia shortly after daybreak,* but the Afghan commander,

---

*These appear to have been Afghans who had been manning the forward positions in front of Ali Masjid and had not been told that the main garrison was decamping during the night.

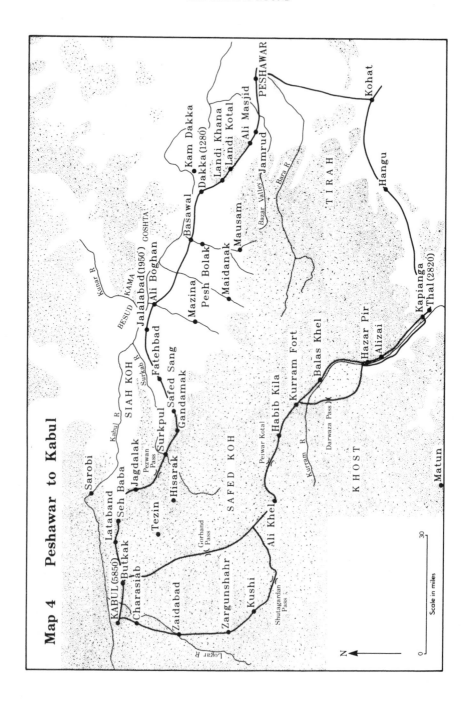

Map 4   Peshawar to Kabul

Ghulam Haidar, and the majority of his regular troops had managed to escape south-westwards across the hills into the Bazar valley.

All that remained now was to occupy Ali Masjid and regroup before continuing the advance to Dakka. For the remainder of the day the main body remained stationary around Ali Masjid while the 1st and 2nd Brigades sorted themselves out. Apart from a small detachment left behind at Panaipal to bring up supplies, the remainder of 2nd Brigade reached Kata Khushtia during the morning of the 22nd. No supplies reached the brigade during the day, but in the evening seventeen captured sheep arrived from Ali Masjid to provide rations of meat. It had proved impossible to get the exhausted supply animals of 2nd Brigade beyond Sapri and the commander of 1st Brigade, being himself short of supplies, promptly appropriated half of 2nd Brigade's supplies when they reached Sapri in order to feed his own men. Thus fed, 1st Brigade continued to its original objective, finally seizing Rhotas peak at about 14.00 hours on the 22nd, joining up en route with the detachment of 20th BNI which had moved on Rhotas via Tabai 24 hours earlier. Large number of Afghans who had been occupying the Rhotas heights were now busy fleeing westwards and some were made prisoners. The signal party was at last able to make contact with Jamrud and thus learn of the fall of Ali Masjid. No practicable route for mules could be found to lead direct from Rhotas to Ali Masjid, and the brigade had to move westwards and then descend the steep Tortang valley in order to link up finally with 2nd Brigade at Kata Khushtia.

On the following day Sam Browne, with the Guides Cavalry, 10th Hussars and 14th BNI, moved on to Landi Khana, leaving 4th Brigade and 11th Bengal Lancers at Ali Masjid and the 1st and 2nd Brigades at Kata Khushtia. On the 24th, Dakka, two miles beyond the western exit of the Khyber, was occupied and the force halted there for three weeks.

The Peshawar Field Force had achieved its objectives quickly and with trifling casualties, despite the fact that it had had only some three weeks in which to get organized. The attack on Ali Masjid left something to be desired as regards execution. Despite the obvious need to co-ordinate accurately the movements of the turning columns with those of the main body, communications between the two halves of the Force had totally broken down on 21 November. The time needed for 1st and 2nd Brigades to move via Lashora and Sapri had clearly been underestimated, partly because inadequate allowance had been made for the British troops being not fully campaign-hardened. (The performance of the Guides and 1st Sikhs provides an instructive comparison.) Why it was necessary to take baggage animals for an operation expected to last only a day, or why Tytler delayed at Lashora for so long, is by no means clear.

Browne's decision to launch and persevere with his frontal attack was criticized at the time,[6] but in the absence of any news from his turning force, he faced a difficult choice. If he had delayed much longer, it would have been too late in the day to attack at all. In launching an attack against such a formidable position he ran the risk of a repulse, something which was to be avoided if at all possible at the beginning of a campaign. In the event, his plan succeeded and he is entitled to the credit which victory brings. The operations had underlined some of the operational defects of the British forces – notably the relative ineffectiveness of the artillery and the poor quality of the transport.

While these events were taking place in the Khyber, the Kurram Field Force was getting under way fifty miles to the south. From Thal, the Kurram valley runs roughly north-west for some 45 miles as far as Kurram Fort. The river here turns due west, but the main route out of the valley into Afghanistan leaves the river and continues north-westwards to the Peiwar Kotal (kotal = pass), roughly 65 miles from Thal. This was Roberts's first objective. Thirty miles beyond the Peiwar Kotal, over a not too difficult route, lay the Shutargardan Pass. Once across this, the route dropped down through the narrow Dobandi defile into the Logar valley from which Kabul could be easily reached.

The Kurram valley itself was mainly occupied by the Turis who, in sharp distinction to their neighbours, were Shiah Muslims. Partly because of this religious difference, the Turis had suffered a good deal at the hands of Kabul and in 1860 had even petitioned to be taken under British rule. Their co-operation in Roberts's advance could be assumed. The real problems lay with the neighbouring tribes on each side. From Peshawar, the route to Kohat lies through the Kohat Pass which was then in tribal territory. In the previous year (1877), it had been necessary to mount a major expedition against the Jowaki Afridis to the east of the pass in order to ensure freedom of movement through it. From Kohat, the road westwards to Thal along the Miranzai valley was dominated on the north by the towering Samana ridge which marked the southern boundary of the Tirah, the mountain fastness of the Afridis, which no British soldier was to penetrate until 1897. In the angle formed by the Miranzai and Kurram valleys lay the territory of the Zaimukhts, notorious for their raiding around Thal and along the road from Thal to Kohat. Bordering on the Kurram valley to the west was the Afghan district of Khost occupied by the Mangals and Wazirs, both exceptionally independent and aggressive. Beyond the Peiwar Kotal, Roberts would encounter the Ghilzais, one of the two great tribal confederations of Afghanistan proper. Roberts thus faced two basic problems – the security of his lines of communication and the problem of transport over the 170 miles or so which separated his main base at Kohat from the Shutargardan Pass. He was authorized to go as far as the Shutagardan, although it was suggested that it might be sufficient to occupy the Peiwar Kotal and the village of Ali Khel, some twelve miles beyond, which marked the boundary between the Jajis, who occupied the area around the kotal, and the Ghilzais. Every effort was to be made to win over the Ahmadzai section of the Ghilzais who were accustomed to wintering their flocks in the Kurram. He was enjoined to avoid Zaimukht territory and to cultivate friendly relations with the local inhabitants. Beyond that, he was given wide discretion in the conduct of his operations and in the subsequent distribution of his troops. Unlike Sam Browne, he had insisted on being given full political powers.

Roberts had had more time than the other force commanders to plan his operations and to make the necessary preparations. Conscious of the need for speed before snow began to fall in the Kurram valley he intended to concentrate on seizing the Peiwar Kotal, leaving Khost to be occupied after the worst of the winter was over. Like Browne, he encountered great problems in obtaining the necessary supplies and in getting them forward to his advanced base at Thal.[7]

Despite the difficulties, the force was concentrated at Thal by 20 November and a trestle bridge had been constructed over the River Kurram, a mile upstream, to enable the force to cross and follow the road up the west bank. The road was actually no more than a rough track, but it presented no serious problems and had the advantage of keeping the force away from close contact with the Zaimukhts and Afridis. Roberts arrived at Thal on the 18th and issued his orders on the 20th for the advance to start the next day.

His force was generally of high quality.* As a result of his Mutiny experiences, he was prejudiced in favour of the so-called 'martial races' – particularly Sikhs, Punjabis and Gurkhas. All of his native infantry were from these races and three of the five he took with him in his advance were experienced regiments of his own Punjab Frontier Force. Of the British regiments, the 72nd and 92nd Highlanders were seasoned, long-service regiments; the 2nd/8th, however, was described by Roberts as 'very sickly, very young and scarcely fit for service'.[8] Nor was he much impressed with its commanding officer; 'Colonel Drew is an officer in whom I have no confidence; his battalion is not in good order and he himself has neither the firmness nor energy required for the efficient command of a young regiment.'[9]

Roberts himself, although technically now a British Service officer, had spent all his career in India, starting in the Bengal Horse Artillery. He had seen much fighting during the Mutiny and had seen active service in Abyssinia in 1867 and in the Lushai Expedition in 1872. But he had spent most of his post-Mutiny service in the Quartermaster-General's Department at Army HQ and he had never commanded troops in the field. He had become a favourite of Lytton's and a close friend of George Colley's. It is clear that he owed his command of the Kurram Field Force to Lytton since he was certainly not the Commander-in-Chief's first choice. He had intrigued with Colley to ensure that, unlike Browne, he was given full political powers and as few detailed instructions as possible.

There was little enough information about the Afghan forces. There was known to be a garrison at the fort at Khapianga, two miles north of Thal, and Afghan troops had watched the construction of the trestle bridge. But precisely how many Afghan troops and guns were in the valley no one knew. Allowing for the troops left behind at Kohat, Thal and the intervening parts, Roberts was taking forward with him some 4,000 fighting men, thirteen guns, 3,000 native followers and 2,000 transport animals.

Promptly at 05.00 hours on 21 November, Roberts's advance guard, consisting of the cavalry, 29th BNI and No. 1 Mountain Battery, moved across the river to the west bank, but they were too late to catch the Khapianga garrison which had fled during the night. The advance guard halted that night at Ahmed-i-Shama, ten miles from Thal, the rest of the 1st Brigade camping at Khapianga. The 2nd Brigade remained at Thal. On 22 November, the advance guard moved on to Hazar Pir, 25 miles from Thal, and 1st Brigade moved to Ahmed-i-Shama. Beyond Hazar Pir, the route left the west bank of the river and struck inland across the

---

*1st Brigade (Brigadier-General Cobbe): 2/8th Foot, 29th BNI, 5th Punjab Infantry (PI) PFF.
2nd Brigade (Brigadier-General Thelwall): wing 72nd, 23rd BNI (Pioneers), 2nd Punjab Infantry PFF, 5th Gurkha Infantry.
Cavalry: 1 squadron 10th Hussars, 12th Bengal Cavalry (BC).
Artillery: F/A, RHA (on elephants), three guns G/3, RA, No. 1 Mountain Battery.
Engineers: No. 7 Company, Bengal Sappers and Miners.
Left at Thal: 21st BNI, wing 5th Punjab Cavalary (PC), No. 2 Mountain Battery; wing, 72nd.
Left at Kohat: 92nd, 28th BNI, C/4, RA.

Darwazai Pass, reaching the river again opposite Kurram Fort, which was occupied by the advance guard on 25 November. The local inhabitants reported that the Afghan forces, numbering some 1,800 men and twelve guns, were retreating over the Peiwar Kotal. The following day, Roberts reconnoitred as far as Peiwar village, twelve miles ahead, from where he could see the Afghans retiring up the valley leading to the kotal.

On the 27th, Roberts's force was concentrated at Kurram Fort and he issued his orders for the advance on the Peiwar Kotal, twenty miles ahead. The squadron of 10th Hussars, two guns of F/A, the three guns of G/3 and the company of Sappers and Miners were to be left at Kurram together with the sick and weakly and all surplus baggage. The European and native field hospitals, which had been set up at Thal, now moved to Kurram in preparation for the attack on the Peiwar Kotal.

At 06.00 hours on the 28th, the main force moved out in two columns towards the Kotal.* The leading troops, accompanied by Roberts, reached the former Afghan camp at Habib Kala, thirteen miles from Kurram Fort and some seven miles from the Peiwar Kotal itself, at approximately 10.15 hours. Receiving reports that the Afghans were retreating in disorder over the pass, abandoning their guns as they went, Roberts decided to push on in the hope of seizing the kotal without opposition.

The approach to the pass lay up a broad valley which gradually narrowed until it came to an end about half a mile below the pass (map 5). From that point, the track climbed steeply up the face of a massive ridge running roughly north-east–south-west. The kotal itself is merely a narrow depression or saddle in the ridge; across it the ground falls away relatively gently into the valley of the River Hariab a mile and a half or so beyond. The track through the kotal was narrow and rocky and unfit for wheeled vehicles; cavalry and infantry had to go in single file.

The south side of the approach valley consisted of a massive spur running out at right angles to the ridge on which the kotal stands. The north side of the valley consisted of a succession of overlapping spurs which all appeared to lead back to the main ridge north of the kotal. Both the main ridge and the spurs were densely covered in pine forest.

Any direct attack up the track to the kotal would be exposed to flank fire from positions on the spurs to north and south, as well as to frontal fire from positions along the main ridge. The kotal itself was commanded to north and south by positions on the main ridge which at this point is some 500 feet above the pass. In effect, a frontal attack would be pushing into a cul-de-sac dominated on all three sides.

In the hope of seizing the kotal quickly – Roberts pushed his leading troops (5th PI and 29th BNI) forward along the northern slopes of the southern spur. Contrary to local reports, Afghan troops and guns were strongly positioned on the kotal and to the north and south, and clearly intent on making a fight of it. The 5th PI and the 29th came under intense rifle and artillery fire from the main ridge and increasingly from the southern spur. The 5th Gurkhas had to be sent forward in support before the advanced troops could be safely extricated. The whole force then

---

*12th BC, 2/8th Foot, wing 72nd Highlanders, 23rd and 29th BNI, 2nd and 5th PI, 5th Gurkhas, four guns F/A, No. 1 Mountain Battery.

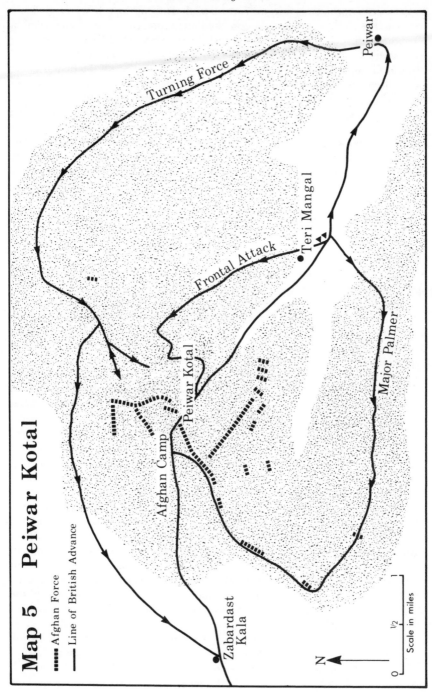

Map 5 Peiwar Kotal

▪▪▪▪ Afghan Force
—— Line of British Advance

Turning Force

Peiwar

Teri Mangal

Frontal Attack

Major Palmer

Peiwar Kotal

Afghan Camp

Zabardast Kala

N

0   ½
Scale in miles

encamped for the night close to Teri Mangal. The Afghans, however, had not finished. They moved a mountain gun along the southern spur and succeeded in dropping shells into the British camp. Little damage was done, but the camp had to be shifted a mile further back, to the irritation of the weary troops.

It was obvious that the Afghans could not now be hustled off the Peiwar Kotal and Roberts confided to his diary that he had a difficult nut to crack. The next two days were spent in careful reconnaissance. Some three miles to the east, the Spingawi valley offered the possibility of an indirect approach. It had been used by Lumsden's party in 1857, and its head, a relatively easy kotal, provided access to the ridge on which the Peiwar Kotal and the main Afghan defences lay. The route itself looked easy and once in possession of the Spingawi Kotal there appeared to be no obstacle to an advance on the Peiwar Kotal from the east. The beauty of this approach lay in the additional fact that it crossed a series of heights, each of which dominated the next one to the south. The plan which Roberts adopted was thus similar in essence to that used by Browne at Ali Masjid. There were, however, three significant differences between the two operations. First, the bulk of Roberts's force was allocated to the turning movement, leaving no more than a token force to fix the enemy's attention to his front. Secondly, Roberts decided to command the outflanking attack himself. Finally, apart from the gun mules and elephants, he took no animals with him.

To disguise his intentions, Roberts arranged for gun positions to be laid out in front of Teri Mangal in full view of the Afghans, and for reconnaissance parties ostentatiously to examine both sides of the main valley. Reconnaissance and local information had suggested that some eight hours would be required for the outflanking force to reach the Peiwar Kotal (the actual distance would appear to have been just over twelve miles). This made no allowance for any serious fighting, but it was not expected that the Spingawi Kotal would be heavily guarded. In order to put the troops of the outflanking column within reach of the Peiwar Kotal by dawn, Roberts left camp at 22.00 hours on the night of 1 December, leaving his camp-fires burning. The column was made up of the wing of the 72nd Highlanders, 23rd and 29th BNI, 5th Gurkhas, 2nd PI, No. 1 Mountain Battery, and four guns of F/A, carried on elephants – in all, some 2,300 men. The troops left with Cobbe for the frontal diversion consisted of the 2/8th Foot, 5th PI, 12th Bengal Cavalry, the remaining two guns of F/A and three guns of G/3, which had come up from Kurram – in all about 870 men. Major A. P. Palmer, with a number of Turi levies, was to operate in a wide, encircling movement round the right flank of the Afghan position, seizing what opportunities he could to divert and embarrass the Afghan right wing. The Afghan forces were estimated at 1,800 regular troops, with eleven guns, plus an unknown number of tribesmen. The opposing forces appeared not unequally balanced and Roberts was taking a gamble in leaving Cobbe with such a small force. But his troops were in good condition and he had chosen to lead the turning column himself because this was where the risks and the need for quick decisions would lie.

The route up the Spingawi Valley proved extremely difficult, the troops having to scramble over ridge upon ridge of loose rocks. Roberts soon began to suspect that the march was being deliberately slowed down by the Pathan sepoys of 29th BNI who were leading the column. His suspicions were confirmed when two shots were fired from their ranks with the obvious intention of alerting their Afghan co-religionists. It was a very critical moment for Roberts. The majority of his Indian troops were Muslims and he had no means of knowing whether the disaffection now evident in the 29th was widespread. But he replaced the 29th with the 5th Gurkhas and the advance continued.[10] Roberts had intended to halt the troops for an hour's rest, but because of the slow progress he pressed on. Just before 06.00 hours, the leading troops of 5th Gurkhas reached the foot of the Spingawi Kotal. They were not detected until within fifty yards of the first barricade on the kotal. In face of heavy fire from the alerted enemy, the kotal and its defences, including two guns, were quickly seized by the 5th Gurkhas, aided by the 72nd Highlanders, and a heliograph signal was flashed back to the camp at Teri Mangal.*

By 09.00 hours, Roberts was ready to resume his advance along the main ridge towards the Peiwar Kotal. He led the advance himself with the 29th, followed by the 72nd, 5th Gurkhas, 2nd PI and four companies of the 23rd Pioneers. A mile beyond the Spingawi Kotal the advance was held up by intense fire from strong enemy forces posted on the far side of a deep ravine. Despite every effort, and the arrival at about noon of the four guns of F/A to add their weight to the fire of the mountain battery, little progress could be made. In contrast to the Khyber, the dense pine woods which surrounded the Peiwar position offered good cover to the defenders and greatly reduced the effectiveness of artillery fire. For the moment the attack was stalled; it remained to be seen what relief could be provided by the diversionary frontal attack.

At about 05.00 hours, Cobbe's five guns had moved out from the camp at Teri with orders to silence the Afghan gun on the south spur and then to concentrate on the Afghan defences on the kotal itself. Shortly after 06.00 hours, Cobbe's infantry advanced along the northern side of the valley, seizing successive spurs until by midday they were no more than 1,400 yards from the kotal itself. Here the direct advance halted for the moment. The 5th PI, however, continued to move up a spur trending away to the north-east which appeared to offer the prospect of reaching the main Peiwar ridge just north of the kotal. In fact, the spur trended ever farther away from the kotal and led directly to the left flank of Roberts's line of advance. By midday the two halves of the force were in contact. The advance of the 5th Punjab Infantry had disclosed a position from which direct fire could be brought upon the Afghan camp and baggage behind the Peiwar Kotal at a range of 1,200 yards. Three guns of No. 1 Mountain Battery were therefore moved across from the Spingawi plateau and opened a telling fire. In the meantime, the companies of 2/8th had inched their way forward to a position on the north side of the main valley from where they could keep up a steady fire on the kotal defences less than half a mile away.

By 12.30 hours the Afghan fire was weakening and men were beginning to stream away from the kotal, but Roberts was still unable to make progress against the opposition in front of him. Behind the main ridge on which the Peiwar Kotal stands, the ground falls away into the valley of the River Hariab which flows south-westwards to cross the road from the Peiwar Kotal to the Shutagardan Pass just

---

*Captain John Cook of the 5th Gurkhas won the VC here for gallantry in charging the enemy and saving a fellow officer's life.

short of Zabardast Kala. At about 13.00 hours Roberts took the bold decision to break off his own attack and to move the major part of his force back and round into the Hariab valley, thus cutting off the Afghan retreat. The move was decisive. When the Afghans grasped Roberts's purpose, the retirement from the kotal became a general retreat. Seizing their chance, the 2/8th, supported by 12th BC and the five guns of F/A and G/3, moved directly forward and occupied the kotal at about 14.30 hours, Major Palmer and his levies having just beaten them to it. The Afghan regular troops fled down the main road to the Shutagardan pursued by the 12th Bengal Cavalry, while the tribal irregulars dispersed rapidly into the hills. Roberts camped that night in the Hariab valley, due north of the kotal, while Cobbe bivouacked on and around the pass itself.

The victory had been neat and timely, at a cost of only twenty dead and 72 wounded. A reinforcing Afghan mountain battery had already reached Ali Khel, an infantry battalion was waiting to cross the Shutagardan and a cavalry regiment and a battery of horse artillery were following up. With winter and these reinforcements approaching, any delay by Roberts could have had serious results. It was clear from the quantity of guns and stores captured that the Afghans expected and intended to remain. The Afghan force had been considerably larger than assumed, having been reinforced by four regular regiments; Roberts was, in fact, outnumbered in regular troops by about 3,500 to 3,100, irrespective of tribal levies. In consequence, the British success in storming such a strong position made a powerful impression upon the Afghans and the surrounding tribes.

The actions at Ali Masjid and the Peiwar Kotal have many points in common in addition to the basic similarity of plan. Roberts even suffered much the same signalling breakdown as Browne. What distinguished the two actions was Roberts's own leadership. His plan was a bold one because, as far as he knew, there was no great disparity between the size of the forces of the two opponents. In splitting his force and employing the bulk of it in an outflanking move, he was taking a risk for which Hanna, always his most bitter critic, severely criticized him. But by leading this move himself he was able to influence events decisively at the two critical points: first, in electing to push on up the Spingawi Kotal at dawn with the element of surprise still on his side, and secondly, in deciding to switch the whole direction of his flanking attack when he saw that he was making real progress. Both reveal the true nature of generalship.

The force remained on and around the Peiwar for four days, collecting the abandoned guns, equipment and stores, sending casualties back to Kurram Fort where the field hospitals were now established, bringing up supplies from the same place and improving the road on each side of the kotal. On 6 December the bulk of the force moved to Ali Khel and on the following three days Roberts, with an escort, reconnoitred as far as the summit (11,000 feet) of the Shutagardan Pass, establishing the fact that the route was by no means difficult and the pass not nearly so formidable a position as the Peiwar Kotal. Armed with this knowledge and bearing in mind that winter was rapidly approaching (early morning temperatures were already well below freezing-point), Roberts decided against occupying the Shutagardan. The primary tasks now were to construct proper winter quarters for the troops to be left on the Peiwar Kotal and in the Kurram valley, and then to explore Khost.

Four hundred and fifty miles to the south, the third prong of the invasion was taking shape. While Biddulph laboured at Quetta to prepare a base for a large force, Lieutenant-General Stewart left Multan and moved forward with the first division of the Kandahar Column. Stewart was one of the most respected figures in the Indian Army. He was known as a calm, level-headed officer, a good organizer, not afraid to take decisions and of absolute integrity. But, like Roberts whose close friend he was, he had seen little active service apart from the Mutiny and a staff job in the Abyssinian Expedition, and he had never commanded troops in action. Ironically, his main claim to public fame was the fact that he had been Chief Commissioner of the Andaman Islands when Mayo was stabbed to death there by a convict in 1872.

His immediate problem was communications. The railway from Multan ended at Rohri on the east bank of the Indus. From there, a steam ferry plied across the river to Sukkhur which was the terminus of the Indus Valley State Railway from Karachi.[11] From Sukkhur, a gruelling march of 160 miles across largely waterless desert brought the troops to Dadar; Quetta lay 90 miles further on. Until the railway was extended from Sukkhur to Sibi in the winter of 1879–80, all supplies had to be moved from the Indus to Quetta by bullock-cart or pack animal; the troops had to march or be carried in native carts. Huge numbers of animals would be required for all purposes and the native owners in Sind had long memories of the enormous mortality among hired animals during the First Afghan War.

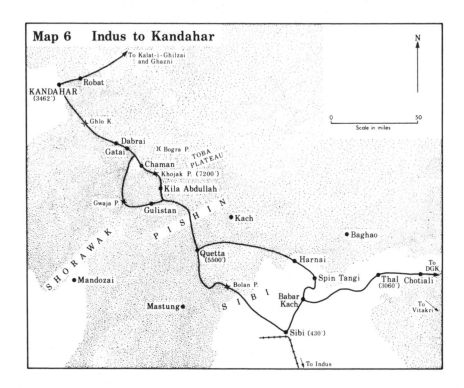

Map 6   Indus to Kandahar

Stewart and his staff reached Quetta in advance of the main body on 8 December and immediately assumed command of what was by now termed the Southern Afghanistan Field Force. His own division, of which he retained command, became the 1st Division of the Force, and Biddulph's force became the 2nd. A reserve division of Bombay and Madras troops began to assemble along the Indus, under the command of Major-General Primrose.

Stewart was not pleased with what he found at Quetta. Biddulph's troops had been under the impression that Stewart's own division was to be merely the garrison for Quetta and had consequently left the preparation of the base to them. Stewart complained that this had 'caused officers to neglect the most obvious duties and precautions and might, under less favourable conditions, have had the most serious consequences'.[12] He was perhaps unfair to Biddulph. Quetta had been occupied only two years before and when Biddulph arrived it housed only a squadron of cavalry, a battery of artillery and two battalions of infantry. He was faced with the task of creating a base capable of accommodating a force of 13,000, without the assistance of a staff and with the additional responsibility of reconnoitring and preparing the route towards Kandahar. He also faced a major problem of communications back to Sukkhur where supplies needed at Quetta were piling up for want of transport. Despite, or perhaps because of, Stewart's sterling qualities, he was not always the easiest man to satisfy and relations between him and Biddulph were not always sympathetic.

Biddulph and Sandeman, the Political Agent in Baluchistan, had already reconnoitred as far as Kushlak on the road towards Kandahar. On the evening of 19 November Biddulph received orders by telegram to prepare to cross the frontier on the morning of the 21st. Leaving behind a small garrison, he moved out of Quetta on the 20th. Before him lay the Khwaja Amran range, the only serious physical obstacle before Kandahar.

The two most obvious routes over the Khwaja Amran were the Khojak Pass, which had been used in the First Afghan War, and the Gwaja Pass to the west. The latter was much the easier but was believed to lack adequate supplies of water. The initial decision went therefore in favour of the Khojak Pass despite its difficulties and the effort which would be needed to rescue the road from the dereliction into which it had fallen since 1842. On 12 December, a small force moved out to occupy the Khojak and to begin work on improving the road. By the 14th the pass was fit for cavalry, infantry and pack transport, and the covering force moved on to occupy Chaman. The road over the Khojak was still extremely steep on the Kandahar side and quite unsuitable for artillery or wheeled vehicles. To make it so would take another fortnight's work, so as an immediate measure a slide was constructed at the most difficult point of the descent and guns and vehicles were lowered down the slide on ropes; with practice the time taken to lower a gun or vehicle was only nine minutes. On 21 December, the main body of the 2nd Division crossed the pass and camped just beyond.

It was clear that an alternative to the Khojak was required in order to relieve congestion, and work began on improving the road over the Gwaja Pass where adequate supplies of water had now been found. Work went on apace in improving the main Khojak Pass route, preparing a road for wheeled vehicles and providing a second track for pack animals.

It was not until 1 January 1879 that Stewart issued his orders for the advance on Kandahar.[13] The 2nd Division was to move via the Khojak; the 1st Division under Stewart himself would take the Gwaja Pass route. Each division consisted of one cavalry and two infantry brigades, mainly of Bengal Army regiments, but including 3rd Sind Horse and 29th Bombay Native Infantry (BoNI). The divisional advance guards moved out on 1 and 2 January, followed at a day's interval by the main bodies. There was no opposition until 5 January when some fifty miles from Kandahar a large force of Afghan cavalry was encountered at the Ghlo Kotal. In a sharp little action, the Afghans were forced to retreat and on the following day the two divisions of Stewart's force linked up at Abdur Rahman. Continuing on parallel roads, the leading brigades of the force entered the city on 8 January. It had been almost, but not quite, a picnic. While the only casualties were the eleven men wounded in the action on 5 January, the mortality among baggage animals had been enormous. Nearly 12,000 camels alone had died as a result of the intense cold, biting winds and mistreatment.

By the time that Stewart reached Kandahar, the political scene in Afghanistan had changed. Sher Ali had fled from Kabul with the remaining members of Stolietov's mission on 13 December, after hearing news of the British successes at Ali Masjid and the Peiwar Kotal which placed the invaders within striking distance of his capital. He was now in Afghan Turkestan and Kabul was in charge of his son, Yakub Khan. The news of the British advances and the Amir's flight had shattered whatever administrative unity there was in the country and tribal independence had already begun to reassert itself. But for the moment it was not clear how this situation could be manipulated to achieve the British objective. Moreover, winter was close at hand. All three invading forces therefore paused to consolidate their positions, to secure their lines of communication, to explore the surrounding country and generally prepare for the further advances which might be required.

The Peshawar Valley Field Force had halted at Dakka for three weeks, busying itself with improving its communications, building up its supplies, and carrying out minor punitive expeditions against the Shinwaris and Zakkha Khel Afridis. Already it was beginning to be seriously troubled by attacks on its supply routes, led by the Zakkha Khel who inhabited the Bara and Bazar valleys south of the Khyber Pass. Early in December, the 2nd Division was ordered forward from Rawalpindi to take over responsibility for the lines of communication between Peshawar and Ali Masjid. Jalalabad, the chief town of the whole region between the Khyber and Kabul, at the junction of the Rivers Kabul and Kunar, some forty miles on, was a more suitable strategic objective than Dakka. Accordingly Browne was authorized to occupy it which he did on 20 December. Sickness having now removed some of Browne's original regiments (including 14th Sikhs and 81st Foot) and with the length of his communications growing, some further reorganization was necessary. The 3rd and 4th Brigades were amalgamated under Appleyard and the resulting force now came under Maude, being based at Ali Masjid. Tytler, with a reorganized 2nd Brigade, remained at Dakka and Basawal and a new 3rd Brigade was formed at Jalalabad under Colonel Jenkins, consisting of the Guides Infantry, 1st Sikh Infantry PFF and No. 4 Mountain Battery. Macpherson's 1st Brigade remained unchanged. Maude's 2nd Division became effectively responsible for the lines of communication as far as Landi Khana, and the 1st Division for the remainder.

Jalalabad proved to be a miserable, dirty town, its defences decayed and dilapidated. There was no trouble with its inhabitants and, in true British fashion, the troops were put to work improving the drainage and roads. In the expectation of a long stay, the 10th Hussars sent back for its band and a supply of tennis-balls. Tytler's men at Dakka had more serious business. The constant depredations of the Zakka Khel Afridis cried out for punishment and on 1 December a column under Tytler had carried out a small punitive expedition, without significant effect. On the advice of Cavagnari, Maude was now ordered to invade the Bazar valley, in co-operation with a column from 1st Division under Tytler which was to move via the Sitsobi Pass to cut off the Afridi retreat. Maude started on 19 December and successfully occupied the valley, destroying a number of villages and towers. But the hostile sections of the Zakka Khel refused to submit, and Tytler's force was fiercely attacked while retiring. The expedition had not tamed the Zakka Khel and a second expedition became inevitable.

In January the weather in this area of Eastern Afghanistan is generally clear but bitterly cold at night, with some snow. While the commanders waited for a development in the political situation, the troops were employed in erecting winter quarters and improving communications. By the end of January, a telegraph line ran from Jamrud to Dakka and was supplemented by a heliograph link for fine days. Wheeled transport could now run the whole way from Peshawar to Jalalabad. To the west, Cavagnari had established a regular flow of information from Kabul. Since the cold was killing off the transport animals, all the camels of the 1st Division, except for 1,500 required to enable a part of the force to move at short notice, were sent back to bring up supplies as far as Dakka. From time to time small forces had to be detached to punish attacks on the line of communications and to break up hostile gatherings. Rumours abounded as to the situation in Kabul. The regular regiments there were reported to be disaffected and deserting. Yakub himself was reported to be trying to mobilize the Ghilzais against the British, but the Ghilzais apparently were not keen to play.

The time had come to have another go at the Zakka Khel who had persisted in raiding convoys, cutting up followers and attacking pickets in the Khyber Pass. This time the expedition was on a more ambitious scale. Cavagnari and Colonel MacGregor, who had been put in charge of communications between Jamrud and Jalalabad, believed that a temporary occupation of the Bazar and Bara valleys was the best way of bringing the Afridis to heel. Maude's plan involved a triple-pronged invasion, with strong columns operating from Jamrud, Ali Masjid and Basawal. In agreeing the plan, Simla specifically limited the operation to ten days, thus in Maude's view effectively destroying the possibility of occupying the Bara valley. Nevertheless, the Jamrud Column* under Maude himself marched on 24 January, the Ali Masjid Column† under Appleyard the next day. These two columns united on the 26th and occupied the central plain of the Bazar valley,

---

*1/5th Fusiliers, 1/25th Foot, 24th BNI, squadron 13th Bengal Lancers, two guns D/A, RHA (on elephants), two guns 11/9 RA, detachment Madras Sappers and Miners – 1,235 men.
†51st Foot, 6th BNI, 2nd Gurkhas, the Mhairwarra Battalion, two guns of 11/9 and a detachment of Madras Sappers and Miners – 1,205 men.

being joined there by the Basawal Column.* Maude now faced a dilemma. The destruction of the villages in the valley by the Zakka Khel themselves, the steady massing of the tribal forces and the continuous sniping made it clear that a further advance into the Bara valley beyond would be bitterly opposed. Maude believed that to do so would bring on a general Afridi war and he was conscious of the Indian Government's expressed wish that collisions with the border tribes be avoided if at all possible. He distrusted the advice of the junior political officer attached to him and he asked Cavagnari to come to see the situation himself. Cavagnari refused and Maude then put the matter direct to the Government of India, asking for clear instructions as to whether he was to persist in forcing his way into the Bara valley in view of the likely consequences. The situation was resolved on 31 January by Sam Browne's ordering the urgent return of Tytler's column. There was no alternative but to conclude a hasty and limited settlement with the Zakka Khel and retire as quickly as possible.

Roberts and Stewart had insisted upon full political control. Sam Browne had been forced to accept political control resting with Cavagnari and his staff. The result was inevitably friction and distrust. Boyce Combe was no doubt typical of most officers in his reaction: 'It is simply sickening to see how we are fettered by the politicals, who are a red rag to all of us.'[14]

The recall of the Basawal column was caused by rumours of a large-scale attack on either Dakka or Jalalabad by the Mohamands living north of the River Kabul, assisted by their Utman Khel neighbours. Reports on 6 February that the tribesmen had reached the districts of Kama and Ghosht in the angle of the Rivers Kabul and Kunar immediately north-east of Jalalabad, caused Browne to dispatch columns across the river the next day. From Jalalabad, Macpherson, with a strong force of cavalry and infantry amounting to some 1,250 men, was ordered to move north-east across the two rivers to come in behind the tribesmen occupying Kama. From Basawal, a force of some 450 men under Tytler was to move via Chardeh on Ghosht while two squadrons of cavalry and two guns of I/C, Royal Horse Artillery, from Jalalabad, under Charles Gough, were to seize the fords over the River Kabul at Ali Boghan and be ready to co-operate across the river with the other two forces. Macpherson's force left at 04.15 the next morning, the plan being to push his cavalry (a troop of 10th Hussars and 100 sabres of the 11th Bengal Lancers) ahead as fast as possible to seize a position at Telian, on the edge of the hills which at this point came down to within five miles of the north bank of the River Kabul. The infantry would follow up, trapping the Kama raiders between the hills and the river. The raiders had, however, begun to retire during the night and only scattered parties remained to be engaged by the carbines of the cavalry and by a couple of rounds from the mountain battery. The Guides Cavalry alone of Tytler's force managed to cross the river but found no opposition. Gough stayed on the south bank since there was clearly nothing for him to do.

The Mohmands and Utman Khel had come down to co-operate with the local Shinwaris, Khugianis and Ghilzais in attacking the British, but the local tribes had abandoned their share in the project, disheartened by the death of the Mir Akhor,

---

*1st/17th Foot, 4th Rifle Brigade, 4th Gurkhas, 45th BNI, detachments of 27th BNI, Guides Cavalry and Madras Sappers and Miners, with the remaining two guns of 11/9 – 1,285 men.

a religious leader who had been active from the beginning in whipping up Afghan opposition to the invaders. Unsupported, the Mohmands had drifted home. Matters remained generally quiescent on the military front until the middle of March, although petty attacks on convoys and mail carriers were endemic. In one such attack on 31 January, Lieutenant Hart of the Royal Engineers won the Victoria Cross for saving the life of a trooper of the 13th Bengal Lancers when attacked by tribesmen. A short expedition into the Laghman valley at the end of January against the powerful and troublesome Ghilzai chief, Asmatullah Khan, temporarily pacified the area without a shot being fired.

The harsh reality behind all this activity was that the British commander and his troops were operating largely blind. Cavagnari and the politicals had virtually no experience of, or contacts with, the tribes around Jalalabad. A rudimentary system of paid spies brought in a certain amount of information and rumour, but in an intensely hostile country all that the British knew for certain was what lay within the range of their guns. Consequently they were in a position of having to react to events, rather than anticipating or dictating them. 'An army might be collecting within a few miles without our knowing it, as we are not allowed to reconnoitre in certain directions for fear of complications,' wrote one observer, 'and the road to Cabul has not been looked at beyond the first twelve or fifteen miles.'[15]

For the Kurram Valley Field Force, December and January had been busy months. Following his reconnaissance of the Shutagardan Pass, Roberts decided to explore a route from Ali Khel back to Kurram Fort which by-passed the Peiwar Kotal. This route ran south-eastwards from Ali Khel across the Sapri Pass and then down through a long, narrow defile to Karaia on the River Kurram, 21 miles west of Kurram Fort. The route had been followed by an Afghan mountain battery en route for Kurram Fort three years earlier, and was assumed to be relatively trouble-free since it lay within the territory of the Jajis and Chakmannis whose chiefs had already visited Roberts. Roberts left Ali Khel on 12 December accompanied by a wing of the 72nd Highlanders, the 5th Gurkhas, the 23rd BNI and No. 1 Mountain Battery. The route proved extremely difficult, very steep in places and very icy. In the narrow defile leading out of the Sapri Pass, the column was continuously fired upon by Mangal tribesmen, and six men were killed or mortally wounded, and two others wounded. The column finally reached Kurram Fort on 20 December. The Sapri route was clearly impracticable in the face of opposition and the force was lucky to have escaped without more serious losses.

While work went on in preparing hutting and supplies for the winter, Roberts decided to carry out the second part of his instructions and visit Khost before the snow put an end to serious movement. Khost was Afghan territory, occupied by the extremely aggressive and independent Mangals. Unless and until it was brought under peaceful control, it formed a continuing threat to the safety and stability of the Kurram valley. Akram Khan, the Afghan Deputy Governor of Khost, was prepared to try to maintain order until British troops could arrive, provided that his personal safety was guaranteed as well as his eventual evacuation to Kabul or to British territory. It was important to provide him with some tangible British support as quickly as possible.

Roberts left Hazar Pir for Khost on 2 January 1879 with a squadron of 10th Hussars, three troops 5th PC, Nos. 1 and 2 Mountain Batteries, a wing of the 72nd

Highlanders and the 21st and 28th BNI – in all, about 2,000 men. No maps of any kind were available but the force reached Matun, the main settlement, on 6 January without incident. The general atmosphere, even so, was hostile and unstable. Matun was a collection of some thirty villages lying in a narrow plain surrounded by hills on three sides. At daylight on the morning after Roberts's arrival, the villages on three sides of the camp were seen to be occupied by masses of tribesmen clearly working up to an attack. The British force was in an awkward position, outnumbered and isolated. Roberts by tradition and experience was a firm believer in the principle of taking the initiative and attacking the enemy. The major threat was a heavy concentration of tribesmen in the low hills to the north-west of the camp. The squadron of 10th Hussars and the three troops of 5th PC, were dispatched against this concentration. Dismounting, the troopers opened fire with their carbines. Alternatively firing and moving forward, and assisted at one point by an effective mounted charge uphill by a troop of 5th PC, the cavalry began to force the tribesmen to retire. Six companies of 28th BNI and No. 2 Mountain Battery then arrived in support, but all that remained to do was for the guns to shell the enemy now retiring farther into the hills. Under cover of this fire, the troops were slowly withdrawn to camp and were not followed up. Meanwhile, from villages to the south and east, the camp had come under persistent fire. The 21st BNI was dispatched to drive out the enemy from these villages which were burnt as retribution. The action then came to an end. The British casualties were two dead and six wounded; enemy casualties were unknown but included 85 prisoners. On the following evening an unhappy incident occurred. Believing that local tribesmen were trying to release the prisoners, the guard opened fire; nine prisoners were killed and five injured.

Roberts remained in Khost until 28 January, exploring and mapping the district, but he could not keep his force there indefinitely. Given the strategic importance of Khost, the apparent alternatives were to leave behind a British garrison or to attempt to construct some form of native administration. A suitable garrison could hardly be less than an infantry regiment, a squadron of cavalry and two guns, and even then it would be in a perpetually hazardous situation; resupply would be potentially a major operation each time. Roberts could not, in any case, spare so large a diversion from his forces. He therefore fell back on a plan to leave a native British official, Sultan Jan, with a force of native levies, in charge of Khost. Sultan Jan was an Afghan, of the Sadozai branch of the Duranis, and it seemed possible that he would be acceptable to the tribal heads of Khost, some of whom were to be given cash allowances to assist. In retrospect, the scheme appears foredoomed to failure, and so it proved. Roberts had barely commenced his return march on 28 January when he was forced to return at maximum speed to Matun in response to a call for help from Sultan Jan who was in imminent fear of attack and convinced now that without a British garrison he could not govern. Having rescued his nominee, Roberts evacuated Khost and left it to its own devices. Little had been achieved except a better knowledge of the area, at the expense of the hostility of yet another large section of the Pathan tribes.

For Roberts, the expedition had produced an irritating and embarrassing quarrel with Macpherson, the war correspondent of the London *Standard*, who had accompanied the force. Macpherson's dispatches were highly critical of Roberts's conduct of the expedition. More especially, he had made much of the deaths of the captured tribesmen and of an alleged order to the cavalry to give no quarter during the action on 7 January. Roberts therefore enlisted the aid of Colley to get rid of Macpherson on the grounds that his dispatches were false and that he had added to a telegram after Roberts had approved it for dispatch. Despite Macpherson's removal, the incident continued for some time to dog Roberts's footsteps. Questions were raised in the House of Commons about the Khost expedition and Roberts was at pains in future to ensure that as far as possible those war correspondents, such as Hensman and General Vaughan, whom he allowed to accompany him were on his side. Months later, in Kabul, he was answering insinuations that Hensman had been carefully chosen to accompany him to Kabul because he could be trusted to put Roberts over in a favourable light. That was not wholly untrue.

The winter had now well and truly set in, with thick snow on the Peiwar Kotal. With the prospect of further active operations in the spring, the troops in the Kurram Valley Force concentrated on making themselves comfortable. A regular mail-cart service now ran from Kohat to Thal, taking only seven hours for the 63 miles, but in vivid contrast the bullock-carts carrying supplies and equipment took a fortnight. For Roberts and his Principal Commissariat Officer, Captain Badcock, transport was a ceaseless preoccupation. Both Roberts's and Sam Browne's forces required enormous numbers of pack animals to meet daily stores requirements and to build up depots to support the expected advances in the spring. Supplies of food and forage in the Kurram valley itself were non-existent and were becoming increasingly scarce around Kohat. Roberts and Browne found themselves competing for supplies and transport animals, exposing starkly the Achilles heel of the Anglo-Indian Army. Nevertheless, great strides had been made in communications. At the end of January, that most useful regiment, the 23rd Pioneers, had started to build a road up the east bank of the River Kurram, from Thal to Kurram Fort. Completed by the end of February, the new road was 51 miles long, roughly the same as that on the west bank, but a good deal easier, particularly for wheeled traffic, since it avoided the Darwazai Pass and the need to ford the river opposing Kurram Fort. But the necessity of keeping the lines of communication secure, particularly between Kohat and Thal, tied down large numbers of troops. Early in February, contingents of state troops from the protected Sikh states of Nabha, Faridkot, Patiala and Nahun, arrived at Kohat and Thal. The men were of the same quality as those enlisted into the regular Sikh regiments and they had been hastily equipped with Enfield rifles from the arsenal at Ferozepore. They were led by their own officers but a number of British officers were attached to exercise general supervision. These contingents, totalling some 600 cavalry and 1,700 infantry with seven very ancient guns, proved exceptionally useful and popular. By shouldering the main burden of road protection between Kohat and Kurram Fort, they released valuable numbers of regular troops for the field.

At the other end of the front, Stewart, having occupied Kandahar without difficulty, proceeded to reconnoitre in force towards Kalat-i-Ghilzai and the Helmund. He himself took the 1st Division to Kalat-i-Ghilzai, while Biddulph led the 2nd Division minus one brigade to the Helmund. Stewart's force encountered no opposition, but the supply and transport situation proved exceptionally difficult.

The cold was intense, occasionally reaching 29 degrees of frost, and the animals died in huge numbers.* Stewart was at his wits' end to feed his troops. By the time that he reached Kalat-i-Ghilzai he could no longer move his whole division. When he retired a substantial force had to be left behind until transport could be scraped together to retrieve it.

There was clearly no prospect of being able to advance on Ghazni or Kabul until the spring because of the supply situation, and the whole enterprise had been risky and largely pointless.[16]

Biddulph's expedition fared little better. Its main object had been to tap new sources of food and forage but in this it was unsuccessful. The force managed to feed itself only by splitting up into small foraging parties and in so doing Biddulph ran real military risks. By the middle of February he could no longer maintain himself on the Helmund and he was able to retire only with the aid of supplies sent from Kandahar. The only serious fighting took place when the rearguard, consisting of 3rd Sind Horse and 118 rifles of 29th BoNI, under Colonel Malcolmson of the Sind Horse, was attacked by some 1,500 tribesmen. Malcolmson seems to have been surprised, but he handled his men well. There was a spirited charge by the cavalry and the attackers were driven off at a cost of some 200 dead. At the beginning of March, both divisions were back in Kandahar.

It had become patently clear that Kandahar and its environs could not support Stewart's present force and the problem of supply from Quetta was fast becoming insuperable through wastage of bullocks and camels. Supplies were piling up which simply could not be moved forward. By this time, the possibility of a satisfactory political settlement with the new Amir, Yakub Khan, was beginning to emerge. Accordingly, Stewart was authorized to send a large part of his force back to India. The lack of a suitable direct route between Quetta and the Punjab connecting with the railway at Multan and avoiding the Bolan Pass, had been a source of frustration since the campaign began. Stewart seized the opportunity to send Biddulph, and the troops returning to India, via the Thal–Chotiali route to Dera Ghazi Khan, linking up with a force from the Kandahar Reserve Division which was being sent to Vitakri. Biddulph's force, in three columns, totalling some 3,000 men, left Khushdil Khan Kila at intervals between 11 and 22 March. Apart from an attack on the first column by some 3,500 tribesmen, which was repulsed without serious difficulty, the force reached its objective of Loghari Barkhan without trouble and linked up there with the Vitakri force which brought much needed supplies. From there, part of the force went on to Dera Ghazi Khan and the railhead at Multan; the remainder turned south-east to Mithankot whence the railway was reached at Khanpur.

The troops from the Reserve Division remained for the moment at Vitakri which had appeared to offer possibilities as a cantonment, strategically placed to dominate the route between Quetta and the Punjab. It proved, alas, to be extremely unhealthy and was quietly abandoned at the end of the year. The Thal–Chotiali route had proved at first hand more difficult than expected; with the decision to build a railway from Sukkhur, to Sibi, and Quetta, it lost its potential

---

*A/B, RHA had lost 110 camels out of 249 by the time it reached Kalat-i-Ghilzai: *Letters from Lieutenant P. F. P. Hamilton, Lieutenant E. O. F. Hamilton from Afghanistan, 1878–80.* Privately printed, Dublin, 1881, p. 17.

importance and was not developed. Biddulph's traverse had produced a good deal of useful information about an area largely unknown to the British hitherto, but it had done so at the cost of antagonizing and unsettling the local Pathan and Baluch tribes.

Even with the departure of Biddulph's force, Stewart had some 10,000 men at Kandahar, Quetta and along the lines of communication between. There was little to do apart from constructing quarters for the troops* pending a resolution of the political impasse at Kabul so Stewart took the opportunity to conduct a series of reconnaissances of the country on each side of the route between Quetta and Kandahar. A sharp reminder of the effect of such reconnaissances on the tribes was provided at the end of March. Sandeman was keen that in any future re-arrangement of territory the district of Shorawak, lying between Quetta and the Registan desert and occupied by a Pathan tribe, the Baraich, should come under British control. A reconnaissance party exploring Shorawak was fiercely attacked during a dust storm on 27 March by a large force of the Baraich. The escort – 30 sabres of 1st Punjab Cavalry and 176 rifles of 30th BoNI (Jacob's Rifles) – was exceptionally well-handled and the attackers were dispersed with a loss of some 90 killed at a cost of only seven wounded.

At the end of March 1879, the military situation had stabilized. At Kandahar, Stewart retained a strong force of roughly three brigades with roughly the equivalent of another brigade and a half in Pishin and at Quetta. He was some 370 miles from his original railhead on the Indus, and although the Indian Government had by now decided to build a line at least as far as Quetta, this offered no very early end to his dependence upon animal transport. Whether or not he would be able to move on Kabul, if required, depended upon the speed with which supplies and transport could be concentrated at Kandahar. Winter had begun to give way rapidly to spring; by the beginning of June, the daily temperature in the sun would be over 100° Fahrenheit, and campaigning would become correspondingly more arduous.

In the Kurram, Roberts had been strengthened by the arrival of the remaining wing of the 72nd Highlanders together with the 92nd Highlanders, 14th Bengal Cavalry and 11th BNI. The arrival of the Punjab Chiefs' Contingents in February had largely solved the problem of protecting the lines of communication, and despite persistent attacks on supply convoys and stragglers he was well-placed to advance as soon as the weather improved. At his advance base of Ali Khel, he was only 80 miles from Kabul by a comparatively easy route, and he had accumulated some two months' supplies.†

Sam Browne at Jalalabad faced the most difficult situation. His line of communication back to his base at Peshawar was only 88 miles in length but around it clustered some of the most turbulent and formidable of the transborder tribes. In particular, the Khyber Pass was the preserve of the Afridis who, despite Cavagnari's bribes, were unable to resist the temptation to attack convoys. Two punitive expeditions had now failed to subdue them. North of the River Kabul, the Mohmands remained a constant menace. From the Khyber to Jalalabad, the road

---

*The head native foreman on the new cantonment had done the same job for Nott forty years earlier.
†He had also received a battery of two Gatling guns.

passed through the territories of the predatory Shinwaris and Khugianis. Ninety miles ahead of Sam Browne lay Kabul, but to get there he would have to traverse a series of difficult defiles in which Elphinstone's army had perished in 1842. Lytton was not anxious to undertake an advance to Kabul but he was prepared to do so if necessary.[17] Browne had accumulated a fair stock of supplies and ammunition, but was still desperately short of transport. It remained to be seen whether the politicals could capitalize on the military's successes so far and thus avoid the need for a spring campaign.

NOTES

1. Quoted in Mary Lutyens. *The Lyttons in India*. London, 1979, p. 153.
2. G. W. Forrest. *Life of Sir Neville Chamberlain*. London, 1909, p. 485.
3. Of the Bolan itself, a contemporary observer wrote 'In winter there is not a blade of grass or a mouthful of food for a man or beast for the whole of the 60 mile defile. The track in one march crosses the river fourteen times. There is nothing the weary traveller can see but the bare hill on either side and the detestable shingle at his feet. The Pass narrows as it reaches the summit and the incline increases, the shingle becoming deeper and more fatiguing.' Captain Hoskins, RE, quoted in G. R. Elsmie. *Field Marshal Sir Donald Stewart*. London, 1903, p. 216.
4. Ross grumbled to Lumsden, the Adjutant-General, that '[Cavagnari's] measures and proposals are a little wild and are generally very suddenly conceived, and however beneficial they may be in the punishment of refractory border villages they are in my opinion very unsafe as regards a more formidable enemy'. Letter dated 10 October 1878 – HP, vol. 12, ff. 25–29.
5. Lytton described Sam Browne to Cranbrook as 'weak in Council and not much of a Departmental Administrator, he is a brilliant frontier officer, full of go and vigour but not rash'. Maude was described in the same letter as intelligent and energetic but very deaf and hot-tempered. Lytton to Cranbrook, 8 November 1878, LP 518/3, p. 806.
6. For example, by Colonel Ball-Acton, commanding the 51st Light Infantry. See *Colonel Ball-Acton. An Appreciation*. Privately printed, 1906, p. 79.
7. Transport was to remain a problem. By May 1879, the Kurram valley and Khost operations had absorbed some 14,000 camels, 2,000 mules or ponies and more than 2,000 bullock-carts. Some 10,000 of these animals had died, been abandoned or

stolen. See Major J. A. S. Colquhoun. *With the Kurram Field Force 1878–79*. London, 1881, Appendix 1.
8. Diary for 4 November 1878 – RP 7101-24-92-18.
9. Confidential reports – RP 7101-23-48.
10. The Pathan companies of the 29th were in a bad state. A jemadar who had discovered the identity of the offenders by sniffing the rifle barrels kept quiet and during the subsequent fighting a party of eighteen Pathan sepoys deserted and found their way back to camp. One sepoy was hanged at Kurram Fort, and the jemadar and the remainder were transported to the Andaman Islands. Subsequently a havildar was found to have stolen a substantial part of the Force's treasury which he was supposed to have been guarding. The Sikh companies of the 29th had given no cause for concern and the regiment subsequently served creditably throughout the rest of the war. Roberts attributed the trouble in part to poor selection of native officers and NCOs – see RP 7101-23-148. *Confidential Reports on Officers of Kurram Force, first campaign*.
11. Travers wrote that this railway was 'managed by Government on economical principles, which means about as badly as it possibly can be. There are insufficient engines, wretched stations without platforms, old carriages and such a scarcity of engine drivers that men quite unfit for the work are put on.' Diary, 18 November 1878.
12. Stewart to Government of India. RP 7101-23-154-1, 14 January 1879.
13. Stewart ascribed much of the delay to the defective organization of the artillery; 'My idea is that in these days an artillery that is practically tied down to bullocks is simply an encumbrance and we should have been in Candahar a fortnight ago if the guns could get along like the other branches – and field artillery ought to do this.' (Stewart to Adjutant-General, 1 January 1879). Elsmie, op. cit., p. 235.
14. *Letters from B.A.C.* [Boyce Albert Combe,

9th Lancers] (*Afghanistan, 1878–80*). Printed for private circulation. London, 1880.

15. Combe, op. cit., p. 25.

16. Writing to his wife, Stewart admitted that he did not know what to do after he got to Kalat-i-Ghilzai except to return to Kandahar; 'It has been rather a risky trip this, as we have only two or three day's supplies in hand, and are living from hand to mouth on what we can pick up . . . A fall of snow would cut us off entirely from our base and source of supply.' Elsmie, op. cit., pp. 239, 245.

17. Lytton to Haines, 18 March 1879 – HP, vol. 19, ff. 5–18.

CHAPTER 6

THE END OF THE BEGINNING

'Tain't so much the bloomin' fightin', 'though there's enough o' that. It's the bloomin' food and the bloomin' climate. Frost all night except when it 'ails, and bilin' sun all day, and the water stinks fit to knock you down. Tain't no bloomin' picnic in these parts, I can tell you.'

Rudyard Kipling *Drums of the Fore and Aft*

The Amir replied to Lytton's letter of 31 October 1878 two days before the ultimatum expired. The reply reached Lytton at the beginning of December. As soon as he had seen the way the wind was blowing, Kauffmann at Tashkent had advised Sher Ali to make peace with the British. That was sensible advice but it ignored the pressures on the Amir. He was not in good health – the ceaseless exertions and anxieties of the years after 1863 when he was trying to consolidate his claim to the throne had sapped his vigour. He was in the grip of a deep personal sorrow as a result of the death of his favourite son, Abdullah Jan, only some seven weeks before. As a result, he faced the prospect of being succeeded by Yakub Khan, that 'undutiful son, that ill-starred wretch' as he had described him to Lytton, who had caused him so much trouble over the last few years and prevented his enjoying that period of relative stability and peace to which he could reasonably have looked forward after 1867. It was not the least of Sher Ali's complaints against the British that they had interfered in his attempts to deal effectively with Yakub's insubordination. But the factor which weighed most in the Amir's mind was that peace with the British meant accepting British officers in Afghanistan. That meant an end of true independence, the weakening of his own authority and the revival of faction. He considered himself, not unreasonably, the injured party. He had throughout wanted only to be left alone; it was the British who had persisted in badgering him and interfering in his affairs, while refusing to give him the clear-cut guarantee of support which he had repeatedly sought. His reply to Lytton rejected suggestions that he was hostile to the British. He justified the rebuff to Chamberlain's mission on the grounds that its reception could only have affected the independence of his government. If the Government of India were prepared to maintain its friendship, he would even now be prepared to receive a purely friendly and temporary mission, with a small escort of twenty–thirty men such as the Russians had brought.

By the time this reply reached Lytton it was too little and too late; Browne was already at Jalalabad and Roberts had occupied the Kurram valley. The British war machine was rolling ponderously forward and could not be stopped without major concessions on Sher Ali's part which would inevitably destroy the stability of his rule.

It is impossible now to know exactly what Sher Ali thought of his military prospects. The Afghan army had undergone considerable improvement in recent years and, in terms of equipment and supplies, was not markedly inferior to the Anglo-Indian armies. Undoubtedly, the terrain favoured the defence and the Amir could rely upon the transborder tribes to make life difficult for the British along their lines of communication; every Afghan was conscious of the fate of Elphinstone's army in the passes between Kabul and Jalalabad in 1842. But Sher Ali had taken no real steps to mobilize his forces or strengthen his defences, and he seems to have accepted events with a certain weary fatalism. If he had any hope of repelling the British invasion it must have disappeared with the news of Browne's speedy victory at Ali Masjid, followed by the news of the unopposed occupation of the Kurram valley and Roberts's success at the Peiwar Kotal. There was only one thing that could now redress the balance – Russian intervention. Stolietov's mission still lingered on in Kabul under Rosgonov although Stolietov himself had returned home in August. A week after the action at the Peiwar Kotal, Sher Ali wrote to Kauffmann asking for the dispatch of all available Russian troops to Afghan Turkestan. Two days later, on 10 December, he announced his decision to go to St. Petersburg to lay his case before the Tsar and the other European Powers. How far he was influenced in this by Rosgonov is difficult to determine. Rosgonov himself was under instructions to return to Tashkent, but Sher Ali was reluctant to let him go. It may be, therefore, that Rosgonov encouraged Sher Ali to go to St. Petersburg as a means of ensuring his own return. But the Amir was no fool and he was well-informed about outside events. The idea of appealing to Britain's most powerful opponent, and one still smarting from a major diplomatic defeat at the Berlin Congress, could well have been his own. An earlier letter of Stolietov's could in any case be interpreted as conveying a hint of Russian support.[1]

Time pressed if he was to cross the Hindu Kush before the snows set in. He left Kabul on 13 December, taking with him the remaining members of the Russian mission. By 1 January 1879 he had reached Mazar-i-Sharif in Afghan Turkestan, 350 miles from Kabul. The move was fatal. Having decided to leave Afghanistan, he had had no option but to release Yakub Khan from house arrest and appoint him, in effect, Regent while he was away. The British now no longer needed to deal with Sher Ali at all – they could justifiably deal only with the effective ruler, Yakub. By removing himself from Kabul, Sher Ali had played into British hands because it was the essence of the British Government's public case that its quarrel was with Sher Ali and not the Afghan people. The point was not lost on the Afghans themselves. With the Amir's departure from Kabul, internal support began increasingly to swing towards Yakub Khan.

At Mazar-i-Sharif, where he was forced to rest, Sher Ali received a body-blow to his hopes in the shape of three letters from Kauffmann. The sum of Kauffmann's advice was that the Emperor had decided against the dispatch of Russian troops to aid the Amir; that in these circumstances Sher Ali should at all costs remain in

Kabul and treat with the British in order to preserve his kingdom's independence, and that, while Kauffmann himself had received instructions to welcome Sher Ali at Tashkent, he had no instructions about helping him to go on to St. Petersburg. The Amir was already in poor health and the Russian defection finally destroyed his spirit. Refusing food, medical aid and consolation, he died on 21 February at the age of 55.

It is impossible to withhold sympathy and respect from Sher Ali. He was not as great a man as his father, Dost Mohammed, or his cousin and successor, Abdurrahman. He lacked the former's charm and subtle intelligence and the latter's grim determination. But his character and achievements were not negligible. He had fought stoutly for nearly five years to establish his hold on the throne. Despite many ups and downs he had never lost heart and, having finally won through, he had gone on to govern Afghanistan and to maintain its territorial integrity for more than nine years. Above all he had shown a fierce desire to retain the independence of his country. Despite disappointment at the rebuffs and lack of warmth that he had generally encountered from the British, he had never been hostile to them, and if, in the last resort, he was not prepared to compromise the independence of Afghanistan by accepting a permanent British presence he can hardly be said to have been wrong. It was his basic misfortune, and that of his country, to be caught up in a power struggle between Russia and Britain. A cleverer or more ruthless ruler might have survived, but there was no dishonour in failure.*

His death and the automatic accession of Yakub Khan to the throne of Kabul resolved the political impasse in which the Indian Government found itself. Yakub's long history of opposition to his father left him able to pursue a new policy without incurring charges of disloyalty. The occasion of Sher Ali's death provided a ready pretext for re-opening communications between the two sides which had virtually ceased since December.

At that time an attempt to open discussions with Yakub, following his father's flight from Kabul, had been rebuffed. Yakub might have disagreed with his father over many things but he was an Afghan, first and foremost, and he bitterly resented the British invasion. In consequence, Lytton had looked around for an alternative candidate and had settled on Wali Mohammed, Sher Ali's half-brother, who was prepared to adopt the role of Shah Shuja.[2] Even so, Lytton had been forced to recognize that Wali Mohammed was not capable of ruling Kandahar and Herat as well as Kabul.

Faute de mieux, there appeared therefore no alternative to a policy of splitting up Afghanistan. But a policy of disintegration was a self-defeating one. If Britain

---

*British opinion then and since has predictably given Sher Ali a bad Press. It is worth noting as an antidote the pen-picture given by Chetan Shah, the Amir's physician and a native of India; 'As to his general character, he has many good parts. He is wise, shrewd, hard-working, humorous, independent and above religious prejudice; but at the same time he is proud, fond of praise, stern and stony-hearted. He is very suspicious and has perfect faith in none ... The Amir is not only very intelligent but keeps himself well-informed as to what is going on in other countries. He has a good knowledge of geography, especially of Europe, with the modern history of which he is also well-acquainted ... The Amir employed the whole of his day and some little part of his night in business, and the greater part of all this in looking after his arms, field-pieces, soldiers, finances and politics. He is also fond of play and jokes but these he manages to have at the same time when carrying on business.'   (Official History, vol. 1, pp. 255–6)

feared Russian influence over a united Afghanistan – and that was essentially what the war was about – that fear could logically only be increased if Afghanistan were left weak and divided. The basic illogicality of a policy of disintegration was a measure of the political difficulty in which Lytton now found himself.

Yakub's accession to full power offered a way out. His pedigree and career ensured him a good chance of maintaining a unified Afghanistan and although he was bitterly opposed to the British invasion he could not fail to see the chaos into which the country was drifting. Even before Sher Ali's death, Yakub had put out tentative feelers in the direction of peace negotiations, and on 26 February he wrote formally to Cavagnari at Jalalabad informing him of Sher Ali's death – 'My worthy and exalted father has . . . obeyed the call of the summoner, and throwing off the dress of existence, hastened to the region of divine mercy' – and seeking an end to hostilities. With Lytton's agreement, Cavagnari sent Yakub a letter of condolence and followed this up on 7 March with a statement of the essential preliminary conditions on which negotiations must be based:

1. The renunciation by the Amir of authority over the Khyber and Michni Passes and the surrounding tribes.
2. Pishin, Sibi, and the Kurram valley as far as the Shutagardan Pass to remain under British protection and control.
3. The regulation of the Afghan Government's external relations in conformity with British advice and wishes.
4. Permission to station British officers, with suitable escorts, in Afghanistan.[3]

Surprisingly, Yakub made no trouble over the last two conditions. Conducting his foreign relations in accordance with British wishes had been something that Sher Ali had always been prepared in practice to do. The stationing of British officers in Afghanistan, however, was the issue on which the Peshawar Conference had come to grief and the one on which Sher Ali had been totally immovable. It might, therefore, have been expected to be the major obstacle in the present negotiations. In fact, Yakub seemed relatively relaxed, possibly calculating that resistance on this point would be ultimately useless and that it would be better to give way gracefully in order to secure concessions elsewhere; possibly calculating also that the presence of British agents might prove only a temporary state of affairs whereas loss of territory was likely to be permanent. He stipulated only that the officers should reside in Kabul and must not interfere in the internal affairs of the country. It was on the territorial conditions that he argued most vigorously. Loss of territory was something which had an immediate impact on his authority within Afghanistan. Surrendering control of foreign relations was something that the average tribesman would not bother much about; giving up territory was an unmistakable sign of defeat and Afghan resentment was bound to focus on the ruler who had had to concede it. On a more personal level, Yakub Khan could not fail to be conscious that he was the direct descendant of Ahmed Shah Durani, the creator of Afghanistan. To surrender what his ancestors had accumulated was something which went against his deepest instincts. He argued, therefore, very forcibly that since he was prepared to accept the stationing of British officers in his country and British control of his foreign policy, thus removing British fears of Russian influence, he could reasonably expect to gain, rather than lose, territory.

On the British side, Lytton was determined that the opportunity to gain a more strategically desirable, or, in the fashionable jargon of the times, 'scientific' frontier should not be lost. To resolve this deadlock, Cavagnari proposed that he visit Kabul to carry on negotiations there. To offset the loss of territory it might be possible to offer a strengthened guarantee against external aggression such as Northbrook had wanted to give in 1873. At the end of March, Yakub himself wrote offering to receive a British mission at Kabul.

The cards were not all on the British side. Although Roberts in the Kurram was in no particular difficulty and was busy completing his build-up of troops and stores ready for an advance in April, his colleagues at Kandahar and Jalalabad were by no means so comfortably placed. At Kandahar, Stewart struggled incessantly with the problem of getting his supplies from the Indus up the Bolan Pass and on to Kandahar. The mortality among the transport animals continued to be enormous and the civil authorities were becoming reluctant to denude their districts of animals which were needed to maintain the civilian economy. A decision had been taken to extend the railway system to Quetta but the survey could not be completed until the autumn, after the hot weather was over, and construction could not start until the winter of 1879–80.[4] From Quetta onwards to Kandahar, the convoys were constantly subject to the threat of attacks by bandits and hostile tribesmen. Although the security problem was never of the same magnitude as on the Khyber line, it necessitated constant vigilance and the employment of numerous detachments of troops.

For Sam Browne at Jalalabad, the situation was a good deal more serious. He was surrounded on all sides by fiercely independent tribes some of whom, like the Bazar valley Afridis, had never accepted the rule even of Kabul. To protect his lines of communications to Peshawar required a whole division of troops under Maude and even so the situation was highly unstable. On 17 March, a surveying party under Captain E. P. Leach of the Royal Engineers was fiercely attacked by Shinwari tribesmen at Maidanak some fourteen miles south-south-west of Basawal.[5] Leach with great coolness succeeded in extricating his force, despite fierce hand-to-hand fighting in which knives and even stones were used. It was due to his leadership that the infantry escort escaped annihilation and he subsequently received the Victoria Cross; we shall meet him later at Maiwand. The sad rhythm which had already established itself on the frontier produced an immediate punitive reaction. Browne was anxious for obvious reasons to avoid hostilities with the Shinwaris as a whole. Tytler was therefore dispatched on 21 March with a force of 1,100 men and four mountain guns to seek reparation, without major bloodshed if possible. In this he was successful, penetrating as far as Maidanak where he blew up a number of towers, levied a fine, completed the survey started by Leach and withdrew without having fired a shot.

In the meantime, Shinwaris had attacked a foraging party near Deh Sarakh, four miles east of Maidanak. No sooner had Tytler returned to his base at Basawal than he was sent off to punish this second outrage. This time, misled by the ease with which he had punished the Maidanak attack, Tytler found himself with a serious fight on his hands. He had taken with him only 150 cavalry, 500 infantry and two mountain guns. Leaving Basawal just after midnight on 24 March, he reached Mausam, the village mainly involved, with the cavalry just after daybreak. The village itself was on rising ground and fortified in the usual tribal manner. To east and west, two large watercourses (nullahs) protected its flanks, constricting the ground on which the troops could advance and impeding the cavalry's mobility. Dense masses of tribesmen occupied the plain on the far side of the western nullah, on the flank of the direct approach to the village. Tytler estimated that he was faced with some three thousand Shinwaris. He could do nothing until the infantry and guns arrived. When they did, he ordered the infantry, supported by the guns* to make a direct assault on the enemy in front of the village, while the cavalry crossed the western nullah and attacked the enemy there. The cavalry succeeded in getting close to its target unobserved, since the tribesmen were busy firing at the advancing infantry, and charged, totally dispersing the enemy concentration and killing some fifty of them before the rocky hillsides prevented further pursuit. Seeing this, the tribesmen in front of the village retired and Tytler was able to occupy it and blow up its towers in retribution for the original attack.

But he was not out of the wood. His retirement was fiercely followed up by the tribesmen who repeatedly came to within eighty yards of his rear and flanks. Not until he reached Pesh Bolak, five miles from Mausam and roughly the same distance from Basawal, did the attacks cease. When he did get back to Basawal, it was only to discover that in the 24 hours he had been gone, yet another attack had taken place on a supply party, two men of the 17th Foot having been killed and 44 camels stolen. British losses at Mausam were two killed and twelve wounded, and the Shinwaris lost at least 160 killed. Tytler's force had been in a critical situation as a result of miscalculating the likely opposition. Only cool leadership had extricated it without a disaster. It was a vivid illustration of the difficulties and dangers which surrounded Browne's force, problems which were likely to increase the farther he pushed forward and the longer the campaign lasted.

A further illustration came at the end of March when Browne learned of two threats developing ahead of him. Asmatullah Khan, with some 1,500 followers, had come down into the Kats Laghman, an alluvial plain on the north bank of the River Kabul some miles west of Jalalabad, with the object of stirring up the local tribesmen against the British. In parallel, the Khugianis, a Pathan tribe living south of the Kabul road, were assembling near Fatehbad some sixteen miles south-west of Jalalabad.[6] Browne dispatched three columns under Macpherson, Major E. A. Wood (10th Hussars) and Charles Gough respectively, to disperse these hostile gatherings. Wood and Macpherson were to operate against Asmatullah Khan and the general plan was for Macpherson's force of infantry and guns to move westwards along the south bank of the River Kabul and the Siah Koh mountains beyond, and take up a position on the south bank of the river. There it would cut off Asmatullah's probable line of retreat in face of Wood's cavalry column moving westwards along the north bank. Macpherson left Jalalabad at 21.00 hours on 31 March with a wing of the 4th Rifle Brigade, a wing of the 4th Gurkhas and another of the 20th Bengal NI, accompanied by the Hazara Mountain Battery and a company of the Bengal Sappers and Miners. After a difficult and tiring march, the head of the column reached the objective at 13.15 hours on 1 April, only to find that its quarry had flown. The exhaustion of his troops after

---

*It was noticeable that at a range of 750 yards the 7pdr shells failed to penetrate the thick mud walls.

their difficult march of some 25 miles made both pursuit and retirement impractic-able, and Macpherson camped where he was, to await the arrival of his rearguard and supplies. During the night he was ordered to return to Jalalabad, sending his guns to join Gough. Macpherson was back at Jalalabad on the evening of 2 April meeting on the way his rearguard and supplies; they had missed the route twenty-four hours earlier and blundered into Gough's column at Fatehbad.

Wood's column had suffered a disaster. He had left camp half an hour after Macpherson to cross the River Kabul by a ford some two miles east of Jalalabad. At this point the river was about three-quarters of a mile wide, but divided into two channels by an island. Across the northern channel the ford was not a straight line but V-shaped. Above and below it were rocks and rapids and the water was running with great force because of the melting of the snows in the mountains; the trestle bridges which normally existed at this point had been removed precisely because of the swollen level of the river. To add to the difficulties, darkness was falling. The column reached the island without difficulty and the leading squadron (11th Bengal Lancers) successfully crossed the northern channel. A number of baggage mules missed the ford and in the darkness were followed by the squadron of 10th Hussars. In tight-packed formation, men and horses were immediately swept away by the fierce current into deep water and on to the rocks below the ford; an officer wrote, 'It seemed as if they had all suddenly set to galloping down stream and they were out of sight and it was all over in a few minutes.' Heavily weighed down with equipment, unable to swim and hampered by the panic-stricken horses, 47 officers and men (out of 75 in the squadron) were drowned or kicked to death by their horses; only nineteen bodies were ever recovered. 'As daylight came and the banks lower down were searched, the bodies were found jammed amongst the boulders and under the rocky banks. The men were in full marching order, khaki, with putties and warm underclothing. They had their swords on and carried their carbines slung over their shoulders and their pouches were full. A man so accoutred simply had no chance against the swollen river.'[7] While rescue operations were under way, Browne reinforced Wood with another squadron of 11th Bengal Lancers, and Wood pushed on towards Macpherson, only to find Asmatullah gone.

Gough's column, consisting of four squadrons of cavalry, the equivalent of one and one-half battalions of infantry and four guns – in all about 1,500 men – left Jalalabad at 01.00 hours on 1 April. the cavalry reached Fatehbad shortly after daybreak and camped just beyond to await the arrival of the infantry, guns and transport. Gough used the day to reconnoitre the surrounding country. Early on 2 April, he sent a cavalry patrol westwards along the road to Gandamak and another patrol southwards towards Khuja, the main centre of the Khugianis. The latter reported large numbers of tribesmen assembling some five miles from Gough's camp to give battle, a fact which Gough could soon see for himself. Following the traditional principle of always attacking an Asiatic enemy, Gough left a squadron of cavalry and 300 infantry to guard his baggage and moved off to deal with the tribesmen. Numbering some 5,000 they were drawn up on the edge of a plateau behind strong stone breastworks. Their flanks were protected by steep bluffs and from their position, the ground sloped down gradually towards Gough's position. He thus faced the task of attacking, frontally and uphill, a very strong position held by overwhelmingly superior numbers. To retreat was likely to lead to a large-scale uprising all around Jalalabad. In its way, the problem was as difficult a one as faced any tactical commander during the war.

Gough, with his long experience in India, was more than equal to the occasion. His tactics were basically those of William the Conqueror at Hastings. He sent forward his cavalry and guns to within a mile of the enemy, with orders to the guns to fire a few rounds and then retire with the cavalry. He hoped to lure the Khugianis out of their position, giving his cavalry and infantry a chance to get at them. The trick worked. The tribesmen rushed forward to attack the retiring cavalry and guns and were taken in flank by the infantry who had moved unseen up a nullah on the enemy's right. A fierce hand-to-hand struggle took place but the enemy were gradually driven back. At the psychological moment, the three squadrons of cavalry charged the enemy's left and shattered it. The tribesmen fled for the cover of their original breastworks but were given no time to rally and unite. The position was speedily occupied by the cavalry, followed by the infantry and guns who opened fire on the fleeing enemy. In the ensuing pursuit, little quarter was given or expected – an observer wrote that, 'Everyone is full of the pluck of these fellows who, in all cases when overtaken, stood at bay and fought like men. It was rather curious to see a fellow, armed only with a large knife, dancing round and round and keeping off three or four Hussars, who could not get their horses to face him, although it always ended in his being cut down or shot.' The Khugianis subsequently attributed most of their losses to the cavalry. Gough lost only six killed and forty injured; the Khugianis' loss was put at over 300 killed and perhaps 900 injured. Lieutenant Walter Hamilton of the Guides Cavalry won the Victoria Cross on this occasion. Two days later, Gough, reinforced by the remainder of the 2nd Infantry Brigade under Tytler, penetrated to Khuja and blew up its walls and towers. It was the end as far as the Khugianis were concerned; on 6 April, they surrendered and promised to give up all hostile action. No further trouble was experienced from them.[8]

Apart from the military problems, Browne faced immense logistic difficulties. He had not had an adequate supply of animals when he was originally ordered to advance and the situation had deteriorated as his lines of communication lengthened. Compounding the problem was the habitual carelessness and neglect with which the transport animals were treated, resulting in a huge mortality rate. So when Browne was asked early in March to submit plans for the advance of his 1st Division to Kabul he was forced to admit that an advance was impossible because of the supply difficulties. Even without a chain of posts between Jalalabad and Kabul, he estimated that the 1st Division, numbering some 8,000 men and 2,100 troop animals, would require the equivalent of 11,000 camel-loads to get it to Kabul with adequate supplies. Against this requirement, he possessed the equivalent of some 3,500 loads; by denuding the 2nd Division of transport, he could bring this figure up to 7,500. None of these figures made allowance for animal wastage. The most that he could contemplate was an early move to Gandamak which was at least cooler and presumably healthier. His new Chief of Staff, Colonel MacGregor, on joining, reported to Army HQ that the transport system had totally broken down.[9]

At the beginning of April, the improved military situation around Jalalabad and the need to exert some further political pressure on Yakub Khan combined to justify the advance to Gandamak. On 12 April, Browne moved from Jalalabad, reaching Safed Sang thirty miles from Jalalabad and three miles short of Gandamak two days later. By the end of April, he had roughly 5,000 men there, well short of the full strength of the 1st Division, but as many as he could feed even with the aid of all available mules and camels from Maude's 2nd Division. The valley of Gandamak is shady and well-watered, but Browne preferred a position at Safed Sang where there were good supplies of water and where he commanded all the surrounding country. But Safed Sang proved also stony, treeless, extremely dusty and very exposed. Part of the force was therefore located in Gandamak itself and on the Nimla plateau further to the east, where Babur had once laid out a beautiful garden which still flourished, famous for its narcissi and avenues of plane trees. Four miles from Gandamak the bleached bones of Elphinstone's soldiers still covered the hill where the remnants of his ill-fated army had made their last stand; it now fell to the 17th Foot to put these bones finally to rest.

At Gandamak, Browne's force was nearly two-thirds of the way from Peshawar to Kabul which now lay only seventy miles ahead. As the crow flies he was only some 25 miles away from Roberts's position on the Peiwar Kotal and Roberts in turn was about ninety miles from Kabul. But whereas Roberts's route to Kabul via the Shutagardan Pass and the Logar valley was comparatively easy, Browne faced an extremely difficult series of defiles which offered excellent defensive positions to the Afghans. It had been intended that on the departure of the 1st Division for Gandamak, Maude's 2nd Division would extend its line of communications responsibilities to include Jalalabad. But when the time came, Maude found himself too stretched to do so and accordingly a garrison from the 1st Division had to be left at Jalalabad, with intermediate garrisons between there and Gandamak at Fort Rozabad and Fort Battye, respectively twelve and twenty-one miles from Jalalabad. Some measure of the problems caused by Browne's long and difficult communications is given by the distribution of troops. In and around Gandamak, he had the equivalent of two cavalry regiments, seven and one-half infantry regiments and twenty guns – in all, about 5,000 men; the remainder of the 1st Division, comprising the equivalent of one cavalry and two infantry regiments with three companies of sappers and miners and two guns – in all, 1,600 men – was occupying Jalalabad and the intermediate posts. Between Jalalabad and Jamrud, Maude disposed of roughly two and one-half regiments of cavalry, nine and one-half regiments of infantry and 24 guns, a total of about 6,300 men.

At Gandamak, Browne had managed to concentrate a good deal less than the full division of men which he had reported as the minimum necessary for him to occupy Kabul. MacGregor suggested as an alternative that Roberts move northwards via the Lakarai Pass to link up with Browne at Tezin. Roberts preferred to move via the Shutagardan Pass, ostensibly because an advance on Kabul from two directions would greatly ease food and forage problems by tapping wider and different areas. One may suspect that he also valued his independence as a commander.[10] There was in any case a basic problem in timing. Roberts, having succeeded in collecting an adequate supply of transport, was anxious to advance as soon as possible lest his transport force should start wasting away. Browne felt

107

forced to delay his advance until he had collected enough transport to sustain his force for a reasonable minimum period. From this logistic dilemma, the military commanders were rescued by Yakub Khan.

On 7 April, Cavagnari had written to the Amir, conveying the British Government's acceptance of Yakub's proposal that a British envoy should visit Kabul. The British acceptance sparked off a lively discussion in Kabul. Some of the Amir's advisers were in favour of his rejecting the British approach and seeking Russian support. No one could guarantee the present safety of a British mission in Kabul where passions ran high as a result of the British invasion and Afghan defeats. Cavagnari's messenger, Bakhtiar Khan, managed in consequence to persuade Yakub to offer to visit the British instead. In view of the danger to a British envoy in Kabul, Lytton agreed that this was the preferable course and on 29 April Yakub wrote saying that he would leave Kabul in four days' time:

> 'The Munshi above mentioned [Bakhtiar Khan] has strung one by one on the thread of description the pearls of your friendly hints and the verbal messages with which you, actuated by the motives of most sincere friendship, entrusted him, and thereby he has opened the door of happiness and joy to the face of my heart inasmuch as the grasp of the desire of having an interview with the officers of high rank and holding a happy conference with them, has taken hold of the skirt of my heart. I will, please God, set out from the capital, for my destination on Monday the 3rd May 1879.'[11]

The first part of the war was now effectively beginning to draw to a close. Before we consider the peace negotiations, we need to look at one further passage of arms which typified the unstable situation in which the Peshawar Valley Field Force found itself. The occupation of Gandamak coincided with rumours that the Mohmands were gathering across the River Kabul from Dakka with the object of crossing the river and attacking the British lines of communications. The local Khan asked for protection against the insurgents whom he reported as being within three miles of his village. The commander of the post at Dakka, Lieutenant-Colonel Barnes, had a garrison of some 800 cavalry and infantry with six guns to protect the hospital and stores depot there and to keep open the road on each side of Dakka. There was obviously something to be said for supporting the local, apparently loyal inhabitants so on 21 April, Barnes took a small force consisting of two field guns of C/3 RA, a squadron of the 10th Bengal Lancers and three companies of the Mhairwarra Battalion, eastwards along the south bank of the river as far as Kam Dakka some seven miles away. Apart from a few shots from across the river he encountered no opposition, but the villagers were unanimous that large numbers of Mohmands were assembled across the river ready to attack them. On the advice of the Political Officer at Maude's headquarters, Barnes arranged for two companies of the Mhairwarra Battalion, under Captain O'Moore Creagh, to march from Dakka the same evening to protect the village. Fortunately as it turned out, Creagh decided to leave trenching tools behind and to take extra ammunition instead. With his 138 men, he reached Kam Dakka just before midnight, ready to occupy and fortify it to protect its inhabitants.

To his surprise, he was refused admittance, the villagers claiming that a British force, without guns, would only make matters worse vis-à-vis the Mohmands. Creagh was in no position to force his way in and he camped for the night outside. Early next morning he again demanded entry and was again refused. Even at this stage, he was not particularly worried and sent a message back to Dakka saying that all was well. Shortly thereafter the situation deteriorated. Large numbers of Mohmands were seen crossing the river to attack him and the villagers were showing clear signs of changing sides. At 08.00 hours, he was reinforced by a detachment of 37 men from Dakka with additional supplies of ammunition, but the detachment commander thought that the route to Dakka was now cut off and no further reinforcements would be likely to get through that day. Creagh's troops were already being forced back and it was clear to him that he had no option but to find a suitable defensive position and fight it out, in the hope that a messenger whom he had dispatched to Dakka for help would get through.

He selected a small graveyard, between the river and the Dakka road, and his men built a breastwork from stones lying about, and laid in a stock of water. No sooner were these preparations complete than the position was surrounded by the Mohmands and villagers. Totally isolated, the small force found itself fighting for its life. Using crops and other cover, the attackers were able to get to within one hundred yards without difficulty and from there they were able to launch direct assaults on the defenders lining the breastwork. The fighting was hand-to-hand, bayonet against knife or sword, and although Creagh's troops succeeded in holding their position, it was clear that without reinforcement they were bound ultimately to be overwhelmed. By three o'clock in the afternoon their ammunition was running out. The fury of the Mohmand attacks showed no sign of decreasing and every man knew that it was now only a matter of time.

In the fashion of schoolboy fiction, help arrived in the nick of time. Maude at Landi Kotal was already uneasy about the situation which appeared to be developing in the Dakka area and, from past experience, distrusted the optimistic advice of the 'Politicals'. He had accordingly dispatched a column of eight companies of infantry, two mountain guns and a handful of cavalry under Colonel Norman to reconnoitre north-westwards from Landi Kotal towards the Kam Dakka area. On the morning of the 22nd the two mountain guns, escorted by a company of the 12th Foot under Major Dyce, had reached Haft Chah, on the Landi Kotal–Dakka road, roughly midway between the two and some five miles south-south-west of Kam Dakka; Norman with the remainder was near Sarobi, due east of Creagh's position. When Creagh's message about the worsening situation at Kam Dakka got through to Barnes, he immediately telegraphed Maude who ordered Dyce and Norman to move directly to Creagh's aid. At the same time a small column consisting of a troop of 10th Bengal Lancers and two companies of infantry under Captain Strong set out at once from Dakka. Strong, having the easiest route, was the first to arrive, just as Creagh's ammunition ran out; 'on its left lay the Kabul River, winding through yellowing cornfields; the mountain slopes and the plain at its feet crowded with blue-togared Mohmands and gay with red and white banners. But the point that drew all eyes was the graveyard with its improvised defences behind which glimpses could be caught of the gallant Mhairwarras, some with bandaged limbs and heads, firing slowly into the surging throng which threatened every moment to overwhelm them.'[12]

Recognizing the critical nature of the situation, Strong left one company to guard the pass over which he had just come, and with the other company (also Mhairwarras) made a dash for Creagh's position which he succeeded in entering.

Shortly afterwards, the troop of 10th Bengal Lancers arrived and, placing himself at its head, Strong charged the besiegers, driving many into the river and breaking up the enemy concentration. He was supported by the remnants of Creagh's gallant infantry who charged out with the bayonet. Seizing the opportunity, Creagh then withdrew his and Strong's troops from the graveyard area and linked up with the company guarding the pass. They were by no means out of danger. The withdrawal brought the Mohmands back again to attack the combined force, and ammunition was still in short supply. At this point, Dyce arrived. The guns quickly re-dispersed the tribesmen and the whole force now withdrew slowly. Encumbered with the wounded and constantly harried by the tribesmen, it reached Dakka at 20.00 hours.

Next day a strong force of infantry, cavalry and artillery under Lieutenant-Colonel Sillery from Dakka reoccupied the ground at Kam Dakka. The guns shelled some tribesmen seen on the north bank of the river, but otherwise there was no sign of resistance. Sillery was joined in the afternoon by Norman's force which finally reached Kam Dakka after a long, exhausting march through the Loi Shilman valley and over the Shilman Gakkhe Pass.

Creagh and Strong lost between them only six killed and eighteen wounded; the tribesmen lost at least 200 killed. Creagh, rightly, received the Victoria Cross; his reputation was made and he was to end up as Commander-in-Chief, India. Strong received, somewhat unfairly, only a recommendation to the Commander-in-Chief for favourable consideration.

The happy outcome of this desperate affair should not be allowed to obscure the nearness of the gap between victory and disaster. Creagh and Strong had acted with great coolness and judgement, when a mistake could have been fatal. Maude and Haines were in retrospect bitterly critical of the political advice which had put Creagh's force in such jeopardy.

The affair demonstrated the constant danger which surrounded small detachments along the line of communications and emphasized Browne's uneasy situation. If stronger forces had been available initially at Dakka, effective support could have been given to the inhabitants of Kam Dakka and the Mohmands possibly prevented from crossing the river. But already more than half of the Peshawar Valley Field Force was tied up in Line of Communications duties and it was not possible to be strong everywhere. What Browne might well have considered was establishing a small number of mobile columns based at suitable points rather than a series of static garrisons.

His situation was, however, about to be relieved. On 8 May, Yakub Khan reached the British camp at Gandamak and was received with appropriate honours.[13] Some 4,750 men were on parade for the occasion and no doubt the point was not lost on the Amir. Whatever Yakub hoped to secure in negotiation, Lytton at least was clear on what terms could be offered. He had taken the prudent opportunity to clear his policy with the Cabinet.

On the British side, the negotiations were conducted by Cavagnari and initially attended by Yakub Khan's advisers. But the talks made little progress, the Amir fighting hard against any cession of territory. On the 17th, Cavagnari, who had little respect for his opponents or their arguments, had a private interview with the Amir.[14] Cavagnari was prepared to concede that Pishin, Kurram and Sibi should be assigned, not transferred, to British control and any surplus of revenue remitted to the Amir. Agreement was reached on this basis. This opened the way to quick agreement on the other outstanding points including the proposal for a telegraph line from Kurram to Kabul. The treaty was signed at Gandamak on 26 May and immediately dispatched to Simla where Lytton ratified it on 30 May. The ratified treaty was presented to Yakub Khan at Gandamak on 6 June.

From the British point of view, the treaty could be regarded as a relatively generous one. The Amir did not formally lose any territory; instead the Kurram valley, Sibi and Pishin came under 'the protection and administrative control' of the British Government. In the case of the Khyber and Michni Passes, the British had never accepted that these were Afghan territory, and control of these passes and of the surrounding tribes was to remain in British hands. The Amir lost control of his own foreign policy, had to accept a British representative in Kabul and the possibility of British agents elsewhere, and had to agree to some not very onerous conditions about freedom of commerce and the institution of a telegraph line from the Kurram to Kabul. But he gained an annual subsidy of six lakhs of rupees and a somewhat strengthened guarantee of protection against external aggression. Above all, Afghanistan was to remain united instead of partitioned.

Even from the Afghan point of view it might have been worse in view of the military balance and Lytton clearly assumed that the Amir would be satisfied and grateful. But that was looking at it through the eyes of the victor and in any case politically it was much in Lytton's interest to persuade the world that it was so. Even if he professed to be content, Yakub can hardly have overlooked the sombre realities of the situation. His Afghan subjects were not likely to appreciate the practical difference between outright annexation and 'protection and administrative control' – and indeed since the British quietly annexed Kurram, Sibi and Pishin outright in 1887, the distinction proved of no real significance. All that the Afghans were likely to see was that extensive and important areas to which they had a more or less valid claim were now permanently in the hands of the British who had a well-deserved reputation for not letting go of anything that they had seized. Above all, Yakub had had to agree to the stationing of a British envoy in Kabul and to the reception of British agents elsewhere whenever the British Government required it. His father had resisted all British pressure for this because he saw correctly that it meant at that time the disappearance of Afghan independence. His son could have had no illusions about the effect of this aspect of the treaty upon the prestige and stability of his rule, particularly in those areas such as Herat and Afghan Turkestan which had been untouched by the war and had not experienced the reality of British military power.[15]

For the moment, the issue for both sides was how to get the British forces out of Afghanistan as quickly as possible. For the Indian Government, the economic and financial burden of the war needed to be relieved as quickly as possible. In the Punjab and Sind, agriculture and commerce had been severely damaged by the voracious demands of the army for transport animals of all kinds. Because of the military demand, supplies and foodstuffs in these areas had enormously increased in price and everywhere in India the provincial administrations had had to cut back on improvements and reforms because of the financial drain of the war. Unfortunately, the need for early withdrawal clashed with climatic realities.

By the beginning of June, the hot season was well advanced everywhere on the North-West Frontier. Temperatures of well over 100° Fahrenheit in the shade were being recorded at Jalalabad, and at Kandahar the temperature in the sun reached 125° Fahrenheit. In the Kurram valley, it was cooler and greener: 'Though during the winter the ground seemed to produce nothing but stones, yet now it was covered with every variety of wild herb; mint, sage, thyme, peppermint and worm-wood scented the air as they were pressed under foot, the latter especially grew in large quantities, and filled the breeze with an aromatic odour, almost too strong for some refined tastes. The slopes were covered with a yellow briar rose, but otherwise there were not many flowers, except some small common English ones such as the scarlet pimpernel, forget-me-not, yellow crowsfoot, wild liquorice and a pretty broom; the young grass, too, began to shoot, and made the place look green.'[16] In any case, a good many troops had to be left in the Kurram as a garrison now that it was under British control, and the distances involved in withdrawing the remainder were much shorter than on the Khyber and Kandahar lines. At the other end of the front, it had been decided at an early stage that the troops could not be withdrawn from Kandahar until after the hot weather, in September, and Yakub had had reluctantly to accept the position.[17]

The problems of withdrawal centred on Browne's force. A major worry was cholera which always appeared in the hot weather, and was present now in the Punjab and at Peshawar in epidemic proportions. Cases had already appeared at Jalalabad. On the same day that negotiations started at Gandamak, Lytton held a conference at Simla with the military and medical authorities to discuss the practi-cability of withdrawing the troops by the more healthy route via the Michni Pass. The conference reached no conclusion and a Medical Commission of four doctors was set up to advise on the more basic issue of whether the troops should be withdrawn at all or left where they were until the hot season was over and sickness on the decline. Apart from cholera, which had reached Jalalabad by the middle of May, the medical authorities were worried about other diseases such as typhoid which might spread if the men were kept in tents in the hot weather.

The Surgeon-General of the British Forces (Dr Ker-Innes) summed up the medical dilemma thus: 'The time was May. Cholera was present in the Khyber route and Peshawar Valley; it was extending to the north and even threatening Kabul at a later date. If the troops marched to India, they marched into cholera; if they remained, it advanced on them. But assuming that they remained it would be necessary for them to continue at their posts until October; for past experience has sufficiently shown that cholera, when once it has invaded the Peshawar Valley, may be expected, speaking broadly as the result of past experience, to localise itself there from May to November.'[18] The doctors concluded that the medical risks were so evenly balanced that the political and financial need for withdrawal must take precedence. So it was decided to withdraw as quickly as possible; many, including Macpherson and Charles Gough, thought it a bad decision both on medical and political grounds.

The task was a formidable one. Allowing for the retention of garrisons now at Landi Kotal, Ali Masjid and Jamrud, some 9,000 men had now to be moved back to India, together with large quantities of stores. The speed and efficiency of the evacuation contrasted vividly with the delays and difficulties which had beset the advance. Sam Browne's headquarters left Gandamak on the same day that the Amir started back to Kabul. The rearguard under Tytler left Gandamak the following day (8 June). As the troops moved back, the telegraph line was rolled up. The rearguard was delayed for a day or two at Jalalabad while the mountains of stores accumulated there were shipped down the River Kabul by raft to Dakka, forty miles on, but Jalalabad was finally evacuated on 13 June. By the 26th, all men and stores had reached Landi Kotal and the 1st Division had been broken up, leaving behind the equivalent of a brigade to garrison Ali Masjid and Landi Kotal.

But it had been a long, hard march for the troops, in temperatures above 110° Fahrenheit. To the heat, dust and thirst was added the ever-present worry of cholera. By 25 June, 317 cases had been reported, with 199 deaths. The reality behind these figures was graphically described by Combe: 'One night we sent on fourteen or fifteen cases, to travel in the cool; next morning, on arrival, the General and I went to the shed set apart as cholera hospital and saw ten of our men laid out in a row, with just a blanket thrown over them. The Doctor would not let us look at them, as he said it was impossible to recognize them and it was no use running the risk of the shock the sight might give us.'

The very high proportion of deaths revealed the helplessness of medical science faced with a disease of whose very cause it was totally ignorant. Ker-Innes described graphically the state of the British troops as they completed the long march:

'On reaching Jamrud and Hari-Singh-ka-Burj, and especially as they made their final marches, their distress was very apparent. Their clothes were stiff and dirty from the profuse perspiration and dust; their countenances betokened great nervous exhaustion, combined with a wild expression difficult to describe; the eyes injected, and even sunken, a burning skin, black with the effects of sun and dirt: dry tongue; a weak voice; and a thirst which no amount of fluids seemed to relieve. Many of these men staggered rather than marched into their tents and threw themselves down utterly incapable of further exertion until refreshed by sleep and food . . . Nor did the officers appear to be in any better plight.'[19]

Overall, the death rate among British troops on the Khyber line was comparable with that experienced during the Mutiny twenty years before, and some thirty times greater than in down-country cantonments such as Bareilly or Calcutta.

In the Kurram, news of the treaty brought to a halt the preparations which Roberts had been energetically pushing forward for a very early advance on Kabul. Throughout May, reconnaissance parties had been out exploring the country between the Peiwar Kotal and the Shutagardan Pass. Since the Kurram was now to come permanently under British control, it remained important to acquire a detailed knowledge of the geography and inhabitants of the whole area and Roberts himself made a series of reconnaissances in the first half of June. A great deal of useful information was acquired; in particular, he was able to confirm that the Lakarai Pass route did not offer a practicable way of linking up with the troops at Gandamak. Having examined all the routes over the Peiwar range, he was satisfied that the best route for a proper road, capable of taking wheeled vehicles, was up the Spingawi Valley. He was convinced also that the natural route from India to Kabul was via the Kurram and he therefore advocated some form of light railway from Rawalpindi to Kurram.

Apart from a few cases of cholera at Thal, the Kurram valley presented no significant health problems. The heat was bearable – indeed in the upper part of the valley, it was relatively cool even in July. Roberts was therefore in no hurry to move his British troops back. In the middle of July Cavagnari, who had been appointed as the first envoy to Kabul, arrived at Thal en route for his new post. Roberts escorted him as far as the new boundary just beyond Ali Khel where his Afghan escort was waiting to take him on to Kabul. Roberts bade an emotional farewell to Cavagnari:

> 'I could not feel happy as to the prospects of the Mission and my heart sank as I wished Cavagnari goodbye. When we had proceeded a few yards in our different directions we both turned round, retraced out steps, shook hands once more and parted for ever.'[20]

Four days later, Roberts left for a well-earned leave at Simla and then to serve on the commission which Lytton had set up under Sir Ashley Eden to look into the future organization of the Indian Army.

The Second Afghan War was over, or so it seemed, and it was time for the congratulations and rewards to flow. For Lytton the result was particularly sweet. The critics who had prophesied disaster and the generals who had condemned the scale of his preparations had both now apparently been proved wrong. Writing to Eden, he claimed exultantly that it had all been done 'without seriously injuring the Afghan people, wounding their national *amour propre* or bequeathing to them any bitter memories of our presence in their country'.[21] For Disraeli's Government at home, struggling hitherto with the political burden of two wars, it was a relief to be able to claim that one at least had been triumphantly concluded. Parliamentary approval by way of a Vote of Thanks to Lytton, Haines and the troops was followed by a formal dispatch conveying the full and unstinted approval of the Government to the terms of the Treaty of Gandamak and to the general policy followed by the Indian Government. Salisbury wrote privately to Lytton: 'I cannot allow the conclusion of this affair to pass without warmly congratulating you on the great success you have achieved and the brilliant qualities you have displayed. To my eyes the wise constraint in which you have held the eager spirits about you is not the least striking of your victories.'[22]

More tangible expressions of gratitude were forthcoming. Sam Browne was given the Grand Cross of the Order of the Bath and knighthoods were given to Cavagnari, Colley, Stewart, Roberts, Biddulph and Maude. Lesser honours were distributed lavishly to the lesser men. Not everyone was entirely happy. Stewart, for one, was uneasy about the way the fountain of honours had played: 'I have today (31 July) got a copy of the Kabul honours,' he wrote to his wife, 'and I am not at all pleased with the distribution . . . and feel that I have got my KCB on false pretences.' Lytton wrote privately to Cranbrook that Sam Browne should have been court-martialled instead of being given the GCB; he (Browne) had shown himself utterly unfit for any responsible command, had neglected every duty of a commander and displayed almost every disqualification; at the end of the campaign, his troops were demoralized and nearly mutinous through lack of confidence in their commander and his neglect of their simplest requirements. This was all very markedly in contrast to Lytton's early assessment. Browne may not have been greatly talented and there are certain indications that his administrative arrangements were defective, but his performance does not seem to have warranted Lytton's extreme castigation.* The fact is that Lytton despised most of the officers and officials he met – thus he now characterized Maude as a mediocre man whose want of tact and temper was not relieved by any apparent military talent while Haines was described as second-rate and ordinary.[23]

There was actually a good deal to be pleased about. Salisbury had been quick to spot the fact that the successful conclusion of the war had greatly strengthened the British position in Europe: 'the great military success has done us yeoman's service in negotiating with Russia; and I hope that the moderation of the terms will be of no small utility at Constantinople'.[24] Viewed from the narrower, Indian viewpoint, Russian influence had been eliminated at Kabul, a British envoy now controlled Afghan external relations and the three key entry points into India from Afghanistan were securely (and as it turned out) permanently in British hands. These strategic gains did not satisfy the most ardent protagonists of the 'forward school', but they were solid enough to stifle criticism.†

Equally important, the reconstructed Indian Army had emerged from its first major test with a good deal of credit. The transport arrangements had been a near disaster; MacGregor summed up most people's sentiments before the Eden Commission; 'To my mind, the failure of the transport service as an organization has been complete. In fact, I have never been able to ascertain that there ever was an organization.'[25] But that was nothing new; the British Army was suffering much the same problems at that very moment in Zululand. The artillery had been a disappointment – the mountain guns threw a pitifully small shell a very short distance and the field and heavy artillery lacked mobility, but it had not proved critical. Finally, there had been a trickle of desertion among the Pathan sepoys.[26] Overall, however, the native regiments had shown that, properly led, they were more than a match for the Afghans.

If there were a sombre side to the campaign it lay in the effects on the trans-border tribes. Bound by strong ethnic and religious ties to Kabul, they could not fail to be affected by the humiliations inflicted on Afghanistan. Many of them, including some of the most powerful such as the Afridis, Shinwaris and Mohmands, had felt the heavy hand of British military power. There would be long-term effects.

The Russians had watched the campaign closely. Major-General Sobolev, of the Russian Imperial General Staff, summed it up thus:

'The absence of a seriously considered plan of operations, the inability to combine caution with decision, the utter helplessness shown in securing the lines of communication, the miserable condition of the intelligence and scouting services, the inability to arrange for the regular dispatch of transport trains, the want of tact shown to the native population, the burdening of the troops with a mass of unnecessary work in requiring them to defend the Commissariat stores and to make up for the want of

---

*Nevertheless, Eaton Travers recorded in his diary what must have been a popular view in the Army: 'Sam Browne is certainly keeping up his apparently well-earned reputation of being a regular old woman and quite unfit to command an army.' Diary, op. cit., 10 June 1879.
†Thus Haines thought that Khost should have been included with the Kurram and direct control installed over the Thal–Chotiali route. On the other hand, Stewart thought it a mistake to hold the Khyber and the Kurram valley.

transport by manul labour, the subjection of military operations to political considerations – these, in our opinion, are the chief negative deductions which can be drawn from a minute examination of the Anglo-Afghan Campaign of 1878–1879.'[27]

There was a good deal of truth in this, but soldiers are entitled to be judged by results. As the troops and their commanders marched back to India, their mood was justifiably one of relief and satisfaction.

NOTES

1. See text of Stolietov's letter of 8 October 1878 quoted in H. B. Hanna. *The Second Afghan War*, vol. II, p. 152 (London, 1904).
2. Hanna, op. cit., vol. II, p. 166.
3. Cavagnari personally had wanted to go farther and to press for British garrisons at Gandamak and Basawal – Cavagnari to Foreign Department, 6 March 1879 (copy in RP 7101-23-147-2).
4. It reached Sibi at the foot of the hills in January 1880, and Rindli, 19 miles beyond, shortly after. It progressed no farther while the war lasted. Quetta was not reached until 1887.
5. As *The Times* correspondent pointed out, 'The Pathans have an inveterate hatred of the surveyor. They have an idea that the Government sends a surveyor first, then an army.' (*The Times* 8 March 1879). Three weeks before the attack on Leach's party, another surveying party had been attacked at Michni, probably by Afridis.
6. No organized system of military Intelligence existed before or during the war. Such Intelligence as was obtained was acquired through the political officers who were accustomed in peacetime to maintaining their own organizations of paid spies and informers in order to find out what was going on in their areas. How far such a system could be successfully utilized for military purposes depended largely on two factors:
1. the closeness of the link between military commander and political officer;
2. the political officer's depth of knowledge of the district concerned.
The military commander who had political powers as well, such as Roberts and Stewart, were naturally better placed in this respect than the commander like Browne whose political officer (Cavagnari) had independent powers. But either way, as the armies moved deeper into Afghanistan, the political officers' knowledge became less and less reliable. Stewart organized a tiny Intelligence Branch of one officer, one native officer and one native NCO to supplement

the work of the political officers, but there is no evidence that he was significantly better-informed than the other commanders. The history of the war is full of examples of poor Intelligence – Stewart's surprise at Ahmed Khel, Roberts's actions before Kabul in December 1879 and, above all, the events leading up to Maiwand.
7. Surgeon-Major T. H. Evatt. *Personal Recollections*, London. Kipling's poem *Ford o' Kabul River* commemorates this disaster. Only 13 horses were lost, most managing to swim ashore once they were freed from the weight of their riders. A number of obvious precautions, including marking the line of the ford, had not been taken.
8. Combe noted a sombre aftermath: 'a lot of prisoners were taken and the Political who came out next morning wanted to have them *all* shot but this was too much for us and he selected five Moollahs or Priests, and though I could not see the justice of this, the General agreed with him, and I had to get them taken away and shot.' Combe, op. cit., p. 42. It is perhaps not surprising in the light of this that the political direction was not widely trusted by the military.
9. It is not easy to see why Browne should have been in this parlous situation. If the civil authorities in Sind could find 19,000 camels for Stewart, it is hard to believe that adequate numbers of animals for both Browne and Roberts could not have been found around Peshawar. One suspects that Browne was to some extent the victim of his own neglect of the problem.
10. In fairness also, the route over the Lakarai Pass was later examined by Roberts and found to require a good deal of work to make it fit for the passage of troops.
11. Official History, vol. II, p. 136.
12. Hanna, op. cit., vol. II, p. 299.
13. Ball-Acton, who was there, described Yakub as a 'villainous-looking man but, as people say, very melancholy-looking'. Mortimer Durand's view was, 'He is by no means the fine young soldier I used to imagine him; a weak, vacillating face,

pleasant enough at times, but not trust-
worthy or in any way impressive.'
14. In a letter to Lytton on 23 May 1879, he
wrote, 'In fact, I found the whole lot to be
pretty much of the ordinary Afghan stamp,
and that avarice and suspicion were their
leading qualities. Their arguments were so
feeble and far from the point that I at once
made up my mind to deal with the case as if
it concerned an ordinary affair connected
with border Pathan tribes.' Lady Betty
Balfour. *Lord Lytton's Indian Administration*,
p. 322.
Cavagnari himself was strongly in favour of
breaking up Afghanistan.
15. Colquhoun, for example, was struck by
the arrogance of the Herati troops he
encountered after the treaty was signed and
their claim that if they had been at the
Peiwar Kotal it would never have been
taken. Colquhoun, op. cit., p. 382.
16. Colquhoun, op. cit., p. 334, describing
the scenery round Ali Khel at the end of
May 1879.
17. Even so, Stewart's force suffered heavily
from cholera, losing in all 253 men out of
401 attacked.
18. Quoted in Abridged Official History,
op. cit., p. 83.

19. Abridged Official History, p. 88. Ball-
Acton thought that marching in the hot
weather brought on most of the 80 cases of
cholera in his regiment. Ball-Acton, op. cit.,
p. 105.
20. *Forty-One Years in India*, vol. II, p. 179. On
hearing that a Mission was to be located in
Kabul, John Lawrence is reported to have
exclaimed, 'They will all be killed! They will
all be killed!'
21. LP 518/4, p. 469 – Lytton to Ashley
Eden, 14 June 1879.
22. Letter of 23 May 1879, quoted in
Balfour, op. cit., p. 330.
23. LP 518/4. pp. 639 and 146.
24. Salisbury to Lytton, 23 May 1879, op.
cit.
25. Eden Commission Report, Appendices,
vol. IV, p. 1641.
26. The 1st Punjab Infantry, a regiment
with a high proportion of Pathans, had 17
desertions up to the middle of May 1879.
Lieutenant-General C. T. Chamberlain told
the Eden Commission, 'Throughout the war,
there had been an unpleasant feeling of want
of confidence in these classes.'
27. Major-General L. N. Sobolev, *The Anglo-
Afghan Struggle*, St. Petersburg, 1880–82.
English abridgement, Calcutta, 1885.

CHAPTER 7

THE WEB IS SHATTERED

'I think you need be under no anxiety about the satisfactory execution and results of the Kabul Treaty or any troubles in Afghanistan consequent on the withdrawal of our troops . . . The Afghans will like and respect us all the more for the thrashing we have given Sher Ali and the lesson we have taught to Russia . . . The Afghan people certainly do not view us with any ill-will.'

Lytton to Cranbrook, 23 June 1879.

Cavagnari reached Kabul on 24 July 1879 and was lodged with his escort in the Bala Hissar in a large and, for Kabul, relatively luxurious building only some 250 yards from the Amir's own quarters. In contrast to the large escort which had accompanied Chamberlain's abortive mission, Cavagnari had chosen to keep his escort small on the grounds that a large escort would stimulate Afghan resentment and his safety must in any case ultimately depend upon the Amir. Apart from Cavagnari, the mission consisted of a secretary (Jenkins), a doctor (Kelly), 25 men of the Guides Cavalry and 50 men of the Guides Infantry under Lieutenant Walter Hamilton, VC. Cavagnari's primary channel of communication with Simla was by mounted messenger to Ali Khel and from there by telegraph or postal service.

It may be doubted whether Cavagnari was the ideal choice of envoy. Son of an Italian aristocrat and an Irish mother, he had been brought up in England, entering the old East India Company's college at Addiscombe as a military cadet. In 1858, he had joined the 1st Bengal Fusiliers and served through the latter part of the Mutiny. In 1861, like many another ambitious young officer, he had switched to the political service and been posted to the Punjab where he was in charge of the Kohat district from 1866 to 1877, becoming Deputy Commissioner at Peshawar. His years on the Frontier had made him something of a legend for energy and courage. It may have been the vivacity derived from his Italian ancestry which struck a chord in Lytton. Just as Alexander Burnes had become the favourite of Auckland, so Cavagnari had rapidly established himself in Lytton's favour.

Of his ability, charm and knowledge of the frontier there could be no doubt. But he was also self-confident to the point of arrogance, bold to the point of rashness and intensely ambitious. Familiarity with the frontier tribes had bred a degree of contempt which manifested itself in his treatment of the Afghans. Despite public protestations of friendship, it would have been surprising if the Amir had not cherished resentment at the way in which Cavagnari had conducted the negotiations at Gandamak. More generally, Cavagnari was to the Afghans the symbol of their national humiliation. Neville Chamberlain had said of him that he was 'more the man for facing an emergency than one to entrust with a position requiring delicacy and very calm judgement . . . If he were left at Cabul as our agent I should fear his not keeping us out of difficulties.' Combe struck a more sour note which may have been shared by many in the army: 'Cavagnari has made a good thing out of it so far but it is about even betting now that he and his friend Yakub Khan, do not both get their throats cut.'[1]

Cavagnari was well-aware of the critical nature of his position at Kabul but he had decided that the best course was to carry it off boldly, with an outward show of confidence and imperturbability. For the moment, a British envoy controlled Afghan external relations, Russian influence had been decisively eliminated and all this had been achieved by a short campaign at relatively little cost. It was the high-water mark of Lytton's Viceroyalty. Except for the garrison at Kandahar, waiting impatiently for the end of the hot weather before marching back to India, the troops were now all back within the new frontier and Lytton could concentrate upon domestic problems in India.

For the Generals, peace brought mixed fortunes. The campaign had made Roberts. A relatively unknown and junior Major-General at the beginning, his was now a household name. He had proved himself not merely a bold and lucky field commander but able to work easily with the politicos. Barring accidents, his future was assured. If Roberts was a winner, Sam Browne and Maude were losers. His former appointment as Military Member having already been filled by Neville Chamberlain, Browne was appointed to temporary command of the Lahore Division from which he retired a few months later. Maude had proved himself a competent commander and he might have been a better choice than Browne for command of the Khyber force, but he had been unable to get on with the politicals and he would have no other opportunities as a commander. Stewart, by contrast, had had no real opportunities to show his abilities as a fighting commander, but he had demonstrated sound administrative and political skill and these were qualities sufficiently uncommon for Simla to be grateful. Of the other officers, Macpherson, Gough and Tytler would reappear, but Biddulph and the other brigade commanders stayed in India when fighting resumed.

As July drew to a close, the remaining British troops at Kandahar prepared to leave Afghanistan. Yakub's nominee as Governor of Kandahar, Sher Ali Khan, the son of Dost Mohammed's brother, Mirdil Khan, arrived to take over the administration of the city and the surrounding district, and the attention of the British military authorities was increasingly focused on the problem of the cholera epidemic which was raging at Quetta and Kandahar.[2] Detailed plans for the evacuation were issued at the end of August, and the troops began to move back to India. On 4 September, the citadel at Kandahar was finally evacuated and handed over to Sher Ali, and there remained at Kandahar only a regiment of cavalry, a battery of field artillery and two regiments of infantry, under orders to march on 8 September. But on the 5th a signal from Army Headquarters ordered Stewart to concentrate all troops north of the Khojak. Within twenty-four hours, the bazaars of Kandahar were buzzing with rumours of Cavagnari's murder and the massacre of his escort.

With his long Frontier experience, no one could have known better than Cavagnari the delicacy of his position in Kabul. Yakub's authority had been undermined by his consent to the terms of the Treaty of Gandamak. The presence in Kabul of the British agent who had negotiated the Treaty was in itself a constant affront to Afghan pride, and it would have been surprising if, as an Afghan and a Muslim, the Amir had not secretly shared the anti-British feelings of his subjects. Cavagnari himself remained outwardly confident, despite the Amir's deviousness over such matters as his proposed visit to the Viceroy and despite a series of petty clashes between members of the escort and the local inhabitants. At the end of August, he was still expressing optimism: 'I personally believe that Yakub Khan will turn out to be a very good ally and that we shall be able to keep him to his engagements.'[3] But the situation was explosive and the fuse was provided by the arrival of six Afghan infantry regiments on routine relief from Herat early in August. As early as May, the British Agent at Meshed had reported that 'The Kabul and Kandahar regiments of the Herat garrison are in a state of disaffection and disorder. The officers have no kind of authority over them.'[4] Now with bands playing, the regiments marched to the Bala Hissar to demand their arrears in back pay. At the palace, they openly jeered at the Kabul regiments that had been beaten by the British, demanded to know why Cavagnari and his mission were allowed to remain in Kabul, and clamoured to be led against the British. They were temporarily pacified by payment of some of their arrears and were persuaded to go into camp at Sherpur, two or three miles north of the city. Cavagnari was well-aware of what was happening: 'Alarming reports personally reached me today from several sources of the mutinous behaviour of the Herat regiments lately arrived here, some of the men have been seen going about the city with drawn swords, and using inflammable language against the Amir and his English visitors.'[5] One of these reports came from Nakhshband Khan, a retired risaldar-major of the Guides, living outside Kabul. 'Never fear,' he reported Cavagnari as saying, 'Keep up your heart. Dogs that bark do not bite.' Nakhshband Khan retorted that these dogs did bite and there was real danger. 'They can only kill the three or four of us here and our deaths will be well avenged,' replied Cavagnari.[6]

Early on the morning of 3 September, soldiers from the Herat regiments again rioted at the Bala Hissar demanding the remainder of their back pay. They were offered a further instalment but demanded the full amount. What followed is not absolutely clear. Apparently someone cried out that they should go to Cavagnari and demand their money from him. Shouting and yelling, the excited mob of soldiers streamed off to the Residency only a few hundred yards away. At the Residency, Cavagnari firmly declined to meet the troops' demand. There followed some scuffling and attempted looting in the course of which some of the British escort fired shots. It only needed this match to touch off the blaze. The Afghan troops rushed off to collect their rifles and the remainder of their comrades. Cavagnari sent an urgent note to the Amir asking for protection. Within an hour the troops had returned and, aided by some of the citizens, launched a full-scale attack on the Residency and its garrison. Yakub sent no help and the result was inevitable. The Residency was wholly unsuitable for defence. From the cover of surrounding houses on three sides, the Afghans were able to pour in a hail of bullets which gradually destroyed the defenders. In due course, a gun was brought up to pound the defences at close quarters. A series of gallant sallies led by Cavagnari and his British colleagues achieved only the most temporary of respites. Although the buildings had been set on fire, the fight went on until well into the afternoon, the last sortie being led by a jemadar of the Guides. By early evening, the Residency lay gutted and smoking, its inhabitants dead.* They had put up an epic resistance; the military commission, which was set up subsequently by Roberts to investigate and to punish the guilty attackers, summed it up in lapidary prose: 'They do not give their opinion hastily, but they believe that the annals of no army and no regiment can show a brighter record of bravery than has been achieved by this small band of Guides. By their deeds they have conferred undying honour, not only on the regiment to which they belong, but on the whole British Army.' In due course, the whole escort was awarded the Indian Order of Merit, Indian troops not being eligible at that time for the Victoria Cross; and the Corps of Guides was authorized to wear the battle honour 'Residency, Kabul' on its colours and appointments.

It was natural that the British should search subsequently for evidence of pre-meditation and direction. No such evidence was ever found. Given the situation in the summer of 1879, what happened was almost bound to happen and, as we have seen, even Cavagnari himself had no optimistic illusions. The massacre was no more than a bubbling over of Afghan resentment after the humiliation of the preceding campaign. What was Yakub Khan's role? In his apartments in the Bala Hissar, less than 250 yards away, he could hear the shouts and shots which echoed and re-echoed throughout that long-drawn-out day. Yet despite repeated messages from Cavagnari and the urgings of some of those around him, he did nothing except to dispatch his Commander-in-Chief with a copy of the Koran to try to persuade his subjects to desist. To Lytton and Roberts this was proof in itself of his complicity. But could he in fact have done more? He, of all men, had the strongest motive to do so because he knew that the murder of the mission could only provoke a British reaction which would destroy him and possibly the independence of his country. If he failed to intervene effectively, it was surely because he lacked the power to do so. The only troops readily to hand were the regiment guarding the Treasury; that was heavily outnumbered by the mutinous regiments from Herat and its men were in any case sensitive to taunts by the Heratis that they had allowed themselves to be beaten like a pack of women by the British.[7] It may well be that Yakub was pulled two ways, by his feelings as an Afghan and by his fear of the damage to his own position; and it may be that a greater show of vigour might have achieved something. Beyond that, he must be regarded as innocent of any involvement.

Of more interest, perhaps, is why Cavagnari failed to head off the outbreak by agreeing to pay the mutinous troops. He had had authority for some time from Simla to assist the Amir with money as he saw fit. He had deliberately declined to do so, and he refused again when faced by the mutineers. He had preferred throughout to withhold assistance in order to force the Amir to stand on his own feet.[8] According to Sowar Taimur, he did finally send an urgent message to Yakub, offering to pay the troops six months of their arrears. If so, it was by a margin too late. Stewart, observing from Kandahar, put his finger on the nub of the matter: 'If

---

*Some accounts claim that Kelly and some of the escort survived, wounded in the ruins of the Embassy until the next morning. This seems unlikely. Seven members of the escort survived – Daffadar Fateh Mahomed Khan and Sowars Akbar Shah and Narain Singh (who had been out with a grass-cutting party), Sowar Mahomed Dost (buying flour in the bazaar), Sowars Taimur, Hussain Gul and Rusul (sent with messages to the Amir and detained). There is a semi-fictional reconstruction of events in M. M. Kaye's *The Far Pavilions*, London, 1979.

he [Yakub] had not the power to save the Embassy himself, he can be of no real use to us as an ally.'[9]

News of the tragedy reached Captain Connolly, the Political Officer at Ali Khel, on the evening of the 4th and reached Simla by telegraph in the early hours of the 5th. It burst upon Lytton and his colleagues with shattering force. For Lytton, the tragedy was heightened by the emotional link between him and Cavagnari. But he was equally conscious of the implications for the policy he had been pursuing; 'The web of policy so carefully and patiently woven has been rudely shattered. We have now to weave a fresh and, I fear, a wider one from undoubtedly weaker materials,' he wrote to Disraeli the same day. There was to be no cheap success after all. Reforms in India would have to wait, and the strains of a new and more dangerous campaign would have to be faced.

For Lytton and his colleagues, there was never any doubt that Kabul would now have to be occupied, nor any real doubt as to how it would have to be done. Kandahar could be re-occupied in a matter of hours, but an advance from there on Kabul would take weeks, if not months, as supplies would have to be accumulated 400 miles from the railhead on the Indus and Stewart would then have a march of more than 300 miles. On the Khyber line, Browne's original Peshawar Valley Field Force had been dispersed months before and although there was a substantial garrison now at Landi Kotal it would take time to assemble a force of troops and transport sufficiently strong to advance through the defiles which led to Kabul nearly 150 miles away. Only in the Kurram could a substantial force be collected quickly. From the existing advanced base at Ali Khel, Kabul lay only eighty miles away, little more than five days' march across relatively easy country.* Roberts, who was in Simla when the news arrived, had already repeatedly made clear his view that the Kurram route offered the easiest and best line for any advance on Kabul.

Within hours of the news reaching Simla, Lytton had consulted the Commander-in-Chief and orders had gone out to Brigadier-General Massy, commanding in the Kurram in Roberts's absence, to move the 23rd BNI, 5th Gurkhas and a mountain battery to occupy the Shutagardan. It was occupied on the 11th and the force entrenched itself pending further orders.

Haines' plan of campaign provided for Roberts to occupy Kabul with a force of one brigade of cavalry and two brigades of infantry from the Kurram; for Jalalabad to be occupied by a division hastily scraped together under Major-General Bright, and for Kandahar to be reoccupied by Stewart with orders to threaten Ghazni to

---

*'Relatively' is the operative word. Hanna described the route thus: '. . . beyond that pass [Shutagardan], it drops by many steep zig-zags, flanked by overhanging rocks, into the bed of a rivulet, strewn with porphry, hornblende and syenite pebbles of brilliant and varied hues, one of the sources of the Logar River. Following this stream it turns sharply to the right and enters the Dobundi Defile whose stupendous perpendicular sides draw closer and closer together till, at a point called by the local tribesmen the Dur-i-Dosukh, or Gate of Hell, they so nearly meet that man can only pass between them in single file, and baggage animals have often to be relieved of burdens too wide to squeeze through the narrow opening. Emerging out of this gloomy fissure, the track crosses a narrow valley, then threads its way between huge fragments of rock up the face of a high hill to the Shinkai Kotal, and finally descends by a succession of stony shelves to the valley of the Logar where, hidden in a great ravine some three miles long by half a mile wide, the numerous hamlets known by the collective name of Kushi, lie among meadows and orchards.' (Hanna, op. cit., vol. III, p. 57). From Kushi the road to Kabul runs up the Logar valley, through easy country, with only one major potential obstacle, the Sang-i-Nawishta defile, eleven miles from the capital.

distract attention away from Roberts's advance. The problem, as always, was transport and Haines urged the Government to take steps immediately to collect the 20,000 camels which he thought would be required to maintain a force in Kabul. While an advance via the Shutagardan offered the best and quickest way of occupying Kabul, the Pass itself would be under snow after the middle of November. The second priority after occupying Kabul would have to be the establishment of a secure line of communications via the Khyber.

Roberts left Simla on 6 September, and reached Ali Khel six days later where he found nearly 6,000 troops already assembled although desperately short of transport. They were rapidly organized into the 1st Division of the Kabul Field Force, with MacGregor as Chief of Staff. The artillery included two Gatling machine-guns which had arrived in the Kurram in April. Although initial trials had been disappointing because of mechanical defects, aggravated by a shortage of spare parts and tools, hard work by the armourers had improved reliability to the point where Roberts was prepared to take the guns with him despite the general shortage of transport.* To hold the lines of communication from Ali Khel through the Kurram valley back to Thal, Brigadier-General T. E. Gordon was left with a force of some 3,000 men and eight guns.

Roberts's plan was to occupy Kushi, fourteen miles beyond the Shutagardan, guarding the entrance to the Logar valley, with an advance guard under Baker, and to collect there the necessary transport and supplies for a swift move on Kabul. In the meantime, Roberts, with the remainder of the force, would remain in the vicinity of Ali Khel, thus it was hoped, deluding the Afghans into believing that no decisive advance would be made until the spring.

The need of a swift advance and the small size of the force made it essential for Roberts to secure the friendship, or neutrality, of the surrounding tribes. By judicious bribes and promises of liberal payment for supplies and transport, he secured promises of help from the tribes around Ali Khel and from the Ghilzais who inhabited the territory between the Shutagardan and Kabul. For the time being, it was the period of Ramadan when good Muslims fasted during the day, a practice which tended to discourage active campaigning. On the day that it ended (22 September), a party of porters carrying telegraph poles, escorted by a party of the 5th Punjab Infantry, was attacked by Mangals and Ghilzais between Karatiga and the Shutagardan Pass, and largely wiped out.

Baker occupied Kushi, only 44 miles from Kabul, on 24 September. On the 28th, after a stiff fight with Mangal tribesmen in the Karatiga defile, where Colour-Sergeant Hector MacDonald of the 92nd distinguished himself, Roberts arrived at Kushi to find the Amir awaiting him. It is a convenient moment to consider the political aspects of Roberts's advance. While the need for swift retribution was the immediate motive, Lytton and his government were conscious that Cavagnari's death had totally transformed the political situation. The degree of Yakub's implication had not yet been ascertained, but even if he could be shown to be wholly innocent it was transparently clear that he possessed neither the prestige nor the power to rule the whole country effectively in the British interest. The

---

*The Gatling was patented by Richard Gatling in the USA in 1862. It had been used in the American Civil War, in the Khivan Expedition of 1873 and in the Russo-Turkish War of 1877–78. The British Army had taken it on the Ashanti Expedition of 1874 and was currently using it in Zululand.

choice lay between trying to find someone else who could rule effectively or splitting the country up. In the meantime, there was a clear military need to clothe the British advance with some show of legitimacy in order to reduce or confuse Afghan opposition.

The Amir himself had provided the peg on which such a pretence could be hung. In the immediate aftermath of the tragedy, the distraught Yakub had written to Roberts expressing his grief at what had happened and his perplexity about what to do next. In a further letter, expressing his intention of punishing the 'rebels' he ended by saying, 'I trust to God for the opportunity of showing my friendship for the British Government and for recovering my good name before the world.' On instructions from Simla Roberts, therefore, issued a proclamation to the Afghan people, on 16 September, stating that the object of the British advance was to punish those responsible for the murder of the British mission and to strengthen the authority of the Amir, provided that he was prepared to maintain friendly relations with the British Government. The proclamation was at pains to stress that those who had had nothing to do with the attack on Cavagnari's mission and who did not oppose Roberts's advance had nothing to fear.[10]

Whereas in the proclamation of November 1878, the British Government had been concerned to emphasize that its quarrel was directly with the Amir (Sher Ali), it was now claiming to be acting in support of the Amir (Yakub Khan). In parallel with the issue of this proclamation, Roberts asked Yakub to send an agent to him for confidential discussions. Yakub's finance minister, the Mustaufi (Habibulla Khan) and his chief minister, the Wazir (Shah Mohammed Khan) met Roberts at Ali Khel on 23 September. The burden of their argument was that, despite the British proclamation, the Amir and his people feared that the British advance was the prelude to a bloody and indiscriminate revenge for Cavagnari's death. The Amir was perfectly prepared to co-operate with the British and to punish the guilty, but he needed time to disarm his present regular troops and to raise fresh troops who would obey his orders. If he or the British moved precipitately, the Afghan army and the population would rise against the Amir, who was already considered by many as a British puppet, and against the British. With winter coming, Roberts might then find himself in a critical position as regards supplies and communications. A further reason for delay lay in the need for the Amir to establish control over Afghan Turkestan, where Abdurrahman was waiting for an opportunity to pounce, and over Herat.[11]

After consulting Simla, Roberts rejected the Amir's pleas, arguing that British public opinion would not tolerate delay in British troops entering Kabul to recover the bodies of the murdered mission and that the Indian Government could not allow the Amir to run any risks through lack of tangible British support. The second argument was a piece of political sophistry. As the Amir suspected, the British advance was primarily a mission of revenge. There was never any real possibility that the British would be prepared to delay, whatever the Amir's arguments.

The impasse was resolved in dramatic fashion by the arrival in Baker's camp of the Amir himself. (One is reminded, in yet another parallel with the First Afghan War, of Dost Mohammed's submission to Macnaghten in November 1840.) Cavagnari's death had presented Yakub with an almost insoluble dilemma. The

Treaty of Gandamak and the necessity of accepting a British mission in Kabul had seriously weakened his position. His hold over the country had already begun to loosen – in Herat, where his brother Ayub Khan, was intriguing against him, in Zamindawar where his uncle was virtually besieged, and in Afghan Turkestan where Abdurrahman was hovering on the border waiting his opportunity. Effectively only three choices were open to the Amir – to attempt to re-establish his authority by putting himself at the head of a national movement of opposition to the British, to ally himself with the British, or to abdicate and flee the country. If he stayed in Kabul and attempted to ride the tiger of national feeling he might well be unseated by his rivals; and in any case he could have had no illusions about the nature and duration of the struggle which it would be necessary to wage against the British. If he allied himself with the British, he could never again hope to rule in Kabul without their support; he would live in constant fear of the assassin's knife and of a change in British policy. There could be little doubt as to the course that a Dost Mohammed or even a Sher Ali would have taken, but then if Yakub had been like his father or grandfather he would not have been in the position in which he now found himself. What finally tipped the balance in favour of alliance with the British was no doubt an amalgam of fears – fear of the power of the British armies, fear of British revenge, fear of the Kabul mob, fear, above all, of his rivals. It may well have been the news that some of his enemies, led by Wali Mohammed, were already on their way to join Roberts that triggered his final decision. He spent the day of 26 September in his pleasure-gardens outside Kabul and then in the evening took horse and rode through the night up the Logar valley to Kushi where he arrived on the morning of the 27th.

When he met Roberts on the 28th, Yakub deployed fresh arguments in favour of delaying the British advance – in particular, the need to safeguard his family and supporters left behind in Kabul. But if he thought that his accession to the British side entitled him to have his arguments accepted he was sadly mistaken. Roberts strongly suspected the Amir of being involved in Cavagnari's death; he believed that Yakub was secretly plotting to rouse the population against the British and that this was the true motive behind the requests for delay.[12] As a soldier, delay was anathema to Roberts and he was already fretting under the enforced delays to his advance caused by the dearth of transport. With these prejudices firmly in his mind, Roberts was predisposed to reject Yakub's arguments and to form an unfavourable view of his character and personality. Roberts's attitude was further strengthened when on 29 September he met Wali Mohammed at Zargunshahr and received from Yakub's rival a strong warning against trusting the Amir. The Amir was treated with superficial courtesy, but it was quickly apparent that the British guard of honour provided for his camp had a double purpose and that effectively he was now a prisoner. As Roberts put it to Lytton, 'So now there is a Highlander standing sentry in front and a Goorkha in rear of his tent.'

So far as Roberts was concerned, the die was cast. As always, he was impatient to get on and seize the initiative. He had received promises of assistance and supplies from the local Ghilzai chiefs which lightened his worries about the transport shortage. On 1 October, the last of his Kabul Field Force crossed the Shutagardan and the whole force of three brigades was concentrated at Zargunshahr on the following day; it totalled just over 6,600 men and eighteen guns, with some 6,000 followers and 4,400 baggage animals. It was enough to occupy Kabul; the problem was how to keep it concentrated. The 750 camels, 3,000 mules and donkeys and 650 bullocks which Roberts had managed to assemble were insufficient to move the equipment for 6,600 men.* There was nothing for it but to divide the force and to move each half on alternate days.

The final advance began on 3 October when the Cavalry and the 1st Infantry Brigade under Roberts himself moved out of Zargunshahr, only some 35 miles from Kabul. Before leaving, Roberts issued a further proclamation to the people of Kabul.[13] Kabul would be occupied, those guilty of the attack on the mission would be punished and anyone found armed in or about Kabul would be treated as an enemy of the British Government. If the entry of the British force were resisted, Roberts would not be responsible for subsequent events.

The advance was by no means a smooth affair. There was considerable confusion in getting the transport animals over the River Logar at Zaidabad and a considerable quantity of the supplies were stolen by marauding tribesmen. It was midnight, therefore, before the last bullock limped into camp at Safed Sang, two miles beyond the river and some fourteen miles on from Zargunshahr. The fittest animals had then to be fed and rested, and sent back to Zargunshahr to enable the remaining half of the force to move forward to Safed Sang. The implications of Roberts's proclamation were quickly demonstrated. At dawn on the 5th, troops surrounded the village of Koti Khel, whose inhabitants had apparently been firing on the British force; three villagers were killed and five captured, of whom three were immediately shot on Roberts's orders for being in rebellion against their lawful ruler (the Amir).

The advance was resumed at 10.00 hours on the 5th, Roberts moving forward with the major part of the force and all the transport, leaving Macpherson with a rearguard at Safed Sang to protect the reserve ammunition and stores until the transport could be sent back to pick it up. The road to Kabul ran across open, cultivated country some distance to the west of the River Logar. Groups of armed tribesmen sat watching the advance but made no attempt to interfere. Early in the afternoon the advance guard reached a group of villages known as Charasiab, only some six miles from Safed Sang.† In front of it loomed the last major obstacle before Kabul; a crescent-shaped range of hills running roughly east and west, between 700 and 1,500 feet above the plain on which Roberts's force stood. At the eastern end of the hills, the River Logar and the direct road to Kabul forced their way northwards through the Sang-i-Nawishta defile.‡ The actual entrance to the defile was dominated by an isolated hill separating the road at that point from the River Logar. In turn, this hill was dominated by a small, conical hill due south of it. At the western end of the hills an alternative road to Kabul via the Chardeh Plain forced its way through the range, having diverged from the main road near the village of Khairabad some 2,000 yards north-east of Charasiab.

MacGregor immediately pointed out the desirability of occupying the conical hill commanding the Sang-i-Nawishta, but Roberts was handicapped by not

---

*Equivalent to some 2,125 camels; a more normal allocation would have been one camel per man.
†Official documents and the medal clasp spell it 'Charasia' but Hanna (op. cit., vol. III, p. 65) demonstrates convincingly that the name means 'four watermills' (= Char-asiab).
‡Sang-i-Nawishta means 'written stone', referring to a stone recording the construction of the road through the defile in the time of the Mogul Emperor, Shah Jehan.

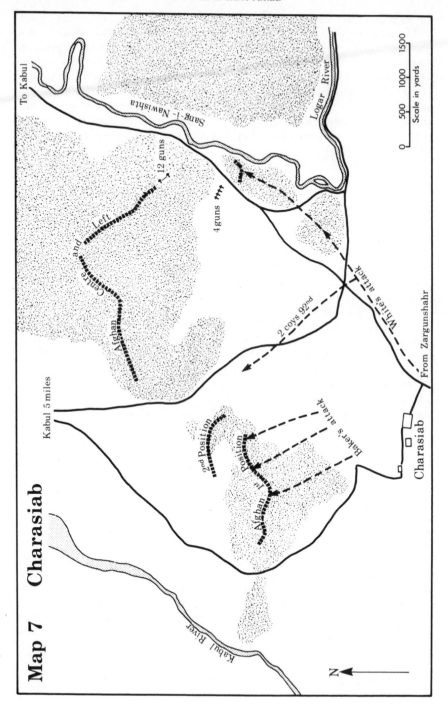

Map 7 Charasiab

having all his force with him. Having reconnoitred along the two roads to Kabul and found no significant opposition, he decided to camp near Charasiab and send back the transport to bring up the rearguard and stores. It was his intention to seize the Sang-i-Nawishta at first light, preparatory to a final advance with his whole force on Kabul, although he had received clear warning from an escaped servant of Cavagnari's that Afghan forces in Kabul were preparing to dispute his advance. As dusk began to close in, parties of Afghans were seen on the hills ahead, a usual sign of trouble, and he had in fact made an uncharacteristic tactical error in not seizing the pass immediately. He was reaping the results of the acute shortage of transport.

At dawn on the 6th, cavalry patrols were pushed forward to reconnoitre and a strong work-party consisting of the 23rd BNI and a wing of the 92nd Highlanders, supported by a small force of cavalry and two guns of No. 2 Mountain Battery, was dispatched under Lieutenant-Colonel Currie of the 23rd BNI to make the Sang-i-Nawishta passable for guns and wheeled transport. But as the sun rose and the shadows retreated, large masses of men could be seen occupying the crest of the range of hills ahead; the deliberation with which they were being deployed and the presence of guns made it clear that Afghan regular troops were present in force.*

Roberts was in an awkward position. He had with him some nine squadrons of cavalry, five and one-half battalions of infantry and sixteen guns, plus two Gatlings – in all about 3,800 men, including sick. He was greatly outnumbered and it would be some hours before he could be joined by Macpherson with the remainder of the force and the reserve ammunition and supplies. Apart from the enemy directly in front of him, he was surrounded by potentially hostile tribesmen who, according to reports he received, had already blocked the road between him and Macpherson. There were, on the face of it, four courses open to him: to attack, to stay where he was, to retreat on Macpherson or to attempt to lure the enemy down into the plain and defeat him there where superior discipline and manoeuvrability could be used to the full. To attack meant launching a small force uphill against a very strong position defended by superior numbers; if the attack were repulsed, the local population would rise and submerge the British troops. To retreat would expose them to immediate attack as they endeavoured to force their way back through a hostile countryside; a feint retreat offered much the same risks. For the force to stay where it was opened up the grim prospect of eventual annihilation as its ammunition ran out. The choice had to be made quickly. Delay and indecision would only multiply the opposition as the population of Kabul and the surrounding villages scented the opportunity and swarmed out to the attack.

Given Roberts's temperament and experience, the choice was not in much doubt. Sending an urgent message to Macpherson to join him before dark, he now considered his plan of attack. The Afghan forces were occupying the whole crescent of hills extending over a distance of some three and a half miles, but with the main centre of concentration, including all the guns, towards the eastern end and overlooking the Sang-i-Nawishta. At the opposite (western) end of the hills, the Afghans held a forward line immediately north of Charasiab, at a distance of

---

*Later information indicates that he was faced by thirteen regular regiments with twenty guns, plus several thousand tribesmen.

some 2,000 yards, with a second line some 600 yards behind. This right wing was clearly the weakest part of the Afghan position and Roberts decided to attack it at once and then roll up the whole position from west to east (map 7).

The attack was entrusted to Baker. In addition to Currie's work-party, he had at his disposal the 72nd Highlanders, six companies of 5th Gurkhas, two companies of 5th Punjab Infantry, a company of Bengal Sappers and Miners, two more guns of No. 2 Mountain Battery, three guns of G/3, and the two Gatlings – in all about 2,500 men. For the defence of the camp and as a reserve, Roberts retained under his personal control F/A, RHA, the remaining three guns of G/3, some 450 cavalry, a wing of the 67th Foot, a wing of the 92nd and a wing of the 5th Punjab Infantry – in all about 1,300 men.

Baker split his meagre force into two. The right-hand column under Major George White of the 92nd consisted of four companies of the 92nd, half of the 23rd BNI, three guns of G/3 and some cavalry. Its task was to threaten the Afghan forces in and around the Sang-i-Nawishta, in order to prevent them advancing on Charasiab; when the moment was ripe, White was to advance and seize the gorge. The remaining troops – the 72nd, six companies of 5th Gurkhas, half of the 23rd BNI, two companies of 5th PI, a company of Bengal Sappers and Miners, No. 2 Mountain Battery, and the two Gatlings, formed the left column which was to attack the Afghan right wing and roll it up.

The action started at about 11.30 with the 72nd Highlanders attacking the centre and right of the Afghan right wing. Little progress was made until the 72nd was reinforced by four companies of the 5th Gurkhas and the two companies of the 5th Punjab Infantry. Despite fierce resistance, this added impetus enabled the attackers to seize the advanced position at about 14.00 hours, just in time to forestall Afghan reinforcements sent down from the main position. Supported by the mountain guns and the two Gatlings (one of which jammed almost immediately) and reinforced by a company of the 23rd Pioneers, the attackers now advanced in a series of short rushes against the second Afghan position 600 yards in rear. The unexpected appearance of two companies of the 92nd from White's force on to the left flank of this position was the decisive factor and the Afghan defenders fled, some northwards across the hills towards Kabul pursued by a wing of the 72nd, the others retreating eastwards to join the defenders of the Afghan main position. They were rapidly followed up and by 15.45 hours Baker was in possession of the right and centre of the entire Afghan position and in a position to attack in flank the remaining Afghan forces still in position above the Sang-i-Nawishta.

While Baker had been attacking the right of the Afghan position, White had pushed forward his cavalry, supported by two companies of the 92nd, to force back the Afghan advanced pickets who were guarding the entrance to the Sang-i-Nawishta and preventing White's guns from getting within range of the main Afghan position on the ridge above. At the same time, he had to deal with the Afghan forces holding the conical hill south of the gorge. Shelling by the three guns of G/3 produced no effect and it became clear that there was no alternative to an infantry assault. White himself led the attack of the two companies of the 92nd: 'The dark-green kilts went up the steep, rocky hill-side at a fine rate, though one would occasionally drop and roll several feet down the slope . . . both sides took advantage of every available atom of cover, but still the kilts pressed on and up, and it was altogether as pretty a piece of Light Infantry drill as could well be seen,' wrote an onlooker.

Unable to resist the impetus of this attack the defenders fled and White found himself master of the hill. His position was not a comfortable one. His tiny force still faced overwhelming numbers of Afghans on the hill to the north who threatened at any moment to advance and overwhelm him. Observers ascribed White's salvation to the fact that he faced Afghan regular troops rather than tribesmen. The Afghans allowed the critical moment for an attack to slip past, and as Baker's attack on the right wing concentrated attention there, White was able to move forward boldly. With great coolness, he detached two companies of the 92nd north-westwards to assist Baker where, as we have seen, their intervention was decisive. His cavalry supported by detachments of the 92nd and 23rd Pioneers, seized the mouth of the Sang-i-Nawishta, capturing six guns on the way. The remaining Afghan forces above the gorge were now under pressure from Baker's troops advancing eastward along the main ridge, and from White's force pushing into the defile. Under this combined pressure, the Afghan forces disintegrated and fled, leaving another twelve guns behind. By 17.00 hours, the whole Afghan position, including the Sang-i-Nawishta, was in British hands. The 5th Punjab Infantry and the 23rd Pioneers camped that night in the plain beyond the defile, facing Kabul. Macpherson arrived at Charasiab the same evening.

Roberts calculated that thirteen regular regiments had been present, together with large numbers of tribesmen, under the overall command of Yakub Khan's uncle, Nek Mahomed Khan, Governor of Kabul. Casualties on the British side were eighteen killed and seventy wounded; on the Afghan side, probably not less than 500 killed and wounded.* It was the most critical action that Roberts had yet fought; failure would probably have meant the total destruction of his force, isolated and divided as it was. While everyone on the British side, from Baker downwards, displayed courage and determination, it was on Roberts that the burden of critical decision fell and he amply deserved the reward of victory.

He now faced potentially the most tricky part of the advance – the occupation of Kabul. The temper of the surrounding population was hostile, there were still large numbers of Afghan troops in and around the city and his force was too small to cope with street fighting in the narrow streets and bazaars. But it was obviously important to try to capitalize on the Afghan defeat by seizing the city quickly. On the morning after the battle, Roberts moved through the Sang-i-Nawishta with the Cavalry Brigade and supporting arms, encountering only minor opposition, and occupied the village of Beni Hissar, three miles beyond the pass and two miles south of the Bala Hissar, intending to concentrate his whole force there before moving to seize Kabul. At Charasiab Macpherson, waiting with the rearguard for transport to move forward, was threatened by large bodies of tribesmen who dispersed only after attacks by the 67th Foot and 28th BNI.

---

*Roberts estimated Afghan killed alone at 300; Duke, *Recollections of the Kabul Campaign, 1879–80*, London, 1883, says that only 100 bodies were counted on the battlefield and that the local inhabitants put the total Afghan loss at 500 killed and wounded; this seems a more likely figure. All twenty Afghan guns were captured.

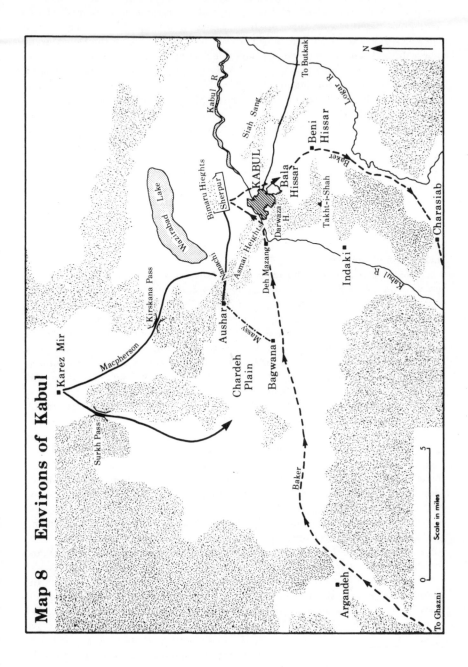

Map 8   Environs of Kabul

Roberts's intention of concentrating his force before seizing the city was almost immediately frustrated. Information reached him that three of the regular Afghan battalions, together with survivors from the battle at Charasiab, had entrenched themselves on the Asmai hills north-west of Kabul overlooking the Deh Mazang gorge through which ran the main road from Kabul to Ghazni. The enemy position also controlled the route northwards to Kohistan and Afghan Turkestan (map 8). Accordingly on the morning of 8 October, the major part of the cavalry brigade, numbering 720 sabres, was dispatched under Massy in a very wide circular sweep to reconnoitre the enemy position and to endeavour to get in behind it to block the lines of retreat towards Bamian and Kohistan. The force moved off at 11.00 hours in such haste that it took with it no rations for the men and only a small amount of grain for the horses. Massy moved in a north-easterly direction, crossed the Siah Sang hills east of the city and then swung westwards towards the cantonment at Sherpur, north of the city, which had recently been evacuated. From Sherpur, Massy could see the entrenched Afghan position on the Asmai hills. There was nothing to be done against it with cavalry so Massy continued westwards round the extreme northern end of the hills and took up a position in the Chardeh plain astride the Ghazni road, due west of the gorge, having warned Roberts by heliograph of the situation.

At Beni Hissar, Roberts, having received Massy's first reports about the enemy position on the Asmai heights, determined to attack immediately. Baker, with the 23rd Pioneers, half of the 92nd and two companies of the 72nd, together with the Gatlings and two mountain guns, was ordered to move westward up on to the Sher Darwaza range of hills which ran northwards towards Deh Mazang, and then move along it to storm the Afghan position. At this stage, both Roberts and Baker were clearly uncertain as to the exact location of the enemy camp, apparently assuming that it lay at the northern end of the Sher Darwaza on the *south* side of the Deh Mazang gorge. Detaching the 92nd to cross the range and along the western face of the hills, Baker himself moved along the crest of the ridge. The going was difficult and it was mid afternoon before Baker finally reached the end of the ridge and was able to see clearly the Afghan position on the *northern* side of the Deh Mazang gorge. The mountain guns opened fire across the gorge, but their shells were too light to make any impact on the twelve Afghan guns opposed to them. By 17.00 hours, the reinforcements which Baker had requested had not reached him and he decided to attack with what he had got. But the troops took time to deploy and with darkness rapidly approaching the attack had to be postponed until next morning. Baker was concerned that the enemy might decamp during the night, and at his request Hugh Gough, with a handful of cavalry and two guns of F/A, was sent off from Beni Hissar to try to block the Kohistan road north of the Asmai heights.

During the night of the 8th/9th, Roberts's force was scattered over the countryside. Baker, with the equivalent of a brigade of infantry, was on the hills west of the city. Two miles west of him, Massy and the cavalry had withdrawn for the night into the shelter of two walled enclosures, where they huddled cold, miserable and hungry. Two or three miles to the north-east of him was Gough with his tiny force, while Roberts and Macpherson remained at Beni Hissar, with the equivalent of an infantry brigade and all the baggage and transport.

Still suspecting that the Afghans might retreat during the night, Baker sent out a strong patrol in the early hours of the morning of the 9th which soon established that the enemy had indeed gone. As soon as Massy learned this from a messenger sent by Baker, his squadrons were sent galloping west down the Ghazni road and northwards in the direction of the Kohistan road. Some 22 miles west of Kabul, the 5th Punjab Cavalry came across and dispersed a small party of the enemy but no other trace could be found. Leaving two squadrons to probe further westwards, Massy retraced his steps and, passing unmolested through the outskirts of Kabul, reached the Siah Sang hills whither Roberts had shifted the British camp during the day.* Like Massy, Gough had found nothing either.

At trifling cost, Roberts was now effectively master of Kabul. The following day, he examined the Sherpur cantonment as possible winter quarters and left the 5th Punjab Cavalry to guard the huge quantity of stores and equipment, including 76 guns, which had been abandoned there. On 11 October, he went with a small escort to inspect the Bala Hissar and the scene of Cavagnari's death. Howard Hensman recorded the scene:

> 'Our first view of the Residency was of the rear wall, still intact, but blackened on the top, where the smoke from the burning ruins had swept across. At each angle where the side walls joined were seen the loopholes from which the fire of the little force on the roof had been directed against the overwhelming numbers attacking them. Every square foot round these loopholes was pitted with bulletmarks, the balls having cut deeply into the hard mud plaster . . . The courtyard of the Residency is about 90 ft square and at its northern end, where formerly stood a three-storeyed building like that I have just described, are nothing but the bare walls, blackened and scarred by fire, and a huge heap of rubbish, the ruins of the roof and walls which fell in as the woodwork was destroyed. Portions of the partition walls still remain, jutting sullenly out from the mass of debris; and these only serve to make the place more desolate. The whitewashed walls on the left are here and there bespattered with blood, and on the raised basement on which the building stood are the remains of a large fire, the half-charred beams still resting among the ashes . . . The ashes were in the middle of the chamber, and near them were two skulls and a heap of human bones, still fetid. It would seem as if a desperate struggle had taken place in the room, the blood stains on the floor and walls being clearly discernible . . . Careful excavation for bodies will also be made among the ruins. It is absurd to talk of the Residency being a safe place for a garrison. It is commanded completely from the walls of the arsenal in the upper Balar Hissar, and also from the roofs of some high houses in the south-west. In addition, houses closely adjoin it on the eastern side; and an attacking party sapping the walls would have have perfect cover in this direction the whole time.'[15]

On 12 October, Roberts, in a full-dress parade, formally occupied the Bala Hissar and on the following day, in a deliberate show of strength, the whole Field Force marched through Kabul. With that, the first phase of the renewed war came

---

*Both Roberts and the CinC were highly critical of Massy's failure to intercept the fleeing Afghans. Roberts had already formed a low opinion of Massy's energy and capacity, as had MacGregor. Hensman thought that Massy could have done very little in view of the difficult cut-up nature of the ground, and Combe, who was with Massy, thought exactly the same. 'We threw out picquets covering as many roads as we could, but the whole country on our side was dense wood and walled villages, so that you could see no distance either way, and I saw at once it was hopeless to think of cutting them off if they bolted . . . It was a pitch dark night, the country full of woods, walled villages, water ruts and ravines; altogether impracticable for cavalry . . .' [Combe, op. cit., p. 80].

to an end, and it is time to look quickly at what had been happening in the Khyber, in the Kurram and at Kandahar.

The news of Cavagnari's death found the British forces on the Khyber line concentrated at Landi Kotal, Ali Masjid and Jamrud. At Landi Kotal, four battalions of infantry, two squadrons of cavalry and two batteries of artillery kept watch on the new boundary with Afghanistan. Farther back, two battalions held Ali Masjid, and at Jamrud there was a squadron of cavalry and two companies of infantry. In the Khyber itself, a force of native levies under a British officer kept the road open. It was immediately obvious that Roberts's advance from the Kurram would have to be supported by an advance on the Khyber line since this was the only practicable line of communication to Kabul once the winter snows closed the Shutagardan. Large additional forces would be required and the initial plan hastily adopted provided for a step-by-step advance, as troops arrived, as far as Jagdalak. Major-General Robert Bright was appointed to command all forces west of the Indus as far as Jagdalak where he was expected to link up with Roberts's troops. Bright's force was styled the 2nd (Khyber) Division of the Kabul Field Force and initially was divided into four brigades:

Peshawar base (Major-General J. C. G. Ross);
3rd Brigade (Jamrud to Basawal) – Brigadier-General J. Doran;
2nd Brigade (Basawal to Jalalabad) – Brigadier-General C. G. Arbuthnot;
1st Brigade (Safed Sang to Jagdalak, with movable column at Gandamak) – Brigadier-General Charles Gough, VC.

The intention was to occupy Dakka immediately, but this hope was frustrated by reports of Afghan regular troops moving towards Dakka from Kabul and of efforts being made to rouse the surrounding tribes. Given the usual impossible situation over assembling transport (most of what had been available having been sent off to the Kurram for Roberts's use), there was no alternative but to postpone the advance until 29 September, when Dakka was occupied by the Guides. By 12 October, Gough had occupied Jalalabad although still in terrible difficulties over transport. Behind him, the 2nd Brigade was moving very slowly into position and Bright, with his HQ, had reached Landi Kotal. Apart from transport, sickness among the troops was severely hampering movement, at least two native regiments being virtually useless for operations.*

On reaching Jalalabad, Gough was ordered to send forward a flying column to Gandamak, 28 miles ahead, to overawe the Ghilzais and intercept fugitives from the action at Charasiab three days earlier. At Gandamak, Gough would be only some twenty miles from Roberts and there was much to be said for keeping the Afghans off-balance by a rapid advance from the direction of the Khyber. But at Jalalabad, Gough had with him only the equivalent of a regiment of cavalry and roughly two and one-half battalions of infantry, and he was reluctant to run the risks which were entailed in extending it as far as Gandamak. He also had only between six and ten days' supplies available. As a compromise, part of his force was moved forward to Fatehbad, roughly half-way between Jalalabad and

---

*On 8 October, the 39th BNI had 470 men in hospital out of a total strength of 550.

Gandamak, and reconnaissances pushed as far as Safed Sang, the former British camp two miles from Gandamak.

In the Kurram valley, Roberts had left behind a sizeable force, but it had to protect a line of communication stretching some 100 miles from the Shutagardan Pass back to Thal. It was perforce distributed in penny packets and almost invited attack from Ghilzais, Mangals and Zaimukhts whose hostility and predatory activities had not altered. Even before Roberts started his advance, the murder of a British officer en route for Kurram Fort had led the Government to sanction in principle a punitive expedition against the Zaimukhts. On the same day that Roberts left Kushi, Mangals and Ghilzais mounted a major attack on the garrison at the Shutagardan under Colonel Money which was repulsed. Twelve days later, on 14 October, simultaneous attacks were made on the posts at Ali Khel, Surkh Kot and the Shutagardan. The attacks were again beaten off but only after some desperate fighting, particularly round the Shutagardan. By the 18th, Money's force, consisting of two battalions of native infantry and four mountain guns, was completely surrounded and its water supply cut off. The Ghilzais now called upon him to surrender, offering him safe passage to Kabul or the Kurram on payment of two lakhs of rupees. Money refused bluntly, but his situation was serious. The rest of Gordon's forces were too fully occupied to relieve the Shutagardan garrison – as it was, the Zaimukht expedition had had to be postponed and the troops under Tytler used to relieve Ali Khel. It was necessary to look to Roberts, assuming that messages sent to him could get through. In fact, the Intelligence reaching Roberts had already led him to dispatch a small force under Hugh Gough to relieve Money. On 19 October, Gough arrived at the Shinkai Kotal, half-way between Kushi and the Shutagardan, whence he was able to open direct heliographic communication with Money. With Gough's support at hand, Money was able to take the offensive and disperse his besiegers. Gough paused long enough at the Shutagardan to bring up a supply convoy from Ali Khel and a draft of some 500 replacements for the regiments at Kabul. The Shutagardan was then abandoned, the 21st Punjab Infantry retiring to Ali Khel, and the 3rd Sikh Infantry, with the four guns of No. 1 Mountain Battery, accompanying Gough back to Kabul. Roberts's line of communication with the Kurram was now severed.

At Kandahar, Stewart had re-occupied the city within 24 hours of receiving the news of Cavagnari's death, and those regiments still north of the Khojak Pass were hastily recalled. By the middle of September, Stewart had the bulk of his original force concentrated at Kandahar and he was making feverish efforts to assemble supplies and transport to enable him to take the field. It was impossible for him to intervene quickly and decisively at Kabul, but an offensive movement towards Kalat-i-Ghilzai might serve to confuse and threaten the Kabul Government and thus help Roberts forward. Accordingly, on 23 September, Hughes' 2nd Infantry Brigade,* with two heavy guns to lend colour to the threat to Kabul, left Kandahar with instructions to proceed up to two or three days' march beyond Kalat-i-Ghilzai. Hughes reached Kalat without difficulty and moved on with the bulk of his force to Ab-i-Tazi, thirty miles ahead and about 120 miles from Kandahar,

---

*2nd Punjab Cavalry, 59th Foot, 3rd Gurkhas (wing), 29th BoNI, G/4, RA (two guns), 11/11 RA (three guns), 6/11 RA (2–40pdr) – total 1,416 men.

THE WEB IS SHATTERED

which he reached on 10 October. The lack of opposition encouraged some discussion between Stewart and Simla as to the advisability of a further advance to Ghazni, only ninety miles from Kabul, but the omnipresent problems of supplies and transport finally ruled this out.

Hughes remained at Ab-i-Tazi for a few days, reconnoitring; he was on the point of retiring when news reached him of a force of Ghilzais assembling to attack his force. He decided to take the initiative and in the early hours of 23 October, a small advance guard under Colonel Kennedy of the 2nd Punjab Cavalry moved out towards Shahjui, twelve miles ahead, where the Ghilzais were reported to be assembling; Hughes, with the remainder of the brigade, followed some hours later. Two miles from Shahjui, Kennedy saw the camp-fires of the Afghan pickets. He had with him two squadrons of his own regiment, two mountain guns of 11/11, RA and roughly a company each of the 59th Foot and the 29th Bombay NI – about 350 men in all. Since the ground on each side of the road was too rough for manoeuvre in the darkness, Kennedy sent forward a squadron of cavalry under Captain J. H. Broome with some infantry to drive in the pickets and press on down the road towards Shahjui. By daylight, Broome had dispersed the pickets and seized a hillock about a mile from the village. Thoroughly aroused, the Ghilzai force of some 200 cavalry and 700 foot advanced to attack his tiny force, but was halted at a distance of half a mile by the appearance of Kennedy with the rest of the force. Under fire from his guns, the Ghilzais retreated. Pursued by Kennedy's troops, they finally turned to stand on a lofty hill some six miles behind Shahjui which had been the site of an old fort. In the action which followed, the hill was gallantly attacked and seized by the company of the 59th under Captain Sartorius, and the enemy cavalry were dispersed after fierce hand-to-hand fighting with the two squadrons of the 2nd Punjab Cavalry.* The Ghilzais fled in all directions, leaving 56 bodies behind, including their leader, Sahib Jan; Kennedy's casualties were two killed and 31 wounded, mainly from the cavalry. Kennedy rejoined Hughes at Shahjui the same day and three days later, having left a garrison to hold Kalat-i-Ghilzai, the remainder of the brigade started its march back to Kandahar.

Thus by the third week in October 1879, Roberts had reached Kabul, but had lost his line of supply via the Kurram valley; he now had to depend for survival upon opening up an alternative reinforcement route via the Khyber. There the advance guard of Bright's line of communications force (now called the 2nd (Khyber) Division, North Afghanistan Field Force) was approaching Gandamak, 63 miles from Kabul. Two hundred and thirty miles to the south-west, Stewart had occupied Kalat-i-Ghilzai and was now the same distance from Kabul.

Nothing could illustrate more vividly Roberts's extraordinarily exposed position. Great risks had been run in reaching Kabul, tactical as well as logistic, and, in the hands of a less determined or less able commander, these could have led to total disaster;[16] they could still do so. One is therefore bound to ask whether it was really necessary to run such risks. No advance, however speedy, could do anything for Cavagnari and his murdered colleagues. If the object has been to demonstrate the implacable might of the British Government, there was a military

---

*Sartorius, who was wounded, received the VC, the first awarded in Stewart's force and the sixth awarded in the campaign as a whole. Stewart thought that the affair had been reasonably well-managed, but that if Kennedy had held his fire a little longer the effect would have been greater – Elsmie, op. cit., p. 295.

case for deferring action until the spring of 1880 when a large force could have advanced with much greater security, and more thought could have been given to the political problem. On the other hand, the moral effect of striking swiftly was great and any delay would have given time to the Afghans to prepare a fiercer resistance when the advance finally started. It was consciousness of these two factors which fuelled Roberts's impatience to get on despite the logistical untidiness and the risks which disturbed more cautious officers such as MacGregor and Hanna. In the final analysis, political pressures permitted of no delay.

NOTES

1. Combe, op. cit., entry for 12 July 1879.
2. Between 24 June and 25 August 1879, Stewart's force had 446 cases of which 272 were fatal. The 3rd Gurkhas lost 16 men in one day. Le Mesurier, op. cit., p. 255.
3. Official History, vol. II, p. 281.
4. Telegram from Agent, 17 May 1879: C2457 – Afghanistan (1880) No. 1, p. 14.
5. Cavagnari to Foreign Department, 6 August 1879. Ibid., p. 18.
6. Ibid., p. 81.
7. One observer reported that only the artillery, the élite of the Afghan Army, was prepared to assist the Amir. But artillery was useless in the circumstances. Abdurrahman suggested that the attack was instigated by Sher Ali's wife, the mother of Abdullah Jan, in order to topple Yakub – Life of Abdurrahman Khan, by Sultan M. Khan, 2 vols., London, 1900. Vol. I, p. 152. Stewart noted that the Wali Sher Ali had received letters which suggested that the Mustaufi was the real instigator.
8. LP 521/1A, p. 85.
9. Stewart to Lady Stewart, 15 September 1879. Elsmie, op. cit., p. 286.
10. Text in Afghanistan (1880), No. 1, p. 63.
11. See Mortimer Durand's notes of the meeting, ibid., pp. 108–110.
12. 'Ghilzais report that Amir has called upon (them) to stop all roads leading from this to Kabul. I am trying to get one of the Amir's letters to this effect.' – telegram Roberts to Foreign Secretary, 17 September 1879. Afghanistan (1880), No. 1, p. 55.
13. Proclamation dated 2 October 1879. Roberts to Foreign Secretary, 13 October 1879 – Afghanistan (1880) No. 1, p. 135.
14. Major R. C. W. Mitford. To Caubul with the Cavalry Brigade, London, 1881, p. 26.
15. Howard Hensman. The Afghan War of 1879–80, London, 1881, pp. 53–55.
16. Cf. MacGregor's comment in his diary for 8 October: 'We have nearly eaten all our provisions and if we were to get worsted, not only would the whole country be up, but we should get no supplies. I hope Bobs' luck will carry him through; but we are playing a risky game' War in Afghanistan 1879–80; the personal diary of Major-General Sir Charles Metcalfe MacGregor. Detroit, 1985. (cited hereafter as Diary).

CHAPTER 8

A RACE OF TIGERS

'We have got into a conflict with a race of tigers and it is only by treating them with a rod of iron they will ever give in.'

MacGregor to Lyall, September 1879.

The period between October 1879 and April 1880 is dominated by two themes – the security of Roberts's force at Kabul and the future political organization of Afghanistan. The arrival in Kabul of Sir Donald Stewart on 2 May 1880, two days after Abdurrahman had been offered the Amirship of Kabul and four days after the fall of Disraeli's Government, effectively marks the end of this period and the beginning of the end of the war.

From a military point of view, the interest of this period lies in Roberts's attempts to dominate the area around Kabul and to open a secure line of communication to India via the Khyber in an effort to create the conditions necessary for a satisfactory solution of the political problem and the evacuation of the country in conformity with the Treaty of Gandamak.

Following the ceremonial entry into Kabul on 13 October, Roberts had three immediate tasks: the security of his force at Kabul, the establishment of a firm line of communications via the Khyber, and the punishment of those responsible for the death of Cavagnari and his mission. The security of his force demanded its concentration in a cantonment which was readily defensible, but from which effective control could be exercised over Kabul and from which a link-up could be effected with Bright's troops. Roberts rejected the Bala Hissar for this purpose on the grounds that it was too constricted and too close to the city, thus reducing its security against sudden attack. Situated as it was on the southern side of the city and hemmed in on the west by the Sher Darwaza heights and on the east by the Siah Sang hills, it did not provide adequate room for manoeuvre either westwards into the Chardeh plain or northwards towards Kohistan.

Although he occupied the Bala Hissar with the 5th Gurkhas and 67th Foot, Roberts decided to concentrate the bulk of his force in the uncom-pleted Sherpur cantonment a mile north of the city. This had been planned by Sher Ali as the main winter quarters of the Afghan army. It was on a huge scale, bounded on two sides by a massive, loopholed wall with towers for artillery at regular intervals; the rear was open but rested on the Bimaru heights, and the east face was incomplete. The main frontal wall facing the city was over a mile and a half long and the whole cantonment was easily capable of taking a very much larger force than Roberts's. European troops could all be accommodated in existing brick buildings, but hutments would have to be built for the native troops. Sher Ali had originally intended to extend the cantonment to include the Bimaru Heights which for the moment provided an open back door. Once this defect was rectified, Sherpur provided Roberts with a secure fortified position, close to the city but giving him ample room for manoeuvre eastwards towards the approaches from Peshawar, northwards towards Kohistan and westwards into the Chardeh plain through the Deh Mazang defile or round the northern end of the Asmai heights.

The wisdom of the decision to use Sherpur instead of the Bala Hissar was underlined by the accidental explosion of massive quantities of ammunition in the Bala Hissar three days after it had been occupied, while the huge amounts of equipment, ammunition and stores left there by Sher Ali were still being checked; seventeen soldiers were killed and a large part of the Bala Hissar destroyed.* Throughout the second half of October work went on at Sherpur constructing hutments for the native troops, building defences along the line of the Bimaru Heights, and collecting supplies and fuel. By 1 November, work had progressed to the point where the existing camp on the Siah Sang hills could be broken up and the troops moved into Sherpur.

In parallel, communications were established with Bright's troops. Roberts had selected Butkak, eight and a half miles east of Kabul on the Gandamak road, as the site of a strong connecting post. This was occupied on 2 November and connected to Kabul by telegraph line the same day. Macpherson with his brigade then moved steadily along the route towards Gandamak, finally linking hands with Gough's advance guard at Kata Sang, nine miles west of Jagdalak, on 6 November. Both Roberts's and Macpherson's examinations had demonstrated the superiority of the Lataband Pass route over that via the Khurd Kabul, and work started on improving the road and extending the telegraph line from Butkak. By 19 November, the line ran uninterrupted from Kabul to Peshawar. Despite an attack on a foraging party on 10 November, which for a time put a company of the 67th in serious danger, the road from Kabul to the Khyber was considered sufficiently secure for Roberts to send back to India all his time-expired, wounded and unfit men, together with his elephants, spare bullocks, and sick transport animals, thus reducing demands on his supplies at Kabul. The total strength of the force in and around Kabul was now just 8,000. Supplies were beginning to come in and although communications with the Kurram had ceased at the end of October, there were good telegraphic and postal communications through the Khyber, letters from Simla reaching Kabul in seven days.†

It had been made clear from the start that a primary objective in seizing Kabul was to mete out retribution on those responsible for the death of Cavagnari and his companions. Lytton and his colleagues, including Roberts, were convinced that the attack on the mission had been stimulated and directed by the Afghan authorities – possibly even by Yakub himself. No Victorian statesman or soldier

---

*Roberts interpreted the construction of Sherpur and the amassing of the very large stocks of arms and ammunition discovered in the Bala Hissar as clear evidence of Sher Ali's intention to fight the British. It is more likely that, given his endemic fear of rebellion, Sher Ali wanted to keep these vital military resources under his immediate control.
†Roberts investigated the use of carrier-pigeons as a back-up in case the other methods of communication were interrupted, but the idea was abandoned as impracticable.

could have doubted that so gross an outrage to a representative of Her Majesty's Government must be punished. Diplomatic tradition, Great Power status and personal sentiment alike cried out for vengeance. Lytton had not minced his words in private to Roberts.

> 'You cannot stop to pick and choose ringleaders. Every soldier of the Herati regiments is ipso facto guilty and so is every civilian, be he priest, or layman, mullah or peasant, who joined the mob of assassins. To satisfy the conventions of English sentiment it will probably be necessary to inflict death only in execution of the verdict of some sort of judicial authority. But any such authority should be of the roughest and readiest kind such as a drumhead Court Martial. It is not justice in the ordinary sense, but retribution that you have to administer on reaching Kabul . . . Your object should be to strike terror, and strike it swiftly and deeply; but to avoid a "Reign of Terror" . . . *There are some things which a Viceroy can approve and defend when they have been done, but which a Governor General in Council cannot officially order to be done.*' [Author's italics].[1]

Even before his advance had started, Roberts had issued a proclamation to the Afghan peoples stating that the object of his expedition was to take public revenge on the murderers of the mission, but making it clear that those who had had nothing to do with Cavagnari's death and who abstained from opposing the British advance had nothing to fear.[2] At Zargunshahr, he had issued another proclamation to the same effect.

> 'Be it known to all that the British army is advancing on Kabul to take possession of the city . . . Therefore all well-disposed persons who have taken no part in the dastardly murder of the British Embassy, or in the plunder of the Residency, are warned that if they are unable to prevent resistance being offered to the entrance of the British Army and to the authority of his Highness the Amir, they should make immediate arrangements for their own safety . . . The British Government desires to treat all classes with justice, and to respect their religion, feelings and customs, while exacting full retribution from offenders. Every effort will therefore be made to prevent the innocent suffering with the guilty. But it is necessary that the utmost precaution should be taken against useless opposition. Therefore, after the receipt of this proclamation, all persons found armed in or about Kabul will be treated as the enemies of the British Government.[3]

Two days after reaching Kabul, Roberts issued yet another, harsher, proclamation.

> 'The force under my command has now reached Kabul and occupied the Bala Hissar; but its advance has been pertinaciously opposed, and the inhabitants of the city have taken a conspicuous part in the opposition offered. They have, therefore, become rebels against the Amir, and have added to the guilt already incurred by them in abetting the murder of the British Envoy and his companions.'[4]

The proclamation went on to institute martial law for a distance of up to ten miles around Kabul, and to institute the death penalty for anyone found carrying weapons within the city or a five-mile radius round it; rewards were offered for the apprehension of anyone concerned in the attack on the mission or who had fought against the British since 3 September, and for the surrender of any articles belonging to the members of the mission or any firearms or ammunition belonging to the regular Afghan army.

It can reasonably be argued that the British were entitled to punish those who had been responsible for the attack on the mission. Whether that entailed the right to invade Afghanistan and effectively usurp the power of the Afghan Government is arguable. To claim the right to execute men who opposed that invasion, on the grounds that they (the British) were acting as the Amir's agents and that resistance to the British was rebellion against the Amir, was dubious and dishonest.* Within days of the formal entry into Kabul, two commissions had been set up. The first, consisting of MacGregor, Surgeon-Major Bellew, and a native member of the Indian Political Service, Mohammed Hyat Khan, was given the job of investigating and collecting evidence against those Afghans suspected of offences under the Proclamation of 12 October. The second commission – in effect, a military court – consisting of Hills (replaced subsequently by Massy), Major Moriarty of the Bombay Army and Captain Guinness of the 72nd High-landers, judged and sentenced those whom MacGregor's Commission sent before it. Significantly, the only member of the Judge Advocate's Department in Kabul was not made a member.

The work of the two commissions suffered from two defects. The first was the lack of reliable testimony. The second was the spirit of vengeance which coloured their judgements. It was impossible that anyone who had seen the gutted wreckage of the Residency, with its nauseating relics, or who had heard the story of the gallant defence made by the members of the mission, could fail to be deeply affected, and in any case Roberts had his instructions.

The problem of obtaining reliable evidence was a serious one. Quite apart from the language problem there was the difficulty of persuading witnesses to give evidence against their fellow-countrymen and, conversely, the difficulty of being sure that the evidence which was given was not actuated by malice or ambition. To obtain evidence at all was not easy, and to start with the commissions had to content themselves with seizing and trying a relatively small number of important officials and personalities in Kabul. Among those immediately detained was the Finance Minister or Mustaufi (Habibullah Khan), the Chief Minister or Wazir (Shah Mohammed Khan), the Governor of Kabul (Yahiha Khan) and his brother, Zakariah Khan, all of whom were suspected, on very little evidence, of being involved in the attack on the mission and in organizing the Afghan resistance at Charasiab. The discovery of the nominal rolls of some of the Afghan regiments which had been in Kabul at the time of Cavagnari's death enabled the commis-sions to extend their work. The surrounding villages were cordoned off by troops and every man whose name appeared on the rolls was detained for trial. To overcome the reluctance of witnesses to testify, Mohammed Hyat Khan was deputed to examine witnesses in secret and to produce their depositions rather than the witnesses themselves, at the subsequent trials. Thus the accused had no means of knowing how the evidence had been extracted or of cross-examining witnesses in order to test their truthfulness and accuracy. These procedures, contrary to all the traditional principles of British justice, although depressingly familiar to students of twentieth-century dictatorships, could hardly have been swallowed had it not been for the harsh spirit of retribution which actuated Roberts himself and a large proportion – perhaps the bulk – of his officers.

*MacGregor, for one, was resolved not to sentence such men to death – *Diary*, p. 108. But despite Roberts's later denials, it is clear that men *were* hanged and shot for opposing the British advance – see, for example, Hensman, op. cit., p. 137.

For the rank and file life tended to be brutal and harsh anyway, and it is unlikely that many of them were worried about the quality of the justice being meted out to Afghan prisoners. In consequence, the work of the two commissions was swift and uncompromising, despite MacGregor's own private reservations.[5] Where possible, MacGregor refused to send forward men whose only crime was to resist the British unless there were a clear statement of evidence and the opportunity of bringing forward witnesses in their defence, but he was powerless to influence the fate of those men who reached Massy's court. There justice was certainly swift and stern, as MacGregor's notes indicate: 'I take the following from the notes of the proceedings of the Commission: (1) Prisoner, Sultan Aziz – Mohammed Hyat states "the city people are unwilling to come forward openly; but I have ascertained beyond doubt that this man was the moving spirit on the night of the 5th to get people to go out and fight us. He was also present himself at the fight [Charasiab] with a standard." Accused simply denies his guilt. The Commission sentence him to be hanged.'[6] The most notorious case was that of the Kotwal (or police chief) of Kabul who was accused of superintending the disposal of the bodies of the Escort and of issuing the proclamation calling upon the population to resist Roberts's advance. There was no convincing case against him, as MacGregor noted: 'There is no direct evidence to prove that the Kotwal ordered it to be made, and therefore there is not enough to hang him, though I daresay that Bobs will do so.'[7] The Kotwal was duly hanged on 20 October.

The individual sentences had to be approved by Roberts but, bred in the harsh school of the Mutiny, he was not a man to flinch from such a responsibility. The condemned men were hanged within 24 hours on gallows set up in the Bala Hissar near the Residency. They were marched there under a guard of British soldiers, followed by a fatigue-party with picks and shovels. The occasion seems to have been anything but impressive: 'Daily, a little crowd of soldiers, camp-followers and traders from the city gathered near the 72nd [Highlanders'] quarterguard from which starts the road down the ridge. The soldiers, in shirt sleeves, and with the favourite short pipes in their mouths, betrayed but faint curiosity, looking upon the culprits with hearty contempt.'[8] Ten men were hanged at a time, and all seem to have met their end impassively.

The work of the two commissions was officially wound up on 18 November, after Roberts had issued a further proclamation, providing an amnesty for all except those directly involved in the attack on the Residency, and recognizing, *inter alia*, that those who had fought against his force were not necessarily rebels against Yakub since they might have believed him a prisoner of the British. It is extremely difficult to discover how many men were executed or in what circumstances. The official report sent to Simla stated that 89 men had been tried and 49 executed. The Official History states that 163 men were tried and 87 executed in October 1879.[9] Hensman and Hanna both refer to large numbers of men being rounded up on 8 and 9 November, of whom 49 were apparently executed. This was clearly in addition to the eleven executions which MacGregor recorded up to 21 October. Roberts, in a letter to the Viceroy, said that 100 men had been executed between 12 October and 12 November.[10] In part, the confusion arises from the fact that men were executed independently of the Commissions. For example, three men were executed at Koti Khel on 4 October during Roberts's advance. Hensman records that five men found with weapons on them were summarily shot by the 14th Bengal Lancers, and that five men were executed at Kabul, apparently without trial, for inciting attacks on the Shutagardan garrison.[13] A further area of confusion arises from the fact that executions were resumed in December after the siege of Sherpur.

Yet despite or because of this formidable catalogue of retribution, two unsatisfactory features remained as far as Lytton and Roberts were concerned. No convincing evidence could be found to connect the Amir and his colleagues with the attack on the Residency, or even to prove that the attack was anything but a spontaneous explosion of popular feeling. After intensively examining the Amir himself, the Commander-in-Chief (Daud Shah), the Mustaufi, the Wazir, the Governor of Kabul and his brother over a period of some three weeks, MacGregor concluded that the exercise was pointless.

> 'The upshot will be, there is no proof of the thing [the attack on the Residency] having been planned, although there are some grounds of suspicion that it was. There is no manner of doubt that the Amir was most apathetic, and did nothing; and there are very strong grounds for suspecting that he was not quite free from conniving at the resistance offered to us at Char Asia. On the whole, he must never be again Amir, and had better be deported to India; the same must be done to the Vazir, Mostafi, Yahiya, Zakariah, and all that breed. The people are the very greatest set of brutes I ever heard of, and it is evident that they hate us – every one of them.'[11]

MacGregor's conclusions are interesting on three counts. Since his view as to the nature of the attack on Cavagnari and of Yakub's responsibility was based upon a closer acquaintance with contemporary evidence than anyone else had or could have in the future, it may be taken as the definitive verdict. Second, it is worth noting the logical difficulties of the British position in claiming that they had advanced on Kabul at Yakub's request while at the same time seeking to prove that he had supported the opposition at Charasiab. If the Amir himself was guilty of opposing the British, how could those Afghans who had fought at Charasiab be guilty of rebelling against him? Finally, in his recognition that the Afghans hated the invading British, MacGregor had put his finger on the second of the unsatisfactory features of the policy of retribution. The more executions that took place the greater the hatred engendered among the population and the fiercer the opposition. It is the classical dilemma of all repressive measures. MacGregor saw the problem only too clearly: 'We are thoroughly hated and not enough feared . . . We have been too cruel yet we have not yet made them [the Afghans] quite acknowledge our supremacy; and they have not yet had time to appreciate our justice.'[12]

Before the work on the two commissions was finished, voices had begun to be raised in India about the hangman's work going on at Kabul. As early as 1 November, the *Bombay Review* had commented.

> 'Now a word about the drum-head exemplary proceedings: it is plain that many facts under this head are being kept back, doubtless under orders from Simla . . . Is it according to the usages of war to treat as felons men who resist invasion? . . . It is plain that the authorities at Simla are bound to let the world know what has been done in this apparently random work of vengeance.'

A week later, the *Review* went further: 'Instead of surprises during the week we have had some more depressing details of military executions with indications, here and there, that our campaign of retribution is sowing a harvest of retribution.' Since Hensman was the only journalist present at Kabul, the information on which these comments were based must have been supplied by officers in Roberts's force. In the middle of November, the weight of *The Times of India* was thrown into the controversy. Welcoming the amnesty, *The Times* commented:

> 'The work of vengeance was so complete as to have become somewhat indiscriminate
> . . . it is to be regretted that a good many innocent persons should have been hanged
> while he [Roberts] was making up his mind as to their degree of guilt. The story of the
> punishment of Kabul will probably be never really known, for with the exception of
> one correspondent, who was specifically admitted to write a pleasant and safe account
> of the affair, the Government thoroughly succeeded in excluding all independent
> witnesses.'[13]

Four days later, *The Friend of India*, a Calcutta newspaper, discussing the matter, said: 'We fear that General Roberts has done us a serious national injury, by lowering our reputation for justice in the eyes of Europe.' Even Lytton was beginning to feel uneasy about what was going on at Kabul.[14] Nevertheless, public interest in India and England had not at this stage been fully aroused. That was to come later, and it will be appropriate then to consider Roberts's defence.

Behind the immediate problems of the security of Roberts's force, and retribution for the death of Cavagnari and his mission, lay the fundamental problem of Afghanistan's future – who was to rule it? Roberts had taken the Amir and his chief ministers along with him in his train to Kabul. While it might suit British purposes to claim that, as in 1838, the British troops were engaged as allies in putting the Amir effectively back on his throne, the reality was that Yakub was a British prisoner under suspicion of complicity in Cavagnari's death. Following his entry into the Bala Hissar on 12 October, Roberts had detained the Mustaufi, the Wazir, the Governor of Kabul and his brother-in-law, pending investigation into their connection with the attack on the Residency and the resistance at Charasiab. There is evidence that the Amir was to be among the detainees,[15] but Roberts appears to have been argued out of this by his political advisers. Nevertheless, as we have seen, MacGregor devoted some three weeks' work in the endeavour to establish a case against the Amir, only to have to admit defeat.

Some hint may have reached Yakub of his proposed detention or he may have realized that he was already a prisoner in all but name. Early on the morning of 11 October he insisted on seeing Roberts and announcing his intention of abdicating, saying that he would rather be a grasscutter in the English camp than ruler of Afghanistan. Yakub claimed later that this abdication had been extorted from him by pressure, but there is no direct evidence of this. On the contrary, the British Government needed to sustain Yakub in office for a few weeks at least in order to give some sort of legal facade to the policy of executing Afghans who had offered resistance to the British advance. The probability is that Yakub's decision to abdicate was taken in a moment of despair, aware as he was of Roberts's suspicions, fearful of being tried and executed, and oppressed by the magnitude of the task of attempting to govern a country which was largely in chaos as a result of the war. As his confidence returned, so it was necessary to explain away his abdication by claiming that it was done under duress.

Roberts refused to accept the abdication pending instructions from Simla. In the meantime Yakub was kept under guard. From the start, Lytton, like Roberts, had been convinced of Yakub's guilt. Before the result of MacGregor's investigations could reach him, Lytton authorized Roberts to make arrangements for the dispatch of the Amir under escort to India and to assume temporarily the government of Afghanistan. Roberts's proclamation of 28 October announced for the first time to the Afghan people that Yakub had abdicated.

> 'I, General Roberts, on behalf of the British Government, hereby proclaim that the Amir, having by his own free will abdicated, has left Afghanistan without a Government . . . The British Government, after consultation with the principal sirdars, tribal chiefs and others representing the interests and wishes of the various provinces and cities, will declare its will as to the future permanent arrangements to be made for the good government of the people.'

Yakub left Kabul for ever on 1 December 1879. Travelling fast, his party reached Peshawar eight days later. The Wazir, Yahiya Khan and Zakariah Khan followed a week later: Daud Shah and the Mustaufi remained at Kabul where they could still be of use to Roberts.

The report of MacGregor's commission was considered in Simla by a committee of experienced officials. They came unanimously to the conclusion that the attack on the mission was spontaneous, but that the Amir and his advisers could have intervened effectively if they had wished and that at the very least they had been culpably indifferent to the fate of the mission. Lytton thought that their verdict erred on the side of leniency, but considered that it provided ample grounds nevertheless for excluding Yakub permanently from thè throne. Lytton did not carry all of his Council with him on this point; at least three Members protested against Yakub's deposition but without success.

The proclamation of 28 October revealed that the British Government had as yet no clear idea of what to do with Afghanistan. Lytton himself had always toyed with the idea of breaking up Afghanistan into three weak states based on Kabul, Kandahar and Herat, but he had allowed himself to be persuaded to give Yakub a chance to show that he could rule a united Afghanistan as an ally of the British. The death of Cavagnari impelled him once more in the direction of a policy of disintegration. 'I do not disguise from myself that we may now be forced to take in hand the permanent disintegration of the national fabric it was our object to cement in Afghanistan and that, in any case, we shall probably be compelled to intervene more widely and actively than we have ever desired to do in that country,' he wrote to Beaconsfield on the day that the news of the attack on the mission reached him.[18]

Cranbrook from the start shared Lytton's view as to the necessity of breaking up Afghanistan, but the Cabinet as a whole was reluctant to abandon the policy which had led up to the Treaty of Gandamak. From Simla, Lytton sought to educate Beaconsfield and his colleagues in the realities of the situation.

> 'I entirely agree with you', he wrote to Cranbrook on 23 October, 'that nothing has occurred, or is occurring, to justify a frightened departure from the lines of a policy

carefully considered and deliberately adopted and followed thus far. The Treaty of Gandamak was undoubtedly the result, the first definite result, of such a policy, and I am confident that any violent deviation from that policy did not grow out of the Treaty, the Treaty grew out of the policy, which always looked and saw far beyond it . . . If, under conditions apparently favourable to its stability, the Treaty could not avert the blow which shattered it to fragments, and suddenly let in upon us that deluge of embarrassments which it was devised to keep out, is it not idle to attempt to cope with those embarrassments by clinging to the fragments of the Treaty? . . . Of course, we cannot recede. But neither can we stand still. We must advance if we would be safe.'

As regards Kabul and the Northern Afghan provinces it is quite premature, quite impossible, to propound *now* a permanent programme. Our action in this direction must be provisional; but although provisional it must also, I think, be prompt, plain and very firm, so far as it goes . . . In the confusion, already general throughout Afghanistan, it is the authority whose first utterance or action is free from confusion that will inspire confidence or commend obedience and thus acquire support.'

The conclusion for Lytton was obvious.

'I think we should instantly take public possession of the authority which falls from the hand of the Amir into our own and promptly, though provisionally, enforce that authority, so far as our practical power of enforcing extends, in every direction . . . The next step will be either to proclaim our permanent retention of that authority or to transfer it, with very careful and copious restrictions, to some form of native government.'[19]

The position to which Lytton was moving was the establishment of separate Afghan states based on Kabul and Kandahar, under British influence backed up by strong military forces within striking distance of the two capitals. There were strong voices among his advisers who wished to go further and annex Kandahar outright, and Lytton himself had by no means ruled out that step. If Kandahar were permanently occupied, he was prepared to contemplate handing over Herat to Persia.[20]

Early in December, the Cabinet came to the same conclusion as Lytton and Cranbrook that Afghanistan must be broken up but, apart from the establishment of separate states based on Kabul and Kandahar, it was still undecided as to what was to happen to Herat and Afghan Turkestan. Salisbury was keen to use Herat to exert pressure on the Russians and with his concurrence, Thomson, the envoy at Teheran, opened negotiations on the basis of the Persians holding Herat in return for giving support to the Turkoman tribes east of the Caspian against Russian pressure.

While the statesmen pondered the political problems, Roberts at Kabul found himself in the middle of a military crisis. At the beginning of November, he had been promoted to the local rank of Lieutenant-General and Bright's division on the Line of Communications now came directly under his command as the 2nd (Khyber) Division of the North Afghanistan Field Force. This was a logical and perhaps overdue step since it had always been clear that the support and reinforcement of the force at Kabul must come in the first instance from Bright's troops; if Roberts had to call up troops from the L of C, it obviously made matters a great deal easier if they were actually under his operational command. The rearrangement was not a moment too soon. When he had fled from Kabul after Cavagnari's death to join Roberts at Kushi, the Amir had left confusion behind him. This had been accentuated by the unexpectedly swift arrival of the British troops. For roughly a month after his arrival Roberts enjoyed a period of peace and quiet at Kabul which enabled him to settle his force into secure winter quarters and to re-establish his line of communications. But it was the lull before the storm. Given the Afghan national character, with its fierce love of independence and hatred of foreigners, it was inevitable that popular feeling would be aroused by the presence of British troops in Afghanistan. The executions at Kabul and the deposition of the Amir added fuel to the smouldering fires of Afghan resentment. As Roberts rather blandly put it later:

> 'The Afghans were waiting on events and the time had not yet arrived when any national movement was possible. But this pause was marked by certain occurrences which doubtless touched the national pride to the quick, and which were also susceptible of being used by the enemies of the British Government to excite into vivid fanaticism the religious sentiment which has ever formed a prominent trait in Afghan character.'[21]

What precipitated events was the need to lay in supplies of food, forage and fuel for the winter. Roberts determined on assembling five months' supplies at Sherpur which would, in the worst case, enable him to hang on until the following spring. This was prudent, but the foraging net had now to be spread much wider than the immediate environs of Kabul which had hitherto served for the daily needs of the force. Since the gathering of supplies on the scale proposed could be accomplished most effectively by the use of native officials, Roberts appointed native governors for Kohistan, the Logar valley and the Maidan area (south-west of Kabul), with responsibility for collecting the normal revenue as well as the extra supplies. There was no question of taking the supplies without proper payment, but it was hardly to be expected that the peasants would be eager to surrender supplies which they themselves might need for the approaching winter.

An isolated fall of snow on 11 November warned Roberts that the collection of his five months' stock of supplies needed to be speeded up.* Reports had come in of particular resistance in the Wardak and Maidan areas and on 21 November Baker, with the equivalent of a brigade, left Kabul with the object of overawing the local population and assisting the Governor (Mohammed Hussein Khan) to collect his quota of supplies; Roberts joined the brigade on the 23rd in its camp twenty-five miles south-west of the capital. Mohammed Hussein Khan had found himself powerless in the face of the stubborn reluctance of the villagers to surrender any supplies over and above the normal revenue demand. There were rumours of large bands of armed men collecting at the instigation of the Mullah Mushki-i-Alam of Ghazni, under the direction of Mohammed Jan, a relative of the Mustaufi's. Baker quickly resolved matters in the Maidan valley by seizing all the headmen, but in the Dara Nirikh Valley further on, a prominent Ghilzai chief, Bahadur Khan, still refused to co-operate. On the 23rd, two squadrons of cavalry sent out to seize him were fired on and forced to retire. On the following day, Roberts, with the bulk of the brigade, destroyed Bahadur Khan's villages, burning

---

*According to Hanna, only 17 days' reserve had been accumulated by the middle of November.

the houses and stores of corn and forage, smashing the cornbins and seizing the livestock.* Three days later, Baker, foraging with a small body of cavalry, was attacked and forced to retire from the village of Ben-i-Badam in the Wardak valley, six miles south-east of Bahadur Khan's villages. Baker revenged himself by burning Ben-i-Badam, whose inhabitants he claimed to be in league with the Mushk-i-Alam ('Fragrance of the World'). Baker now found it prudent to retire, with the results of his foraging and by 2 December was back at Kabul. Two days later, Mohammed Hussein Khan was murdered, apparently by Bahadur Khan's people.

As November drew to a close, reports of opposition and insurrection in the areas around Kabul grew. In practice, the British ruled no further than the range of their guns and accurate, timely Intelligence was virtually impossible to obtain. What Intelligence there was came at second- or third-hand and inevitably lagged behind events. But the general drift of events was unmistakable. To the north of Kabul, in Kohistan, the British-appointed Governor (Shahbaz Khan) was virtually powerless in face of a gradually rising tide of disaffection led by the principal Kohistani chief, Mir Bacha. In the Logar valley, the Governor (Abdullah Khan) had been forced to flee for safety. To the south-west, the Maidan and Wardak districts were in a state of insurrection led by Mohammed Jan, who had commanded the Afghan artillery at Ali Masjid a year earlier. The unifying influence was the Mushk-i-Alam who, from his headquarters at Ghazni, was calling for a Holy War against the foreign oppressors. His influence was wide and deep because many of the leading mullahs at both Ghazni and Kabul had been his pupils.[22] To the east of Kabul, however, the country remained relatively quiet and communications with Gough's head-quarters at Gandamak remained intact.

Roberts was uneasy about the situation. He would have been even more worried if he had known the full extent of the insurrection. For the moment, he was content to send reassuring telegrams back to India, but among his staff there was bitter criticism of the apparent dilatoriness and timidity of Bright's forces in pushing troops forward.[23] At Sherpur, priority had been given to building quarters for the Indian troops and to storing supplies, and work on improving its defences had proceeded with no great urgency. Nothing at all had been done to clear away houses and enclosures which gave cover close up to the walls.

The growing threat could not be ignored indefinitely and on 7 December, Roberts held a Council of War to consider his plan of operations. In essence, it consisted of a pincer movement. Macpherson was to move due west from Sherpur, through the Nanachi Pass, and halt on the edge of the Chardeh plain. Baker was to move due south from Kabul, through the Sang-i-Nawishta, roughly as far as Safed Sang and then turn due west until he reached the Wardak valley close to where the Rivers Kabul and Nirikh joined. He was then to sweep northwards, while Macpherson swept south-westwards, towards Argandeh, crushing between them the insurgents led by the Mushk-i-Alam and Mohammed Jan. To cloak the beginning of these operations a grand review of the whole garrison was to be held the

---

*Roberts's defence of this action in his memoirs (*Forty-One Years in India*, vol. II, p. 258) is not accurate or truthful and has been effectively demolished by Hanna, op. cit., vol. III, pp. 158–9. MacGregor disapproved of burning villages: 'it exasperates them and does not funk them'. *Diary*, p. 128.

following day in the plain north of the Bimaru heights, ostensibly to present medals to four men of the 72nd Highlanders for gallantry at the Peiwar Kotal a year before. MacGregor suggested that the Guides be brought up from Gandamak to Butkak to keep Mir Bacha's men at Baba Kushka from interfering with Macpherson's operations. No sooner had this been agreed than it was discovered that Baba Kushka was a good deal closer to Kabul than had been assumed, so counter-orders went out to the Guides to come to Kabul.

Roberts's plan was bold but risky. It meant splitting his relatively small force at Kabul into three parts. After dispatching Macpherson with some 1,800 and Baker with another 1,250 men, he would be left with only some 2,800 men (including sick) to hold Sherpur. Baker in particular would be operating up to thirty miles from Sherpur. His plan could only be justified on the assumption that the various Afghan forces would not combine and that Baker's and Macpherson's brigades were capable individually of dealing with the forces they were likely to encounter. These were bold assumptions indeed, especially since Roberts actually knew very little about the Afghan forces. Moreover, Baker and Macpherson would be out of contact for most of the time. A striking feature of the plan was its concentration on the situation west and south-west of Kabul at the expense of the threat from Kohistan. An Afghan advance from Kohistan into the Chardeh plain could cut off both Macpherson and Baker from Sherpur where the available troops were inadequate to defend that vast enclosure. The only immediate reinforcements which Roberts could then call upon would be the garrisons at Butkak and the Jagdalak Pass, and the remainder of Charles Gough's brigade at Gandamak. But if the countryside rose it might be impossible for these troops to get through. Since Baker had the farthest to go to get into position for the combined drive, it is surprising that the plan did not provide for him to leave a day ahead of Macpherson instead of the other way about. Eleven months earlier, another British commander, Lord Chelmsford, had elected to split up his force. In their own way, and on their own ground, the Afghans were no less formidable than Ceteswayo's Zulus.

Macpherson moved through the Nanachi gorge on the afternoon of the 8th and camped for the night at Aushar, just beyond the gorge, on the north-eastern edge of the Chardeh plain. Baker left Sherpur the following morning and camped that night at Chikildukhtaran, three miles beyond Charasiab and twelve miles south of Kabul. On the evening of the 10th, after a difficult march, he was in position in the Wardak valley ready to sweep northwards towards Argandeh. Unfortunately by this time the northern half of the pincer movement had become unhinged.

Macpherson had barely started to move towards Argandeh on the morning of the 9th when he was ordered to stay where he was, so as to allow the insurgent forces from the Maidan area to advance deeper into the Chardeh plain and to give Baker more time to get into position. The delay was fortunate because during the course of the 9th, Intelligence reached Macpherson that large numbers of tribes-men were moving northwards from the Maidan valley in the direction of Kohistan, presumably to link up with the Kohistani insurgents under Mir Bacha. Unless this growing menace from Kohistan were dealt with, Macpherson, in moving towards Baker, risked finding himself cut off from Sherpur. He proposed to Roberts that Baker be recalled to Sherpur and directed against the enemy concentration in

Kohistan while Macpherson moved north from Aushar to co-operate. In effect, the original pincer movement towards Argandeh was to be replaced by another pincer movement in the direction of Kohistan. Since Baker was then only some ten miles south of Kabul en route to Chikildukhtaran, he could have been back in Sherpur the same evening, but for reasons which are not clear Roberts decided not to recall him. Instead, he ordered Macpherson to move the next day against the Kohistani force reported assembled at Mir Karez, seven miles as the crow flies north-north-west of Aushar. The intervening country was considered unsuitable for cavalry so Macpherson was ordered to leave the horse artillery battery and two of his three cavalry squadrons at Aushar.

Early on 10 December, with the remainder of his force, he moved back through the Nanachi gorge, deluding enemy observers into believing that he was retreating to Sherpur, and then moved north and west through the Khirskhana Pass until he reached the Surkh Pass which led northward to Mir Karez. By clever tactics, he dispersed the insurgent force outside the northern end of the pass and, following up rapidly, utterly dispersed the remainder of the Kohistani force camped in and around Mir Karez. Macpherson was able to heliograph news of his success to Roberts at about midday. Roberts strengthened the cavalry force at Aushar with another two squadrons from Sherpur and ordered it to intercept the tribesmen who were now in retreat, but the cavalry were unable to get to grips with the tribesmen who had hastily scattered. In the course of the afternoon, Macpherson, who had camped for the night at Mir Karez, was ordered by Roberts to march the next morning towards Argandeh thus reverting to the original plan of driving the insurgents, who appeared to be retreating to the south and west, on to Baker's brigade coming up the Maidan valley. The horse artillery and cavalry left behind at Aushar under Massy were to strike southwards on to the Ghazni road and then move westwards along it meeting Macpherson at a point some three miles from Argandeh and thirteen miles from Sherpur. Massy's instructions, given personally to him by Roberts, were to move cautiously along the Ghazni road, keeping in close contact with Macpherson, and on no account to engage the enemy until Macpherson had done so. Roberts explained to Massy that some 1,500–2,000 Kohistanis were retreating towards Argandeh and it was his [Massy's] task to prevent them breaking back into the Chardeh plain. Roberts had grossly under-estimated the nature of the forces facing Macpherson and Massy. It was not 1,500–2,000 fleeing Kohistanis with which they had to deal, but a force of some 10,000 men from Maidan and Wardak under Mohammed Jan, which had reached Argandeh on 10 December and was preparing to move the next day on Kabul.

At nightfall on the 10th, Roberts's force was split into four. Thirty miles south-west of Sherpur, Baker's brigade was preparing to sweep northwards towards Argandeh and the Chardeh plain; twelve miles north-west of Sherpur, Macpherson was preparing to move towards Baker; just over three miles west of Sherpur and eleven miles south-east of Macpherson, Massy's cavalry force was also making ready to move towards Baker. All being well, these three forces would meet in the vicinity of Argandeh. The remainder of the Kabul Field Force remained behind to guard Sherpur.

The Chardeh plain into which Massy, Macpherson and Baker were to advance, lies due west of Kabul, separated from it by the Asmai and Sher Darwaza heights through which the road to the capital penetrates by way of the Deh Mazang gorge (map 8). Roughly twelve miles from west to east and roughly eight miles north to south, it is bounded on all four sides by hills or mountains, creating in effect a large amphitheatre. The floor of this amphitheatre was densely cultivated with orchards and market gardens, and seamed with a mass of streams and watercourses fringed with willows and poplars. Scattered all over the plain were numerous hamlets and villages. A contemporary observer wrote: 'It looks like what I suppose Lombardy to be; all cultivated, with poplars round many of the fields. The valley looks thick with trees in most parts.' Although flat, it was not good country for cavalry and artillery.

Massy, with a squadron of the 9th Lancers, left Sherpur early on the morning of the 11th and joined the mounted troops at Aushar. Since he and Macpherson were not in visual touch, he dispatched a troop of 9th Lancers to make contact with Macpherson; with the remaining 214 men of the 9th Lancers and 14th Bengal Lancers, plus four guns of F/A, RHA, he moved out across the plain, striking south-west towards the Ghazni road near the village of Kila Kazi. He was within a mile of the village when the advance guard reported large numbers of men three miles ahead. He had bumped into Mohammed Jan's army.

Nevertheless, he continued to advance until he could see that the enemy was in overwhelming force. The four horse-artillery guns were ordered to deploy and open fire at a range of some 1900 yards to try to halt the enemy until Macpherson could arrive. Massy eventually found himself within some 1,500 yards of the enemy. At that point he dismounted fifty men of the 9th Lancers to engage the advancing Afghans with their carbines. 'With any number of standards, white, red and black, they seemed to be making straight for us,' wrote an officer of the 9th Lancers:

'The RHA opened fire, but as they were in such straggling order, only a few were killed; we could see them through our glasses picking them up. We then went on and again opened fire. Their bullets now began to drop in amongst us so that the Colonel ordered me to dismount my troop and open fire to try to check them. This I did but our fire had little or no effect on them. After firing, a few rounds, we were ordered to mount and follow the guns, who had retired some 300 yards. This we did, and on arriving at the guns they opened fire but don't seem to have done much harm. The bullets were now coming in like hail, and knocking the horses down both in the squadron and also the RHA horses.'[25]

When Roberts arrived on the scene at approximately 11.00 hours, Massy was in retreat. Roberts had started out from Sherpur expecting to see Macpherson and Baker between them complete the dispersal of the insurgents. Instead, as he later wrote, 'an extraordinary spectacle was presented to my view. An unbroken line, extending for about two miles and formed of not less than between 9,000 and 10,000 men, was moving rapidly towards me, all on foot save a small body of cavalry on their left flank – in fact, the greater part of Mohammed Jan's army.' It was as critical a situation as Roberts had ever found himself in, but it was a situation designed to bring out his talents as a commander.

He saw immediately that there was no prospect of stopping the advancing enemy with the tiny force available. The immediate task was to get the guns away and then retreat on Sherpur. To do that he must hold either the Nanachi or the Deh Mazang gorges. An officer was sent galloping to Hugh Gough at Sherpur, with an order to hold the Nanachi gorge since that was the direction in which the enemy was pressing back Massy's force. At the same time, Massy was ordered to charge the enemy to give time to get the guns away. The charge of the 9th Lancers and 14th Bengal Lancers had little impact. There was difficulty in rallying the 9th Lancers to make a second charge and thereafter matters degenerated into a rout. In the confusion, the line of the Kabul–Ghazni road was missed. One gun had quickly to be spiked and abandoned in the ditch into which it had fallen. The other three, having made off in the direction of the village of Bagwana on Roberts's instructions, soon found themselves in similar difficulties and also had to be abandoned after being spiked. In and around Bagwana there were scenes of wild confusion as the cavalry tried to get across the deep ditch into which the three guns had fallen. There were scenes also of great gallantry; Lieutenant Hardy of the Royal Horse Artillery refused to leave a wounded fellow-officer, Lieutenant Forbes of the Bengal Lancers, and they died together. The Reverend J. W. Adams, Chaplain to the Force, won the Victoria Cross for pulling men out of the ditch to safety. Those who could not get clear of the village died under the Afghan knives. Those who survived made off in various directions – some towards the Nanachi gorge, some over the Aliabad Kotal, the majority with Roberts in the direction of the Deh Mazang gorge.

While Roberts was retiring towards Deh Mazang, the bulk of Mohammed Jan's army was apparently heading for the Nanachi gorge and Sherpur. If Gough could not hold the enemy at Nanachi, the cantonment at Sherpur must inevitably be overrun. Cut off from Sherpur and each other, Macpherson's and Baker's brigades would be overwhelmed in succession. It was at this point, at about noon, that the situation was transformed by the arrival of Macpherson. He had left Mir Karez at 07.50 hours, heading southwards across the Surkh Pass. Emerging into the Chardeh plain, Macpherson could see groups of tribesmen moving eastwards from Argandeh and could hear the sounds of gunfire away to the east, in the direction of Aushar, where he had left the cavalry and horse artillery. Leaving his baggage train to make its way under escort round the north-western rim of the plain to Sherpur, Macpherson with the rest of his brigade marched at top speed towards the sound of the guns.*

At about 12.30 hours, Macpherson struck the rear of the enemy. The Afghans had assumed that his brigade was moving towards Argandeh and, apparently, had for a time mistaken his advance guard for Kohistani reinforcements. The effect of Macpherson's attack was to deflect Mohammed Jan's forces from the Nanachi gorge and to push them south-eastwards towards the Deh Mazang gorge, leading to Kabul itself. It was this change in direction which Roberts spotted just after midday without knowing the precise cause because in the noise and confusion surrounding him he could not hear Macpherson's artillery. The Deh Mazang gorge was no less vital than the Nanachi since it also led, via the city, to Sherpur. As soon as he spotted the change of direction, Roberts sent an oral message to Hugh Gough, ordering him to seize the Deh Mazang gorge at once with a wing of the

---

*The baggage reached Sherpur only after a stiff fight with part of Mohammed Jan's left wing.

Right: Robert, first Earl of Lytton, Governor-General and Viceroy of India, 1876–80. (National Army Museum)

Right: The Amir Sher Ali. (National Army Museum)

Left: Major Sir Louis Napoleon Cavagnari. (National Army Museum)

Below: The bridge of boats across the River Indus at Attock. (India Office Library)

Right: Ali Masjid – the fort as seen from the eastern side of the Pass. (National Army Museum)

Below right: The interior of the fort at Ali Masjid after its capture in November 1878. (Royal Hussars Museum)

Peiwar Kotal

Above: A group of officers of the 51st Regiment, about 1878. Note the variety of uniforms. (India Office Library)

Left: Peiwar Kotal, 1879. (National Army Museum)

Top right: No 2 (Derajat) Mountain Battery descending the Spingawi Kotal, 1879. (National Army Museum)

Centre right: Men of the 8th (King's) Foot garrisoning the Peiwar Kotal in 1879. (National Army Museum)

Bottom right: Sepoys of the 23rd (Pioneers) Bengal Native Infantry. The men are Sikhs. Note the pioneer tools, the Snider rifles and the native shoes. (National Army Museum)

op left: A Morse telegraph detachment. (National rmy Museum)

entre left: European field hospital at Ali Khel, 879. (National Army Museum)

ottom left: Camel kajawahs in the Kurram, 1879. National Army Museum)

Above: Fort Battye and the scene of the action at Fattehbad. (National Army Museum)

Below: The River Kabul at Jalalabad, showing the scene of disaster to the 10th Hussars on 31 March 1879. (India Office Library)

op left: The Khan of Lalpura and followers. (India ffice Library)

Above: Cavagnari, Jenkins and the Amir Yakub Ali at Gandamak, May 1879. (National Army Museum)

ottom left: The Bala Hissar from the north-east. National Army Museum)

Below: The Bala Hissar, showing (centre) the burned-out remains of the Residency. (National Army Museum)

Top left: Cavagnari and Afghan Sardars at Gandamak, 1879. (National Army Museum)

Centre left: A Gatling gun detachment in Kurram, 1879. Note the Broadwell ammunition drums, introduced in 1872. (National Army Museum)

Bottom: A group of F Battery, A Brigade, Royal Horse Artillery, Major Smith-Wyndham in helmet. (National Army Museum)

Right: Lieutenant-General Sir Donald Stewart. (National Army Museum)

Top left: Roberts (bearded figure with cane under his arm) and staff at Kabul, 1879. Facing him is Macpherson, with Hugh Gough leaning forward in between. Charles Gough is on Roberts's left, with Massy next to him (wearing sword). The clergyman is the Reverend J. W. Adams, VC. Colonel McGregor stands behind Roberts. (National Army Museum)

Centre left: Sherpur (in middle ground) from Asmai Heights, with Bismaru Heights immediately behind Sherpur, December 1879. (National Army Museum)

Bottom left: Sherpur with Sher Darwaza and Takht-i-Shah in the background, December 1879. (National Army Museum)

Above: North-west corner of Sherpur, December 1879. (National Army Museum)

Below: The bridge over the River Kabul between Sherpur and Kabul. Bala Hissar is in the centre middle distance, with Takht-i-Shah on the horizon to the right. (National Army Museum)

p left: 9th Lancers, (Captain Shearburn's troop) Kabul, 1880. (National Army Museum)

ntre left: Lepel Griffin (centre) with staff at Kabul the spring of 1880. (National Army Museum)

Bottom left: Kandahar – the Citadel. (National Army Museum)

Above: Jagdalak Pass. (National Army Museum)

Below: Kandahar – the Shikapur Gate in 1880. (National Army Museum)

Top: Kandahar – the Baba Wali Kotal. (National Army Museum)

Centre: The view from Kandahar looking west. (National Army Museum)

Bottom: A heliograph and searchlight detachment; the officer in khaki is Captain Stratt. (National Army Museum)

72nd Highlanders. Gough, however, was reasonably well-informed of the situation through a picket on the Sher Darwaza heights above the Bala Hissar. Seeing the Afghan tide rolling towards the Nanachi gorge, he had telegraphed for the Guides to march at top speed for Kabul and had re-disposed his forces at Sherpur to meet the expected attack from the west. Even before Roberts's first order reached him, Gough had seen fragments of Massy's force, including the horse artillery teams, arrive in Sherpur and he had been warned by the picket on the Sher Darwaza of the change of direction of Mohammed Jan's forces towards Deh Mazang. He was thus ready to react quickly, and a force of some 200 men of the 72nd Highlanders under their Colonel, Brownlow, managed to reach and seize the Deh Mazang gorge two miles from Sherpur just before the Afghans arrived.

At Sherpur, the news brought by the survivors of Massy's force had produced an atmosphere of alarm and near panic.[26] The crisis, however, was nearly over. Unable to force the Deh Mazang gorge and under fierce attack from behind from Macpherson's troops, Mohammed Jan's forces drifted southwards to occupy the Takht-i-Shah heights overlooking the Sher Darwaza and the Bala Hissar. The deflection of the Afghan forces away from the Nanachi gorge gave MacGregor, the Chief of Staff, the opportunity to retrieve the spiked guns. With the help of survivors from Massy's original force, part of the escort for Macpherson's baggage and some of the cavalry left at Sherpur, he succeeded in dragging the guns back to Sherpur where they were quickly repaired and put back into service, using duplicate parts held in reserve.

By the late afternoon, Roberts and the survivors of Massy's original force were all back in Sherpur. Brownlow's Highlanders held the Deh Mazang gorge while the picket, now reinforced to a strength of some 200, was still in position on the Sher Darwaza heights, less than a mile from Mohammed Jan's forces on the Takht-i-Shah. Macpherson's troops, having in his own words, 'almost boxed the compass and drove – I may say hunted – the enemy in all directions so that by 2 o'clock . . . not an Afghan could be seen on the Chardeh plain', bivouacked in the late afternoon near Kila Kazi. But he was soon recalled to Deh Mazang where his brigade entrenched itself. Apart from Baker's force, Roberts now had his troops concentrated and he was further strengthened at midnight when the bulk of the Guides Cavalry and Infantry reached Sherpur after a forced march from Seh Baba.

It cannot have been an easy night for Roberts. He was now faced with a large-scale insurrection. He urgently needed Baker's brigade, but he had no idea where it was or indeed if it still existed. As an obvious precaution, he telegraphed to Bright, warning him that his 1st Brigade under Charles Gough might be required at Kabul and ordering him to reinforce Gandamak to enable it to be held if the 1st Brigade had to move out. The night passed reasonably quietly apart from a series of determined attacks on the Sher Darwaza post, which Hugh Gough had prudently reinforced.

All told, on 11 December, Roberts had lost 30 killed and 47 wounded, mainly from Massy's original force. But it was not so much the casualties as the transformation of the overall military situation which was the real price of what the Abridged Official History called 'a disastrous engagement'. From a position of dominance, the British force now found itself on the defensive. Whether the balance could be redressed once again in the British favour remained to be seen.

The basic cause of the reverse – faulty Intelligence – is clear. In directing Massy to move across the Chardeh plain to link up with Macpherson, Roberts was under the impression that he was dealing only with remnants of the force which had originally opposed Macpherson at Mir Karez; he was clearly unaware that Mohammed Jan had reached Argandeh on the 10th with a very large force. What probably saved Massy (and Roberts) from total disaster was Macpherson's timely decision to abandon his original objective and march towards the sound of the guns. Looking back, twenty years later, Roberts professed to see nothing wrong with his plans.

> 'Reviewing the incidents of the 11th of December, as I have frequently done since, with all the concomitant circumstances deeply impressed on my memory, I have failed to discover that any disposition of my force different from that I made could have had better results, or that what did occur could have been averted by greater foresight or more careful calculation on my part. Two deviations from my programme (which probably at the time appeared unimportant to the Commanders in question) were the principal factors in bringing about the unfortunate occurrences of that day. Had Macpherson marched at 7 am instead of at 8, and had Massy followed the route I had arranged for him to take, Mahomed Jan must have fallen into the trap I had prepared for him.'[27]

In fact, Roberts had set no trap for Mohammed Jan's force because he did not know where it was or where it was heading. If Massy had followed the route laid down and if Macpherson had marched an hour earlier, it is probable that Macpherson would have seen and attacked the Afghan army before Massy made contact and thus the disaster to Massy's force would have been avoided. To that extent only, Roberts could claim that he was the victim of his subordinate commanders' decisions.

Macpherson attracted some criticism in the newspapers although he, of all the commanders, had little with which to reproach himself, and one may perhaps detect the hand of Roberts's admirers among the staff and assembled newspaper men in Kabul. The main weight of criticism descended on Massy who had already lost the confidence of Roberts and Haines. He was now criticized for departing from the route he had been ordered to follow, for engaging the enemy before he had linked up with Macpherson, for failing to have scouts out, for weakening his force by sending off the troop of the 9th Lancers, and for various other tactical errors. Despite vigorous protest, he was removed from his command in February 1880.[28] His supporters secured him a brigade command in India and he eventually finished up as GOC, Ceylon.

Baker also had had an eventful day. Early in the morning he moved off northwards into the Maidan valley, heading for Argandeh and expecting to crush the insurgents between his brigade and that of Macpherson's. Despite efforts to contact him, he was ignorant of the fact that Macpherson had been re-directed the previous day northwards into Kohistan, and was nowhere near Argandeh as originally planned. As he moved up the Maidan valley, the hills on either side of him were crowned with large numbers of Wardak and Logari tribesmen moving parallel with him. His rearguard and baggage was soon under heavy attack and Baker himself was forced to go back to assist it through the Maidan Pass. In the meantime, his advance guard of cavalry had discovered that the Argandeh Pass was blocked by Afghans and the brigade was cut off from Kabul. Although it was late in the afternoon Baker decided that he could not risk leaving the enemy in possession of his line of advance and in a brilliant, small action, the ubiquitous George White, with some of the 92nd Highlanders, stormed and seized the pass. The brigade then bivouacked, leaving Baker to an anxious night, wondering why Macpherson had not arrived at the rendezvous.

On the following morning, Baker was able to open up heliographic communication with Roberts and learned what had happened the day before. He was ordered to return to Sherpur at once but that was easier said than done. His baggage animals were exhausted and his rearguard under constant attack and making slow progress. So difficult was the situation that at one point he seriously contemplated leaving his baggage behind under guard and pressing on with the remainder of the force. But the need to leave behind a large proportion of his force weighed against this course; he therefore continued his steady march towards Sherpur, via the Deh Mazang gorge, arriving with his main body at about 18.00 hours on the 12th. As they approached Kabul, his men could see fighting going on on the Sher Darwaza heights. His losses since leaving on the 9th had been only three killed and thirteen wounded, but his expedition had accomplished nothing and run considerable risks.

The 12th December had been another unsatisfactory day for Roberts. He had decided that the best way of retrieving the situation was to take the initiative at once. Accordingly, on the morning of the 12th, he dispatched a force of 560 rifles and two mountain guns from Macpherson's brigade, under Lieutenant-Colonel Money, to dislodge Mohammed Jan's forces from the Takht-i-Shah. The enemy position was an exceptionally formidable one – steep slopes strewn with jagged masses of rock and strengthened by sangars thrown up overnight. Starting from Deh Mazang, Money moved up and along the ridge of the Sher Darwaza heights towards the Takht-i-Shah, but was held up by fierce Afghan resistance midway along the ridge. By the time that he had overcome this, it was 15.30 hours, his ammunition was running low, and he was in no position to tackle the even more formidable Afghan position on the Takht-i-Shah itself. He was accordingly ordered to bivouac where he was, Roberts having decided to await the return of Baker's brigade before resuming the attack. Casualties had been negligible (four killed and thirteen wounded), but the objective had not been gained and the psychological advantage lay with the Afghans. MacGregor recorded gloomily in his diary the same night 'That is the second defeat in two days; one more and we shall have to shut ourselves up all the winter.'[29] The troops were still dangerously dispersed, with Macpherson at Deh Mazang, hanging on with only some 300 men, and Money's 550 isolated on the ridge above.

With the arrival of Baker's brigade on the evening of the 12th, an attack could now be launched in strength. The left of the Afghan position rested on the Takht-i-Shah itself, his right occupied a spur jutting out to the east overlooking the village of Beni Hissar. Roberts's plan for the 13th involved a renewal of Money's attack along the main ridge towards the Takht-i-Shah, while a strong force under Baker moved southwards from Sherpur, seized the village of Beni Hissar and advanced westwards up the spur.

Baker's force* left Sherpur at about 08.00 hours. As the advance guard under George White approached Beni Hissar, it could see large numbers of tribesmen leaving the village and climbing up the spur to the west which was Baker's first objective. White immediately saw the need to prevent the tribesmen from reinforcing Mohammed Jan's forces on the spur and the Takht-i-Shah. On his own initiative, he decided to seize the centre of the spur. Supported by the 92nd and Guides, he climbed the front face of the spur and after fierce hand-to-hand fighting, seized the crest.† After a short pause to enable the mountain guns to come up to cover his advance, White moved up the spur, fighting doggedly for each foot of the way, finally reaching the summit of the Takht-i-Shah at about midday. There they found Money's men who had fought their way southwards along the Sher Darwaza ridge. In the meantime, many of the Afghan right wing, cut off from the main force on the Takht-i-Shah by White's bold advance, had re-descended the eastern end of the spur and re-occupied Beni Hissar and the neighbouring villages.

While Baker had thus achieved his aim and seized the whole of the Afghan main position, enemy opposition was revealing itself to be hydra-headed. At the very moment that his troops were occupying the Takht-i-Shah, a large body of Afghans emerging from Kabul had seized two villages on the road to Sherpur, thus cutting off Baker's direct line of retreat. Baker therefore had to use his reserve to storm and seize these villages. Hardly had he done so than he was warned by heliograph from Sherpur that enemy forces were advancing on the rear of the cantonment. In parallel Baker's cavalry, supported by the remainder of the cavalry from Sherpur under Massy, was engaged with enemy forces which had collected to the eastwards around the Siah Sang heights. The city and all the surrounding countryside was in a state of general insurrection and as fast as one gathering was dispersed another appeared in a different direction. Roberts simply did not have enough troops to dominate the whole area.

By the end of the day, all troops had been withdrawn to Sherpur save only for Money's force which, reinforced by the 67th under Macpherson's personal command, continued to occupy a position on the Sher Darwaza heights above the Bala Hissar. But the Deh Mazang gorge had had to be abandoned, and effectively Roberts held no more than the Sherpur cantonment. Casualties during the day had amounted only to fourteen killed and 45 wounded, and since the Afghans had been dispersed wherever they had been encountered, Roberts and many of his officers appear to have been very satisfied with the day's work and confident that the menace which had hung over the British force for the last four or five days had been effectively dispersed. But experienced frontier officers were not so sanguine.

When daylight broke on the 14th, the optimism of the previous evening was seen to have been premature. A mile and a half away to the west of the cantonment the Asmai Heights were crowded with men whose numbers were increasing rapidly and it was obvious that Mohammed Jan was preparing to launch a massive new attack from this direction. There was no alternative but to attempt once again to

---

*5th Punjab Cavalry, one squadron 9th Lancers, 92nd Highlanders, Guides Infantry, wing 3rd Sikh Infantry, 150 men of 5th Punjab Infantry, No. 2 Mountain Battery (four guns), G/3 RA (four guns) – in all about 1,800 men.
†Lieutenant W. H. Dick Cunyngham, 92nd Highlanders, won the VC here.

disperse the Afghans. The task was again given to Baker, some of whose troops had now been in action for four days. The force, which moved out just after 09.00 hours from the Headquarters Gate in the west face of the cantonment, consisted of the 14th Bengal Lancers, the 5th Punjab Infantry, the Guides Infantry and 294 men of the 72nd and 92nd Highlanders, with four guns of No. 2 Mountain Battery and four field guns of G/3, RA – in all, about 1,650 men. Since Macpherson was still in position on the Takht-i-Shah with the 67th and detachments of the 3rd Sikhs and 5th Gurkhas, Roberts retained at his disposal in Sherpur only some 1,700 infantry and two regiments of cavalry, a force quite incapable of defending the cantonment on its own.

The key to the Afghan position was a conical hill at the northern end of the Asmai Heights. The ground prevented the cavalry doing anything except take up a watching position to the north but, covered by the fire of the guns, a party of the 72nd and Guides attacked and seized the hill. They were reinforced quickly by the mountain guns and 100 rifles of the 5th Punjab Infantry. The main body, led by the remainder of the 72nd, 92nd and the Guides, now passed through and worked their way southwards along the heights, assisted by the fire of G/3 and four guns of F/A, RHA which came into action from the south-west corner of the cantonment. At the same time, Macpherson with the 67th moved northwards across the Deh Mazang gorge to attack the rear of the enemy forces on the Asmai Heights, assisted by fire from marksmen of the 67th and two guns left behind on the Sher Darwaza. Under this pressure from front and rear, the Afghan forces crumbled and by mid-morning the whole of the Asmai Heights were in Baker's hands.

The triumph was short-lived. Large numbers of Afghans were already coming down from the direction of Kohistan against the conical hill still held by detachments of the 72nd, Guides, 5th Punjab Infantry and the four guns of the mountain battery. This new Afghan pressure was irresistible and the position had to be abandoned after a most gallant defence, two of the mountain guns being lost in the process.*

The pressures on the British forces were rapidly accumulating. Masses of tribesmen were occupying the Siah Sang heights and moving northwards round the eastern end of Sherpur, presumably to link up with forces from Kohistan in an attack on the rear face of the enclosure. From the Sher Darwaza heights, the gallant Robertson, still in position with his signallers, reported that the crowds of tribesmen moving north and east across the Chardeh plain to join in the fighting reminded him of Epsom on Derby Day! Gough, with a squadron each of the 9th Lancers, Guides Cavalry and 5th Punjab Cavalry, was quite unable to disperse the crowds moving northwards from the Siah Sang Heights. The day was graced by a very gallant charge by Captain Vousden and ten of his 5th Punjab Cavalry sowars which dispersed several hundred Afghans moving along the north bank of the River Kabul near the city. Vousden received the Victoria Cross and the seven surviving men the Indian Order of Merit, but individual actions such as this could not affect the general issue.

At about 14.00 hours, Roberts was forced to bow to the overwhelming Afghan pressure which was building up from all directions and to recall all of his troops to

---

*Lance-Corporal Sellar, of the 72nd, won the VC here.

Sherpur. 'It was a bitter thought', he wrote subsequently, 'that it might be my duty to retire for a time within the defences of Sherpur, a measure which would involve the abandonment of the City and Bala Hissar, and which I knew, moreover, would give heart to the tribesmen.'[30] Faced with tens of thousands of tribesmen, flushed with success and scenting the possibility of annihilation, the retirement was bound to be a delicate operation even for disciplined troops. Nevertheless, by 16.45 hours, Baker's men were back safely in Sherpur. The retirement from the Sher Darwaza and Takht-i-Shah was a more ticklish affair; Macpherson's men had further to go and were bound at some stage to traverse the suburbs of the city. But despite incessant pressure on the rearguard formed by some of the 67th, and the difficulties and dangers created by the narrow streets of Kabul and the orchards and walled gardens beyond, all of Macpherson's men were back at Sherpur by nightfall. 'Thank God we have scraped through that business! At one time I expected we should have been overwhelmed,' said Macpherson's principal staff officer, after he had got back.[31] As Macpherson's troops entered the Headquarters Gate, Gough with the cavalry came through the eastern entrance and Roberts had his whole force assembled for the first time since Macpherson had moved out on the afternoon of 8 December to begin the whole disastrous week of events. There remained the garrisons at Butkak and the posts between there and Jagdalak, amounting in all to some 1,800 men, very nearly a brigade. The troops from Butkak, consisting of the 12th Bengal Cavalry and 50 rifles of the 28th BNI, arrived at Sherpur that night, having miraculously come unscathed through ten miles of countryside swarming with insurgents. The Lataband garrison, 25 miles from Sherpur, consisting of a wing of the 23rd Native Infantry and part of the 28th Native Infantry, with two mountain guns, was believed (not entirely accurately) to be well-provisioned and fortified and capable of retaining its position. Since it was vital for the Sherpur garrison to maintain its link with Bright's troops, Roberts decided to leave the Lataband garrison where it was for the time being.

During the fighting on the 14th, casualties had been 35 killed and 103 wounded. Since operations started around Kabul on 8 December, Roberts had lost 81 killed and 213 wounded. The losses had been heavy and the results had been disastrous. Many must have been bewildered as Combe at the change of fortunes – 'By Jove! and really that is all one has breath to say. A change has indeed come over the vision of our dream – last night we were all cock-a-hoop, thinking ourselves fine fellows, and that all we now had to do was to walk around and burn some villages; and within twenty-four hours we are locked up, closely besieged, after a jolly good licking and all communications with the outer world cut off.'[32] What had gone wrong? In retrospect, it is easy to criticize Roberts's original plan which effectively split up his force into three parts and left each part vulnerable to defeat in detail. 'They [the British casualties] were unusually heavy for Afghan fighting, but have given us valuable experience, as we no longer despise our enemy . . . and we shall no longer send flying columns over the hills and break up our army into three weak parts', wrote Hensman, in implied criticism, after the events of 14 December.[33] He had put his finger on the real causes of the disasters – a basic lack of accurate Intelligence about the enemy's movements and strength, coupled with a good deal of contempt for the Afghans.

The unbroken string of relatively easy British successes which had attended the course of the war would appear to have led Roberts into the classical mistake of underestimating his enemy. There had been tactical errors as well – the failure to tell Baker of the change of plan for Macpherson's brigade on 9 December, and the consistent use of detachments, such as Money's, on 12 December, which were too small for their tasks – but these merely compounded the basic errors. It is unlikely that Roberts, despite his predilection for quick, bold action, would have split up his forces and sent them chasing over the countryside on 9–11 December if he had been aware of the strength and rapidity of Mohammed Jan's movements. Nor would he have persisted in his policy of sending out detachments on 12, 13 and 14 December to seize positions which he could not then hold if he had really appreciated the weight and nature of the forces opposing him. That he was not better informed reflects the fact that, for all their successes hitherto, the British controlled only the countryside immediately within range of their guns.

NOTES

1. Lytton to Roberts, 9 September 1872 – LP 518/4, pp. 732–5.
2. See Chapter 7, n. 11.
3. See Chapter 7, n. 14.
4. Text in *The Anglo-Afghan War, 1879–80* Intelligence Branch, Quartermaster-General's Department. London, 1881, pp. 67–8.
5. Commenting on the Indian Government's orders that justice should be swift, stern and impressive, he wrote in his diary, 'It cannot be short unless we catch men whose guilt is patent . . . I do not believe it ever does good to kill men indiscriminately and I will not lend myself to it.' *Diary*, p. 108.
6. Ibid., p. 112.
7. Ibid., p. 111.
8. Hensman, op. cit., pp. 87–88. Hensman, a war correspondent for the *Daily News*, shared to the full the avenging spirit of Roberts's force. In a revealing passage, he refers to the executed men thus: 'such poor specimens of humanity as those marched daily to execution are of but little account in our sight'. *Daily News*, 15 December 1879.
9. Official History, Part III, Simla, 1885, Appendix A to Chapter 1.
10. Roberts to Lytton, 22 November 1879 – RP7101-23-101, p. 224.
11. *Diary*, p. 120.
12. Ibid., p. 133.

13. *Times of India*, 17 November 1879. The reference is to Hensman.
14. Lytton to Cranbrook, 5 December 1879 – LP 518/4, p. 1077.
15. Cf. MacGregor's diary for 11 October: 'Wrote out programme for tomorrow, when we are to make our entry into the Bala Hissar, never to go out of it again I hope. The troops are to line the road, and a salute is to be fired and the flag hoisted; then we are to go into the Diwan-i-Am, and the Amir and all his people are to be quodded.'
16. There is a detailed eyewitness account of Yakub's abdication by Colonel Sir Neville Chamberlain, written in 1887, among Roberts's papers – see RP7101-23-149.
17. Lytton was critical of the MacGregor Commission's report which he regarded as unjudicial and heavily biased against Yakub. Clearly Lytton would not have been averse to finding Yakub guilty if the evidence had been solid enough to sustain the charge.
18. Lytton to Beaconsfield, 4 September 1879 – Balfour, op. cit., p. 359.
19. Lytton to Cranbrook, 23 October 1879 – see Balfour, op. cit., pp. 376–380.
20. Lytton to Cranbrook, 5 November 1879 – Balfour, op. cit., p. 381. Lytton no doubt received some satisfaction from Roberts's report that he had disinterred the terms of the proposed Russian treaty with Sher Ali. No written

copy could be found, but the alleged terms had been reconstructed from memory by the Mustaufi and the Afghan envoy who was to carry the treaty when signed to Tashkent. The main terms were:

a. Russian control of Afghan external relations;

b. free, exclusive Russian commercial access;

c. Russian assistance to the Amir and his selected heir against all rivals and rebellion;

d. Russian military aid to recover Peshawar in event of an Anglo-Russian war.

Whether Sher Ali ever intended to sign such a treaty remains unproven. Apart from the promise about Peshawar, the terms are not far from being a mirror image of what Lytton had ultimately been prepared to offer!

21. Dispatch No. 1027, dated 23 January 1879 – quoted in Official History, vol. III, p. 80.

22. Hensman reports the arrival of the Governor of Ghazni at Kabul on 18 November, claiming that he had lost control of the city to the mullahs who were preaching a holy war (jihad). Roberts had intended to visit Ghazni with a brigade, but was prevented by the failure to establish a secure L of C via the Khyber.

23. As late as 7 December, when the Mushk-i-Alam was within fourteen miles of Kabul, Roberts could still telegraph to Simla: 'Kohistanis are assembling and inclined to give trouble. Some men under a Mullah,

named Mushk-i-Alam, have collected again near Ben-i-Badam; these people and the Kohistanis are too far away at present to take notice of. I am endeavouring to settle matters without proceeding to extremities.' *Afghanistan (1880)*, No. 1, p. 179.

24. Ball-Acton, op. cit., p. 125.

25. Captain Stewart-Mackenzie, quoted in Major E. W. Sheppard. *The Ninth Queen's Royal Lancers, 1715–1936*. London, 1939, p. 167.

26. 'It was a great relief to find they were not advancing direct on us by the Nanachi Kotal as they had originally intended – for, honestly speaking, I think we should have had a tough job to stop them.' – Gough, 'Old Memories', *Pall Mall Magazine*, March 1899, p. 396. According to Hensman, op. cit., p. 197, Gough had less than one thousand men available for duty but that was a gross underestimate. Including sick, he had some 3,000 at Sherpur.

27. Roberts, op. cit., vol. II, p. 281.

28. The formal grounds for his removal are set out in a letter from the Adjutant-General, India to Roberts dated 9 February 1880. RP7101-23-147-3.

29. *Diary*, p. 136.

30. Roberts, op. cit., vol. II, p. 291.

31. Colonel Lockhart, in conversation with Hanna – quoted in Hanna, op. cit., vol. III, p. 217n.

32. Combe, op. cit., pp. 114–5.

33. Hensman, p. 214.

CHAPTER 9

CRISIS AT KABUL

'We are thoroughly hated and not enough feared.'

MacGregor's Diary

The fortnight which followed the disastrous events of 11 December at Kabul was one of great anxiety for Lytton and his Council. The Viceroy was by no means taken wholly unawares by the crisis. As early as 21 October 1879, he had written to Roberts, 'My fear is that when the Afghan people and tribes have fully realized all that is involved in the Amir's abdication they may begin to form hostile combinations likely ere long to increase our troubles.'[1], and on 9 December, he had told Cranbrook that, 'I have always fully reckoned, as a certainty, upon a general uprising of the country about Kabul next spring; and what has now occurred is only unforeseen in so far as it has occurred much sooner than I expected, with less warning, and on a larger scale . . .'[2] But it was precisely because the outbreak had come much earlier than expected and on a larger scale that a crisis had arisen. He was inclined to blame Roberts for having stirred up trouble by his executions.[3] Lytton and his colleagues could do little to help in the short term. The only reinforcement available to assist Roberts was Charles Gough's brigade at Gandamak; further reinforcements would take weeks to push along the Khyber line. The troops at Kabul would have to sink or swim by their own efforts. There can have been few at Kabul or Calcutta who did not remember uneasily the fate of Elphinstone's army 37 years before. Lytton at least kept his nerve. There were many in India who did not. 'The Anglo-Indian Press has behaved throughout the crisis *ignobly*,' Lytton wrote indignantly; 'In a paroxysm of panic, it has been for the last week daily predicting (with an apparently enthusiastic satisfaction at the prospect) irreparable disasters and now that all its silly predictions are falsified by the event, it systematically ignores our success.'[4]

Bright's 2nd Division had been placed under Roberts's overall command against the very contingency which had now arisen. Between Jamrud and his most advanced post at Jagdalak Fort, forty miles from Kabul, Bright disposed of some 12,000 troops. There had been no major disturbances on the line of communications since it was re-occupied at the beginning of November, but there had been a certain amount of cutting of the telegraph line and stealing. All convoys of supplies and personnel had to be escorted and Bright's force was dispersed between a large number of posts. It was difficult to concentrate a large force quickly. The Commander-in-Chief had recommended in October that a reserve force be assembled near Peshawar in case of an emergency, but his proposal had been rejected.

When on the evening of 11 December Roberts telegraphed Bright warning him that the 1st Brigade might be wanted at Kabul, Gough's troops were split between

Gandamak, Pezwan and Jagdalak. Arrangements were immediately made for the post at Gandamak to be reinforced from Jalalabad to enable Gough to concentrate his brigade. News of Roberts's likely need of Gough's brigade reached Army Headquarters the following day. The C in C at once ordered troops at Lahore, Nowshera and Rawalpindi to be ready to move forward to Peshawar for employment under Bright. On the same day (12 December), Roberts telegraphed Bright instructing him to dispatch Gough and his brigade to Kabul whenever the telegraph line between there and Gandamak was cut.* Two days later, reinforcements having arrived to garrison Gandamak, Gough moved forward as far as Jagdalak with the 9th Foot, 4th Gurkhas, two squadrons of the 10th Bengal Lancers and two mountain guns. There he received a peremptory telegram from Roberts, ordering him to advance at once on Kabul, picking up the Lataband garrison en route and leaving garrisons for those intermediate posts which could be readily held, abandoning the rest. Bright was ordered at the same time to send Arbuthnot's 2nd Brigade forward to Kabul.

Bright had his own problems. The Ghilzais under Asmatullah Khan were reported to be massing for attack near Jagdalak and the news of the Afghan successes around Kabul was beginning to unsettle the tribes all along the Khyber line. Bright pointed out to Army Headquarters that if Arbuthnot's brigade moved to Kabul there would then be no troops between there and Landi Kotal. He pressed for a further division to be mobilized and deployed on the lines of communications before Arbuthnot moved to Kabul. Army Headquarters had already acted on the news from Kabul and the troops previously warned for service at Peshawar were set in motion. Behind them the 8th Hussars were ordered to Lahore, together with the 1st Gurkhas and the remaining elements of the 2nd and 4th Gurkhas. Thus the equivalent of a brigade of cavalry, a brigade of infantry with three batteries of artillery was moving towards the frontier as reinforcements.

Gough had concentrated the major part of his brigade at Jagdalak, forty miles from Kabul, by 16 December, but he could go no further. The telegraph wire on both sides of him had been cut, hostile concentrations of Ghilzais occupied the hills around him and he was under intermittent long-range sniping. He had available only 1,030 infantry (including sappers), 229 cavalry and four mountain guns, and he was short of transport and small-arms ammunition. It seemed madness to him to try to force his way through to Kabul with such a tiny force. Even if he got to Kabul, communications with the rest of Bright's force could not be maintained with the number of troops available. No one could accuse Gough of lacking personal courage, but in the situation in which he found himself he was reluctant to hazard his force. Bright ordered him to stay where he was while the situation was explained to Roberts. While waiting for Roberts's reply, Gough was reinforced by a detachment under Colonel Norman, bringing his total strength up to some 2,100.

It was evident that the forces on the Khyber line of communications were inadequate. Hitherto, for economic as well as political reasons, the Government of India had been reluctant to increase the forces already deployed in the campaign,

---

*It is an illustration of the spontaneous and unco-ordinated nature of the uprising that the telegraph line out of Kabul was not cut for several days after 11 December. The Butkak garrison managed to get back unopposed to Sherpur on the 14th.

but on 21 December, it bowed to further pressure from the Commander-in-Chief and authorized the formation of a second (Reserve) division at Peshawar, under Major-General John Ross, for operations on the Khyber line. To form it, it was necessary to bring up two Madras native infantry regiments and a regiment of the Hyderabad Contingent. The troops already at Peshawar were now gradually pushed up the Khyber line, but it would obviously take time before the effects were felt at the head of the line, at Jagdalak.

On the same day (21 December), Gough had taken the plunge and set out for Kabul. Roberts's reply to Bright had arrived the day before, gallantly carried by an Indian NCO of the 28th Bengal Native Infantry since neither the telegraph or the heliograph was working. It was peremptory: 'Order Gough to advance without delay. This order is imperative and must be obeyed. There is nothing to stop him.' The messenger brought news that the Latabad garrison was on half rations and had supplies for only another two days. At the same time, Gough received three signals from Bright, telling him that he was not to advance on Kabul if there were any risk of a repulse or of his having to abandon his links back to Gandamak. In face of these conflicting orders, Gough did not hesitate. Judging that Roberts and the Lataband garrison were in real trouble, he decided to advance. After leaving garrisons at Jagdalak, Jagdalak Kotal and Pezwan, he had left only some 1,400 men, with four mountain guns.* At Lataband he could pick up the garrison of some 900 men and he hoped to link up there with troops which Roberts had promised to send out to help him in to Sherpur. Nevertheless, it was a perilous enterprise. The problems were compounded by the inevitable paucity of sound transport. Everything that could stagger had to be pressed into service, but it was obvious that many of the animals could not reach Kabul or even Lataband. Gough's instructions were bleak; when it became necessary, tentage would be destroyed first, followed by the rest of the baggage; food and ammunition were to be abandoned only in extremity.

The force reached Seh Baba, ten miles on from Jagdalak, on the afternoon of 21 December, with most of its transport still intact. On the following morning, it set out for Lataband, ten miles further on. Conditions were harsh with snow on the ground, fog and low cloud, and temperatures close to freezing point. Between Seh Baba and Lataband, the transport animals laid down and died in droves; many of those that survived had to abandon their loads. The endless delays caused by the need to redistribute loads and to destroy what had to be abandoned meant that the rearguard did not reach Lataband until nearly midnight.

The Lataband garrison, under Colonel Hudson, 28th BNI, was itself in difficult straits through lack of food and fuel and it had little transport. More equipment had to be abandoned by Gough's troops in order to spare animals for Hudson. At Lataband, however, Gough found the 12th Bengal Cavalry, under Major J. H. Green, which Roberts had dispatched in the early hours of that morning to make contact with the brigade. Green had been ordered to halt at Butkak if it were

---

*10th Bengal Lancers	26
2/9th Foot	500
72nd Highlanders	46
2nd and 4th Gurkhas	788
No. 5 Company Bengal Sappers and Miners	76
Total	1,436

unoccupied by the enemy and the inhabitants appeared friendly; if not, he was to press on to Lataband. Green's ride through hostile country, in darkness and snow, was as hair-raising an enterprise as any during the war. Almost immediately after leaving Sherpur the column was fired on and the alarm given to the surrounding tribesmen. In consequence, the bridge across the River Kabul was blocked and the regiment had to ford the river. The banks were steep and slippery and men and horses fell backwards trying to clamber out. It took two hours for the regiment to cross the river and a number of horses were drowned, leaving the dismounted sowars to make their own, perilous way back to Sherpur. Butkak proved to be occupied by several hundred tribesmen who fired on the regiment as it tried to by-pass the village; at one point the rear squadron had to be dismounted to try to hold off the enemy with carbine fire. Green finally reached Lataband with the loss of three men killed, three wounded and twelve missing, of whom ten ultimately turned up at Sherpur, having had to hide up by day and move by night.

With Green's regiment and Hudson's men, Gough's strength had now risen to some 2,700. As the force moved out on the morning of 23 December it could hear heavy firing from the direction of Kabul. It is not difficult to imagine the thoughts which must have been running through the minds of every man in Gough's column. Were they too late? Was Roberts being overwhelmed even as they struggled to reach him? And if the Afghans had destroyed Roberts, what hope could there be for them? Nevertheless, they pressed on. Butkak, which the cavalry advance guard reached at 11.00 hours, proved to be deserted. From there Gough was able to heliograph Sherpur asking for further orders. He must have been enormously relieved when his message was acknowledged, but no orders followed so he sent a further message, saying that he would carry on to the River Logar, the last significant obstacle before Sherpur, and communicate again there. The reply from Sherpur was cut off by cloud almost as soon as it began, but the exchange of signals showed that some portion at least of Roberts's force still hung on at Sherpur. At the bridge over the river, empty fortifications showed that the Afghans had intended to dispute Gough's passage just as he had feared. He was now only six miles from Sherpur, but the Siah Sang hills cut him off from direct sight or sound of the cantonment. It was now early afternoon, and by the time he had concentrated his troops and transport, it was too late to press on to Sherpur, so the brigade encamped where it was. Gough's anxiety was relieved later that night by a messenger who sneaked into camp with a message from MacGregor. MacGregor reported that there had been heavy fighting and Kabul and the surrounding villages were still in Afghan hands; Gough was to move into Sherpur as early as possible the next morning.

It began to snow during the night and it was still snowing when Gough began the final stage of his advance. In dense fog his men groped their way round the eastern edge of the Siah Sang towards Sherpur through an ominously silent, deserted country. A mile from Sherpur they met a patrol of the 12th Lancers – then Roberts himself. The march was over and the disaster which had threatened every inch of the way had been avoided. Gough had shown great courage and initiative in undertaking the march and the Commander-in-Chief did no more than justice in recording his 'high appreciation of the very able and satisfactory manner in which Brigadier-General Gough conducted this extremely difficult operation', and in calling attention to the conduct of the troops who had had such an anxious, arduous march through hostile country in the depths of the bitter Afghan winter.

The hazardous nature of Gough's position is underlined by Asmatullah Khan's fierce attack on the Jagdalak Kotal garrison on the 23rd. The post, greatly strengthened since previous night attacks, was now manned by some 260 troops, mainly Bengal Sappers and Miners. Although the Ghilzais got to within 150 yards, the defenders were able to maintain their position until relieved from Jagdalak Fort next morning.*

To see Gough's advance in its true perspective we need to look at what had been happening at Sherpur after the disastrous events of 14 December. The situation which faced Roberts on the evening of that day was serious. After four days of continuous fighting, he had failed to disperse the Afghan forces under Mohammed Jan, now swollen by thousands of tribesmen from Kabul and the surrounding districts, scenting victory. Having failed to defeat Mohammed Jan in the open, Roberts's troops now had no option but to sit tight behind their defences and hope either for relief or for an all-out attack.

The Cantonment at Sherpur was to have enclosed an enormous square, having a perimeter of about five miles and taking in the Bimaru Heights to the north (map 9). In December 1879 only the south and part of the west wall were complete. The south face was approximately a mile and a half long; a massive wall, sixteen feet high, pierced at intervals of about 700 yards by three gateways protected by large circular bastions. Between the gateways, the wall was studded with smaller, semi-circular bastions from which flanking fire could be directed against an approaching enemy. At each end was another massive circular bastion. The west wall was very similar, but only about 1,000 yards long, finishing level with the western end of the Bimaru Heights. It had been damaged by an explosion in October just before it was occupied by the British. The east wall had been planned on similar lines, but was incomplete, being nowhere higher than seven feet and lacking bastions. It was only some 700 yards long and finished well short of the eastern end of the Bimaru Heights. The whole of the rear or northern face lay open.

To make the cantonment defensible, it was essential to fortify the line of the Bimaru Heights, and to connect it to the ends of the eastern and western walls. Plans for this had been prepared in November, but although a limited amount of work had been done, the scheme as a whole had been postponed in favour of building winter shelter for the native troops and accumulating supplies. Nothing had yet been done to clear the villages and walled enclosures close to the eastern, southern and western faces, which provided excellent cover for attackers, because Roberts was reluctant to stir up hostility among the local population by large-scale demolition.

The bulk of the garrison was now set to work in earnest, filling in the gaps in the defences. A number of mud towers had already been built on the Bimaru Heights; these were now connected by a continuous line of breastworks just below the crest, and strengthened at intervals by gun emplacements. The centre of the Heights was pierced by a gorge which provided a rear entrance to the cantonment; this was now

---

*Nevertheless, many in Roberts's force clearly thought that Gough could have come more quickly and it may be significant that in due course Gough was omitted from the Kandahar relief force, his place being taken by MacGregor who was promoted for the purpose.

Map 9 Plan of Sherpur

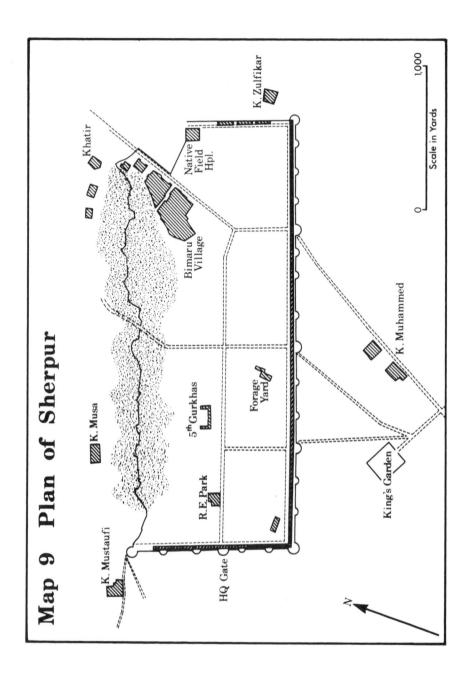

K. Zulfikar

Khatir

Native Field Hpl.

Bimaru Village

K. Musa

K. Muhammed

5th Gurkhas

Forage Yard

R.E.Park

King's Garden

K. Mustaufi

HQ Gate

N

Scale in Yards

1,000

0

flanked with trenches and dominated by a blockhouse. The gap at the north-western corner of the cantonment was closed by a deep ditch backed by a wall of captured gun carriages and limbers and strengthened with wire and timber entanglements. The major part of the work was concentrated on the gap in the north-eastern corner. Here, a small fort, which had been used as a hospital for Indian troops, was sandbagged and strengthened; Bimaru village was loopholed and the eastern end of the Heights connected to the eastern wall by a continuous line of wire and timber entanglements. The southern and western walls needed little work except the barricading of the gateways, the blocking up of various unofficial entrances and the provision of ramps and ladders to provide better access to the tops of the walls.

The available artillery consisted of twelve 9-pounder field guns, eight 7-pounder mountain guns and two Gatlings, together with four Afghan 18-pounders and two 8-inch howitzers which had been found at Sherpur and pressed into service. Four Afghan mountain guns were also deployed, but their ammunition was so unreliable that their value was nil. Two of the 18-pounders and a Gatling were positioned on the southern side of the Bimaru Heights to sweep the face of the defences in the north-west corner. A two-gun battery at the eastern end of the Heights carried out the same function for the north-eastern corner defences. The remainder of the guns were disposed in pairs in the circular bastions along the southern wall and along the line of entrenchments on the Heights, with four field guns in reserve. The guns were fairly well-supplied with ammunition and the infantry had 350 rounds per man, but it was necessary to issue stringent instructions against waste. The last steps were to connect up the various faces of the cantonment by telegraph, and to level a number of buildings and enclosures outside the walls in order to give clearer fields of fire.

All that remained then was to distribute the troops round the defences and to sit tight to await relief or attack. Roberts had available some 7,000 men, excluding sick, to man a perimeter of some 8,000 yards. Some calculated risk might be taken in thinning-out troops along the southern and western walls which were the strongest parts of the defences, but the numbers of troops available was still very small, especially since certain parts of the defences along the eastern face were extremely weak. Indeed, until all the additional work had been done, there is little doubt that Mohammed Jan's forces could have overrun the cantonment with relative ease; by leaving the British undisturbed the Afghans had forfeited a major chance of victory. On the credit side, the cantonment had its own water supplies and Roberts had devoted considerable efforts to amassing stocks of supplies and fuel. Ample stocks of firewood had been found in Sherpur and Roberts calculated that he had food and ammunition for four months. All that he was short of was forage of which he had only some six weeks' supply. It was thus unlikely that he could be starved out; long before then he could expect to have been relieved by Bright. Contrarily, Mohammed Jan would face increasing difficulty in keeping his forces together in the depths of winter. The real dangers lay in a massive attack breaking through the perimeter by sheer weight of numbers or, alternatively, in a series of attacks which exhausted the supplies of ammunition.

Roberts divided his perimeter into five sectors:
1. Macpherson, with detachments of 92nd Highlanders, 67th Foot and 28th Native Infantry, No. 7 Company Bengal Sappers and Miners and four guns held the east wall and the eastern half of the south wall.
2. Colonel Brownlow held the remainder of the south wall and half of the west wall with 72nd Highlanders and two guns.
3. Major-General Hills held the remaining half of the west wall and the western half of the Bimaru Heights as far as the gorge, with 5th Punjab Infantry, 3rd Sikhs, 5th Gurkhas, two guns and a Gatling.
4. Hugh Gough held the remainder of the Bimaru Heights with 23rd Pioneers.
5. Colonel Jenkins with the Guides held the north-eastern angle defences linking Gough's section with Macpherson's.

Baker commanded the reserve which was located opposite the end of the gorge through the Bimaru Heights, and Massy with the cavalry guarded the stores of food and forage in the middle of the cantonment. Roberts himself exercised overall control from the so-called Headquarters Gate in the middle of the west wall – oddly, because there he was as far away as he could be from the weakest section of the defences, along the eastern perimeter. He was, however, linked by telegraph to the sector commanders and to Baker.

Mohammed Jan had his own problems. It was always difficult to keep large assemblies of tribesmen together for very long periods, and, despite heavily outnumbering Roberts's force, the Afghan general possessed neither the disciplined manpower, the equipment nor the heavy artillery to conduct formal siege operations.

For the first two days of the siege, the British force was occupied in strengthening the Sherpur defences, but on 17 December, the cavalry moved out to patrol around the perimeter. This was the signal for huge masses of the enemy to gather on the Asmai and Siah Sang Heights, where they were shelled and dispersed by the guns inside Sherpur, but Roberts was too weak in numbers to risk a more general engagement. The following day, the troops were continuously occupied around Sherpur preventing parties of the enemy getting close up under the walls; some of the Bengal Sappers and Miners levelled enclosures nearby to give a better field of fire. That evening, it started to snow hard. Although there was plenty of firewood available inside Sherpur, little could be done to alleviate the cold and exposure for the sentries on the walls. 'At ten o'clock I visited the bastions held by the 72nd Highlanders, and gained some idea of the work our men are called upon to do. The sentries in their greatcoats were simply white figures standing rigidly up like ghosts, the snowflakes softly covering them from head to foot and freezing as they fell . . .'[5] The Afghan sharpshooters could retire each evening to the warmth of Kabul and the surrounding villages, but Roberts's men could not afford to relax their vigilance. Rumours of impending night attacks added to the strain which began to take toll of the defenders who were already barely adequate to cover the vast perimeter. It was the fear of his force simply wasting away through exposure and sickness which underlay Roberts's peremptory message on 20 December to Charles Gough, ordering him to advance without delay.*

---

*With the telegraph cut, Roberts was dependent upon the heliograph link with Lataband, which in turn depended upon the weather. Thus it was not until the 18th that Roberts learned that Gough was still at Jagdalak.

Roberts had other worries on his mind. He had with him in Sherpur, Daud Shah, Habibullah Khan and other Afghan Sirdars and, deeply distrustful as he was of all Afghans, he was acutely conscious of the potential security risk. If Hanna, who was present as Staff Officer to Hugh Gough, is to be believed, there were fears also about the presence in vital positions at each end of the Bimaru Heights defences of native regiments which contained high proportions of Pathan sepoys. There were also worries about the enormous quantities of combustible stores and ammunition (much of it captured from the Afghans themselves) lying about inside the cantonments.

Although there was no suggestion of any treachery by the sirdars, Roberts took the prudent precaution of confining them under guard. Similarly, although there was no hint of treachery among the native regiments, they were quietly buttressed by the addition of four companies of Highlanders. The arrival of the snow helped to solve the problem of the inflammable stores and supplies.

Having summoned Gough's brigade to join him from Gandamak, there was little that Roberts could do until he arrived. A sortie of 800 men under Baker to destroy the fort of Kila Mir Akbar, east of Sherpur, the dispatch of two convoys of supplies escorted by friendly Hazaras to Hudson at Lataband,* and the threat of a serious attack on the 21st were the main events to break this period of anxious waiting. The news from the enemy camp suggested that while there was dissension between the Ghilzais and the Kohistanis as to who was to rule Afghanistan – the former favouring Yakub Khan, the latter his old rival, Wali Mohammed – both factions remained united in their determination to expel the British.[6] Hensman states that at this juncture Mohammed Jan sent formal terms of capitulation to Roberts; these specified the evacuation of all British troops from Afghanistan, the restoration of Yakub Khan and the surrender of two senior British officers as hostages against the implementation of the terms.[7] This is a mysterious affair. Roberts made no reference to it at the time of his telegrams and dispatches, or later in his memoirs; nor does MacGregor mention in his diary. From Roberts's point of view, the receipt of such proposals involved no discredit, and their apparent rejection could only redound to his credit. Hensman is normally an extremely reliable witness and was possessed of excellent contacts with Roberts's own staff; there is no apparent reason for him to have invented the story, and the reported terms have an inherent plausibility. It may be that the proposals reported by Hensman were indeed discussed in the Afghan camp and duly reported by spies to Roberts, but that since they were not made formally to him by the Afghan leaders he ignored them. Even if they had been put to him formally, it is inconceivable that he would have considered them; the precedents from 1841 were not encouraging.

The unstable situation around Kabul was resolved by Gough's departure from Jagdalak. News of it must have reached Mohammed Jan within a matter of hours from the Ghilzai tribesmen who watched every yard of Gough's march. Although the reinforcements which Gough was bringing with him were too few to change significantly the physical balance of forces at Kabul, the very boldness of the move was enough to tip the psychological balance in the Afghan camp in favour of an

---

*One convoy got through; one was captured and the escorting Hazaras were presumably killed.

immediate assault. During the course of 22 December, Roberts was warned by the servant of one of his cavalry rissalders that an assault was planned for the early hours of the next morning, the signal being the lighting of a bonfire on the Asmai Heights by the Mushk-i-Alam himself. There would be a demonstration attack against the south wall, followed by the main attack against Bimaru village and the east wall; if this were successful, the attack on the south wall would be renewed.

An hour before dawn, the British troops stood to their arms. The scene was described by Hanna who was present.

'In strained expectation, confident of ultimate victory, yet conscious that a life-or-death struggle lay before him, every man's eyes were turned towards the west, watching for the predicted signal; yet when it came, so brilliant, so dazzling was the light that burst forth from the Asmai Heights that, for an instant, men's hearts stood still with astonishment and awe. All saw that light and some fragment of the scene revealed by it, but the watchers on the Behmaru ridge saw all that it disclosed, and never did soldiers gaze upon a more glorious, a more terrible spectacle. At their feet – every nook and corner of the vast enclosure, every defensive work, every group of defenders, clearly visible – lay the cantonments, and beyond, across the snow-clad valley, dotted with villages and forts, every seam and ruck on the rugged, precipitous Asmai Heights shone out as if traced by a pencil of fire, and on those heights, their figures dark against the snow below and the light above, men – watchers and waiters like those who now beheld them – were just starting into fierce motion, ready to throw away their lives in the endeavour to break through the obstacles that lay between them and their hated foe.'[8]

From Kohistan, from Maidan, from the Logar valley, from Wardak, the tribes-men had flocked in to join the inhabitants of Kabul and its surrounding villages and the regular Afghan troops. From the east, the Ghilzais who had been besieging Hudson at Lataband and preparing to resist Gough's crossing of the River Logar had come to join the attack on Sherpur. The Afghans had perceived that this was their supreme opportunity to destroy Roberts's force. Roberts himself estimated the enemy numbers at 60,000, and even if this were an overestimate it is clear that the garrison was outnumbered several times over. The Afghans could, moreover, concentrate their attack. Against the sheer weight of this attack, the defenders must rely upon the advantages of fixed defences and discipline.

The attack was spearheaded by *ghazis*, religious fanatics who were prepared to throw away their lives with reckless abandon, secure in the knowledge that a place in Paradise awaited those who died for the Faith. The guns on the Bimaru Heights fired star shell to illuminate the ground in front of the eastern defences and, using the illumination thus given, the Martini-Henry and Snider volleys began to crash out with relentless precision, while the British artillery scourged the attackers with case-shot and high explosive. Spasmodically, the rattle of a Gatling gun added to the general din. Daylight saw the attack raging unabated. By now it was general around three sides of the perimeter, only the defences along the Bimaru Heights being left alone. But it was against the eastern perimeter that it was pressed home hardest.

This was defended by some of the most reliable of Roberts's troops – the Guides, 28th BNI, 92nd Highlanders and 67th Foot – but at about 09.00 hours, some three hours after the fighting had started, the Afghans succeeded in occupying a position very close to the eastern end of the Heights, opposite the gap between the Heights and Bimaru village. Gough signalled for reinforcements, but was told that he must hold on at all costs since the attack was now general against most of the perimeter and Roberts had too few reserves to risk using them up in one sector. At about 09.30 hours Baker was directed to release a few men from the reserve to assist Gough and Jenkins, and Hills, whose sector alone was virtually untouched, released a wing of the 3rd Sikhs. At about 10.00 hours, the attack slackened and when it was resumed an hour later it was not pressed home with the same determination as earlier. As yet unperceived by the British, some of the tribal contingents, including the large force from Kohistan, had begun to retire, having obviously concluded with the volatility which is characteristic of the Pathan that the attack had failed.*

Roberts, displaying that sense of timing which is the mark of the born tactical commander, now ordered four guns of G/3, RA, escorted by 5th Punjab Cavalry, to move out through the gorge in the Bimaru Heights to bring flanking fire to bear on the position gained by the Afghans near the eastern end of the Heights. Deprived of the flank protection which the retreating Kohistanis should have provided, the Afghans began to evacuate this position. Just after midday, Roberts, sensing that the turning-point had arrived, dispatched the remainder of the cavalry under Massy through the gorge, followed by Baker with the Sappers and Miners, part of the 92nd Highlanders, 3rd Sikhs and two guns. Leaving Baker to sweep through the villages and enclosures east and south-east of the cantonment, Massy sent the 14th Bengal Lancers northwards to block the road to Kohistan (although it was too late to intercept the retreating Kohistanis), and the Guides Cavalry to block the road to Butkak; the 5th Punjab Cavalry and the 9th Lancers were dispatched round the eastern end of the cantonment to occupy the roads leading southwards to Kabul.

By now the Afghan forces were in full retreat and the 67th Foot were able to move out of the eastern defences and co-operate in destroying nearby villages and forts, while the 5th Punjab Infantry attacked and occupied temporarily Kila Mahomed Sharif, south of the cantonment, which had been a particular nuisance throughout the siege. Throughout the afternoon, the work of dislodging the enemy from positions around the cantonment went on. The work appears to have been pursued with grim severity. No quarter was given: 'All stragglers were hunted down in the nullahs in which they took shelter, and then dispatched. Two or three lancers or sowars were told off to each straggler, and the men, dismounting, used their carbines when the unlucky Afghan had been hemmed in.'[9] Hanna thought that it recalled the days of the Mutiny when no quarter was given to rebels. Late in the afternoon, the troops were recalled and manned the perimeter of the cantonment as before, but the immediate cloud of anxiety and uncertainty which had hung over the garrison had been dispersed. The Afghans had made a supreme effort, they had fought long and bitterly and had suffered very heavy losses. The reaction which followed their defeat was therefore all the more severe and it was clear that the great tribal combination could not be brought together again for some considerable time to come. In the meantime, the British could only grow

*Charles Gough's advance may also have played a part.

stronger. The point was driven home when Charles Gough marched unopposed into Sherpur early the next morning.

In his subsequent dispatch the Afghan losses were reckoned by Roberts at 3,000 and this was probably not far wrong. Despite the ferocity of the assault, the British losses were tiny, totalling five killed and 28 wounded. Attackers and defenders alike had exhibited great gallantry and courage and the completeness of the Afghan repulse ought not to obscure the fact that the issue hung in the balance for the best part of three hours. If the Afghans could have penetrated the perimeter in force at even one point, the garrison must have been overwhelmed by sheer weight of numbers. In retrospect, it is clear that, failing a formal siege attack on classical lines, the Afghans' best chance of success lay in sitting it out and relying upon attrition to wear down the garrison's strength. The size and shape of Sherpur was such that there was no alternative to defending the whole perimeter, large as it was; if the garrison could not do that, it was doomed. But attrition tactics demanded a discipline and cohesion which the Afghans did not possess.

The full magnitude of the victory on the 23rd was not immediately apparent and that evening Roberts was considering plans for capturing the Bala Hissar and clearing the enemy out of Kabul itself. But on the following morning, to his enormous relief, he discovered that, 'The great tribal combination had dissolved, and that not a man of the many thousands who had been opposed to us the previous day remained in any of the villages or on the surrounding hills.'[10] Kabul and the Bala Hissar were quickly re-occupied. The Afghan insurgents had done a good deal of damage to the houses of British sympathizers and to the Bala Hissar from which all ammunition had disappeared. While Charles Gough's brigade re-occupied the city, Hugh Gough with half the cavalry was dispatched westwards via the Nanachi Pass into the Chardeh plain, and Massy with the other half south-wards via the Sang-i-Nawishta gorge, to harry the retreating tribal forces. But a snowstorm destroyed any chance of success and Mohammed Jan and the Mushk-i-Alam with the young, newly proclaimed Amir, Musa Jan, easily made good their escape to Ghazni.

A sombre aftermath of Roberts's victory was the immediate re-establishment of the Military Commission under Massy to punish Afghans caught under arms. But before we return to its further activities, it is necessary to look briefly at what had been happening elsewhere in Afghanistan. At Kandahar, following the return of Hughes' brigade from Kalat-i-Ghilzai, a period of almost total inactivity set in. Apart from the occasional fishing and shooting expeditions, there was little for the troops to do, and boredom and frustration were the order of the day. Stewarts' force was too weak in numbers and too far away to attempt any move which could be of significant assistance to Roberts at Kabul. In the absence of an active military role, the presence of the troops at Kandahar was primarily an element in the political game which Lytton and his colleagues were engaged in playing in the endeavour to achieve an acceptable system of government for Afghanistan. The British and Indian Governments had agreed upon a policy of splitting up Afghanistan, with Kandahar as an independent state under British domination. For this purpose, British troops would need to be based permanently within effective striking distance of Kandahar itself. In turn, this demanded good communications from India. In October 1879 construction started on a railway line from the Indus to Sibi, at the foot of the Baluchistan mountains. Extension to Quetta and even Kandahar was an obvious move and by the end of the year it had been agreed that the extension should run via Harnai to Gwal in the Pishin valley, since the more obvious route up the Bolan Pass was prone to floods and snow blockages.

Towards the end of December Lytton agreed that the Bengal troops in Southern Afghanistan should be replaced by troops from the Bombay Army. The Bengal force thus relieved could then move on Ghazni, if the situation required it, or return to India. As a first step, Brigadier-General Phayre's Bombay brigade, on the lines of communication, would be moved up to occupy Quetta and Pishin, while the Bombay reserve brigade, quartered along the Indus under Brigadier-General Burrows, should take the place of Phayre's troops on the lines of communication. A reserve division of Bombay troops was to form at Jacobabad. There for the moment we may leave the Kandahar force, beset with boredom but now with an early prospect of release.

With the departure of Roberts from Ali Khel at the end of September 1879, en route for Kabul, the Kurram valley was effectively cut off from the main stream of the war, a point which was driven home when the Shutagardan Pass was evacuated following the attacks on it in the middle of October. In these circumstances, it was questionable whether the Kurram should not be evacuated altogether. It was of no economic importance, it tied down substantial numbers of troops, and it brought the Indian Government into further conflict with the tribes, notably the Zaimukhts and Mangals.

On 14 October, while Money at the Shutagardan Pass was engaged in extremely critical fighting, the garrison at Ali Khel was repulsing a heavy attack by Mangals and Jajis. No sooner had this crisis disappeared than Balas Khel, further back in the Kurram valley, commanding the main route into Zaimukht territory to the east, was threatened by a body of some 3,000 tribesmen. Faced with these difficulties, Brigadier-General Gordon, commanding in the Kurram, was unable to assist Money despite the latter's critical situation. The evacuation of the Shutagardan and the return of the 21st BNI to the Kurram eased matters, but the problems were still serious and, at Gordon's insistence, the post at Ali Khel was also given up;* the Peiwar Kotal now marked the effective limit of the British advance in the Kurram.

Within the valley, the problem of the Zaimukhts remained. The opening of the new and principal road up the east bank of the River Kurram, close to Zaimukht territory, had increased temptation as far as the tribesmen were concerned. The list of convoys attacked and stragglers murdered grew continuously. The murder of Surgeon Smyth in June 1879 had already led to a decision in principle to mount a punitive expedition against that tribe. The murder of Lieutenant Kinloch of the 5th Bengal Cavalry while he was riding between Chapri and Mundari on 29 September precipitated matters and Brigadier-General Tytler was ordered to prepare an expedition. A proclamation was issued, listing the various misdeeds of the Zaimukhts, warning other tribes against giving them help and setting out the

---

*Lytton complained bitterly to Haines about Gordon's alarmism and general jitteryness. The latter was accordingly replaced in general command of the Kurram by Brigadier-General Watson early in November.

objectives of the expedition, namely, to protect British communications in the Kurram valley and, specifically, to construct a road from Balas Khel to Torawari, in the heart of the Zaimukht country. But Roberts's force had so denuded the Kurram of stores and transport that the Zaimukht expedition could not start until the second week in December. In the interim, a small force under Lieutenant-Colonel Rogers successfully dispersed the tribal gathering threatening Balas Khel, and in a daring raid into Zaimukht territory, Major Davidson and a squadron of the 18th Bengal Cavalry seized twelve men suspected of being involved in a serious attack inside the Kurram. Almost simultaneously, a troop of the 18th Bengal Cavalry led by Risaldar Nadar Ali Khan dispersed a very large assembly of Zaimukhts who were menacing the post at Chapri.

Following a series of careful reconnaissances, Tytler finally moved from Balas Khel on 8 December. The Zaimukhts were expected to be able to put some 3,500 fighting men into the field, and the terrain was a difficult and dangerous one, comprising a series of valleys divided by high, rugged mountains and approached through narrow defiles. The reconnaissances had shown, however, that some of the tribe at least were not prepared to fight and those that were did not possess modern weapons. Nevertheless, Tytler, an experienced frontier soldier, was not prepared to take any chances and his force numbered some 3,200 men with six mountain guns.* With this force, he intended to penetrate to Zawo, the most distant and inaccessible of the valleys, which the Zaimukhts looked upon as impregnable. He reached Chinarak, eight miles from Zawo, with little difficulty on 12 December. Leaving a substantial part of his force to protect Chinarak, an important road junction, he set out on the 13th to attack Zawo, which lay at the head of a ravine some eight miles long which at one point was only some ten feet wide. It took him two days in face of strong opposition, compounded by the exceptional difficulty of the track. Having burned the houses and destroyed the forage, Tytler was back at Chinarak on the 15th.† He then moved eastwards towards the territory of another tribe, the Orakzais, who, despite the proclamation, had mustered in support of the Zaimukhts. Before he could attack them he received an urgent order to break off the operation because his troops were required to make a demonstration towards the Shutagardan Pass to help Roberts who was by now in trouble at Kabul. Tytler was in a difficult position; he could not ignore the urgency of the order to retire, but to do so without securing the submission of both the Zaimukhts and Orakzais would nullify the purpose and results of the expedition, as well as endanger his regiment. He therefore released the 13th BNI and the squadron of the 13th Bengal Cavalry to join the troops in the Kurram, while retaining the rest of the force facing the Orakzais. This firm front did the trick; both the Orakzais and Zaimukhts submitted and by 23 December the force was back at Thal. Losses had been insignificant – two killed and two wounded – but Tytler himself, exhausted by twelve months of hard campaigning, succumbed to an attack of pneumonia some seven weeks later.

---

*85th Light Infantry, 4th Punjab Infantry, 29th BNI, 13th BNI (wing), 20th BNI (wing), 1/8 RA (four guns), No. 1 Mountain Battery (two guns), detachments of 2/8th Foot, 1st, 13th and 18th Bengal Cavalry, half No. 8 Company Bengal Sappers and Miners – in all, 3,226 men.
†The attack on Zawo was assisted by the accurate fire of 1/8 RA's new 7-pounder jointed guns (Kipling's famous 'screw guns'), making their appearance in action for the first time.

The conclusion of the Zaimukht expedition offered an excellent opportunity to withdraw from the Kurram valley. Watson, who had succeeded Gordon in overall command in the Kurram, recommended evacuation. Service there was both unpopular and unhealthy as far as the native regiments were concerned. The 1st Bengal NI, for example, had 250 men in hospital or on sick leave; the 21st BNI had 200. Potential recruits were refusing to join these regiments while they were stationed there. Contrary to the opinion which Roberts had expressed at the conclusion of the first Kurram campaign, the weight of senior military and political judgement was now in favour of evacuating the valley and relying upon the Khyber route as the main line of communication with Kabul. But Lytton himself was reluctant to abandon the route on which he and Roberts had placed such store, and the Kurram continued to absorb large numbers of troops until the end of the war.*

At Kabul, Roberts was determined to avoid being placed in jeopardy a second time. He now had more than 10,000 men available and with these, and civilian labour, he put in hand a very extensive programme of defensive works. Every village and enclosure within a thousand yards of Sherpur was now levelled; a trench and wall were constructed along the entire length of the Bimaru Heights, and the gaps in the defences of Sherpur filled in. Roads to take artillery were laid out around the whole cantonment. Outside Sherpur, a fort to hold half a battalion was constructed at the northern end of the Siah Sang hills, and to the eastwards, the village of Kala Ibrahim Khan was fortified to protect a new, permanent bridge over the River Kabul south of Sherpur. In this way Roberts hoped to prevent any force gathering to attack the south face of Sherpur and to protect communications from Sherpur to the Bala Hissar and to India. To the west, a large fort on the Asmai Heights commanding the Deh-i-Mazang gorge and a series of blockhouses and towers on the Sher Darwaza, above the Bala Hissar, completed the programme. Roberts aimed to hold all the commanding heights around the city, not only to dominate Kabul but to prevent Sherpur from being directly invested. But to hold this ring of fortifications as well as Sherpur required very considerable numbers of troops and in the event of a renewed large-scale attack Roberts would have found it as difficult to defend this extended position with 10,000 men as to defend Sherpur with 7,000. The shrewd and experienced Hindu merchants of Kabul took the same view – 'You want more men if you are to hold Kabul and keep out the enemy. What are ten thousand to fifty thousand? There must be twenty thousand to guard Sherpur and the city.' – and promptly decamped to Peshawar and safety.[11]

Roberts was determined to retain the initiative, and two days after the repulse of the great attack Baker left Sherpur with a force of some 2,000 men and four guns to destroy the villages of Mir Bacha, the Kohistani leader, and to carry off as many supplies as possible. Mir Bacha himself escaped but his villages were levelled, and the vineyards and orchards destroyed. Overawed by this heavy hand, other villages yielded up the supplies demanded by Baker even though this meant hardship and the slaughter of their livestock because there was no longer enough forage to feed

---

*Lytton believed that while a railway through the Kurram as far as the Peiwar Kotal was practicable and relatively easy, a railway through the Khyber was impossible. Today there is still no railway through the Kurram valley whereas a railway through the Khyber was opened in 1925.

it through the rest of the winter. On 31 December, the day after Baker returned, a second expedition left for the Chardeh plain to destroy the village of Bagwana whose inhabitants were thought to have taken an active part in the fighting on 11 December. The village was burned and four headmen taken to Kabul and hanged for alleged complicity in the deaths of Lieutenants Forbes and Hardie. The lines of communication were now re-established, Butkak being re-occupied on the 26th, Seh Baba on the 30th and Lataband on the 31st.

In Kabul, the hangman was again at work. On 26 December, Roberts had issued yet another proclamation, proclaiming an amnesty for all those who submitted quickly, but excepting the Mushk-i-Alam, Mohammed Jan, Mir Bacha, Samander Khan of Logar, Tagir Khan and the undiscovered murderers of Mohammed Hussein Khan, the former British-appointed governor of Maidan; however, anyone who rebelled again would be punished. At the same time, the Military Court was re-established to punish men guilty of offences under the proclamation of 28 October 1879 which forbade, *inter alia*, the carrying of arms in the vicinity of Kabul. In his earlier return, covering the period up to 18 November 1879, when the Court had been wound up for the first time, Roberts showed 49 men as having been executed. In his return of 27 January 1880, he claimed that from first to last, up to 26 December 1879, 87 men had been executed, implying that in the second and final phase of the Military Court's operations 38 men had been hanged.[12] But there is reason to doubt the figure of 87 as the sum total of executions. It clearly does not include ten men executed on 30 December 1879 for being armed when caught during Mohammed Jan's retreat on the 24th, nor the four headmen from Bagwana executed on 3 January 1880. Hensman records in vivid detail the shooting of eight Kohistanis without trial on 13 December 1879, and there may well have been other similar cases.[13] The comment in the Calcutta newspaper *The Englishman* on 12 January 1880 that 'so numerous have these hangings been that they excite but little attention' may well have been superficially true as regards Kabul, although even there officers such as MacGregor were deeply disturbed.[14]

It was certainly not true of the United Kingdom. On 1 December 1879, an article in the influential *Fortnightly Review* by the journalist Frederick Harrison had bitterly and forcefully criticized the trials and executions in Afghanistan. Public interest in the matter was suspended during most of December as the British public followed with bated breath the drama at Sherpur, but once that was over, public anxiety re-asserted itself. A meeting of the Peace Society on 29 December called upon people to 'repudiate a system of terrorism which could only find a parallel in the worst times of Barbarian conquest', and Henry Spurgeon, the famous Baptist preacher, used similar colourful language four days later. More to the point, a number of politicians, including Lord Ripon, began during January to attack with increasing fierceness the whole justification and conduct of the war. A memorial, signed by many of the leading men of the day, including John Morley, Joseph Chamberlain, the historian, J. A. Froude, the Bishops of Oxford and Exeter and the Duke of Westminster, was sent to the Prime Minister, calling for an end to the invasion of Afghanistan. Harrison weighed in with a second article, criticizing in detail the operation of martial law at Kabul.

Roberts and the Government of India were by now seriously disturbed by the agitation. In a letter dated 10 January 1880 which was read to both Houses of

Parliament, Roberts claimed that no one had been executed simply for fighting against the British, and that his measures were essential for the safety of his force. On 6 February 1880, *The Times* published a telegram from Roberts's orderly officer, claiming that no one had been executed unless convicted of being involved in the attack on Cavagnari's mission. That was patently untrue and it was clearly necessary now for a more considered official report. Roberts's report of 27 January 1880 reached the War Office only on 12 March. Significantly, it was forwarded by the Government of India without comment. It lists in detail the 87 men claimed to have been executed up to 26 December 1879.[15] Quite apart from the total number executed, the report was inaccurate on the number of villages burned, omitting in particular the village of Beni Badam burned by Baker on 28 November 1879. What is particularly interesting is the apologia which Roberts advanced in the report. He cited three justifications for the imposition of martial law.

1. It benefited the Afghans themselves since it provided peace and order.
2. It was necessary in order to control the natural Afghan fanaticism.
3. By banning the carrying of arms on pain of death, it had led to an absence of attacks on British troops.

Specifically Roberts claimed that no one had been executed solely for fighting at Charasiab, but only if he had been involved in the attack on the Residency as well. But he also claimed that the mere possession of mission property was justification for assuming the person's presence at the attack. He went on finally to claim that to question the good faith and integrity of Massy's Military Court meant discrediting all military courts.

Roberts's report closely reflected advice which he had been receiving privately from Lytton. The latter advised Roberts not to attempt to justify executions on the ground that anyone who fought against the British was a rebel against the Amir; in Lytton's view, that argument simply was not tenable. Instead, he counselled Roberts to justify his actions by reference to the need to safeguard his force, isolated in the heart of hostile country, an argument which he thought could hardly fail.[16] Roberts also had the benefit of Lepel Griffin's literary skill in drafting his defence.[17]

The report was received in London less than a fortnight before Parliament was dissolved. In the General Election which followed, Gladstone and the Liberals were swept into power. In the excitement of replacing old policies and men with new, the executions at Kabul, having played their part in the Conservative defeat, were quietly forgotten.

It is difficult now to reach an accurate, unbiased view. Roberts himself was undoubtedly acting on the instructions of the Government of India, issued in the emotional atmosphere which followed Cavagnari's death. Those instructions, backed up by Lytton's private admonitions, required him not only to punish individuals swiftly, sternly and impressively, but to regard the Afghan nation as collectively responsible and to consider some formal act of retribution against the city of Kabul itself either by way of a fine or by demolishing the Bala Hissar.[18] Like any military commander, Roberts had a duty to ensure the security of his troops in hostile territory. On a deeper level, it would be foolish not to recognize that in most British eyes at that time the Afghans ranked as savages – alongside Zulus,

Maoris, Burmese, Ashantis and, in due course, Fuzzy-Wuzzies and Dervishes – in whose case the sanctity of human life was considered a good deal less important than in the case of Europeans. Swift, harsh justice, involving the execution of prisoners as a warning or in retribution, was therefore both relatively common-place and unremarkable in 'colonial' campaigns. In India, moreover, this attitude was powerfully influenced by memories of the Mutiny only twenty years earlier. Nevertheless, the number and nature of the executions at Kabul is not easily paralleled in nineteenth-century British colonial warfare, and the strength of the agitation in England was evidence of a public consciousness that things had been allowed to go too far. Despite Roberts's assertions, it is difficult to believe that there was any strong proof against many of the men executed for their alleged participation in the attack on the mission. There must be a strong suspicion that many were hanged simply for opposing the British or as an example to others. Stewart at Kandahar disapproved publicly of executing men simply for fighting against the British and this condemnation particularly upset Roberts. Abdurrahman never forgave Roberts for the executions.[19]

It is necessary finally to look at events along the lines of communication. The move of Charles Gough's brigade, coupled with the news of Roberts's plight at Kabul, set off a series of determined attacks on the detachments left behind. On 23 December, the day of the great attack on Sherpur, some 3,000 Ghilzais under the persistent Asmatullah Khan attacked the garrison at the Jagdalak Pass, but were repulsed after eight hours fighting, for the loss of two killed and two wounded. On the following day, two posts near the Charagali Pass, four miles south-east of Ali Boghan, were attacked but without significant loss. Five days later, on the 29th, Asmatullah Khan struck again, at the post at Jagdalak itself, but was beaten off with help of reinforcements from Pezwan; on the same day, a small punitive expedition under Lieutenant-Colonel Mackenzie of the 3rd Bengal Cavalry left Jalalabad to punish a group of villages believed to be responsible for the attacks on the Charagali posts. The villages were occupied and hostages taken without incident. By the end of December the situation along the lines of communication had temporarily quietened down. Work was going on to strengthen the various posts and reinforcements were gradually working their way forward from Peshawar. In Simla, Kabul and Kandahar, thoughts could now turn to the shape of the spring campaign.

NOTES

1. Quoted Balfour, op. cit., p. 389.
2. Ibid., p. 383.
3. 'But privately, my impression is that the Kabul executions were unwise and that they may have tended to precipitate the recent hostile combination.' – Lytton to Cranbrook, 31 December 1879. LP 518/4, p. 1143.
4. Balfour, op. cit., p. 394.
5. Hensman, op. cit., p. 238.
6. Mohammed Jan went so far at this time as to proclaim Musa Jan, eldest son of

Yakub, as Amir, and his supporters plundered Wali Mohammed's property in Kabul.
7. Hensman, op. cit., p. 245.
8. Hanna, op. cit., vol. III, pp. 243–4.
9. Hensman, op. cit., pp. 254–5.
10. Roberts, op. cit., vol. II, p. 306.
11. Hanna, op. cit., vol. III, p. 276. See also Hensman's comment: 'It may be a small matter, after all, that these terror-stricken Hindus turn their faces eastwards; but it should be remembered that, all through the

troublous times of the Durani Dynasty, their forefathers, and they themselves, have remained in Kabul, and they are only leaving the city now, because they do not believe in the power of the British to hold it against another army of 50,000 Afghans.' Hensman, op. cit., pp. 292–3.

12. *Dispatch from the Government of India, including a copy of the report of Lieutenant-General Sir Frederick Roberts, KCB, VC, dated Kabul 27 January 1880* – C-2523 (1880).

13. Hensman, op. cit., pp. 228–9.

14. Combe's reaction may well have been widely shared among the officers of the force: 'I have all along been dead against the indiscriminate hanging and shooting of the common prisoners, who merely obeyed orders in fighting us, while the headmen who gave these orders were simply placed under arrest, and it is absurd to call these people "rebels" and "insurgents".' (op. cit., p. 137).

15. A telegram from Roberts dated 23 January 1880 had given 97 executed but this, it was now claimed, included some double-counting.

16. Lytton to Roberts, 5 January 1880. LP 518/6, p. 16.

17. Lytton to Egerton, 4 January 1880. LP 518/6, p. 9.

18. Instructions from Government of India to Roberts, reference A-505 dated 29 September 1879 – *Afghanistan (1880)*, No. 1, pp. 97–99.

19. Roberts's autobiography, *Forty-One Years in India*, virtually ignores the whole subject of the executions, apart from one footnote. Curzon at a later date recorded an extra-ordinary conversation with Abdurrahman in which the latter fantasized about the prospect of Roberts being tried before Parliament for his crimes – a curious but vivid expression of Abdurrahman's bitterness against Roberts. See Curzon, Hon. George, *Letters of Travel*, London, 1923.

CHAPTER 10

A RAM IN A THICKET

'We have found in Abdul Rahman a ram caught in a thicket.'

Lytton to Cranbrook

When the smoke had cleared away from the events of December 1879, it could be seen that the basic situation remained little changed. The British forces controlled the country only as far as the range of their guns, and no comprehensive solution to the problem of who was to rule Afghanistan was in sight. A decision had been taken in favour of splitting up the country, and a ruler of sorts (the Sirdar Sher Ali) had been found for one fragment, Kandahar. But there was no obvious candidate for Kabul and the only solution so far thought up for Herat was to offer it to the Persians. As yet only a small part of the country had been traversed by British troops. Little was known of what went on in Herat and nothing at all about Afghan Turkestan. As in 1841, the British held Kabul but did not control Afghanistan, and in the absence of a stable government to which power could be transferred, they faced a huge and continuing drain in money and troops. The war had already created a deficit on the Indian budget and set back urgently needed reforms and improvements. If this were to continue, there would be a risk of serious native discontent which might threaten the whole fabric of British rule. More immediately serious were the possible effects on the Indian troops themselves. As early as 9 December 1879, Lytton had told Cranbrook, 'I consider that our greatest danger at the present moment (and it is, I think, a very real and imminent one) is the danger of wearing out our native army. I do not think that we can employ native troops for lengthened periods beyond the North-West Frontier without serious risk of injury to their spirit. While they are actually fighting, they will keep in fairly good heart, but what tries and disgusts them is picket and escort duty during the long, dead seasons of trans-frontier service . . .'[1] That did, perhaps, rather less than justice to the Indian soldiers, but it was true that some regiments on active service were finding it difficult to attract recruits, and Stewart made the same point to Ripon a few months later.[2]

In early December the Cabinet had decided on a basic policy of breaking up Afghanistan, but on Lytton's advice it had deferred consideration of the detailed arrangements until the dust had settled around Kabul. Lytton had firmly rejected Afghan requests for the restoration of Yakub, whose abdication was now publicly proclaimed to be irrevocable, but he had assured the Afghans that Britain was willing to recognize anyone else who might be selected by the Afghan people as ruler of Kabul, provided that he was prepared to rule in friendship with the British. In a private letter to Cranbrook, Lytton explained that he would not restore Yakub because the latter had Cavagnari's blood on his hands and could not be trusted to accept the policy of disintegration; even if Yakub did accept this policy, he would be soon swept away by the Afghans themselves.[3] At some point between the end of December 1879 and the beginning of February 1880, Lytton appears to have decided on a policy of scuttle. The first indication of this was the appointment of Lepel Griffin, a member of the Political Department, to take charge at Kabul of all political matters, in close co-operation with Roberts. 'After lengthened consideration', wrote Lytton in his slightly exaggerated way, 'I have come to the conclusion that there is only one man in India who is in all respects completely qualified by personal ability, special official experience, intellectual quickness and tact, general common sense and literary skill, to do for the Government of India what I want done as quickly as possible at Kabul, and that man is Mr Lepel Griffin.' There is some evidence that Griffin and Roberts had not hitherto been on good terms, but they worked together closely and amicably at Kabul. Griffin's formal instructions were not given to him until March, but the essence was conveyed in a letter from Lytton in the middle of February.

> 'I see no reason why you should not, as soon as you reach Kabul, set about the preparation of a way for us out of that rat-trap by making known to all whom such knowledge concerns the cardinal points of our policy viz:
>
> 1st. Non-restoration of the ex-Amir.
>
> 2nd. Permanent severance of Western from North-East Afghanistan [i.e., Kandahar from Kabul].
>
> 3rd. Neither annexation nor permanent occupation of the latter.
>
> 4th. Willingness to recognize any ruler (except Yakub) whom the Afghans themselves will empower to arrange with us on their behalf, for the restoration of their country and its evacuation by our troops.'[4]

Writing to Cranbrook at the same time, Lytton explained that the sole object of the forthcoming spring campaign was to facilitate the early evacuation of the country.[5]

The formal instructions given to Griffin before he left for Kabul set out Lytton's objectives very clearly. They started by stressing the need to settle matters in Afghanistan before the harvest because thereafter the tribes would be restless and free to act against the British forces. Afghanistan must be separated into three or more separate provinces, and it would be necessary to retain a permanent British garrison at, or close to, Kandahar. For Kabul, four courses were theoretically possible – to annex, to occupy indefinitely, to evacuate as quickly as possible or to defer evacuation until a suitable, friendly ruler could be found. The first two courses were unacceptable and even the last course suffered from the fatal defect of lack of finality. Evacuation as fast as possible was thus the preferred solution both because it was in line with previous declarations and because it should lead to a quick overall settlement, relieving the strain on India. Griffin's task therefore was 'to effect the withdrawal of our forces from Afghanistan by next autumn at the latest, making the best political arrangements that circumstances admit for carrying out this withdrawal and for the future administration of the country'. To assist in this, Griffin was authorized to offer the possibility of gifts of money and arms to the new ruler as well as perhaps to some of the leading chiefs. It was admitted that early withdrawal without the certainty of stability was unsatisfactory, but against that it was argued that a great deal had already been achieved in dissipating the Russian threat and in creating peace and security at Kandahar and in Baluchistan.[6]

The defensive note in these instructions and the implicit recognition that speedy evacuation was merely the lesser of a number of evils makes it clear that, behind the bland facade of skilfully drafted argument, we are witnessing Lytton's recognition that his policy had failed. That this recognition owed something to the events of December seems equally obvious. To that extent, the true victors could now be seen to be Mohammed Jan and the Mushk-i-Alam.

Against this background of political expediency, planning was going on for what was intended to be the final military campaign. A major element was the relief of Stewart's Bengal division at Kandahar by Bombay troops, and the subsequent move of the division to Kabul prior to its withdrawal from Afghanistan. As a preliminary, Brigadier-General Phayre's brigade from the Reserve Division on the Indus was ordered forward to Quetta, thus releasing the 3rd Sind Horse, 19th Bengal Native Infantry and 2nd Sikh Infantry to move forward to Kandahar. Behind Phayre, Brigadier-General Burrows, with another brigade from the Reserve Division, moved up to occupy the lower end of the Bolan Pass. These movements were incorporated in the overall plan which the Commander-in-Chief submitted to Lytton early in January 1880. It comprised four main elements:

1. The move of Stewart's Bengal division to Kabul via Ghazni;
2. A march by Roberts's troops at Kabul through Kohistan and Bamian;
3. The move of a force from the Kurram over the Shutagardan Pass to Kabul;
4. Operations by Bright's L of C division against Asmatullah Khan's Ghilzais in the Laghman valley, operations which had had to be postponed when Gough's brigade was summoned to Kabul.

In addition, the Reserve Division at Peshawar was to be ready to operate against the Afridis in the Bara valley, and the Tirah should they give trouble.*

The objectives of this ambitious plan of operations were to consolidate and extend the area of British military dominance and to secure the lines of communications back through the Khyber and Kurram. Stewart's march was the most important element because it would traverse an area which had not hitherto seen British troops and which was, in consequence, the centre of the main opposition movement. Lytton feared that insurrection, still under the nominal leadership of the Mushk-i-Alam, could well revive in the spring. Stewart's move was intended to nip that in the bud. The advances into Kohistan and Bamian were intended to serve the same purpose by overawing areas which had been prominent in anti-British activity, but which had not as yet felt the heavy hand of a British presence.

Stewart and Roberts were asked for their detailed comments and plans. Stewart was perfectly prepared to carry out his part of the operations although he was still unclear as to its precise objectives. He could not move until the necessary Bombay troops had arrived to relieve him at Kandahar and he foresaw in any case great

---

*Much to Lytton's consternation, Haines proposed to take personal charge of the operations, basing himself at Kabul. Lytton had a poor opinion of Haines as a field commander and believed that the Commander-in-Chief was being manipulated by an ambitious Adjutant-General (Lytton to Cranbrook, 16 March 1880 (LP 518/6, pp. 178–183)). Haines was eventually argued out of the idea, but it left some ill-feeling between him and the Viceroy. Lytton's judgement in this case was clearly right.

difficulties in assembling all the necessary transport. Allowing for these factors and the impending onset of the snowy season, he nominated 21 March as the earliest suitable date for the start of his march.

For his part, Roberts was prepared to undertake operations in Kohistan and Bamian. To do so, he would have to evacuate Sherpur because it required too large a garrison and concentrate his troops and stores in a new, entrenched camp on the Siah Sang heights and in the Bala Hissar. He would require reinforcing at Kabul by a heavy battery, some garrison gunners and two more regiments of native infantry. Another four regiments of native infantry, two regiments of British infantry and a section of mountain artillery would be required for the lines of communication between Jamrud and the Lataband Pass. He would also need the equivalent of another 3,800 camels. Roberts did not want the reinforcements for Kabul sent up during the winter months because of supply problems; he therefore fixed on 21 March as the earliest date on which his operation could start.

In the meantime, preparations were pushed ahead at Kabul. The sick and wounded were evacuated to Peshawar, the 12th Bengal Cavalry, 14th Bengal Lancers and 5th Punjab Cavalry were sent back to rest and recuperate before taking the field again, and a mounted infantry corps was formed from the available infantry regiments. By intensive efforts, fifty days' supply of food was accumulated and convoys from India replenished ammunition stocks and brought up warm clothing for the force. Meanwhile the garrison kept itself amused with snow fights, skating, concert parties (that of the 72nd Highlanders was particularly famous) and Christy-minstrel bands. Inevitably the officers had established a Club; true it was only a large marquee dug into the ground, but it provided a place for officers to meet, smoke, exchange news and drink the whisky and champagne which appeared to form an essential part of the stores of any British army wherever it happened to be.

In the early part of March, both the L of C forces and Roberts's own force at Kabul were reorganized, on the insistence of the Commander-in-Chief. Ross's Reserve Division at Peshawar was absorbed into the L of C force under Bright who now became Inspector-General of Communications and directly responsible to Army Headquarters. The line from Jamrud to Butkak inclusive was now divided into three sections:

1. Jamrud – Basawal inclusive, under Brigadier-General W. A. Gib with HQ at Landi Kotal;
2. Basawal– Safed Sang, Brigadier-General Doran, with HQ at Jalalabad;
3. Safed Sang – Butkak inclusive, Brigadier-General R. Sale-Hill, with HQ at Safed Sang.

The movable columns at Jalalabad and Gandamak were placed under the command of Brigadier-General Arbuthnot.

The force at Kabul was divided into two infantry divisions, the 1st being commanded by Roberts directly and the 2nd by Ross, together with the Cavalry Brigade under Hugh Gough in place of Massy. The whole force was formally re-named the Kabul Field Force.* During the course of March, substantial reinforce-

---

*It had previously been the 1st Division of the Eastern Afghanistan Field Force, Bright's L of C troops having formed the 2nd Division. The change of title reflected the transfer of responsibility for the L of C to Army Headquarters.

ments reached Kabul, bringing the total strength of the Force up to just over 12,000 men. Bright's L of C force now numbered some 16,000 and the Peshawar District Force, which now constituted the immediate reserve, some 5,800.

The overall plan of operations submitted by the Commander-in-Chief was approved by the Government of India towards the end of February. No sooner had it been adopted than it began to fall apart because of insuperable difficulties over transport. The Kurram Force had been chronically short of transport ever since Roberts had begun his advance in September, and half of what was now left was useless. The proposed advance of a column to Kabul would have meant leaving the remainder of the troops in the Kurram totally destitute of transport. In any case, Watson's troops were so weakened by sickness that he could not put together a force strong enough to fight its way if necessary over the Shutagardan. This element of the plan therefore had to be abandoned. In substitution, Roberts was ordered to occupy Kushi and the Shutagardan in order to reopen communications with the Kurram.*

Bright's force was reasonably well-off, but it depended heavily on hired transport and if this were withdrawn, as it was expected to be in April when the owners resumed private trading, the Khyber line would be short of the equivalent of 2,500 camels. In these circumstances, operations in the immediate future against the Bara Valley or Tirah Afridis could not be contemplated.

At Kabul, Roberts now calculated that he was at least a thousand camels short of his needs; later, more thorough investigation raised this figure to more than five thousand. The projected operations into Kohistan and Bamian had to be abandoned. At the beginning of April, Roberts was left only with the task of pushing forward a force to Sheikabad some forty miles from Kabul to meet Stewart.

Of the grand design there remained only Stewart's move from Kandahar to Kabul and the projected expedition into Laghman. Before dealing with Stewart's move and with the political developments which were quickly to overtake the need of extensive military operations in Northern Afghanistan, we need to look briefly at events along the Khyber line of communications.

At the beginning of 1880, Bright had nearly 15,000 men deployed on the line from Peshawar to Seh Baba, manning some sixteen major posts, with a substantial reserve at Peshawar. Despite constant patrolling and escorts, it was not enough to prevent repeated attacks on the telegraph line and against stragglers. The smaller posts remained under constant threat of attack, and until Bright was strong enough to mount punitive expeditions against the more aggressive local chiefs, this situation was likely to continue. Moreover, for the constant vigilance a price had to be paid. In the first week of January, the 6th Dragoon Guards lost five men drowned in an exact repetition of the disaster to the 10th Hussars almost a year earlier. Again, the native cavalry who were leading crossed safely.

The Mohmands remained Bright's biggest problem. Naturally aggressive, the temper of their chiefs had not been improved by Roberts arresting Yakub Khan's wife who was suspected, with reason, of aiding and abetting Mohammed Jan and the Mushk-i-Alam; she was, however, the daughter of the leading Mohmand chief,

---

*This too was later countermanded.

the Khan of Lalpura. Early in January, there were reports that the Mohmands were assembling on the north bank of the River Kabul near Jalalabad with the intention of crossing the river and attacking the posts south of it.

On 12 January, a party of four hundred Mohmands crossed the river and attacked the post at Ali Boghan, but were driven off. The next day a relief force from Jalalabad failed to catch the party, but shelled very large groups of tribesmen seen across the river. On the next day (14 January), matters took a more serious turn when some 5,000 Mohmands were discovered encamped just west of Kam Dakka while another 3,000 occupied the Gara heights, three miles south-east of Dakka Fort.

Their combined menace obviously required prompt action. Ross, who was still responsible for the Dakka sector, quickly arranged for a pincer attack from Dakka and Landi Kotal, designed to catch the Mohmands between the two forces with only the river as a line of retreat. Colonel Boisragon (20th BNI), commanding at Dakka, was directed to attack the enemy on the Gara heights, while Brigadier-General Doran, moving northwards across country from Landi Kotal, was to attack the enemy force at Kam Dakka. Once the latter had been occupied, the enemy on the Gara heights would have their retreat across the river cut off.

Success obviously depended upon good co-ordination between the two British columns. Boisragon left Dakka Fort early on the morning of the 15th with 900 men.* By midday, he was in position south-east of Dakka, facing the enemy who had fortified their position on the Gara heights. Having carefully studied the ground beforehand, Boisragon was able to put in a well-coordinated attack, using his artillery to ease the path of the infantry. By 14.30 hours, he was in possession of the enemy position for the trifling loss of one killed and three wounded. Unfortunately the second arm of the pincers was not in position. Doran's advance guard had left at 04.30 hours to seize the Anjiri Kandao Pass, six miles north of Landi Kotal.[7] His main force followed an hour later.† Progress in the dark was very slow and it was not until after 08.00 hours that the column was concentrated on the pass. At 08.45, it started off again. The track down from the Anjiri Kandao was a mere goat track, narrow and steep, so that the men could move only in single file, and the battery mules and transport animals could hardly be got along at all. Although Doran could hear Boisragon's guns four miles to the west, he was unable to make speed because of the difficulty of the route. It was not until 13.00 hours that he reached the Shilman Pass, the last major obstacle before the river. It was occupied by the enemy but they were quickly swept away. Doran was then able to communicate with Dakka Fort by heliograph and learned of Boisragon's success. From the Shilman, Doran could see down the ravine which led to the River Kabul, where large numbers of the enemy were visible retreating along the south bank of the river. Having wasted time searching for his baggage which had become detached, Doran did not start down the ravine, to Kam Dakka, until 15.20. The route was as difficult as any encountered previously and although the Shilman is only some two and a half miles from Kam Dakka as the crow flies, Doran did not

---

*144 sabres 6th Dragoon Guards and 17th Bengal Cavalry, 710 rifles of 25th Foot, 8th and 30th BNI, four guns I/C, RHA – about 920 men.
†20 sabres 17th Bengal Cavalry, 1,200 rifles 5th Foot, 25th and 31st BNI, 1st and 4th Madras NI, thirty men C Company Madras Sappers and Miners, two guns 11/9 (Mountain), RA – about 1,300 men.

reach the village until 18.20 hours, where he met Boisragon's troops. The retreating enemy could be seen crossing the river and on the opposite bank.

The two British columns camped for the night at Kam Dakka, cold and foodless because the baggage had not arrived. The unfortunate Colonel Hodding and the Madras Infantry, in charge of Doran's baggage, had had a dreadful day. The path beyond the Anjiri Kandao was very nearly impossible for animals and a false alarm of an enemy attack caused a panic among the civilian drivers, many of whom deserted, causing animals and loads to be lost over the precipices. By nightfall the baggage was still on the pass. On the 16th, despite assistance by sappers from Landi Kotal, it managed to struggle on only another four miles and it was not until late on the night of the 17th that the major part reached Kam Dakka; the last of it did not get in until the morning of the 18th, having taken three days to cover the seventeen miles from Landi Kotal.

In the meantime, the troops had constructed two rafts and on the 17th, Boisragon's troops crossed the river and seized the village of Rena. Next day, Rena was burned and its tower blown up; Boisragon was back at his base at Dakka that afternoon. Doran returned via the Gara Pass and Haft Chah, reaching Landi Kotal the same afternoon, his baggage having this time prudently taken the long route round via Dakka. Despite the failure of the continued operation, the Mohmands had suffered a severe defeat, losing some 500 killed and wounded. For the moment they were shocked and cowed.

Towards the end of January, Bright was able to carry out the expedition into the Laghman valley, both north and south of the river, which had had to be postponed when Gough's brigade was summoned to Kabul. A column of some 2,500 men, accompanied by Bright himself, traversed the valley and occupied Asmatullah Khan's fort for nearly a month. No opposition was encountered from the Ghilzais who were no doubt digesting the effects of Roberts's success at Kabul and Ross's more recent operations against their Mohmand neighbours. But trouble along the Khyber line was hydra-headed. No sooner had the Mohmands and Ghilzais been put down than the Safis threatened the post at Seh Baba, which had to be reinforced. As a precaution, Pezwan and Jagdalak were strengthened and the 1st Gurkhas were ordered up from Jalalabad, but on 22 March Lieutenants Reid and Thurlow of the 51st Infantry were attacked while riding between Jagdalak Fort and the Jagdalak Pass. Thurlow was mortally wounded and Reid, despite a gallant effort to rescue his brother-officer, was forced to retreat in face of a large band of Ghilzais. The very next morning, 150 transport animals were stolen between Pezwan and Gandamak and the following day (24 March), the Mohmands were reported to be collecting opposite Jalalabad again. They dispersed before Doran could get at them.

Then, on the night of 26 March, a force of some 1,200 Shinwaris and Khugianis launched a determined attack on Fort Battye, nine miles east of Gandamak. But for the fortuitous presence of 150 men of the 31st BNI, en route for Gandamak, the original garrison of 100 men of the 4th Madras NI and 50 sowars of the 4th Bengal Cavalry must have been overwhelmed. As it was, the attackers managed to seize the southern wall of the fort and the transport lines and were ejected only with great difficulty. The Khugianis had obviously recovered from their defeat by Gough a year earlier, and it took another expedition, using the two movable columns from Jalalabad and Gandamak, and much destruction of villages, to bring them to heel and agree to pay a fine of 5,000 rupees. On 11 April, Arbuthnot and the movable column from Gandamak of some 2,200 men, accompanied by Bright himself, left Gandamak for the Hissarak valley to punish the Ghilzais under Mazullah Khan for the attack on Thurlow and Reid. The expedition encountered continuous opposition and suffered a minor reverse when a strong reconnaissance force under Colonel Ball-Acton was halted short of its objective and forced to retire. Mazullah Khan's fort was blown up, but neither he nor his clan submitted.

The reorganization and strengthening of the forces along the Lines of Communication in March and the creation of two movable columns under Arbuthnot had undoubtedly improved the security of the Khyber line. The fact remained that the tribes along the route were unsubdued. With 16,000 men deployed, Bright was unable to halt the steady stream of petty attacks. The daily grind of furnishing pickets and convoy escorts, interspersed with frequent rapid movements to counter threatened attacks on the posts, imposed a heavy strain on the troops particularly as the hot weather approached. It was important therefore from a military point of view to be able to see some solution to the political impasse.

The re-appearance of Abdurrahman Khan on Afghan territory offered such a vision. The son of Sher Ali's brother and rival, Afzal Khan, and the cousin of Yakub, he had lived quietly under Russian protection since Sher Ali's final triumph in 1868. He had resisted spasmodic Russian pressure to try his luck again in Afghanistan, preferring to wait until the right moment arrived. That moment had now come. Early in February rumours reached the Indian authorities that he had crossed the border and entered Afghan Turkestan. Letters to his mother, living in Kandahar, indicated that he was interested in negotiating for his accession to the throne of Kabul. The opportunity was too good to miss and Lytton accordingly proposed to Cranbrook that Abdurrahman be recognized publicly as the legitimate heir of Dost Mohammed and offered the throne of Kabul. Cranbrook was by no means happy about the prospect of Abdurrahman as ruler of Kabul in view of his long stay with the Russians, but he was persuaded to agree.[8] On instructions, Griffin invited Abdurrahman to 'submit any representations that you may desire to make . . . with regard to your object in entering Afghanistan',[9] In line with the situation, very clear instructions were given to Roberts and his commanders that they were not to provoke further conflict; petty punitive expeditions, likely to provoke ill-feeling were to be scrupulously avoided.

. Neither Griffin nor Lytton had yet grasped the measure of the man. He was, in fact, an exceedingly able politician, and he had had long years of exile in Samarkand in which to plan his tactics when the chance finally came. Even before Griffin's letter reached him, he was in touch with the chiefs in Kohistan, claiming that he had come to save Afghanistan from its present misery and degradation and declaring that he was ready to lead a holy war against the British unless they were ready to listen to his representations.

This was powerful, persuasive propaganda, calculated to appeal to a wide audience in Afghanistan. Almost before Griffin's letter had reached Abdurrahman, Lytton was writing in some alarm to Cranbrook: 'The situation has within the last three weeks changed very considerably in favour of Abdul Rahman, and my present fear is that the wrecks and refuse of the Ghuzni faction will ere long rally to his standard, placing him in a position to appear suddenly before Kabul at the head of a united nation and dictate terms to us, instead of accepting them from us.'[10] It was against this new and rapidly evolving political background that Stewart began his march from Kandahar on 29 March.

The railway line from Sukkhur, begun in October 1879, reached Jacobabad by the beginning of November 1879, and Sibi on 14 January 1880. The engineering aspect was easy since it was built basically over flat desert, but the administrative problems of maintaining a force of some 5,000 labourers and 2,000 animals in a bare, waterless desert were substantial. The laying of 133½ miles of track in 101 days was a remarkable achievement by any standards, but there had been no time to build proper earthworks and bridges and the line was very vulnerable to flooding from the Indus.* Administratively, therefore, it made a great deal of sense to use troops from Bombay in Southern Afghanistan.

The obvious candidate to succeed Stewart in command at Kandahar was Phayre. Lytton, however, thought him deficient in tact, good temper and sober judgement.[11] Instead, Major-General Primrose, a British Army officer in command of the Poona Division, was appointed, despite some reservations about his health; Phayre was in due course promoted to Major-General and given charge of the lines of communications. Because Primrose was not conversant with the political scene, the political powers which Stewart had hitherto wielded himself were entrusted to St John. This was a change which was to have significant results.

At the end of the first campaign, Sher Ali, an elderly cousin of the Amir Sher Ali, had been installed as Governor of Kandahar and left in control. He was now the obvious choice for ruler of that separate state of Kandahar which the British Government had decided to set up. Sher Ali was not himself a strong figure and he had no widespread basis of support, being regarded by most Afghans as a British puppet. But he was the best, if not indeed the only, candidate available and since it was the intention to maintain a British force permanently in the region of Kandahar, these defects were not considered fatal. Stewart was consulted at the end of 1879 as to the precise form and responsibilities of the new authority in Kandahar. He thought that Sher Ali should be given authority over the existing province of Kandahar, extending westwards as far as Farah on the far side of the Helmund, eastwards as far as Pishin (which, however, together with Sibi, was to be administered by the British under the terms of the Treaty of Gandamak), and northwards to include Kalat-i-Ghilzai. Under this arrangement Sher Ali would have a territory of some 70,000 square miles with a population of between half a million and a million inhabitants and an annual revenue of £200,000. Since the province was already in some ways the most prosperous in Afghanistan, the new state appeared a viable proposition. Stewart favoured giving Sher Ali complete autonomy save only for the conduct of foreign relations which should be the responsibility of a British Agent. The Wali should have his own military force to keep order, but ultimate responsibility for securing the state against external attack would rest with the British garrison.

---

*A line up the Bolan Pass was completed in 1886 but washed away in 1890. A second line, using a different alignment, was finished in 1895, and is still in use. The alternative route to Quetta, via the Harnai valley, was opened in 1887, but permanently severed by floods in 1942.

These views were endorsed by the Government of India and largely embodied in a letter which Lytton wrote to Sher Ali on 13 March 1880, telling him that he had been recognized as the independent ruler of the province of Kandahar, the precise limits of which remained, however, to be determined.[12] Sher Ali cannot have been in much doubt as to the nature of the poisoned chalice which was being pressed upon him. Even before Stewart had left Kandahar, the Wali's troops had mutinied at least once and clearly demonstrated their total unreliability. Far away on the western horizon, a tiny cloud no larger than a man's fist was beginning to rise again in the shape of Ayub Khan, the Governor of Herat and brother of Yakub. Four months earlier, Stewart had been sufficiently alarmed to recommend preparations against a possible advance by Ayub, but Lytton had taken a more optimistic view and the scare had subsided. Now it was rising again.

Against this background Stewart set to work to organize his move to Kabul. He proposed to take with him all the Bengal Army regiments except the 19th Native Infantry and the Heavy Battery (6/11, RA, equipped with 40-pounders and 6.3-inch howitzers) which were to return direct to India. He was overruled on this latter point – wisely as it turned out – by the Commander-in-Chief who felt that Stewart's force was by no means over-strong for the task it faced. How soon the force could move depended upon how quickly the necessary transport could be assembled and how soon the necessary Bombay replacements could arrive at Kandahar to take over. A drought at Kandahar meant that there were no animals for purchase and only a few for hire locally, so that Stewart was forced to rely upon those already available. By using hired transport to the maximum on the lines of communication and by retaining at Kandahar all Government-owned animals, he managed to assemble enough animals to make his advance practicable. Even so, he was able to carry only seven days' rations for the native troops and followers (although nearly two months' supplies for the British troops). Since the march to Kabul was likely to take at least a month, he would have to live off the country for a large part of his requirements. But for the newly completed railway to Sibi, the task of assembling adequate supplies and transport would have been almost impossible.

The movement of Bombay troops up the lines of communication was hampered both by transport difficulties and by heavy snowfalls in the passes. It was further complicated by the need at the same time to provide troops to protect the working parties engaged on extending the railway from Sibi to Quetta via the Harnai valley. It was not until 9 March that Phàyre arrived at Kandahar with part of the 1st Bombay Native Infantry and 5/11, RA, and assumed formal command of the garrison pending the arrival of Primrose. It was not until the 21st that Stewart was in a position to tell Simla that he would definitely march for Ghazni on the 29th.

The nature of what Stewart was proposing to do has been overshadowed subsequently by the drama of Roberts's march in the reverse direction five months later. In some respects Roberts had the easier task. His force was larger, he had been able to select his regiments carefully from the large selection available around Kabul, his route had already been explored by Stewart's force and as a result of Ahmed Khel he could expect much less opposition; finally he had the powerful assistance of Abdurrahman. By contrast, Stewart was launching himself largely into the blue. Once he left Kandahar, he would be on his own, forced to live off the country and facing an unknown degree of opposition. It was by any standards a risky venture, and not the least remarkable aspect is that it was undertaken without Stewart's having any clear idea of the Government's plans and objectives. No instructions at all reached him from Simla until 28 March, the day before he left, when he received a telegram telling him that a column from Roberts's force at Kabul would meet him at Ghazni. Stewart replied at once, pointing out that he had still not received any orders or details of the campaign now being set in motion. He was not clear whether he was to be required to halt at Ghazni or to go on to Kabul or the Kurram. He did not want supplies or troops pushed forward to Ghazni from Kabul at this stage. If, when he got to Ghazni, he needed supplies either from Kabul or the Kurram he would fetch them himself. In the meantime, he recommended that because of supply difficulties round Ghazni, any supporting troops from Kabul or the Kurram should not go beyond Kushi.[13]

Lytton thereupon minuted the Commander-in-Chief setting out concisely the Government's plans and objectives.

> 'It is essential that General Stewart should be at once fully informed of the entire plan of operations, and of the political objects desired by the Government of India. The latter may be thus summed up; The Government is anxious to withdraw as soon as possible the troops from Kabul and from all points beyond those to be occupied under the Treaty of Gandamak, except Kandahar. In order that this may be done, it is desirable to find a ruler for Kabul, which will be separated from Kandahar. Steps are being taken for this purpose. Meanwhile it is essential that we should make such a display of strength in Afghanistan as will show that we are masters of the situation and will overawe disaffection. But it is not desirable to spread our troops over a large tract of country, or to send small columns to any place where they would encounter opposition and increase the hostile feeling against us. All that is necessary from the political point of view is for General Stewart to march to Ghazni, break up any opposition he may find there, or in the neighbourhood, and open up direct communications with General Sir F. Roberts at Kabul . . . It is not desirable that Sir D. Stewart's troops should remain for long at Ghazni; and it is, therefore, necessary that all military dispositions should be made with a view to enabling him to leave Ghazni as soon as he has put down any open opposition that he may find there. It is very desirable that the conduct of operations in Afghanistan should, as soon as possible, be brought under one head. Sir D. Stewart should, therefore, assume the supreme command as soon as he is in direct communications with Kabul.'[14]

These instructions reached Stewart two days out of Kandahar. The interesting features are the belated recognition of the need of a unified command in Afghanistan, and the remarks about small columns. It is tempting to read both as reflecting in some sort a disillusionment with Roberts's operations since September.[15]

Stewart's force ultimately totalled 7,249 men, with 7,273 followers and more than 11,000 animals of all kinds.* This was a very large assembly to feed off the country, and to ease the supply problem the force was to move on two parallel

---

*Cavalry Brigade (Palliser) – 19th Bengal Lancers, 19th BNI, A/B RHA.
1st Brigade (Barter) – 1st Punjab Cavalry, 2/60th Rifles, 15th and 25th BNI, 11/11 RA.
2nd Brigade (Hughes) – 2nd Punjab Cavalry, 59th Foot, 2nd Sikh Infantry, 3rd Gurkhas, G/4 RA, 6/11 RA.
Divisional Troops – 4 and 10 Companies, Bengal Sappers and Miners, Ordnance and Engineer Field Parks, Field and General Hospital.

routes, astride the River Tarnak until just short of Ghazni. To further ease the supply situation, the main part of the force was divided into two brigades moving with a day's interval between them.

The advance began on 27 March when the two companies of Bengal Sappers and Miners moved out of Kandahar to improve the road on the right bank of the Tarnak to make it suitable for the Heavy Battery. The next day Brigadier-General Barter's brigade began its move along the left bank, and on the 30th, Brigadier-General Palliser's brigade, accompanied by Stewart and his staff, began to move up the right bank, followed on the 31st by the rear brigade under Hughes. Palliser and Stewart reached Kalat-i-Ghilzai on 6 April followed the next day by Hughes. Barter camped eight miles to the east of the city. The force now halted waiting for supplies ordered from Kandahar. Stewart took the opportunity to pick up the two companies of the 59th Foot and two guns of 11/11 (Mountain Battery) RA which had been garrisoning Kalat-i-Ghilzai,* to transfer the Heavy Battery to the rear brigade, thus giving more time for the road to be smoothed out for it, and to send back weak or sickly men and animals. At the same time, he telegraphed to Simla, saying that he hoped to be at Ghazni on 21 April and recommending that the supporting column from Kabul meet him at Sheikabad, forty miles from Kabul, bringing with it ten days' supplies for his British troops. The supplies from Kandahar failed to reach him and he recommenced his march on 8 April, although henceforth he had no more than two days' supplies with him for his native troops. He still had with him some 7,200 troops, 6,400 followers and 8,700 animals. From Kalat-i-Ghilzai onwards he was heading into territory which the British had not traversed since 1842.

The weather was good – frosty at night, but sunny and warm by day – and the roads reasonably easy, but signs of opposition were beginning to appear. From Kalat-i-Ghilzai onwards, Barter's brigade was shadowed by a rapidly growing force of tribesmen. The British scouts were encountering parties of armed tribesmen in all directions; in consequence reliable Intelligence was virtually unobtainable, but there was a general expectation of a fight before the force reached Ghazni. Until now, Stewart had been inside the province of Kandahar, and the Wali Sher Ali had been able to ensure reasonably adequate local supplies. Forty miles beyond Kalat-i-Ghilzai, the force crossed the boundary into the province of Ghazni which hitherto had remained totally independent of British authority and was the centre of the opposition led by the Mushk-i-Alam and Mohammed Jan. The force now found itself moving through country where a 'scorched earth' policy had been implemented; villages were deserted, crops and animals removed or hidden. Stewart was forced to scavenge for supplies.[17] From newly ploughed fields, from freshly dug groves, from dung heaps, from underground canals, stores of grain and flour were uncovered enabling the troops to be fed; but there was not enough to give followers a full ration and they were reduced to eating whole grains of wheat sweetened with sugar.[18] Seventy miles from Ghazni, Barter's brigade joined up with the main force and Barter and Palliser's brigades then halted at Jan Murad to allow Hughes to catch up. Stewart himself was feeling the strain of the warm

---

*They were replaced at Kalat-i-Ghilzai by two companies of the 66th Foot, two guns of C/2 RA and the 29th Bombay NI.

weather and the poor food, and the troops were tired from the constant strain of having to scavenge over long distances to find food and forage on top of the daily marches.

At Jan Murad, Stewart found himself with some highly dubious allies in the form of Hazaras who seized the opportunity of the British presence to pay off old scores against their Afghan enemies by looting and destroying their villages and killing any Afghans who fell into their hands. As Stewart ruefully recognized, it was likely to be the British who got the blame, but there was probably not a great deal that he could have done about it and it is doubtful whether the depredations of the Hazaras materially increased the already manifest Afghan hostility to the British troops. The Afghan force which had been shadowing Barter was still there and appeared to be contemplating an attack but retired when Barter moved out against them. When Stewart resumed his march on 18 April, a force of some 9,000 tribesmen moved parallel with the column at a distance of some eight–ten miles. That night they camped some four miles to the south-east of Stewart's camp at Mashaki, but they had gone when dawn broke on the 19th.

Despite the logistic difficulties, Stewart had now covered about 195 miles and was only some 25 miles from Ghazni. At Kalat-i-Ghilzai he had received a letter from Lytton urging him not to linger at Ghazni, but to push on as quickly as possible in order to take over military and political control at Kabul.[19] A column was already on its way from Kabul to Sheikabad to support Stewart if necessary.

The deserted villages through which Stewart was moving was evidence enough of the basic hostility which surrounded him, and the gatherings of tribesmen who had hung around his column at a discreet distance showed the sort of opposition he might expect to encounter. Once at Ghazni, however, he was only some 90 miles from Kabul. If the Afghans were to make a serious attempt to halt his advance it could be assumed that they would do it either at Ghazni itself, which was a renowned fortress, or just before. Stewart had no information about likely opposition other than what his mounted scouts could discover as they moved ahead and on the flanks of the division.[19]

When it moved off at daybreak on 19 April, the division was strung out along the road over a distance of six miles. The advance guard, under Palliser, consisted of the 19th Bengal Lancers, six guns of A/B, RHA, 19th BNI and the two companies of Bengal Sappers and Miners. This was followed by Divisional Headquarters, escorted by 50 sowars of the 19th Bengal Lancers, a company of the 2/60th Rifles and a company of the 25th BNI. Then came the main body under Hughes, consisting of the 2nd Punjab Cavalry, 59th Foot, 3rd Gurkhas and 2nd Sikh Infantry, with the Heavy Battery (6/11, RA) and G/4, RA. This was followed by the huge baggage train, with Barter's brigade bringing up the rear.

Six miles beyond Mashaki, the hills to the west came close to the Ghazni road and a large spur jutted out eastwards across the road. Divisional Headquarters and the main body had halted and were breakfasting about two miles short of this spur when Palliser's brigade major arrived at a gallop with the news that the position immediately to the front and left of Palliser's advance was held by strong forces of enemy foot and horse. Stewart had the fleeting hope that they were Hazaras, but he was quickly disillusioned. It was clear that the enemy would have to be attacked and dispersed before the division could continue its march. Orders were immediately dispatched to Barter to send forward two squadrons of the 1st Punjab Cavalry and half of his infantry. But Barter was six miles away and only the cavalry could be expected to reach Stewart in under two hours. As Stewart explained to his wife, he did not expect the enemy to attack so he decided to carry the attack to them without waiting for Barter.

Continuing his advance, he began to deploy some 1,400 yards short of the spur (map 10). The horse and field batteries were deployed astride the road, facing roughly northwards, supported by 2nd Punjab Cavalry, one squadron of 19th Bengal Lancers and a company of 19th BNI. Hughes was directed to deploy his

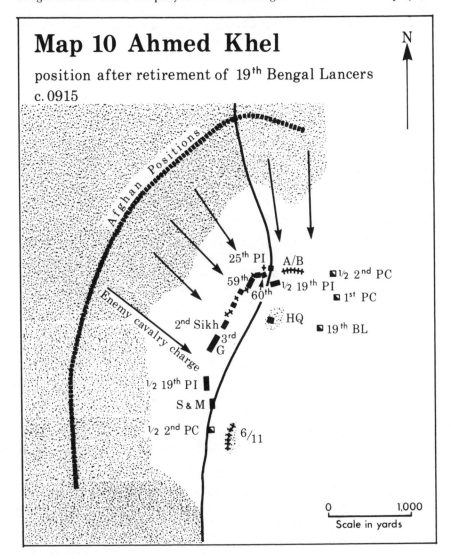

Map 10 Ahmed Khel

position after retirement of 19th Bengal Lancers
c. 0915

N

Afghan Positions

Enemy cavalry charge

25th PI   A/B
59th   ½ 19th PI   ■½ 2nd PC
60th   ■ 1st PC
2nd Sikh   ■ HQ
3rd   ■ 19th BL
G
½ 19th PI ■
S & M ■
½ 2nd PC ■   6/11

0   1,000
Scale in yards

infantry for attack in line west of the road facing westwards, with one and a half squadrons of 19th Bengal Lancers at the southern end of the line protecting the left flank of the infantry. The Heavy Battery was placed to the east of the road on the far left of the line, with a large gap between it and the 19th Bengal Lancers. Stewart, with his staff and escort, took position on a knoll to the east of the road, roughly behind the centre of the infantry, with six companies of 19th BNI and his own escort in reserve close by. He planned to assault the enemy on the hills west of the road with his infantry, supported by the fire of the Heavy Battery, and then roll up the Afghan position from south to north, while keeping the enemy on the spur due north of him in check by the fire of the other two batteries, and by the cavalry. Before he could complete his deployment, a huge mass of men foamed over the crest of the hills and charged straight down upon his deploying infantry. Simultaneously a large body of horsemen debouched from two ravines on the enemy's right flank and struck the squadrons of Bengal Lancers. At the far end of the line a mass of some 2,000 horsemen emerged from behind the spur and galloped down on the batteries, intent upon cutting in on the rear of Hughes' infantry.

The effect of this massive and well co-ordinated concentric attack was shattering. The Bengal Lancers, struck before they could get up sufficient momentum to charge, were hurled back in total confusion on the 3rd Gurkhas at the left-hand end of the infantry line. The Gurkhas, caught while deploying, were in turn broken up and forced back upon the 19th BNI, in reserve behind them. Stewart immediately deployed half of the 19th and the two companies of Sappers and Miners to reinforce the firing-line. The remainder of the 19th BNI and the two companies of Stewart's escort were deployed to protect G/4 and A/B which were firing case-shot and shrapnel as fast as the guns could be loaded in an effort to halt the Afghan attack. Every man that Stewart had available was now in the firing-line, but nothing seemed able to stop the tide of the Afghan advance. 'The scene was one which defies description. Such an enormous body of Ghazi swordsmen had not been brought together since the battle of Meeanee,' wrote Chapman. 'Their bravery was magnificent, and the fury of their onset tried the nerves of our troops for a few minutes, for nothing stopped them short of death.'[20] Another observer (Captain Elias, of the 59th Foot) wrote, 'Most of them were big men, with long white robes flowing in the wind, right arms with swords or other weapons extended, and trying to guard their bodies (against Martini-Henry bullets!) with shields. Anyone with the semblance of a heart under his khaki jacket could not help feeling something like pity to see them advancing with their miserable weapons in the face of our guns and rifles, but their courage and numbers made them formidable.'[21]

At this point, a tactical error in ordering the 59th Foot, in the centre of the infantry line, to take up a fresh position brought Stewart's force to the verge of total disaster. The 59th was struck by the tidal wave of Afghan swordsmen before all the men had had time to fix bayonets and while they were still attempting to get into formation; it began to give ground.* On the extreme right flank, the field and horse artillery batteries, having run out of ammunition, had been forced to retire, the Afghans being within thirty yards of the guns. On the left flank, the Afghans,

---

*Kipling's short story *The Drums of the Fore and Aft* appears to have been loosely based upon this incident.

having smashed the 19th Bengal Lancers and temporarily disordered the 3rd Gurkhas, had swept over and through the medical posts behind the firing-line and reached the knoll occupied by Stewart. The battlefield was covered in a dense fog of flying dust, whipped up by a strong wind, so that it was difficult to tell what was happening. The break-up and annihilation of Stewart's force was now extremely close.[22]

Luckily discipline and firepower began to reassert themselves in the nick of time. Both the 3rd Gurkhas and the 59th recovered their cohesion and began to pour crushing volleys into the attackers. The 2nd Punjab Cavalry, charged into the enemy horsemen on the extreme right flank, temporarily relieving the pressure at that end of the line and enabling G/4 and A/B to be redeployed to assist the infantry. Two squadrons now relieved the shaken Bengal Lancers at the other end of the line, and the Lancers, joined by two squadrons of the 1st Punjab Cavalry from Barter's brigade, took over the job of clearing the right flank. On the left flank, the 2nd Punjab Cavalry, assisted by some well-aimed shells from the Heavy Battery, dispersed some Afghans still trying to outflank the British left to get at the baggage. With the infantry line now standing firm and sweeping the ground with their volleys, assisted by four guns which had been re-deployed from G/4, RA, the Afghan attack began to slacken and then to turn into a rout, the tribesmen dispersing in all directions. Stewart, conscious of the vulnerability of his baggage train, limited his pursuit to the right flank where the cavalry cleared the ground as far as the River Ghazni. Some 2,000 Hazaras, however, had followed the battle from a distance and they fell on the fleeing Afghans, butchering them in large numbers.

The fight had lasted barely an hour and was over long before the bulk of Barter's infantry, forced marching from the rear, could reach the scene. Excluding the 1st Punjab Cavalry, Stewart's force had totalled some 2,800 men and he had lost seventeen killed and 124 wounded, a remarkably small number in view of the fierceness of the fighting. Not surprisingly, the heaviest loss was among the 19th Bengal Lancers who lost five killed and 42 wounded. The Afghan force was estimated at about 15,000, consisting mainly of Ghilzais. Their dead lay thickly scattered in front of where the infantry had stood; 1,200 bodies were actually counted on the field and their total casualties were probably about 3,000. There had been great gallantry shown on both sides and if, in the end, discipline and better weapons had pulled the British through, it had been only by the very narrowest of margins.[23]

Ahmed Khel was the only major action fought by Stewart and it would be difficult to think of a more tactically inept affair. Caught on the march with less than half his troops with him and with the remainder strung out behind him to a distance of six miles, one might have expected Stewart to halt and concentrate his whole force. He had the whole day in front of him and ample time to reconnoitre and settle his plan of action. Instead, by continuing to push forward, he deprived himself of Barter's support and was caught in the act of deploying. In retrospect he was not too happy about the conduct of some of his troops – 'Some of the cavalry did not do very well,' he wrote in his diary, 'nor did some of the other troops. They were hardly prepared for a rush of some 2,000 swordsmen who dashed upon the line without check.'[24] But it was his own fault that they were not properly prepared and in the end it was only the disciplined steadiness of regiments such as the 2nd Sikh Infantry which saved him. He had been totally surprised and very nearly paid the penalty.[25]

Stewart remained on the battlefield for two hours, collecting his dead for burial or burning and treating his wounded. By the time he moved off at about midday, Barter's brigade had come up and the division was at last properly concentrated. It camped that night at Nani, about ten miles from Ahmed Khel. Two days later, on 21 April, it camped outside the walls of Ghazni, some 223 miles from Kandahar and only 90 miles or so from Kabul. Despite its dilapidated appearance, Ghazni might still have been a difficult proposition to take if resolutely defended and there was a good deal of relief when no opposition was encountered. The news of Ahmed Khel had obviously had its effects on the population of the city, but Afghan hostility generally remained strong in the area. The day after his arrival, Stewart received Intelligence that Roberts's old antagonists, the Mushk-i-Alam and Mohammed Jan, had assembled a force estimated at 30,000 close to Ghazni. The advance guard of some 6–7,000 were located by cavalry patrols the same day at the villages of Arzu and Shalez, only five miles north-east of the British camp.

Stewart quickly decided to disperse this gathering and Palliser moved out before dawn on the 23rd with four battalions of infantry, two regiments of cavalry and two batteries, in all 2,800 men. Three miles from Ghazni, the force topped a ridge and saw below it, at a distance of about two miles, the two villages about half a mile apart and occupied by an Afghan force estimated at some 6,000. The villages were strongly enclosed in the usual mud walls, and the surrounding ground was either cultivated, with innumerable channels and ditches, or marshy. It was clear to Palliser that an attempt to capture the villages could be an expensive business. He decided to shell the Afghans out into the open where he would be able to use the superior firepower and manoeuvring ability of his troops. But at ranges of between 1,400 and 1,800 yards, using high explosive and shrapnel, the guns were unable to make any significant impression. By 08.30 hours, Palliser had been forced to withdraw the batteries and heliograph for reinforcements. By the time that 450 men of the 59th Foot and 3rd Gurkhas had reached him, the enemy numbers had been swollen by local tribesmen who flocked in in full view of the British troops. Palliser now withdrew to his original position some 2,500 yards from the villages hoping that the enemy might be tempted out by this apparent retreat. When this did not work, Palliser signalled Stewart for instructions. Stewart now decided to take all available men and assume command of the operations himself. Having already sent a wing of the 19th Bengal NI to guard the gates of the city, he had to leave the camp in the hands of two companies of the 3rd Gurkhas, the two companies of Sappers and Miners and the Heavy Battery, under Major Tillard, of the Heavy Battery. Tillard did what he could to entrench the camp and to put up barricades of camel saddles, but there was no possibility of his defending the camp against a serious attack.*

---

*'We had left our camp seven miles behind, not very strongly protected. What if the whole affair had been a ruse to inveigle us out, while a large force came down from the hills in our absence and burned all the tents and stores, etc?, but the Afghans are not an enterprising enemy, and there was probably nothing to fear.' Elias, op. cit., p. 674. Stewart was either lucky or clever on this occasion; we may perhaps give him the benefit of the doubt.

Stewart reached Palliser at about 11.00 hours with G/4, RA, the equivalent of a battalion of infantry and the 19th Bengal Lancers, bringing the total force available to just over 4,000. He immediately decided to take Shalez, sending Barter to attack it from the rear while Hughes attacked it frontally; the 2nd Punjab Cavalry, with two guns, was sent to observe and mask the village of Arzu. Barter and Hughes had no sooner begun to move, just before midday, when the Afghans began to evacuate both villages, demonstrating yet again their sensitivity to being cut off. Within the hour, both villages were in British hands. Stewart's casualties were two killed and eight wounded; the Afghans were estimated to have lost 150 killed and 250 wounded. News of the defeat now caused the main body of the insurgents, which had apparently been planning another Ahmed Khel, to disperse.

The remainder of Stewart's short stay at Ghazni was taken up with finding a governor for the province. He was well-aware of the futility of leaving behind a mere British puppet and, correspondingly, of the difficulty of finding a suitably independent ruler who could nevertheless guarantee the stability and security of the area. Stewart finally hit upon a prominent sirdar, Mohammed Alam, who was willing to accept the task subject to a guarantee of support from Stewart and subject also to the heir-apparent to the throne of Kabul – Musa Jan, Yakub's son – residing at Ghazni under his (Mohammed Alam's) protection. Stewart agreed to both conditions, believing that the most important thing was to achieve an immediate period of tranquillity at any cost. Given this, he was confident that the Afghans would soon see the advantage of permanent peace and stability. To this end, he advised the Hazaras, who were alarmed at the prospect of being left to the uncertain mercy of their Afghan neighbours, to make their peace with the new Governor who had professed his willingness to meet the Hazaras half-way.

On the point of leaving Ghazni, Stewart now received his first formal instructions from Simla since leaving Kalat-i-Ghilzai. They directed him to open up communications with Ross, who had left Kabul with a force to meet him, and then to proceed immediately to Kabul to assume supreme command. He was not to withdraw the Ghazni force via the Kurram until he had had an opportunity to assess the situation in Northern Afghanistan. He was ordered to breach the walls of Ghazni before withdrawing to render the city defenceless. Stewart replied on the 24th, saying that he proposed to base the Ghazni division temporarily in the Logar valley. He expected Afghan opposition on the Shutagardan route to the Kurram. In a further signal, he reported that instructions had reached him too late to do anything about the walls of Ghazni, but that since the Ghazni defences were contemptible anyway, it was not important.

Stewart was already in communication by heliograph with Ross who had arrived at Saidabad, some forty miles to the north, on 23 April.* The Kandahar division left Ghazni on the 25th and halted that night about fourteen miles north of Ghazni. The same evening, Major-General Hills and Major Kinloch, the Political Officer with Ross's column, rode into camp, thus linking up the two forces. Three days later, Stewart handed over command of the Ghazni Field Force temporarily

---

*Contact was established on the 22nd when Ross's column spotted a light flashing from the Sher-i-Dahan Pass some 50 miles away to the south. Ross thus learned of the fight at Ahmed Khel and was able to heliograph the news back to Kabul. This is an interesting illustration of the range of the heliograph in suitable country.

to Hughes and accompanied Ross's column northwards to Argandeh where he met Roberts on 1 May. They reached Kabul together on 2 May and Stewart assumed overall command of all the forces in Northern Afghanistan.

In the month since he had left Kandahar, the general political situation had changed significantly. Early in the New Year, the Mustaufi had volunteered to meet the leading Afghan chiefs to attempt to reach agreement about the future of the country. In March, the Mustaufi met Mohammed Jan, the most influential of the chiefs opposing the British. A month later, on 4 April, the Mustaufi re-appeared in Kabul with the news that Mohammed Jan and other leaders were ready to discuss matters with the British. Lepel Griffin, on behalf of the British Government, made it clear that separation of Kandahar from Kabul was a fixed point in British policy, but this was by no means acceptable to the Afghan chiefs. A meeting was arranged for 13 April, but on the 11th a document, signed by a con-siderable number of chiefs, representing Duranis, Ghilzais, Mangals and Tajiks, was handed to Griffin. This requested the restoration of Yakub as Amir of a united Afghanistan, the withdrawal of British troops, immediate economic assistance because of the devastation already caused and agreement that any Agent of the British be a Muslim. In face of this pressure for a return to the *status quo ante bellum*, it is not surprising that the meeting on 13 April, from which Mohammed Jan and the leading Durani chiefs conspicuously absented themselves, proved fruitless. Griffin made it clear that the Government was prepared to accept anyone except Yakub as ruler of Kabul, but Kandahar would in any event be separated. As Roberts recognized, the arrival of Abdurrahman was creating intense excitement among the Afghan population. The air was thick with rumours of chiefs and tribesmen flocking to join him.

Eight days later, Griffin received Abdurrahman's reply to his letter of 1 April. It cleverly suggested a united Afghanistan under the joint protection of Britain and Russia.[27] This was clearly unacceptable and Lytton instructed Griffin to tell Abdurrahman that the British Government would not allow Kandahar and Kabul to be re-united nor agree to a joint Anglo-Russian protectorate. It was prepared to hand over Kabul and the rest of the country without conditions if Abdurrahman was prepared to come to Kabul to receive it, but in any event it proposed to evacuate the country by October 1880. If he did not look sharp, the Ghazni faction might seize Kabul ahead of him. Lytton claimed that the renewed campaign had had only two objects – to avenge the deaths of Cavagnari and his companions, and to secure the strategic safeguards sought under the Treaty of Gandamak. Both had now been achieved and there was thus no need or intention to haggle with any prospective new ruler, let alone enter into a treaty with him.[28]

Lytton told Cranbrook complacently the same day that, 'We have found in Abdul Rahman a ram caught in a thicket.'[29] Since it was Lytton himself who was struggling to free himself from the entanglement in Afghanistan while Abdurrahman was moving forward effortlessly on a swelling tide of tribal support, it might be thought that the description was less appropriate to him than to Lytton.

Griffin conveyed the gist of Lytton's instructions to Abdurrahman in a letter of 30 April 1880, but, with Roberts' concurrence, he deliberately omitted the points about Kandahar and the intention to evacuate the country by October. Lytton was predictably angry when he discovered this, but it is impossible not to feel that Griffin and Roberts had the better grasp of the situation. Given the Government's decision to evacuate in a matter of months, come what may, Griffin's negotiating position was increasingly based upon bluff. Once Abdurrahman realized that time was on his side, there would be nothing to negotiate about.

On the military front, events at Kabul were primarily concerned with preparations for meeting and co-operating with Stewart. Roberts planned to leave strong garrisons to occupy the Bala Hissar and an entrenched camp on the Siah Sang hills, and to use the remainder of his troops for operations in the field. A number of fresh regiments had reached him so that by the end of March his force numbered over 12,000 men. He had also received large reinforcements of transport animals, bringing his numbers up to about 11,000, a significant proportion of which were suffering from sore backs and mange. There was still a good deal of vagueness as to the operations Roberts was to undertake. Army Headquarters' idea was that he should occupy the Shutagardan Pass and positions leading to it in order to support Stewart when he reached Ghazni and in case it was decided to withdraw part of his force to India via the Kurram. Roberts was reluctant to do this. He doubted whether Stewart would require any direct military support since the activities of the Mustaufi should prevent any opposition at Ghazni, and he claimed that political events would require most of his force to stay in or around Kabul. He won this particular argument; assistance to Stewart was to be limited to a column under Ross, advancing as far as Sheikabad, roughly midway between Kabul and Ghazni. Matters remained quiet around Kabul and supplies were coming in satisfactorily although Roberts remained cautious in view of his experiences: 'This very important matter is, and must continue to be, a source of grave anxiety to any one commanding a large force in an enemy's country; especially a country like Afghanistan, where, even in a few days, and with little or no previous warning, great pressure may be successfully brought to bear against those upon whom we are dependent.'[30]

Stewart having announced that he expected to reach Ghazni on 21 April, Ross left Sherpur on the 16th with a strong column numbering nearly 4,000 men. He took with him ten days' supplies of tea, sugar and rum for Stewart's troops, but he had only four days' ordinary supplies for his own force so that he was compelled to rely upon foraging for local supplies. He found the people in the Maidan hostile and there were reports of a tribal force gathering in the Logar valley, to the eastward, to attack him. A foraging-party was forced to retire by a body of tribesmen led apparently by the same Bahadur Khan whose villages had been burned by Baker in November, and a reconnaissance party was fired upon. Ross was forced to send out columns to blow up towers of the guilty villages and to bring in supplies forcibly. Nevertheless, he reached Saidabad, four miles south of Sheikabad, on the 23rd without further serious incident although continuously sniped at, and established contact with Stewart.

To the east of him, in the Logar valley, events had taken a more serious turn. Four days after Ross had left Kabul, a smaller force of two squadrons of the Guides Cavalry, a wing of the 92nd Highlanders, the Guides Infantry and two horse artillery guns – in all about 1,200 men – under Colonel Jenkins of the Guides, had left for Charasiab to overawe the Logar valley tribesmen and prevent them attacking Ross. Jenkins camped on 21 April south of Charasiab, near the village of Chikildukhtaran, some twelve miles from Sherpur. Here he received news that a large force under Mohammed Hassan Khan, the ex-Governor of Jalalabad, which had set out to attack the rear of Ross's column had returned, and was now camped about twelve miles away. The following day Jenkins found that a range of hills, some 1,500 yards in front of him, and commanding the road southwards through the Logar valley, was in hostile hands. The force remained camped near Chikildukhtaran because its presence tended to divert hostile attention from Ross's column. At 02.00 hours on the 25th, Jenkins was warned by a friendly chief that Mohammed Hassan was now only six miles away and intended to attack at dawn. He immediately dispatched a messenger to Sherpur and the camp stood to arms. The baggage was sent back a mile to the rear under guard of one and one-half companies of infantry, a picket was ordered forward on to the range of hills to the southwards to give warning of the enemy approach and a cavalry patrol was sent southwards along the main road to reconnoitre. When dawn broke, the hills in front were seen to be swarming with Afghans and the picket was retiring to camp, closely followed by the cavalry patrol which was being pursued by a very large body of tribesmen.

To meet this attack, Jenkins deployed four companies of the Guides Infantry and two companies of the 92nd across the front of his camp. More Guides Infantry, in approximately company strength, occupied two small forts west of the camp to guard against an outflanking attack. The infantry in the firing-line were able to get some cover from ditches and water channels. There was no cover, however, for the cavalry which provided Jenkins' only reserve. They were forced to keep on the move to reduce casualties. At about 05.15 hours, the two guns of F/A, RHA opened fire on the masses of the enemy clustering on the forward slopes of the hills ahead, and the Afghans replied with a steady fusillade of rifle fire. As the day wore on, the enemy numbers were swollen by tribesmen coming in from the surrounding country, and they gradually worked themselves forward until some of their standards were within two hundred yards of the British line. As they began to lap round Jenkins' right flank, another small detachment of the Guides was sent to occupy a second village to the right rear of the camp. By now, Jenkins was facing some 5–6,000 Afghans. He dared not risk attacking the enemy in front of him for fear of being outflanked and cut off from Kabul. But he dared not retreat either since this would have brought the enemy straight down on him, with the near certainty of a disaster. Luckily the Afghans showed no enthusiasm for coming to grips: 'At one moment, they rose up all round with a shout and threatened to break over us like a great wave,' an officer present wrote. 'Men felt for their pistols and instinctively tightened their grip on their swords; but it turned out that even the Ghazis down below were in no hurry to face the bayonets of our slender fighting-line; and the human froth above subsided as quickly as it had risen.'[31]

Nevertheless, Jenkins' force was in an extremely serious situation, with the enemy numbers increasing hourly. Some time between 09.00 and 10.00 hours, he managed to get a heliograph message back via the signalling-post on the Sher Darwaza heights, saying that he was holding his own so far, but that the enemy were being reinforced. He must have been relieved to learn that a force under Macpherson had already left Sherpur to assist him. At Kabul, Roberts, with his force reduced by the dispatch of Ross's and Jenkins' columns, was facing the possibility of a renewed attack on Sherpur by the Kohistani chief, Mir Bachar, still smarting under the destruction of his villages for their part in the attack on Sherpur on 23 December. But clearly Jenkins could not be left exposed to annihilation and Macpherson accordingly left Sherpur at 09.00 hours with the 45th BNI, the remaining four companies of the 92nd and two guns of No. 2 Mountain Battery. At the Bala Hissar, he picked up 129 men of the 2nd Gurkhas and a troop of the 3rd Punjab Cavalry, bringing his force up to roughly 1,100 men.* Hugh Gough followed in support with three squadrons of cavalry, a wing of the 28th Bengal NI and four horse artillery guns.

At about noon Macpherson emerged from the Sang-i-Nawishta gorge where he got a good view of the situation. Leaving two companies of the 45th to hold the defile and protect his line of withdrawal, he headed to join Jenkins. Having sent back the baggage to Sherpur, Macpherson, after consulting Jenkins, decided to attack the Afghan left and roll it up while Jenkins, reinforced by three companies of the 45th BNI, attacked the enemy in front of him. The plan went smoothly: the Gurkhas, three companies of the 45th and a wing of the 92nd supported by four mountain guns, fell on the Afghans' left wing and smashed it while Jenkins, with three companies of the 45th, the Guides and four companies of the 92nd, launched a frontal assault on the Afghan right and centre. By early afternoon the enemy force had been totally dispersed and the hills to the south thoroughly cleared of tribesmen. The cavalry and the horse artillery pursued for four miles down the road. By 16.00 hours, Jenkins' and Macpherson's forces were re-assembled on the site of the original camp where Roberts, who had come down from Sherpur, congratulated them on the victory. By 20.00 hours, the troops were back in Sherpur. British casualties totalled four killed and 34 wounded; Afghan casualties were estimated at 200 killed alone.

Ross at Saidabad had not been free from difficulties either. On both 25 and 26 April, he had had to send out strong columns to disperse hostile gatherings occupying the hills west of his camp. When he finally marched for Kabul on 29 April, accompanied by Stewart and his staff, he left behind a column under Charles Gough to punish villages which had been responsible for this opposition.

It remained to be seen whether Stewart could now bring about the installation of a stable native government at Kabul and a peaceful British evacuation.

---

*The staff work seems to have been poor. Two guns of 6/8 RA never got into action because their orders arrived too late. The guns of No. 2 Mountain Battery, having been warned at 08.15 hours to stand by, received no order to move and managed to join Macpherson only by luck.

NOTES

1. Lytton to Cranbrook, 9 December 1879 –
Balfour, op. cit., p. 394.
2. See p. 217 below.
3. Lytton to Cranbrook, 20 January 1880 –
Balfour, op. cit., p. 397.
4. Lytton to Griffin, 16 February 1880 –
Balfour, op. cit., p. 408.
5. Lytton to Cranbrook, 18 February 1880 –
ibid., p. 409.
6. Instructions quoted in Balfour, op. cit.,
pp. 403–8. The omission of any reference to
Herat reflects Lytton's view that with
Kandahar secured, Herat was not important: 'My own opinion is that the importance
of Herat is entirely relative; and that if the
British power were firmly established at
Kandahar, you could afford to regard with
indifference what happens at Herat.' (House
of Lords, January 1881).
7. Norman's march to Kam Dakka in April
1879 (see page 109) had followed a different
route as far as the Shilman. Doran's route
via the Anjiri Kandao was presumably
chosen because it appeared the quicker, and
time was of the essence if Doran and
Boisragon were to co-ordinate their attacks
successfully. Bright was highly critical of
Doran's apparent failure to reconnoitre the
route beforehand, the difficulty of which was
well-known – See Bright's dispatch of 5
February 1880, copy in RP 154–1.
8. Lytton's proposal in a telegram of
14 March 1880 and Cranbrook's reply on
15 March 1880 – *Afghanistan (1881)*, No. 1 –
*Further Correspondence relating to the affairs in
Afghanistan.* (C-2776), p. 10.
9. Griffin to Abdurrahman, 1 April 1880 –
Balfour, op. cit., p. 142.
10. Lytton to Cranbrook, 12 April 1880 –
Balfour, op. cit., p. 413.
11. Lytton to Sir Edwin Johnson, 19
February 1880 – LP 518/6, p. 119.
12. *Afghanistan (1881)*, No. 1, p. 13.
13. Telegram, Stewart to Viceroy, 29 March
1880 – Official History, vol. IV, p. 212.
14. Minute from Lytton's Military Secretary
to C in C, 30 March 1880 – *Afghanistan
(1881)*, No. 1, p. 15.
15. Hanna, op. cit., vol. III, pp. 315 and
316n, takes this view and specifically
ascribes the change of tone at Simla to the
replacement of Colley as Military Secretary
by Brackenbury, and to the arrival of Major-
General G. R. Greaves as Adjutant-General
in India. But Hanna is always keen to
detect criticism of Roberts.

16. 'After leaving Kelat-i-Ghilzai we found
the entire country deserted; the villages for a
hundred miles had been abandoned, and the
people had gone taking flocks and herds and
household goods but burying their precious
things, with grain and flour, in the fields,
under the hearths, or even under dung-hills
...' General E. F. Chapman, *Blackwood's
Magazine*, February 1902, p. 260. Chapman
was Stewart's Chief of Staff on the march.
17. 'Sir Donald Stewart's March from
Kandahar to Kabul'. *Macmillan's Magazine*,
May 1881.
18. Quoted in Elsmie, op. cit., p. 326.
19. 'Our absolute ignorance of the country
was our greatest difficulty, the systematic
desertion carried out by the enemy having
made it impossible to gain even the smallest
information.' General Chapman, op. cit.,
p. 261.
20. Chapman, op. cit., p. 262.
21. RUSI Journal, vol. XXIV, pp. 669–70.
22. 'At this moment the situation was most
critical, for both flanks of the extended line
were turned and the troops were somewhat
shaken by the vehemence of the attack.'
Official History, op. cit., vol. IV, p. 233.
23. Hamilton, of A/B, RHA, wrote 'I only
saw two Afghans ask for mercy, and one
cannot help admiring their reckless bravery;
and the way, and the order, in which they
advanced, deserved success.' Hamilton, op.
cit., p. 36.
24. Elsmie, op. cit., p. 331.
25. 'We did not expect the enemy to fight
that morning' – Stewart to his wife, 20 April
1880. Ibid., p. 334.
26. 'Certainty of Sardar Abdul Rahman
being at Kunduz causes a good deal of
excitement all over the country; the
Kuhistanis are nearly all looking to him and
no doubt a large majority of Afghans
generally would join him, should he make
his appearance at the head of a force, as
deliverer of his country' – Roberts to QMG
16 April 1880 – Official History, vol. IV,
p. 61n.
27. Text in *Afghanistan (1881)*, No. 1, p. 46.
28. Lytton to Griffin, 27 April 1880 – text in
Balfour, op. cit.
29. Lytton to Cranbrook, 27 April 1880 –
ibid., p. 4.
30. Dispatch No. 1339 to Army Headquarters, 17 April 1880.
31. Lieutenant G. Robertson, *Kuram, Kabul
and Kandahar*, Edinburgh, 1881, p. 181.

CHAPTER 11

THE BEGINNING OF THE END

'If ever there was a mere geographical entity, it is Afghanistan. It is as idle to talk of
the national sentiments of the Afghans as it would be to talk of the corporate feeling of
the parish of Marylebone.'

Lytton in House of Lords, January 1881

With Stewart's arrival at Kabul at the beginning of May 1880, the
curtain went up on the last act of the drama which had started at Ali Masjid
nineteen months earlier. A new and dominant figure had arrived on the stage in
the shape of Abdurrahman; a hitherto leading player, Lytton was about to take his
departure. On 28 April, Disraeli's Conservative Administration had been defeated
by the Liberals at the polls, a defeat in large measure attributable to the
unpopularity of the war in Afghanistan and to the devastating use which
Gladstone had made of this in the famous series of speeches generally known as
the Midlothian Campaign. Gladstone, the new Prime Minister, announced that
Lord Hartington would be taking over as Secretary of State for India in place of
Cranbrook, and that Lord Ripon had been appointed Viceroy in place of Lytton.
Another leading actor, Roberts, now found his part diminished by the arrival of
Stewart to take over the role of supreme commander in Northern Afghanistan with
full political as well as military powers.*

Stewart assumed command of all troops in Northern Afghanistan, including
those on the Khyber line of communication. The whole was now to be known as
the Northern Afghanistan Field Force, of which the two divisions of Roberts's
Kabul Field Force now became the 1st and 2nd Divisions, and Stewart's old
division, to which Hills was now appointed, the 3rd; the Khyber Line Force under
Bright retained its name. The Kurram Force was also to come under Stewart
should communications be re-opened between the Kurram and Kabul; in practice
it remained an independent command until the end of the war. For the time being,
the 1st and 2nd Divisions, with Roberts now acting in effect as a corps commander,
remained in and around Kabul while the 3rd Division camped at Hissarak with one
brigade deployed to watch the Logar valley to the east.

Stewart, well aware of the drain on Indian resources caused by the war, and of
the difficulties of keeping the regiments on active service up to strength and in
good morale, was anxious to reduce the number of troops in Afghanistan.[1] He

---

*Roberts was deeply upset at his supersession; 'I am personally much distressed at the idea of being
superseded by Sir Donald Stewart. Having been here from the beginning, I certainly hoped to see the
ending of the business,' he wrote to Griffin (RP 101, p. 419). He intrigued with Griffin and the Viceroy to
get all political powers entrusted to Griffin, but Stewart made it clear that he would resign rather than
agree to Griffin's having full political authority. No more was heard of the suggestion.

promptly stopped work on the very extensive fortifications which Roberts had put in hand at Kabul and planned to reduce the number of regiments, particularly cavalry. In this, however, he failed; troops could not be withdrawn until there was greater peace and stability and of that there was as yet no sign. The arrival on the scene of Abdurrahman and the knowledge that the British were negotiating with him had caused uncertainty and turbulence among the local population. This aggravated Stewart's difficulties in obtaining local supplies to feed his troops, now approaching 20,000 (with an equivalent number of followers). This was a large burden in any circumstances for such a poor country as Afghanistan and fuelled the hostility of the local inhabitants who reacted by preventing such supplies as were available reaching Kabul. This was particularly true in the area south-west of Kabul. Early in May, Baker, with a very strong brigade and accompanied by Roberts, left Sherpur for a wide sweep south down the Logar valley, then westwards into Hissarak, then northwards through Maidan to Kabul, arriving back in the early part of June. Apart from temporarily relieving the immediate supply problem at Kabul and paying off old scores against the Ghilzai chief, Padshah Khan, by destroying one of his villages, it is not clear how much value the expedition served. It did very little to pacify the country; Hill's division in Hissarak continued to live in a state of near-siege, its pickets sniped by day and night, local supplies scanty and difficult to procure and convoys from Kabul few and far between and having to be strongly escorted every inch of the way. Such contacts as there were with the local tribesmen indicated that very little would be required to provoke renewed large-scale hostilities throughout the Logar valley and Hissarak.

Lytton had offered to stay on until the autumn in order to spare Ripon the ordeal of coming out in the hot weather, provided that he (Lytton) was not required to do anything which he could not honestly support – he was, no doubt, thinking primarily of any proposal to restore Yakub Khan. The offer was politely rejected and Ripon arrived at Simla on 8 June. The instructions which Ripon brought with him and the advice which he received from Lytton[2] coincided on two major issues only – the need to bring the war to an end and evacuate Afghanistan as quickly as possible, and the need to keep out Russian influence. On all other issues the policies were diametrically opposed.[3] Whereas Lytton and Cranbrook were wedded to the concept of splitting up Afghanistan and separating Kandahar from Kabul, Ripon and Hartington believed basically in the unification of the country. Ripon's instruction did not exclude the possibility of restoring Yakub (and according to his short-lived Private Secretary, 'Chinese' Gordon, that was Ripon's intention for a time): to Lytton such a move would have been the ultimate betrayal.[4] On the timing of the evacuation, Hartington believed that it could not be as immediate as Lytton hoped and might have to be delayed until the autumn which indeed was what Lytton himself had originally laid down as the target. For the moment, the new administration was prepared to continue the negotiations with Abdurrahman; it had little option since negotiations had reached an advanced state and apart from Yakub no other conceivable candidate was on the horizon.

Abdurrahman had already proved a shrewd negotiator. He had replied to Griffin's letter of 30 April which had urged him to come to Kabul, by seeking clarification about the future position of Kandahar, the presence of a British agent in Afghanistan, the British attitude on his future relations with Russia and the benefits and services which Afghanistan would receive and be expected to provide. In the meantime, he continued to move slowly and deliberately towards Kabul, steadily gaining in support as more and more chiefs, afraid of missing the bandwagon, came over to his side. His reluctance to come immediately to Kabul had caused Stewart to doubt his good faith and to recommend breaking off negotiations, but Ripon was prepared to give Abdurrahman the benefit of the doubt. Griffin was now authorized to tell him that since Persia and Russia were pledged not to interfere, the ruler of Kabul could have no dealings with any Power except Britain; the British would assist against unprovoked external aggression; that there was now no wish to station a British officer as envoy in Afghanistan although it was for consideration whether there would not be mutual advantage in having a Muslim agent at Kabul; and that while Kandahar must remain separated, Abdurrahman was free to try to secure his rule over the rest of the country.[5] [On the face of it, Ripon's acquiescence in the continued separation of Kandahar seems paradoxical, but it reflected no more than Ripon's belief that undertakings had been entered into with the Wali, Sher Ali, which it would be dishonourable to break.] The letter, however, crossed with one from Abdurrahman announcing that he was on the point of starting for Kabul and expressing himself generally satisfied with the assurances already given by the British Government. But he was careful in a subsequent letter to refer to his having been promised 'the boundaries of Afghanistan which were settled by treaty with my most noble and respected grandfather, Amir Dost Mohammed'.[6] He would not, and could not, acquiesce publicly in the separation of Kandahar. Not only was it the ancient home of the Durani Royal Family, but he knew that a divided Afghanistan could only lead to a renewal of these dynastic struggles which had taken so much of the time and energy of both his uncle and grandfather. To him the Kingdom of Kabul without Kandahar was like 'a head without a nose or a fort without a gate'.[7] He professed to be ready to leave Herat to Ayub Khan if the latter were prepared to be friendly.

Taken in conjunction with information that he was appealing to all the leading chiefs for support for a march on Kabul, Abdurrahman's letter revived doubts as to his good faith. He was told bluntly that it was essential for him to come to Kabul quickly, otherwise the British would evacuate the country and leave the population to choose its own ruler.[8] The threat was not an empty one; Abdurrahman, as a Durani, could not count automatically upon the support of the Ghilzais who, if they were in favour of any ruler at all, supported Yakub. In the meantime Abdurrahman was still north of the Hindu Kush and his deliberately leisurely approach towards Kabul was increasing the restlessness and general hostility of the tribes around Kabul.

On 18 June, Hills moved northwards to Charasiab in the hope that supplies would be easier there, but this proved a vain hope and by the 26th he was back at Zargunshahr. At roughly the same time, Charles Gough was engaged on a wide sweep west through the Chardeh plain and then north to Kohistan, partly to tap fresh sources of supplies and partly to damp down the rising tide of agitation. Moving westwards along the northern rim of the Chardeh plain, he camped at the entrance to the Bektut valley in the north-west corner of the plain. Rumours of a hostile gathering in Maidan to the south-west resulted in a detached force under Colonel Norman reconnoitring southwards as far as the Kotal-i-Safed Khak, some five miles beyond Argandeh. Shots were exchanged with a large body of tribesmen who retired without offering serious resistance. Norman then rejoined Gough and the brigade moved northwards to Karez-i-Mir, the village occupied by Macpherson in December 1879. Mir Bacha, that persistent antagonist, was reported to be in the area, and cavalry patrols sent out to the north towards Istalif were fired on. But generally Gough had a quiet time, remaining in the general area to the north of Kabul until the end of July awaiting Abdurrahman's appearance. Meanwhile, at the beginning of July, a brigade under Macpherson moved out to Abdul Gafar in the Chardeh plain, six miles from Sherpur, to keep an eye on the tribal gathering which still hung about in Maidan. To strengthen the forces left at Sherpur, the 19th Bengal Lancers were called up from the 3rd Division.

Hills' move northwards to Charasiab in the middle of June had temporarily left a vacuum which was quickly filled by assemblies of tribesmen. These for the most part quickly dispersed on the return of the division, but substantial groups were reported in the vicinity of Patkao Shahana, a village some four miles from Kushi. They were reported to be awaiting reinforcements from Roberts's old antagonist, Mohammed Jan. Hills determined to disperse these gatherings before they became a serious menace. Palliser accordingly left camp early on the morning of 1 July, with the 1st Punjab Cavalry, two squadrons of 2nd Punjab Cavalry and two squadrons of 19th Bengal Lancers, in all 577 sabres. Cresting a ridge two miles north of the village, Palliser found a mass of some 1,500 tribesmen retreating in a body eastwards towards the Altimur Pass. Leaving one squadron to cover the village, Palliser charged at once with the remaining six squadrons and despite the roughness of the ground totally dispersed them. Afghan casualties were estimated at not less than 200, while Palliser lost three killed and 29 wounded. The force was back in camp by 18.30 hours, having covered forty miles during the day. It was the most brilliant cavalry action of the war and effectively removed the menace which had hung over the Logar valley.

It is necessary to look quickly at events in the Kurram and on the Khyber line of communication before returning to Kabul where the effective conclusion of the war was now coming in sight. The winter in the Kurram had been exceptionally severe and although it had effectively prevented any hostile action, it had played havoc with the physical condition of the troops. In the middle of January, the ill-fated 29th Bengal NI, for example, was reported as having only 200–300 men fully fit and the regiment urgently needing replacement. The command situation also needed sorting out. Watson, as a Brigadier-General, nominally held military and political command in the valley, but another Brigadier-General (J. J. E. Gordon)* was joint military commander. The troops available amounted in effect to a division, but for command purposes Watson himself had only three staff officers (a Brigade Major and two Deputy Assistant Quartermasters-General).[9] At the end of April, therefore, Watson was given the temporary rank of Major-General and a full divisional staff. The opportunity was then taken to divide the available troops into

---

*Not to be confused with T. E. Gordon, Watson's immediate predecessor.

an Upper Kurram Brigade and a Lower Kurram Brigade under Gordon and Brigadier-General H. L. R. Newdigate respectively.

The spring passed uneventfully, being disturbed only by a clash between a squadron of the 18th Bengal Cavalry and a force of some 600 Wazirs near Thal. May opened badly with an attack by a band of marauders on the post at Chapri, eight miles north of Thal. They got into the post, killing a sentry in the process, and then proceeded to kill Lieutenant Ward of the Transport Department, two sepoys and eight dhooli-bearers besides wounding sixteen soldiers and followers. The garrison was clearly slack and the raiders were not pursued. Investigation showed them to be from Khost and they were reported to have lost eight killed and wounded.* Two days later, on 3 May, reports of an impending attack by a force of Wazirs on the posts at Chapri, Manduri and Badshah Kot led to the posts being reinforced and plans made to intercept the attackers. The attacks did not materialize and it seems that the Wazirs had been thwarted by reinforcement of the posts. At the end of May, Gordon led a raid on a village three miles south of Ali Khel to try to capture a Jaji chief, Nanak, notorious for his anti-British activities. Nanak himself escaped, but in retribution his tower was blown up and the inhabitants of the village disarmed. This was effectively the end of hostilities in the Kurram although sniping and rumours of attacks persisted. The main preoccupations before the valley was evacuated in October were serious outbreaks of rinderpest and foot-and-mouth disease among the transport animals and the prevalence of virulent malaria among the troops.

Attacks and counter-attacks continued along the Khyber lines of communication until the end of the war. By the end of March 1880 Bright disposed of a force of 16,000 men and 28 guns, the equivalent of two divisions, but it was not enough to prevent constant attacks. For the troops life consisted of a wearisome round of guard and convoy duty in weather getting steadily hotter; by June, Ball-Acton was recording shade temperatures of 110° Fahrenheit at Jalalabad. The attacks continued. On 5 May a stores convoy was attacked by Ghilzais near Rozabad and lost three men killed and wounded. Two days later Ghilzais raided the commissariat cattle yard at Jalalabad itself and carried off 1,000 head. Despite pursuit the raiders got away into the Laghman with 800 head which were not recovered. Two days later Doran reported that a fanatical priest, the Mullah Khalil, who had been preaching a holy war, had succeeded in gathering together a force of tribesmen and freebooters and was occupying the districts of Besud and Ghoshta on the north bank of the River Kabul opposite Jalalabad. This could not be tolerated without undermining the confidence of the native administration at Jalalabad and the local population.

Besud, in the angle between the west bank of the River Kunar and the River Kabul, was not easy country over which to operate. The hills came down close to the river banks and the strip of plain thus left was used at this season for rice growing; it was wet and swampy with numerous water channels and ditches. Because the rivers were swollen by melting snow from the mountains the trestle bridges west of Jalalabad had been dismantled to prevent them from being swept

---

*The garrison consisted of 30 men of the 1st Bengal Cavalry and 50 men of the 5th BNI. The post commander was placed under arrest, but was subsequently released and returned to duty.

away. Doran ordered rafts to be constructed to ferry troops over the river, and on 14 May, 200 men of the 1st and 4th Madras Infantry were ferried across to occupy a fort on the north bank. Over the next four days they were reinforced by a squadron of the Central India Horse, 400 men of the 5th and 12th Foot and two guns of No. 1 Mountain Battery. On 19 May Doran set out with these forces to attack the Mullah Khalil. Because of the nature of the ground he had first to move westward before he could swing northwards. The enemy, to the north-east of him, were thus in a position to attack Doran's bridgehead before he could get back to defend it. Doran decided to strike quickly at the insurgents before they were aware that he had left his bridgehead.

Leaving a small garrison at the bridgehead, which could be supported by artillery fire from Jalalabad across the river, Doran set off before dawn on the 19th with some 670 men. At about 06.00 hours he was close to the edge of the hills to the north where he found the enemy, 2,000 strong, moving steadily southwards towards the bridgehead, blissfully unaware of his presence. He waited to let them get further out into the plain and as soon as the Afghans discovered his presence and came to a halt he moved his infantry and guns forward to within 700 yards and commenced to pound the enemy with artillery and rifle fire. Under this hammering they rapidly broke and fled northwards towards the hills whereupon Doran launched the Central India Horse at them. A portion of the enemy force barricaded itself within a nearby fort. The guns were brought up to pound it at a range of thirty yards and the surviving defenders were then rushed and bayoneted. The remainder, shattered by the cavalry charge, took refuge in the hills. By 10.00 hours Doran's force was on its way back to its bridgehead, having killed at least seventy of the enemy for the loss of six wounded. As further punishment, two forts belonging to the insurgents were destroyed during the next three days. By this time, the River Kabul had risen alarmingly and Doran faced the extremely difficult task of getting his troops back to the south bank. Using rafts and twenty elephants, the infantry, guns and baggage were got across in the course of two days for the loss of one man. The Central India Horse swam their horses across, some troopers doing the trip as many as ten times in order to bring horses and baggage ponies across.

Simultaneously, operations were taking place at the other end of the L of C, in the 1st Section, now commanded by Brigadier-General W. A. Gib. Reports having been received of a hostile gathering under the Mullah Fakir at Shershai, about eight miles south of Ali Boghan, Gib moved out from Pesh Bolak on 18 May with a mixed force of about 1,000 men.* The enemy were not found at Shershai where Gib halted for the night, but were reported to be at Mazina nearly seven miles further south. Moving off again at dawn on the 20th, over difficult country, Gib came in sight of the enemy at about 07.30 hours. The tribesmen were strongly posted in an area littered with forts, walled enclosures and orchards and broken up by innumerable water courses and terraced fields. They were in defiant mood, beating drums, waving their standards and firing on a flag of truce which the Political Officer sent forward. Using four companies of the 14th Foot, supported

---

*135 men 8th Hussars, 110 men 5th Bengal Cavalry, 450 men 2/14th Foot, 266 men 32nd BNI (Pioneers), four guns L/5, RA.

by two companies of the 32nd Bengal NI and the four guns of L/5, RA, Gib attacked the left flank of the enemy. Despite stubborn resistance, the tribesmen were steadily driven back. By 13.00 hours the position was in Gib's hands. Further parties of Afghans who now appeared were in turn attacked and dispersed. On the following two days a number of towers were blown up as punishment and by the evening of the 22nd the force was back at Pesh Bolak. Gib's casualties were two killed and seven wounded; the Afghans lost at least 120 killed, 200 wounded and some prisoners. Gib attributed much of his success to the effective gun fire.

The threats to the L of C continued however. The Mullah Khalil had moved eastwards across the River Kunar into the district of Kama (the scene of Macpherson's operations in February 1879, see p. 9l), where he had assembled a force of Mohmands. Action against him had to be postponed for a few days because of the swollen state of the River Kabul, but at the beginning of June Doran crossed into Kama with No. 2 Movable Column. The Mullah Khalil's forces dispersed as a result of the British concentration and Doran had to content himself with blowing up towers belonging to some of the local Mohmand chiefs who had supported the Mullah. Simultaneously Arbuthnot, with No. 1 Movable Column, was conducting a short incursion into the Laghman where the ubiquitous Asmatullah Khan and the Mullah Fakir were reported to be stirring up trouble.

June proved a particularly troublesome month. Trading caravans were raided near Ali Masjid on the 5th and 9th, and on 12 June Gib reported that the Afridis were gathering in strength in the Bara valley to attack communications between Landi Kotal and Jamrud. At the other end of the line, a convoy was attacked between Jagdalak and Pezwan on the 19th, two soldiers being killed; ten days later another convoy was attacked by 200 tribesmen in nearly the same place, three men of the 31st Bengal NI being killed and three wounded out of a total escort of about twenty, and a considerable amount of property being stolen. At the same time Asmatullah Khan was rumoured to be hatching mischief in the Tezin area and the posts at Jagdalak and Seh Baba were reinforced. On the last day of June the daily convoy between Pezwan and the Jagdalak Kotal was attacked. July was to prove no better.

The fragile nature of the lines of communication between Peshawar and Kabul is readily apparent, as is the heavy demand on the troops manning the route, but it is worth noting that throughout the war there was no major disaster to a convoy. It is easy to see, nevertheless, why Lytton and his military colleagues were anxious about the effect of the constant patrolling and escort duty on the native troops.

The absence of any feasible candidate other than Yakub, the steady swing over of tribal support to Abdurrahman and the continuing signs of hostility to the British presence had produced a situation in which the acceptance of Abdurrahman as Amir at Kabul had become the only practical course. Despite continuous pressure from Griffin, the Afghan contender continued to take his time over coming to Kabul. All the while he was steadily assembling support. By the middle of July he was in Kohistan, telling the chiefs there that he came with friendly intentions towards the British and calling upon them to refrain from hostile actions. Those who had held aloof, like Mohammed Jan and the Mushk-i-Alam, but who were now growing war-weary, moved to accept Abdurrahman. For the British Government, the overriding consideration was speedy evacuation of the country and Stewart was told on 20 July to settle the political arrangements quickly. Formal recognition of Abdurrahman was left to his judgement but there were to be no negotiations; Abdurrahman had to take the offer of the throne on British terms or leave it. If he declined, Stewart was authorized to assemble the leaders of the Sher Ali family party and transfer power to them if they could form a workable government. The political problem could not under any circumstances be allowed to delay evacuation of the troops.

Stewart and Griffin wasted no time. Two days later Griffin addressed a large meeting of notables and chiefs at Sherpur, including a delegation from those attending Abdurrahman, telling them that satisfactory arrangements had been made with Abdurrahman and of the intention to evacuate Northern Afghanistan speedily. The first convoy of sick and invalids left Kabul six days later. On 29 July Gough's brigade, camped in Kohistan, caught the sound of the joyful fusillade of rifle shots which marked the new Amir's arrival at Istalif. Two days later Griffin met him at Zimma, sixteen miles north of Kabul. Griffin was greatly impressed.

'Amir Abdul Rahman Khan is a man of about forty, of middle height and rather stout. He has an exceedingly intelligent face, brown eyes, a pleasant smile, and a frank, courteous manner. The impression that he left on me and the officers who were present at the interview was most favourable. He is by far the most prepossessing of all the Barakzai Sirdars whom I have met in Afghanistan, and in conversation showed both good sense and sound political judgement. He kept thoroughly to the point under discussion and his remarks were characterized by shrewdness and ability.'[10]

Allowing for relief at the fact that the hitherto unknown candidate had turned out so well, this was still a considerable encomium from an experienced official. Griffin formally handed over a letter from the Viceroy in Council recognizing Abdurrahman as Amir of Kabul. The new Amir was told that he would receive a gift of ten lakhs of rupees and all the Afghan guns and equipment left at Sherpur and in the Bala Hissar; a formal treaty would have to await the establishment and consolidation of his rule. The British were still hedging their bets.

Griffin's prompt call on Abdurrahman was largely due to the devastating news which had reached Stewart on 28 July of the defeat and dispersal of Burrows' brigade at Maiwand. Within 24 hours of the information reaching Stewart from Simla, the bazaars of Kabul were buzzing with the news. Stewart was rightly apprehensive about its effect on the delicate negotiations with Abdurrahman: 'This is the worst misfortune that can happen to us here. It is impossible to say how Abdur Rahman will take it.'[11] In fact, Abdurrahman made no attempt to increase his demands or to put obstacles in the way of the British withdrawal. Given his views about Kandahar he may well have welcomed the indication that, even with a British garrison, the province could not stand on its own. He probably calculated also that the British would now be bound to attack and destroy Ayub in order to regain prestige and that this could only help him (Abdurrahman) by removing his most dangerous rival. The cards were in any case all beginning to fall his way. On 4 August, the Mushk-i-Alam, Asmatullah Khan and other important dissidents wrote to Griffin, saying that they were prepared to accept any ruler that the British should choose, in order to put an end to the prevailing uncertainty among the people.

With Abdurrahman safely in the bag, Stewart could concentrate upon the military problem which faced him. Immediately on hearing the news of Maiwand, he had ordered Hills, Gough and Macpherson back to Kabul where their troops were concentrated by 5 August. Two questions now had to be faced: whether to continue as planned with early evacuation of Northern Afghanistan, and secondly what assistance, if any, could be offered to Kandahar. The intention to evacuate had already been announced and much preliminary movement had already taken place. To reverse this decision would be to throw into doubt British good faith and to undermine Abdurrahman's position. Instability and uncertainty could only increase the risk of another insurrection at a moment when the British needed to concentrate on the crisis at Kandahar. Moreover, the longer the delay at Kabul the greater the strain upon the Indian economy and upon the troops. Stewart had little difficulty in concluding that early evacuation should proceed and both Ripon and Hartington agreed.* Since a good deal of work had already been done in dispatching surplus stores and personnel down the line to Peshawar, Stewart was able to confirm 10 August as the date for the final evacuation of Kabul. There still remained confusion as to the limits of the evacuation. Instructions sent to Stewart in June had ordered him to retire no further than Gandamak. For a variety of sound reasons – military, political, sanitary – Stewart was determined to withdraw completely to the boundaries established by the Treaty of Gandamak. Army Headquarters, however, was not told until 9 August of Stewart's intention, and his detailed timetable for evacuation was not received until the day after he marched out of Kabul. He was right in his judgement and his failure to tell Simla what he intended was probably because he wanted to present a *fait accompli* with no further room for argument. Both the Commander-in-Chief and the Viceroy were angry but had to acquiesce as Stewart no doubt calculated. In the event, it had no permanent effect on his relations with Ripon.

As regards Kandahar, Stewart knew at first hand the difficulties of pushing reinforcements quickly up the Bolan Pass route. He also knew at first hand what was involved in marching from Kabul to Kandahar. From the first he had believed that a force from Kabul might be required to relieve Kandahar and he put in hand arrangements for such a force within hours of receiving the news of Maiwand.[12] Roberts shared this view, having in addition reservations about the quality of the Bombay troops who might be employed via Quetta. Simla had no difficulty in deciding that it was from Kabul rather than Quetta that early relief for Kandahar must come, and orders reached Stewart on 3 August. The choice of commander was left to him, although reading between the lines one can detect Simla's preference for Roberts to be used. It could only be him or Stewart. Whoever went would have the chance of excitement and distinction; whoever stayed would have the anxious and burdensome taks of getting the troops back to India without serious loss from disease or from the tribesmen clustered along the route from Kabul to Jamrud. With rare generosity, Stewart gave the command of the Kandahar relief force to Roberts. It was clearly the right decision. Stewart, on the evidence, was not the equal of Roberts as a field commander but, equally, the

---

*As an interesting example of the speed of communication, Stewart telegraphed his view to Ripon on 5 August, Ripon signalled London the same day and Hartington's approval was received at Simla on the 6th. It says something also for Victorian decision-making.

delicate task of evacuation required administrative and political gifts which Stewart had in supreme measure.[13]

The choice of commander dictated the choice of troops because Roberts had strong prejudices in favour of Highlanders, Sikhs and Gurkhas, and against Pathans who had let him down at the Peiwar Kotal and whose kin formed the major element of Ayub Khan's army. Other considerations such as the need in fairness to repatriate those troops who had been in Afghanistan the longest had to give way to the purely military. Roberts was given the pick of the troops and transport at Kabul, but he elected to take no wheeled transport or guns. Since Ayub's guns had largely decided the issue at Maiwand, Roberts's decision to take with him only the relatively feeble mountain guns seemed questionable, not least to the Commander-in-Chief. But Roberts and Stewart counted on the relieving force's not meeting serious opposition before reaching Kandahar and thereafter being able to use Primrose's artillery; they placed greater emphasis upon mobility and speed.

The force finally selected consisted of a division of three infantry brigades under Macpherson, Baker and MacGregor, a cavalry brigade under Hugh Gough and three batteries of mountain artillery; Ross went along as infantry divisional commander and *de facto* Second in Command. The force totalled almost exactly 10,000 men with eighteen guns, 7,800 followers and more than 8,000 ponies, mules and donkeys.* Two hundred rounds of rifle ammunition per man were taken for the infantry and 540 shells for each battery. A limited amount of supplies, including mutton on the hoof, was taken along, but Roberts planned largely to live off supplies gathered along the way. Abdurrahman had arranged to send one of his own officials as well as the Mushk-i-Alam's son to organize collection; it was, after all, in his interest to see Ayub defeated quickly.

It was a force of exceptionally high quality; Roberts had selected as far as possible regiments he knew. Some, like the 72nd Highlanders, the 23rd Pioneers and the 5th Gurkhas, had served under him since the start of the war and had been present at all his major actions. Others, such as the 92nd Highlanders, the 9th Lancers and the 3rd Sikh Infantry, had been with him since his advance on Kabul in September 1879. Three regiments – the 2/60th Rifles, 15th and 25th BNI – had marched from Kandahar to Kabul with Stewart only four months before and would now be retracing their steps. Of the regiments which had not served directly with Roberts before, the most interesting choice was the Central India Horse which, coming relatively late on the scene from its remote cantonments in the jungles of Central India, had quickly won a high reputation for efficiency and was now rewarded with selection for this élite enterprise. Virtually all of the native troops were Gurkhas, Punjabis or Sikhs.

The subsequent history of the Kandahar Relief Force will be dealt with in due course. For the moment, we need to consider the final evacuation of Northern Afghanistan. In the middle of July, there were some 20,000 troops around Kabul

---

*Cavalry Brigade – 9th Lancers, 3rd Bengal Cavalry, 3rd Punjab Cavalry, Central India Horse.
1st Infantry Brigade (Macpherson) – 92nd Highlanders, 23rd and 24th BNI, 2nd Gurkhas.
2nd Infantry Brigade (Baker) – 72nd Highlanders, 2nd and 3rd Sikh Infantry, 5th Gurkhas.
3rd Infantry Brigade (MacGregor) – 2/60th Rifles, 15th Bengal (Sikh) NI, 4th Gurkhas, 25th BNI.
Artillery – 6/8 RA, 11/9 RA, No. 2 Mountain Battery.

and another 14,000 on the lines of communication back to the Frontier. Allowing for Roberts's Kandahar force, Stewart had to move some 24,000 men with immense quantities of stores and transport roughly 170 miles in the middle of the hot season.* The logistic problems involved were compounded by the fact that Roberts's force had skimmed off the fittest men and animals.

The logistic problem was in some ways potentially less serious than the military one. Even though Abdurrahman and his officials would be keen to remove any obstacles to the speedy homeward passage of Stewart and his troops, the risk of attack from the tribes along the route remained a very real one. They had all to some degree felt the heavy hand of the British during the course of the war and the temptation to harry and plunder the retreating convoys would be very strong. At the beginning of July, a small punitive expedition under Colonel Ball-Acton had burned three villages in the vicinity of Pezwan in retaliation for recent attacks, but met stiff resistance in doing so. Throughout July, incursions along the L of C had continued – telegraph wires cut, posts attacked, the raft service engaged in ferrying stores and sick from Jalalabad to Dakka continually fired upon and temporarily halted. And rumours circulated that the Afridis were gathering in the Tirah to attack posts in the Khyber Pass.

The first essential was to evacuate stores and sick personnel while the L of C were still adequately guarded by fighting troops. Cavalry and artillery were likely to be less valuable than infantry during the homeward march and there was a good case for thinning out their numbers in advance. Large convoys of sick and followers left Kabul on 28 and 29 July, followed on 4 August by No. 4 Mountain Battery and on the 5th by 6/11 and 12/9 RA; G/3 RA and A/B RHA left on succeeding days. With them went the 19th Bengal Lancers, half of the 2nd Punjab Cavalry and virtually all the Sappers and Miners. Some 3,000 men were thus on their way down the line. Concurrently stores were being evacuated at depots down the route. As in the previous year's withdrawal a raft service between Jalalabad and Dakka, a distance of some thirty miles proved extremely useful.

Stewart was thus able to keep very closely to his timetable for evacuating Kabul itself. On 6 August he issued his farewell order, thanking the troops at Kabul and especially those manning the lines of communication for their services and extending good wishes to those who were going with Roberts. Two days later the Kandahar Relief Force moved out. On 9 and 10 August, the last convoys of sick and stores left Kabul. There remained only the fighting troops, now down to some 6,700. The last days were complicated by a serious dispute between Stewart and Lepel Griffin over the demolition of the fortifications which Roberts had had constructed around Sherpur and Kabul and the handing over of arms to Abdurrahman. At root, the dispute arose from acutely differing perceptions of Abdurrahman's chances. Griffin was convinced that the new Amir had the necessary intelligence, shrewdness and force of character to rule Kabul securely

---

*Stewart and the authorities at Simla had clashed over the desirability of marching in the hot season. Stewart believed that, on balance, the discomfort which the troops would suffer was outweighed by the likely reduction in the incidence of disease. His view prevailed but it is interesting to contrast it with the experience of the similar withdrawals in June 1879 (see page 113 above). A plan to move part of the Kabul troops back to India via the Kurram was abandoned, because it would have delayed evacuation, and with the detachment of Roberts's force it was no longer physically necessary to have a second line of evacuation.

provided that he was given the necessary British support. To destroy the fortifications at the very moment when he was poised to assume the throne and further to refuse him arms and ammunition to enable him to support himself in power would, in Griffin's view, deal his chances a mortal blow.[14]

Stewart, distrusting all Afghans, had no great belief in the new Amir: 'Griffin is much taken with Abdur Rahman's intelligence and nice manners. Unfortunately, like all Afghans, he wants everything from us, and all he has to give in exchange is the chance of his friendship. The fact is, we have made a mess of the whole business, I fear, and have been wasting our time on a man who has no real strength of his own.'[15] Stewart took the view that to leave behind arms and ammunition and fortifications which could one day be used against British troops was military folly. From this view he refused to shift, arguing that it was basically a military, not a political, matter and one for him to settle, not Griffin. Stewart's view was initially upheld in India where lack of faith in Abdurrahman was general. Griffin, however, stuck obstinately to his guns and insisted that if he was to be overruled his protest should be formally recorded in writing. The hint was not lost on Simla and Stewart was instructed to come to an agreement with Griffin. Stewart thereupon told his political adviser that if there were clear evidence that the Amir attached real importance to the fortifications being handed over intact, he (Stewart) would be prepared to agree to this. Griffin was an experienced official, wise in the ways of getting things done. The same evening he wrote to the Amir, outlining the type of letter needed. It duly arrived the next morning and Stewart gave in. As Griffin put it slyly, 'If he [Stewart] thought the Amir's letter a strangely timely one, he never showed any surprise.' Not only were the fortifications left intact, but Stewart handed over thirty Afghan guns which Roberts had found earlier at Sherpur, and five lakhs of rupees.

History will show that Griffin was right, and Stewart wrong, about Abdurrahman's character and chances; indeed, with all the advantages of hindsight, it comes as a slight surprise now to realize that there were ever doubts on the matter. But Stewart showed good sense in bowing in the end to Griffin's judgement.

The final act of the Kabul drama took place on 11 August. The baggage left at 05.00 hours and a few hours later the new Amir and Stewart met for the first and last time outside the Headquarters Gate of Sherpur, Roberts's command post during the siege. Abdurrahman had asked for the interview but initially at least he seemed at a loss for words. But just as Stewart rose, impatiently, to leave, the Afghan found the right words to express a deep appreciation of the British Government's action in placing him on the throne of his ancestors, and his firm intention of living permanently in friendship with the British. At the end of this meeting, Abdurrahman rode back to his camp outside Kabul to prepare for his ceremonial entry into the city the next day, while his officials took over the Bala Hissar, Sherpur and the remainder of the fortifications from their British opposite numbers. Under the command of Hills, and accompanied by Stewart, Griffin and their staffs, the British troops finally moved off down the road to India, only a day behind Stewart's original timetable.

As far as Seh Baba, three marches from Kabul, the country was relatively open and the troops moved as a division. Beyond Seh Baba the hills closed in and movement of the force in one body became extremely difficult. In addition to the troops themselves, there were some 3,000 native followers and a huge congerie of transport animals of every description – camels, elephants, donkeys, ponies, bullocks, mules – with a wide variety of wheeled vehicles. A considerable number of Kabulis – Afghans as well as Hindus – had decided to accompany the force, fearing for various reasons the arrival of Abdurrahman; they brought with them their own animals. All of these had to be protected and camping grounds and water supplies found for them at the end of the day. As always, Stewart's force suffered from massive transport problems. Many of the animals were under-nourished and exhausted, Roberts's force having taken the best. Under the daily strain of marching they laid down and died in droves; one convoy alone lost 185 camels out of 407 getting through the Lataband Pass, two days' march out of Kabul. The strain was greatest on the rearguard who had, in effect, to sweep up behind the rest of the force.

> 'It is impossible to describe in adequate terms the difficulties and perplexities which devolve upon the rearguard of an army marching by confined, waterless roads in a mountainous region under a broiling sun. Loads get displaced and must be readjusted; a pony or a camel casts its load, which must be replaced or transferred to another animal, or a wheel comes off in the narrowest and most difficult part of the road. Each and every such incident causes a check along the whole line and a huddling together of animals ensues; ponies and mules begin to fight and kick; weak and jaded followers declare they cannot march, but they must be got on somehow. Such, in a few words, are some of the ever-recurring dilemmas which, from morn till night, tax the patience and endurance of a baggage or rearguard.'[16]

From Seh Baba, the division therefore moved by brigades, Charles Gough's 1st Brigade picking up the tedious task of rearguard. Immediately ahead of the leading troops of the Kabul division the troops of Bright's L of C force were also steadily retreating. The whole operation was controlled by telegraph, each major unit reporting its position daily to Stewart's Headquarters; the rearguard rolled up the telegraph lines as it passed. Inevitably, some stores – particularly food and grain – had to be left behind because there was not enough transport to move it, and although attempts were made to hand it over to the Amir's agents, most of it was plundered by the local tribesmen; at Basawal, Khugianis and tribesmen from Hissarak came to blows over sharing the loot. But of actual attacks on the British forces there were none although all along the route groups of tribesmen gathered to watch the retreat and the route had to be properly picketed all the way.

As far as Jalalabad, the 2nd (Hughes) and 3rd (Colonel Daunt) Brigades alternated in the lead, Divisional Headquarters travelling with whichever brigade happened to be in the middle. From Jalalabad, the 2nd and 3rd Brigades moved by detachments, the 1st Brigade alone continuing to move basically as a brigade until the end. Stewart left the force at Jalalabad, and on 31 August at Peshawar handed over command of all troops in Northern Afghanistan to Bright, and then left for Simla to report to the Commander-in-Chief and the Viceroy.*

---

*Where he was promptly offered the post of Military Member on the Viceroy's Council in succession to Johnson who had resigned as a result of the financial blunder over the cost of the war.

As each regiment emerged from the Khyber, it came under the control of the Peshawar District Commander and camped at Hari Singh-ki-Burj, just outside the mouth of the pass, some four and a half miles from Peshawar. To avoid congestion, the troops were then fed forward as fast as possible across the Indus at Attock and Khushalgarh, and thence to their new stations in India.

Gough's brigade reached Landi Khana on 4 September, the 2nd Battalion of the 9th Foot being the last unit to leave Afghan territory. The effective frontier with Kabul now ran through Landi Kotal where, throughout the autumn and winter, Gough remained with a brigade of fresh troops garrisoning that station, Ali Masjid and Jamrud. The arrival of Gough's original 1st Brigade at Hari Singh-ki-Burj on 7 September effectively marked the end of the evacuation of Northern Afghanistan.

It had been a very well-managed and successful operation. Twenty-four thousand men with large quantities of stores and equipment had been withdrawn through difficult country, at the height of the hot season without significant loss. Apart from a small number of cholera cases there had been very little sickness. The arrangements for feeding the troops had been very successful – indeed, with the necessity of using up supplies rather than leaving them to the local population, the troops were probably better fed than they had been at any time before. There had been no attacks on the columns as they wound their way back through the defiles to India and this could largely be attributed to the careful military precautions taken and to the fighting qualities which the troops had already displayed. Boyes was justified in claiming that 'It is not too much to say that the return of the Afghan Field Force to India in 1880 under General Sir Donald Stewart is one of the most striking examples on record of how a highly disciplined, well-organized force in the hands of a skilful General successfully overcame the greatest difficulties.'[17]

In parallel, Watson evacuated the Kurram valley. The enthusiasm with which initially Lytton and Roberts had propounded the use of the Kurram as the future main line of approach to Kabul had not been shared by all experienced Frontier officers. The Commander-in-Chief, for one, had never been an enthusiast; he had always taken the view that the route over the Shutagardan Pass and in particular the steep western descent to Kushi made it a difficult and therefore unreliable main artery of communication.[18] Experience had proved his point. Within days of Roberts leaving Kushi in September 1879, his rearward line of communication over the Shutagardan had been cut and never effectively re-established, tribal hostility and the winter snows proving obstacles which could not be overcome. Roberts himself had reluctantly swung round to the Commander-in-Chief's view.[19] But if the Kurram was no longer to be regarded as a main artery to Kabul, it became a cul-de-sac, of no practical value, absorbing large quantities of troops.* Earlier in the year Watson had already pressed unsuccessfully for the evacuation of the Kurram.

The change of Viceroy and the settlement in Northern Afghanistan altered the whole situation. 'As a line of military communications, experience has condemned

---

*At the beginning of August 1880, the forces in the Kurram had reached a total of 8,679. *Official History*, vol. V, p. 107.

it [Kurram],' wrote the Commander-in-Chief, 'and I abandon it as such without the slightest regret.'[20] Watson was equally forthright: 'I know of no reason for keeping troops any longer in the Kurram.'[21] He advocated handing the valley over to Wali Mohammed. At the end of August, however, he was ordered to tell the Turis and Jajis that the British intended to evacuate the valley and leave the tribes to form their own independent government. By the beginning of September 1880 the evacuation of stores from the upper end of the valley was in progress, as a preliminary to a general withdrawal. The Peiwar Kotal itself was evacuated on 12 September and the defences destroyed, the troops falling back on Shalozan amid torrential rains but without molestation. On 6 October Watson was ordered to evacuate the whole of the Kurram. He arranged for the Turis and Bangash to take over the various fortified posts and to garrison them with tribal levies, in return for which he handed over 5,000 rupees and a quantity of rifles and ammunition captured originally from the Afghans. Kurram Fort was evacuated on 16 October and by the 21st the troops were concentrated at Thal which became brigade headquarters for the time being. The Kurram had played a valuable role in the early stages of the war, but it had been kept on too long and had absorbed too high a proportion of the army's resources to no very good purpose.

NOTES

1. 'It would be impolitic to keep the native regiments another winter in this country. They are very home-sick and it will not do to try them too much. The hardships they have undergone have had a marked effect on the popularity of the Service and nothing should induce your Excellency to sanction our remaining in Afghanistan another winter.' Stewart to Ripon, 11 June 1880, Quoted in Elsmie, op. cit., pp. 360–1. Combe noted the same point: 'A great pity they cannot relieve some of the regiments up here; they have been too long at it, are sick and weary of the business, and are all very weak in numbers.' (op. cit., p. 181).

2. Text in Balfour, op. cit., p. 428–34.

3. Ripon had been Under-Secretary of State for India for six months in 1861, and Secretary of State from 1866–68. In consequence he had been deeply influenced by John Lawrence.

4. Roberts, hitherto a firm believer in Yakub's guilt, had changed his tune and now agreed with Stewart and MacGregor that the best thing to do would be to send for Yakub.

5. Griffin to Abdurrahman, 14 June 1880 – *Afghanistan (1881)*, No. 1, p. 47.

6. Abdurrahman to Griffin, 22 June 1880 – ibid., p. 48.

7. See Sultan M. Khan, *The Life of Abdur Rahman* (London, 1900) vol. 1, pp. 195 and 208 for his views about Kandahar.

8. Griffin to Abdurrahman, 2 July 1880 –

Afghanistan (1881), No. 1, p. 48. In fact, preparations for the evacuation of Kabul had been going for a month, with the dispatch of engineer and ordnance stores back to India.

9. Strength on 1 April 1880 was 7,393, consisting of three cavalry regiments, the equivalent of nine battalions of infantry, four batteries of artillery and a company of Bengal Sappers and Miners. This includes Kohat which came under Watson.

10. Griffin to Foreign Secretary, Simla, 4 August 1880 – Official History, vol. V, p. 97. No British official had met him before.

11. Diary, 28 July 1880. Elsmie, op. cit., p. 372.

12. 'Making preparations for sending a force to Kandahar via Ghazni . . . Everything must give way to the military necessities of the case.' – Diary for 29 July 1880. Elsmie, op. cit., p. 376. Nevertheless, Stewart showed some signs of wavering thereafter until orders from Simla settled the matter.

13. Abdurrahman makes quite clear in his autobiography (Sultan M. Khan, op. cit., vol. II, p. 155, for example) his intense distrust and dislike of Roberts.

14. 'I was certain . . . that if the fortifications had been blown up, and this insulting display of distrust had been shown to our chosen nominee in the sight of all Afghanistan, Abdur Rahman would never have established himself at Kabul . . .' Sir

Lepel Griffin, 'Afghanistan and the Indian Frontier' *Fortnightly Review*, November 1901.

15. Elsmie, op. cit., p. 374.

16. Lieutenant-Colonel W. J. Boyes, *The Return March to India under Sir Donald Stewart in 1880*, JRUSI, vol. XXXVII (1893), Boyes, as DAAG was responsible for organizing the march.

17. Ibid., p. 131.

18. 'The Shutagardan must ever be considered a bad line of military communications . . . The variation of altitude in the short distance which separates Habib Killa from Kushi is surely in itself prohibitory of all thought of a railway beyond Kurram . . . Unless a transport train far more extensive and more efficiently organized than any we have seen in the last campaign were available to him, a commander who would advance to Kabul by this line would find enormous difficulties in his way, for, having expended the limited number of days' supply he could hope to carry with him he must, of necessity, become dependent on the means of some other column, operating either by the Ghazni or by the Jellalabad road.' Minute of 25 August 1879.

19. Memorandum dated 12 May 1880 – Official History, vol. V, p. 13.

20. *Afghanistan (1881)*, No. 1, p. 86.

21. Ibid., p. 94.

CHAPTER 12

DISASTER IN SOUTHERN AFGHANISTAN

'It got beyond all orders an' it got beyond all 'ope;
It got to shammin' wounded and retirin' from the 'alt.
'Ole companies was lookin' for the nearest road to slope;
It were just a bloomin' knock-out – an' our fault.'

Rudyard Kipling *That Day*

Since its bloodless occupation in January 1879, Kandahar had become a back-water. Apart from Hughes' expedition to Kalat-i-Ghilzai in the autumn of 1879, there had been no military activity of significance. The extension of the railway to Sibi early in 1880 had eased the supply problem. Although the supply line to Kandahar was roughly twice the length of that from Peshawar to Kabul, the Brahui, Baluch and Pathan tribes through which the line ran were a good deal more pacific and less formidable than those along the Khyber route. The Khan of Khelat, through whose territory the road to Kandahar passed, had proved a helpful ally and the lines of communication to Kandahar had not seriously been threatened. Nevertheless it remained necessary to escort convoys and guard the roads. In the spring of 1880, there were some 12,000 troops with 20,000 transport animals in Southern Afghanistan.

By Afghan standards, Kandahar itself was a pleasant and fertile place. The River Argandab which flowed just west of the city provided ample water for irrigation and Kandahar was famous for its orchards. 'Villages cluster around the city on three sides,' wrote Le Mesurier in 1879. 'Cornfields, orchards, gardens and vineyards are seen in luxurious succession, presenting a veritable oasis within the girdle of rugged hills and desert wastes all round.'[1] It was the alleged richness and fertility of the province of Kandahar which had been one of the strongest arguments of those who favoured its occupation and retention. Experience showed that this aspect had been somewhat exaggerated. On closer acquaintance the city proved to be a good deal decayed, its fortifications dilapidated and its streets narrow and filthy. While Kandahar itself produced fruit and cereals in abundant quantities, the rest of the province, as Biddulph had discovered in 1879, was by no means prosperous and outside Kandahar supplies were not plentiful. For the troops the biggest problem was boredom. The troops on the lines of communica-tion had at least the constant daily grind of patrol and escort duty; for the troops at Kandahar, there was nothing except kit parades and sentry duty interspersed with the occasional expedition to bathe and fish in the river and perhaps a sports day.

At Kandahar, under Lieutenant-General Primrose, was the major part of two British infantry battalions (2/7th and 66th), the equivalent of two native infantry regiments (the 1st and elements of the 19th and 30th Bombay Native Infantry (BoNI)), the equivalent of two regiments of cavalry (3rd Sind Horse, elements of the Poona Horse and 3rd Bombay Light Cavalry), together with E/B, RHA, 5/11 (Garrison), RA, two guns of C/2, RA and No. 2 Company of the Bombay Sappers and Miners. Kalat-i-Ghilzai was garrisoned by two companies of 66th Foot, 29th BoNI, a squadron of 3rd Sind Horse and two guns of C/2, RA. Some 6,500 men were employed in garrisoning posts along the route back to Sibi, along the lines of the railway under construction via Harnai and in the Thal–Chotiali district covering the routes from Quetta to Dera Ghazi Ghan and the railhead at Multan. From Sibi back to the Indus at Sukkur, further quantities of troops were employed in L of C work. A Reserve Division of Bombay troops (but including the 1st Madras Cavalry) was distributed between Karachi, Hyderabad and Jacobabad. The majority of the troops were widely dispersed in small garrisons. It would be difficult to concentrate a force to strengthen the garrison at Kandahar if that should be needed.

In the middle of March 1880, marauders from the Kakar tribe of Pathans had killed Captain Showers near the Khojak Pass and gone on to attack a survey party under Lieutenant Fuller, RE. The first task of the Bombay troops at the beginning of April had been to recover Showers' body. A fortnight later, on the night of 16 April, tribesmen incited by a local mullah attacked the post at Dabrai between Chaman and Kandahar, garrisoned by some tribal levies. Major S. J. Waudby, 19th BoNI, commanding that section of the L of C, with an escort of five men, had arrived that day at the post on his way back to Kandahar. Warned of the attack by a friendly chief, Waudby put the post into as good a state of defence as he could, barricading the entrance with bags of grain. Just before midnight the tribesmen attacked and, after a desperate resistance by Waudby and his five men, overran the post. The levies fled at the outset and the only unwounded survivor was a sowar of the Sind Horse who managed to escape and bring the news to Kandahar; one other soldier was later found severely wounded but lived to tell the tale. Waudby had sold his life dearly, using a pig-sticking spear when his ammunition ran out. Eleven attackers were subsequently found dead around the post, together with many wounded. As punishment, a force from Gatai and Chaman supported by some of the Wali's troops destroyed a fort belonging to a chief known to be implicated in the attack and took the chief back to Kandahar for trial by the Wali.

Throughout April and May there was a groundswell of tribal hostility which showed itself in wire cutting, attacks on stragglers and the plundering of unescorted convoys. A convoy from Kandahar to Kalat-i-Ghilzai was attacked by Ghilzais in the middle of April and communications between the two places blocked. Colonel Tanner, commanding at Kalat-i-Ghilzai, surrounded the offending villages, took prisoners and recovered some of the stolen transport animals. On his way back, he dispersed a force of tribesmen attempting to bar his way, killing the leader, a local mullah. At the beginning of May three officers returning to Kandahar were fired on close to the city, one being seriously wounded, together with a sowar of the escort. None of these incidents was especially significant in itself although the attacks near Kalat-i-Ghilzai empha-sized the continuing independence and hostility of the Ghilzais despite the passage of Stewart's force. Taken together, they were no more than might have been expected given the unwelcome presence of an alien force in Afghanistan and the temptation to plunder which this offered tribesmen used to scratching a poor living from barren soil. But behind the attacks lay the de-stabilizing influence of Ayub Khan at Herat.

In some ways Ayub was the most interesting figure to appear on the Afghan side during the war. Aged 29, he was the younger brother of Yakub Khan. During the days of Yakub's opposition to their father, Ayub had sided with his brother and had had to go into exile in Persia for his pains. Upon Yakub's accession to the throne, Ayub resumed the governorship of Herat. He had been by all accounts a strong critic of Yakub's action in signing the Treaty of Gandamak and was suspected of implication in the murder of the previous Governor of Herat (Fakir Ahmed Khan) a supporter of Yakub.[2] The regiments which had mutinied at Kabul and killed Cavagnari and his companions had come from Herat, and although there is no evidence of Ayub's direct complicity, it is unlikely that he was surprised or disappointed by events in Kabul. The British occupation of the capital and the subsequent deposition and exile of Yakub produced a new situation. Ayub was probably as outraged as other Afghans by Yakub's exile. But if the throne of Kabul were vacant Ayub had as good a claim to the succession as anyone.* In Herat, a province so far untouched by the war, he had an existing power base of troops and resources which was stronger than that of any potential rival.† Once he decided to make a bid for the throne, Kandahar automatically became his most probable first objective. It lay on the main road to Kabul; it was the ancestral seat of the Duranis, a point of great emotional significance; and of all the provinces of Afghanistan, it was popularly considered the richest. The installation of Sher Ali, an elderly uncle of Ayub's, as British puppet there was likely to strengthen rather than diminish Ayub's ambition.

As early as December 1879 rumours had reached Kandahar that Ayub was contemplating an advance. Stewart had taken the threat seriously enough to recommend laying in supplies along the road from Kandahar to Girishk on the Helmund in case a force had to operate there. He was right to do so because, as we now know, Ayub had already dispatched his own agents to Farah to lay in supplies for an advance on Kandahar. But there was a counter body of opinion at Simla and elsewhere which believed that the inherent rivalries between the Herati and Kabuli regiments at Herat would make it impossible for Ayub to advance. Lytton accepted this view, which was strengthened by the fact that the rumours came to nothing.

The appearance of Abdurrahman as a claimant to the throne transformed the scene. He and his father, Afzal, had fought bitterly to take the throne from Ayub's father, Sher Ali. It was not to be expected that Ayub would accept Abdurrahman's candidateship tamely. It has been argued that Ayub committed a major blunder in this case in not moving from Herat directly against Abdurrahman as soon as the latter crossed the Oxus into Afghan Turkestan when he was still without any significant measure of support.[3] The opportunity if it existed was let slip. Ayub knew that the Ghilzais were opposed to Abdurrahman and he may well have

---

*At the meeting which Griffin held with various chiefs at Kabul on 13 April 1880, Ayub's name had been specifically mentioned as one of those whom the British Government would be prepared to consider (see page 198 above).

†In March 1878, Indian police reports indicated that in the province of Herat there were seventeen regiments of regular infantry, four troops of horse artillery, two mountain batteries and four bullock-drawn field batteries (or 44 guns in all, some breech-loading).

thought that with Herat and Kandahar solidly in his possession, it would be possible to reach an accommodation with the Ghilzais thus making his position virtually impregnable. We know very little directly of Ayub's thinking. Not having fought the British, he may have shared the prevailing feeling of his own troops that the British could be beaten, and the departure of Stewart's division might have encouraged him in this belief. But there is also a hint in his correspondence that he expected the British to co-operate and allow him to take over Kandahar and perhaps Kabul in succession to Yakub.

Throughout the early part of 1880 rumours of an advance by Ayub were prevalent in the bazaars of Teheran and Kandahar. To counter-balance this there were continuing reports of fierce dissension between Ayub's Kabuli and Herati regiments. The general view of the Indian authorities was that while an advance by Ayub could not be discounted, the dissensions among his troops were likely to prevent it. But reliable news from Herat was extremely difficult to get especially since the Wali's discontented troops in the Zamindawar district prevented some of it getting through to Kandahar. The Wali himself had better reason than the British authorities to fear the effect of a move by Ayub and he was better able to assess the truth which lay behind the conflicting reports of Ayub's intentions. On 24 May, following news from his son that Ayub intended to leave Herat in the middle of June, the Wali asked the British Resident (St John) for a British brigade to be dispatched to Girishk – on the River Helmund, eighty miles to the west of Kandahar – to bolster up his own authority in the area. Unless the British made their support clear, the Wali argued, the countryside would rise in support of Ayub and his own troops would desert.

The forces immediately available to Primrose at Kandahar totalled about 4,800 men. At Kalat-i-Ghilzai, eighty miles to the north, there was a garrison of approximately 1,000. Spread back along the lines of communication to Sibi were another 5,400 men. It would be difficult to concentrate a strikeforce quickly from these L of C garrisons.[4] Already Phayre and Sandeman had asked for a further 900 troops to protect the railway line being built via the Harnai valley. They had suggested that if there were any probability of Kandahar being attacked, a complete brigade should be ordered up from the Reserve Division on the Indus. But nothing had yet been done.

The obvious successor to Stewart at Kandahar had been Phayre, but he had a reputation for being unable to get on with the politicals and the natives. Primrose, the other contender, a British Service officer who had been commanding the Poona Division at the beginning of the war, was reputed to be in bad health so Lytton's initial choice was Bright. But when the Governor of Bombay reported in response to a query from Simla that Primrose was actually in strong health as well as being a man of discretion, the choice finally fell on him.[5]

The infantry brigadiers, Burrows and Brooke, had spent most of their careers in staff jobs (they had been respectively Quartermaster-General and Adjutant-General of the Bombay Army when posted to Kandahar), and had seen little or no active service. The cavalry brigadier, Nuttall, had spent much of his service in civil police appointments and had never served in the cavalry. Political control was in the hands of a relatively junior political officer, St John, who had been Principal of the Native College at Ajmer before the war started.

222

The Wali's views were duly reported to Simla by St John who recommended that a brigade be dispatched. Haines did not think that the Kandahar force was strong enough to detach a brigade and suggested that the Reserve Division on the Indus be mobilized as soon as it was known for certain that Ayub contemplated a move on Kandahar. He was afterwards to complain that if this advice had been followed there would have been no disaster. But as Ripon pointed out caustically, mobilization was not the same as actually dispatching troops to Kandahar. In any case, all that was done for the moment was to send a reconnaisance party under Major Leach, VC to the Maiwand area, half-way to the Helmund, to assess its suitability as a camping ground for a brigade. Preparations were also made to move up two native regiments from the L of C to Kandahar when required. The Wali now left to join his troops in Zamindawar, on the far side of the Helmund.

Ayub's advance guard actually left Herat on 9 June, his main body following six days later. While he made steady progress towards the Helmund, the authorities at Kandahar remained in a state of blissful ignorance. It was not until 21 June that St John received reliable news from the Wali about Ayub's preparations and plans; the Wali again pressed for the support of a brigade. St John still hoped that the Wali would be able to stop Ayub without British troops getting involved, but he recommended that a force be moved up to support the Wali and stiffen the morale of his troops. Primrose was averse to moving troops in the prevailing hot weather and Simla preferred to wait for further authentic Intelligence of Ayub's movements.

On 27 June, when Ayub was already half-way to the Helmund, St John repeated his advice: 'I recommend dispatch of brigade to Maiwand if only to confirm fidelity of Wali's troops, overawe Zemindar tribes and establish confidence here.' Primrose now told Army HQ in Simla that he was arranging to move a brigade to Girishk on the Helmund, and to fill the gap left at Kandahar by moving up the 4th BoNI from Quetta and withdrawing a wing of the 29th from Kalat-i-Ghilzai.

Information about Ayub's advance had also reached Simla from Teheran, and Ripon and Haines agreed that some action was now necessary. Primrose's proposals were considered inadequate and on 2 July he was authorized to send a brigade to Girishk and to move up to Kandahar a brigade from the Reserve Division. The same day St John reported that Ayub's force consisted of ten regiments of infantry, 2,500 cavalry and six batteries of guns – in all, some 6–8,000 men.[6]

The Government's decisions had come dangerously late. The railway to Sibi could not move cavalry or guns because of inadequate rolling-stock; it could move infantry quickly provided there were no serious breakdown. But floods had already produced one break in the line, and when the troops reached Sibi there was still a march of some 160 miles to Quetta. Ripon was uneasy about the safety of Kandahar and asked Haines specifically whether Primrose had enough British troops. Haines replied somewhat ingenuously that there were enough provided that Ayub did not appear in greater strength than expected.[7]

Burrows was nominated to command the Girishk brigade, with Nuttall in command of the cavalry. The force consisted of two regiments of cavalry (3rd Bombay Light Cavalry and 3rd Sind Horse), two regiments of Bombay Native Infantry (1st (Grenadiers) and 30th (Jacob's Rifles)), one regiment of British

223

infantry (the 66th, minus two companies), half of the 2nd Company, Bombay Sappers and Miners and E/B, RHA – a total of some 2,500 men and six guns.* Supplies were taken for one month. Primrose retained in Kandahar only the 2/7th Foot, a wing of the 19th Native Infantry, the Poona Horse and some miscellaneous troops, totalling approximately 2,300 all ranks. After the event, there were those like Stewart who thought that Primrose should have sent all or nothing; in fairness, there was no reason for Primrose to suppose at the time that a strong brigade was not adequate for the task.

The 3rd Light Cavalry and the 3rd Sind Horse had served in the Abyssinian Expedition of 1868 although they had seen little fighting. More recently the Sind Horse had distinguished itself in action near Maiwand in February 1879. The 66th was an extremely reliable, steady regiment which had been in India since 1870. It lacked two of its companies which were garrisoning Kalat-i-Ghilzai. The Grenadiers was one of the oldest Indian regiments and had always borne a high reputation, but apart from minor operations in Aden in 1865 it had seen no active service since the Mutiny. The 30th had seen no active service at all since it was raised in 1858, and it was known to contain a high proportion of young, untrained Pathan recruits.[8] A potentially significant weakness in both of the native infantry regiments was the fact that many of the officers had been with them for a short period only. The force would be operating at the height of the hot season, in a basically unfriendly country where forage would be difficult to obtain. Nevertheless it was encumbered with a large baggage train.

Nuttall's cavalry left Kandahar on 4 July, followed next day by the remainder of the brigade. The whole force was concentrated on the Helmund opposite Girishk on 11 July (map 11). Burrows and St John arrived to find the Wali's troops increasingly restive over the news of Ayub's approach. It was agreed that the Wali would move his troops back across the river where they would be quietly disarmed by the British force. Before this could be carried out the Wali's troops mutinied. The infantry and guns fled towards Herat, the majority of the cavalry towards Kandahar. Burrows pursued the rebels across the Helmund and after a sharp fight, recaptured the guns and killed or wounded fifty of them. The bulk of the mutinous infantry nevertheless managed to join Ayub. A disturbing aspect of the affair was the unsteadiness shown by the 30th; 'When the 30th Native Infantry came up, without an order and the enemy a long way out of range, they commenced a wild, irregular fusillade, many of the men firing up in the air, and some of them not even placing their rifles to their shoulders! I am not certain whether I mentioned these circumstances to General Burrows but it made a great impression on me at the time and I thought then that if it came to hard fighting, the regiment would be difficult to keep in hand.'[9]

The recaptured artillery (four smoothbore 6-pounder guns and two smoothbore 12-pounder howitzers) were formed into a separate battery, manned by a detachment from the 66th, under the command of Captain J. R. Slade of E/B. Because the mutineers had taken away the horses, the ammunition wagons could not be retrieved and only some fifty rounds per gun were finally brought away.

---

*The figures given on page 485 of the Abridged History do not include all the staff and over-estimate the strength of the 66th.

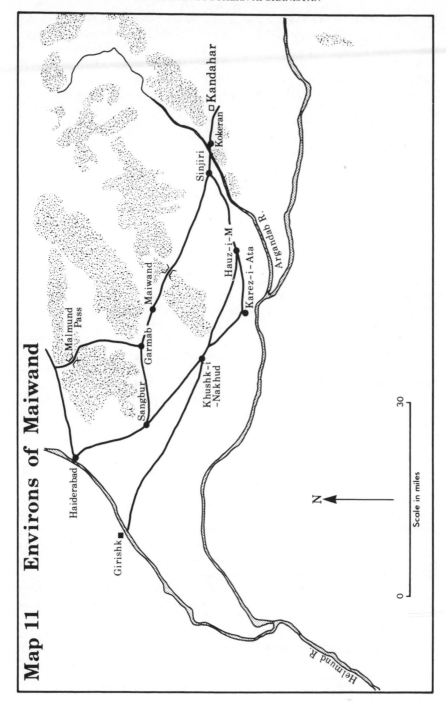

Map 11   Environs of Maiwand

Burrows was now in an awkward situation. He was eighty miles from his nearest supports at Kandahar, with a 25-mile wide stretch of waterless desert immediately to his rear. The Helmund was fordable almost everywhere and in the absence of reliable Intelligence, he could not hope to cover all the points at which Ayub might cross.[10] With the disintegration of the Wali's force and the disappearance of his authority in Zamindawar, there was in any case little point in remaining on the Helmund. Burrows therefore decided to withdraw some 35 miles to Khushk-i-Nakhud where supplies should be more readily obtainable. His reasoning was summarized in St John's telegram to Simla on 17 July: 'The river offering in its present condition no obstacle in any place to the passage of troops, the Wali's army having ceased to exist, and reports reaching me from different quarters that Ayub's intention was to cross further north, if at all, General Burrows determined, rightly in my opinion, to fall back on Khushk-i-Nakhud, where several roads from Helmund to Kandahar meet, where supplies are abundant and communication with Kandahar easy.' The move back to Khushk-i-Nakhud was completed by the 17th, the Wali and some of his men accompanying the force.* On the same day Ayub's cavalry reached the Helmund at Girishk. His main force arrived three days later and encamped between Girishk and Haiderabad.

The position at Khushk-i-Nakhud was a sound one strategically. There were five routes by which Ayub could advance on Kandahar. Two of them – the main road from Girishk and the road from Haiderabad through Sangbur – passed through Khushk-i-Nakhud. The other three – the southern road along the River Argandab, the road through Sangbur and Maiwand, and the route through the Malmund Pass – were all within striking distance. But the odds had clearly worsened. Not only had Ayub been reinforced by the remnants of the Wali's infantry, but the disappearance of the Wali's authority and the retreat of the British force had stirred the countryside and brought tribesmen flocking to join Ayub.

The original purpose in dispatching the brigade had been to bolster up the Wali's authority in Zamindawar. Now that that authority had disappeared, a new situation arose demanding a re-assessment of Burrows' objective. On 15 July, the Commander-in-Chief had telegraphed to Primrose: 'Wali's troops having deserted, the situation has completely changed. General Burrows must act according to his own judgement, reporting fully. He must act with caution on account of distance of support.'[11] These were not particularly helpful instructions but at least they appeared to give the man on the spot full liberty of action. For some days after the disappearance of the Wali's troops, optimistic reports about Ayub's intentions continued to come in. Sandeman, watching anxiously from Quetta, felt obliged in consequence to warn Simla that 'the movement in Ayub's favour is more extended and determined than, I think believed at Kandahar'.[12] His warning was underlined by St John's telegram the same day, reporting the movement of considerable numbers of tribal cavalry and 'ghazis' to join Ayub on the Helmund and Ayub's intention to attack Burrows at Khushk-i-Nakhud.

Simla was beginning to concentrate on the idea of Burrows attacking Ayub. The Commander-in-Chief had already asked Primrose for his views on whether Khushk-i-Nakhud was the best position 'for covering Kandahar and striking a

---

*Hanna says that Malcolmson of the Sind Horse and Anderson of the Grenadiers pressed for an immediate retreat to Kandahar. Hanna, op. cit., p. 393.

blow at Ayub should he cross the Helmund'. Primrose replied on the 19th, 'General Burrows at Khushk-i-Nakhud is within fair supportable distance from Kandahar . . . an impression is abroad that he [Ayub] will not meet our troops in the open but that if he crosses the river at all he will do so to the north of Girishk and perhaps make for Ghazni for political reason.'[13]

Burrows was actually some 46 miles from Kandahar, and reinforcements, particularly of infantry, could not reach him in less than three days. It was not, however, unreasonable to believe that Ayub might be making for Ghazni. The Ghazni faction, which had been led by Mohammed Jan and the Mushk-i-Alam, was still very much in being and were strong supporters of Yakub, Ayub's brother. If Ayub could reach Ghazni and come to some arrangement with the forces there, he would be in a strong position to bid for the throne of Kabul against Abdurrahman. We do not know for certain what Ayub's objective was, but the fact that he was to take the northern route through Maiwand, rather than the direct route through Girishk and Khushk-i-Nakhud, suggests that he may indeed have been seeking to avoid the British and move straight on to Ghazni. Primrose's signal certainly embodied St John's view.

The effect of Primrose's appreciation was reflected in the Commander-in-Chief's reply on the 21st: 'It is of the utmost importance that Ayub should not be allowed to slip past Kandahar towards Ghazni without being attacked.'[14] This was followed the next day by an even stronger hint: 'You will understand you have full liberty to attack Ayub if you think you are strong enough to do so. Government consider it of the greatest possible political importance that his force should be dispersed and prevented by all possible means from passing on to Ghazni.'[15] These telegrams were duly copied to Burrows at Khushk-i-Nakhud.* Clearly Simla was now apprehensive lest Ayub succeed in making common cause with Mohammed Jan and the Ghazni faction and overturn the settlement being worked out with Abdurrahman.

That Burrows understood what was expected of him is clear from his narrative report after the battle: 'My instructions were to strike a blow at Ayub Khan and prevent his passing on to Ghazni.' The situation was summed up realistically by an officer of the force, writing on the 21st: 'We are now awaiting Ayub Khan who is about thirty miles off, with 36 guns and about 6,000 infantry. It will be a stiff fight if he comes to the scratch as this is a perfectly open country and we have only 1,500 infantry, 500 sabres and six guns.'[16]

On 19 July, Burrows had moved camp some three miles nearer to Girishk and two days later, on receipt of a report that Ayub contemplated a night attack, he had moved his force again, into some adjacent stone enclosures. The position was not a good one tactically, but Burrows had in any case no intention of fighting there.[17] A reinforcement of fifty sabres of the 3rd Sind Horse arrived on the 24th, escorting nine men of E/B who brought horses and equipment for the smoothbore. To supplement St John's spy system, daily cavalry patrols were now sent out to

---

*Burrows had taken three heliographs with him, but from Khushk-i-Nakhud was unable to make contact with Primrose. There was not enough telegraph wire available to link him with Kandahar. All messages therefore had to be taken by mounted messenger, which caused a delay of at least 24 hours each way. The equipment was destroyed by a shell during the battle.

Sangbur (some fourteen miles to the north-west, on the main road from Haiderabad), Garmab[18] (roughly the same distance to the north, covering the exit from the Malmund Pass) and to Band-i-Timur (to the south-west, on the river road).

Intelligence now began to accumulate about Ayub's movements. On the 21st St John reported rumours that Ayub intended to move via Sangbur. Two days later the Sangbur patrol encountered enemy cavalry only three miles from camp and on the 25th the same patrol was attacked as it approached Sangbur, losing two men. The same day a patrol to Maiwand learned that Garmab was occupied by Ayub's men and that his main force was expected there on the 26th and at Maiwand on the 27th.[19]

All of this would seem now to have added up to a fairly clear indication that Ayub intended to take the road through Sangbur and Maiwand and that he was probably only a day or so away. Once it was clear that Ayub would not be using any of the southern routes, Khushk-i-Nakhud lost much of its value and Maiwand became the best position. Unfortunately Burrows was not inclined to believe this information and decided to await further news. On the morning of the 26th Sangbur was reconnoitred and found empty, and a spy reported that the Malmund Pass had been clear the day before. But late on the afternoon of 26 July news was received from another spy that Maiwand was now occupied by irregulars and Garmab by a strong force of enemy cavalry.

The information from spies that evening was that Ayub and the main body would be moving through the Malmund Pass that night to rendezvous at Maiwand whence he intended to advance on Ghazni via the Khakrez valley. His force was estimated at 3,500 regular infantry, 2,000 cavalry, 5,000 ghazis and 34 guns.[20] Burrows had already told Primrose that he intended to attack Ayub if the latter advanced on Maiwand or Khushk-i-Nakhud.[21] He decided therefore to move on Maiwand the next morning at 06.30 hours. His orders to that effect were issued at 22.30 hours on the 26th. In fact, Ayub had reached Sangbur shortly after the regular British patrol had left. On the morning of the 27th, therefore, Ayub and Burrows were moving on the same point (Maiwand) but, at roughly right angles with each other. Burrows had if anything slightly the shorter distance to go, but he was encumbered by baggage and likely to be the slower of the two.* The question is therefore why Burrows did not move on the night of the 26th as St John, Leach and Slade apparently pressed him to do. Burrows never explained his thinking. Perhaps he thought he had more time than he actually had. Perhaps he was reluctant to accept the risks and confusion inherent in a night move across hostile country.

The brigade fell in at approximately 04.30 hours on 27 July. A troop of 51 sabres of the Sind Horse under Lieutenant A. M. Monteith† moved out to picket a small hill three miles to the north-west, commanding a view of the approaches from Sangbur and Maiwand, and a troop of the 3rd Light Cavalry under Lieutenant Geoghegan moved out to a point some one and a half miles north of the camp to act as an advanced screen to the main force when it moved off.

*According to Leach's map, Khushk-i-Nakhud to Maiwand is about thirteen miles; Sangbur to Maiwand is about sixteen miles.
†There were three Lieutenants Monteith present – A.M., J. and E.V.P. There were also present two Royal Artillery subalterns named respectively Fowle and Fowell.

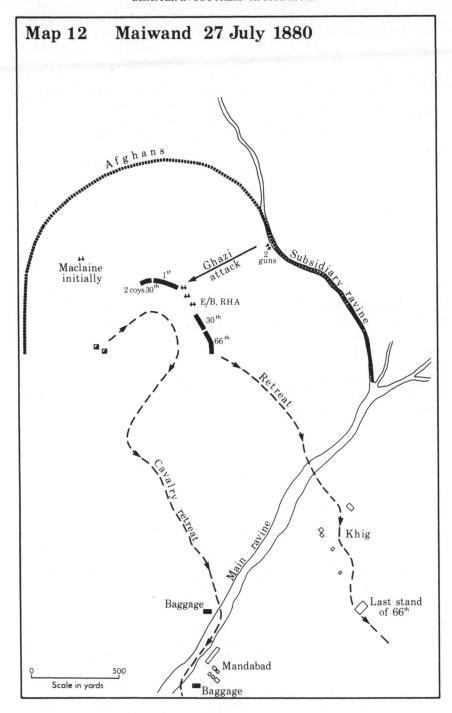

Map 12   Maiwand   27 July 1880

Afghans

Maclaine
initially

1st

2 coys 30th

Ghazi
attack

2
guns

Subsidiary ravine

E/B, RHA

30th

66th

Retreat

Cavalry retreat

Main ravine

Baggage

Khig

Last stand
of 66th

0   500

Scale in yards

Mandabad

Baggage

The brigade was to have moved off at 06.30 hours, but it does not appear to have left until about 07.00 hours having been delayed by assembly of the baggage train.* The column was led by a squadron of the 3rd Light Cavalry, accompanied by two guns of E/B under Lieutenant Maclaine. They were followed at a distance of 500 yards by the two remaining squadrons of the Light Cavalry, accompanied by a second section of E/B, under the battery commander, Major Blackwood. Burrows and the Brigade Staff accompanied the cavalry. Then came the infantry in parallel columns, with the smoothbores and the Sappers and Miners between the columns. The rearguard consisted of 96 sabres of the Sind Horse under Lieutenant-Colonel Malcolmson with the remaining two guns of E/B under Lieutenant Osborne. The baggage train of more than 2,000 animals was on the right flank of the main column, escorted by some 200 infantry. All told, the main column covered a distance of just over a mile. (The detailed composition and strength of the brigade is given in the appendix to this chapter.)

The column halted twice to allow the baggage train to close up, the second halt being made at approximately 08.45 hours at the village of Mushak, some six miles from the starting-point. Officers had their breakfasts, but the native infantry did not apparently fall out for a meal nor is it clear whether they even managed to refill their water bottles. During the halt a spy arrived from Sangbur, having gone first to Khushk-i-Nakhud, with the startling news that Ayub's main force was approaching Maiwand, which had already been occupied by his advance guard.

Burrows was now roughly half-way to Maiwand and he decided to push on, apparently hoping to forestall the main enemy force. The column moved off at about 09.15 hours. Three-quarters of an hour later, by which time it had covered another two miles, both Monteith and Geoghegan, from their positions ahead of the column, reported large masses of men moving across the head of the column, in the direction of Maiwand. Burrows and Nuttall came forward to see for themselves, but visibility was bad because of heat haze and dust, and Major Hogg was dispatched further forward to get a closer view. As Hogg watched, the leading groups veered off to the north, leaving a screen of horsemen to observe the British. No guns or infantry were yet visible but it was clear that Burrows had stumbled on Ayub's army on the march.

Immediately to the front of the British force, at a distance of about a mile, lay a small village, Mandabad,† and away to the right another straggling village, Khig (map 12). On the far side of the villages lay a large ravine, some 15–25 feet deep and 50–100 feet wide, running in a generally north-easterly direction. Beyond Khig a narrower subsidiary ravine diverged at right angles and ran north-westwards towards the enemy position. The ground in the angle between the two ravines was a flat plain, extending northwards to the hills beyond Maiwand, with occasional

---

*Burrows, in his narrative, says 06.30, as does Hogg, and one or two other officers. The majority of observers put the time at 7 or even later, and in view of the mass of baggage to be loaded this is more probable.

†The plan of the action accompanying Leach's narrative, prepared from a sketch made when Daubeny's column subsequently visited the battlefield in September, records this village as Mahmudabad, but I have followed the Official History in referring to it as Mandabad.

irregularities giving some protection to men lying down, but none against artillery fire.*

Burrows never made clear what his analysis of the situation was at this moment or how it determined his actions. It may be that he thought that he still had time to reach Maiwand before Ayub's main force, with its artillery, arrived, and that it was only after his troops had crossed the main ravine that he realized from the numbers facing him that he could not do so. That was Griesbach's impression. If, however, Burrows had already determined at that stage to stand on the defensive it is surprising that he should have ignored the tactical advantages of occupying the ravine and the enclosures of Mandabad. What Burrows now did was to order Blackwood, with Fowell's and Maclaine's sections, forward across the ravine, escorted by a troop of the 3rd Light Cavalry. Blackwood, with Fowell's two guns, appears to have opened fire at approximately 10.50 hours, (according to Hogg's watch), from a position about 500 yards beyond the ravine.† Maclaine, with his two guns, crossed the ravine some distance west of Fowell and then proceeded at a gallop to the left front where he came into action about a mile beyond the ravine and some 1,700 yards from the nearest enemy.

Maclaine's action mystified many people at the time and has done so ever since. Burrows claimed in his official report of 5 September that Maclaine's action was wholly unauthorized and committed the whole force to advancing to support him, thus giving Burrows no time to reconnoitre, plan his action or refresh his men. But he does not make this claim in his dispatch written on 30 August 1880, and Leach is quite clear that the infantry were already crossing the ravine when Maclaine's guns opened fire.‡ Since Maclaine was taken prisoner later the same day and subsequently murdered we cannot know the truth. The most likely explanation is that, having been ordered across the ravine by Blackwood, Maclaine misunderstood his orders and advanced too far, instead of keeping in alignment with Fowell's section.§ Both Leach and Slade thought that Maclaine should have been supported rather than withdrawn; the Official History (vol. V, p. 338) takes the same view. The point is debatable.

Blackwood had opened fire at nearly the maximum range of his guns, and throughout the day the poor visibility made accurate judgement of range difficult. He therefore obtained Burrow's permission to move forward, finally coming into action some 2,000 yards beyond the ravine, at a range of some 2,000 yards. Osborne's section was now brought up from the rear and a succession of messages

---

*The general area had been visited by Biddulph's brigade in January 1879, when Malcolmson and the 3rd Sind Horse had been present (see Chapter 6). In June 1880 Leach had conducted a specific reconnaissance of the Khushk-i-Nakhud and Maiwand areas.

†It is impossible to harmonize the various accounts of Blackwood's movements. What is clear is that Blackwood's original position beyond the ravine was too far away from the enemy for effective shooting, that he therefore moved forward some distance to his final position where he was then some 2,000 yards from the ravine, and some 2,000 yards from Ayub's centre. See the accounts of Fowell, Mayne, Hogg, Oliver, Currie and St. John.

‡Colonel Maxwell in his My God – Maiwand! (London, 1979) has argued that Maclaine did not move until the rest of the brigade had started to cross the ravine. This seems to ignore the evidence of Harris, Oliver and J. Monteith and involves misquoting Leach. The point is, however, irrelevant to the question of Maclaine's action.

§Leach conjectured that Maclaine's action was the result of disappointment on 23 July when his guns had been ordered out to support the cavalry and then withdrawn without firing a shot. Thus Maclaine was determined to get to grips this time. Reports and Narratives, p. 11. The Official History (vol. V, p. 338) suggests that Maclaine had had an earlier disappointment on 14 July.

to Maclaine brought him back to a position on Blackwood's left, the whole of E/B being then in echelon from left to right, with Henn's half-company of Sappers and Miners as close escort. As they came up, the infantry formed a line on each side, but to the rear, of the guns, the Grenadiers on the left of the guns, and the four right-wing companies of the 30th immediately to the right, with the 66th on the extreme right. The four left-wing companies of the 30th were for the moment kept in reserve. The smoothbores were initially stationed to the left rear of E/B.

The key to Burrows' position and to the battle was the subsidiary ravine which offered a covered approach round his right flank and into the rear of his position. No one on the British side seems to have known of the existence of this ravine until after the battle had started despite Leach's reconnaissance in June. Its importance was recognized immediately by the enemy, however, and the 66th was forced to throw back its right flank more and more to meet the enemy fire from the ravine. The regiment ended up facing east, almost at right angles to the Grenadiers, with the 30th forming the hinge. To the rear of the brigade the baggage near Mandabad was quickly under attack from tribesmen seeping down the subsidiary ravine. Engaged in a separate fight of its own throughout the day, the baggage guard had no thought to spare for the rest of the brigade.*

The left flank ended in air and was early outflanked by dense masses of enemy cavalry. Burrows therefore brought up two of the left-wing companies of the 30th and deployed them on the extreme left of the line. Two other left-wing companies joined the rest of the 30th in the firing-line. There was now no reserve. If the line gave way, the cavalry, distributed in small packets behind the right and left flanks, offered the only chance of retrieving the position.

Ayub had been surprised on the march and he was unable to reply to the British artillery for half an hour. As his guns came up they were progressively extended to their left and attempts were made to push some of them down the subsidiary ravine to enfilade the British line. The regular infantry, consisting of Kabuli and Herati regiments, were massed in the centre. On leaving Herat, Ayub's force appears to have consisted of nine regiments of regular infantry, three of cavalry, some 1,500 irregular cavalry and 36 guns, a total of about 6,400 men. Six guns had been left *en route* at Farah and there had presumably been some wastage of men also. But he had been joined by some 1,500 of the Wali's troops and by large numbers of irregulars,* so that his total force at Maiwand was probably of the order of 10,000–15,000.[22]

Of Burrows' total force of just under 2,600, some 600 were employed on baggage guard, as orderlies or on other miscellaneous duties. The actual force available for the fighting line, excluding officers, was about 1,900, made up of some 350 cavalry, 1,350 infantry, 43 Sappers and Miners and about 190 gunners.[23]

The first phase of the battle was essentially a pounding match between E/B and Ayub's artillery in which the British were totally outclassed. Ayub's guns were more numerous and his six breech-loading Armstrongs threw a heavier shell than

---

*The baggage guard beat off all attacks and Quarry's company of the 66th was the only formed body of infantry to leave the field.

*Most survivors refer to these as 'ghazis'. A ghazi is a special kind of religious fanatic and although no doubt a number were present, the vast majority of irregulars present were almost certainly ordinary tribesmen.

anything on the British side. It proved impossible to subdue them.[24] The 66th and the 30th were partially protected when lying down by a small fold in the ground and suffered few casualties during this phase of the action. E/B, the Grenadiers and the two companies of the 30th on the extreme left, however, had little or no cover and among them casualties quickly began to mount, as also among the cavalry. At approximately midday, Burrows appears to have ordered the Grenadiers to advance, but after going some 200 yards, they were forced by the enemy fire to halt and lie down again.*

To the front, the steady fire of the Grenadiers and the guns of E/B were keeping Ayub's infantry at bay. On the right flank, the devastating volleys of the 66th's Martini-Henrys prevented any attempts by the tribesmen to come to grips. And on both flanks the smoothbore battery was providing valuable protection.

Burrows claimed later that at this stage he was confident of success. In reality the situation was already critical. He was virtually surrounded, he had no reserves and the Afghan artillery fire was beginning to demoralize the Indian soldiers. On the left flank, sepoys from the 30th were beginning to drift away from the firing-line.† Hogg wrote later, 'It was quite clear to me soon after 1 pm that nothing but a miracle could save us.'

At approximately 13.30 hours the smoothbore battery exhausted its immediate supply of ammunition and Slade ordered it to withdraw to the rear to replenish. He went to report to Blackwood and found him going to the rear, severely wounded. Slade then took over command of E/B as well, staying with it since Fowell had also been severely wounded.

The withdrawal of the smoothbores had a serious morale effect on the native infantry who were thirsty, tired and had lost heavily from the Afghan artillery fire. On the left flank, the Afghan cavalry, which had been kept at bay by the fire of two of the smoothbores, began now to close in and present excellent targets to the infantry. Leach suggested to Burrows that the two companies of the 30th should be thrown back to counter this threat. Burrows was not prepared to risk it because these companies had earlier shown signs of unsteadiness when being moved. Leach, who had had some of the 30th with him during his reconnaissance in June and knew the difficulties, then went over to assist Lieutenant Cole, the only British officer with them. With some difficulty the sepoys were induced to start volley firing at 600–800 yards, but many of them were recruits unable to make proper use of their rifles.

On the right flank, enemy irregulars were beginning to overflow on to the rear of the 66th. To clear up this situation Nuttall ordered Lieutenant Smith of the Sind Horse to charge with his troop and half a troop of the Light Cavalry. Smith had considerable difficulty in getting the men formed up and under control,‡ but had just moved off when Nuttall shouted to him to stop. When he returned, Nuttall

---

*Whether this move took place and, if so, for what purpose, is not clear. If it did take place, it must have been to provide the Grenadiers with better cover.

†'Many made little or no use of their rifles, and others, falling out of the ranks for water, remained in rear for far longer than was necessary.' Leach's Narrative.

‡'Observing that there was some delay in carrying out the orders, I rode up to Lieutenant Smith and asked him the cause of it. He said his men were out of hand and asked me to help him. I observed that most of the men had carbines instead of drawn swords. I spoke to them severely and got them to return carbines and draw swords.' – Hogg's Narrative.

told him that he had halted the charge because of the presence of a ravine in front of it.

The moment of crisis was rapidly approaching. Ayub had succeeded in bringing two of his guns down the subsidiary ravine to a position only some 200–300 yards from the British centre.* With the crews largely protected by the ravine, these guns began to inflict serious damage, particularly on the Grenadiers who had no natural cover. At about 14.30 hours the fire of Ayub's guns momentarily slackened as though his ammunition had run out. Burrows' hopes were, alas, misplaced. Huge masses of tribesmen suddenly spilled out of the subsidiary ravine and swept diagonally down on the British centre and left.

Without waiting to receive the charge the two companies of the 30th, now led by a solitary native officer, disintegrated, exposing the left flank and rear of the Grenadiers. Almost surrounded, the adjutant of the Grenadiers attempted to form battalion square. In the noise and confusion, the native officers lost control and succeeded only in getting the regiment into a V-shaped formation, with its rear completely exposed. Heat, thirst and the battering they had received from the enemy's guns now took their ultimate toll. Densely packed and exhausted, the men were unable to use their weapons and were cut down at will.†

As soon as he saw the left wing dissolve, Slade ordered E/B to fire one more round and then to withdraw. But the guns, which had been slightly in advance of the infantry, were now almost surrounded and Maclaine, whose guns were the farthest advanced, failed to get his away. Leach and Slade both recorded that the final shots were fired at a range of only 15–20 yards.

The disintegration of the left wing and the withdrawal of E/B infected the remainder of the 30th, which retired in haste on to the left-hand companies of the 66th.‡ In a matter of minutes the line had dissolved. The only means of restoring the situation appeared to be by a cavalry charge. Leach received Burrows' permission to order Nuttall to charge immediately.

Leach took the message personally over to Nuttall who was then about a quarter of a mile south-west of the Grenadiers. Nuttall asked Leach where he was to charge and Leach pointed in the direction of Maclaine's captured guns which were visible beyond the Grenadiers.

Because the cavalry had been split into penny packets earlier on, Nuttall was only able to assemble the equivalent of two squadrons (Mayne's squadron and Geoghegan's troop of the Light Cavalry and A. M. Monteith's troop of the Sind Horse), about 150 sabres in all. The battering they had received from the Afghan artillery had affected the men's morale: 'I saw how hesitating their manner was and that they did not like the job,' Hogg wrote. Nuttall led the charge which struck

---

*Colonel Maxwell has demonstrated by personal inspection that these guns were much closer than originally thought at the time and shown in Leach's map.

†'Sudden as had been the panic among the Grenadiers, they were still standing, apparently irresolute but so closely packed that defence was hopeless. I question whether bayonets were fixed; and if they were, they were little used . . . The indifference of the men to death was most extraordinary and numbers were cut down without a struggle.' – Leach's Narrative. The effect of having so few British officers also told at this point.

‡It is clear that the 30th were already unsteady. Mainwaring, their Colonel, in his narrative said, 'Judging from the conduct of the remainder of the regiment which was under my personal command . . . it was the unsteadiness of young soldiers on first going into action and not the unsteadiness which is caused by alarm. The remaining six companies were so far unsteady that it was almost impossible to stop the laughing and talking in the ranks; and the eagerness of the men to advance made it very difficult to keep the line properly dressed.'

the enemy surrounding the Grenadiers, but it was not pushed home with any real vigour. Hogg, who was an interested onlooker, reported that, 'instead of going straight to their front and trying to smash clean through the whole line of Ghazis, they stopped short with a small band who were actually inside the Grenadier square, cutting the men down, and as soon as they had disposed of these, they wheeled to the right about and retired without orders, and in spite of their officers.'[25] Burrows then rode up and according to his own account ordered Major Currie to charge again with some of the Light Cavalry still at hand. Currie denied hearing any such order and was specifically exonerated on this charge at his subsequent court-martial in March 1881. Burrows then rode on to Nuttall and asked him to charge again. Nuttall said that this was impossible because the men were out of hand but that he would try to rally them on the retiring guns.* The day was now clearly lost and Burrows galloped back to do what he could to save the Grenadiers. The cavalry continued to retreat although some of the troopers appear to have dismounted to fire their carbines. The cavalry was finally assembled in reasonable order on the far side of the main ravine near Mandabad.

The precise sequence of events after the line gave way is impossible to establish. Slade appears to have reformed the remaining four guns of E/B some hundreds of yards to the rear of their original firing position, and refilled some of his limbers, the remainder having to be abandoned. He then retired the battery to the far side of the main ravine, picking up the smoothbores en route, and came into action again with both batteries, to try to cover the infantry's retreat. He was soon forced to retire to prevent being encircled by the Afghan horse. The smoothbores were by then completely out of ammunition, but E/B came into action twice more.

The infantry split up. Some of the Grenadiers, with the remnants of Cole's companies, fell back in the general direction of Mandabad. The remainder of the Grenadiers, with the 66th, were forced off to the right in the direction of Khig. The Sappers and Miners also appear to have retired on Khig since it was there that Henn, their commander was killed.

The native infantry were exhausted and seemingly overwhelmed by the disaster. They could not be induced to re-form or to defend themselves, and the bulk of their casualties occurred during this phase of the battle. In particular, very few, if any, of the seriously wounded got away.† Those retiring in the direction of Mandabad appear to have crossed the main ravine just to the east of the village, and then headed in the general direction of Kandahar.

The 66th and most of the Grenadiers crossed the ravine opposite Khig.‡ Leach gives the impression in his narrative that initially the 66th moved forward, wheeled round in column and then retired in formation. This seems inherently

---

*Burrows admitted at Currie's court-martial that the latter might not have heard the order in the prevailing noise and confusion. Hogg, ibid., was quite sure that after the first charge there was no way of getting the men to face the enemy again. It seems very doubtful whether a second charge could have made any difference.

†Anderson says in his narrative that at least 250 of the Grenadiers, including all the dangerously wounded, were killed before they could get back across the main ravine. The distance from the Grenadiers' original position to the ravine was about a mile.

‡Talbot's plan in 'Reports and Narratives' shows all the infantry retreating through Khig. Clearly the majority did so, but some of the Grenadiers certainly retired close to Mandabad – see Lieutenant-Colonel Griffiths' and Leach's narratives. The *Abridged Official History* (p. 520) has Burrows and some of the 66th retreating through Mandabad, but this is quite clearly wrong – see Note 27 below.

improbable and is contradicted by most other accounts. In particular, Slade, writing subsequently to his mother, said that Burrows had told him that the 66th had been disorganized by the recoil of the Grenadiers and the men had retired in small groups, fighting as they went. Colonel Mainwaring of the 30th said in his narrative: '. . . the pressure from the two Native regiments on both its [66th] flanks pushing it to its immediate front and it may thus be said that the 66th never retired at all', which may be the explanation of Leach's impression.

Khig itself consisted of a number of walled enclosures, and parties of the 66th and Grenadiers halted at successive enclosures to fire on their pursuers. Desperate attempts were made to reform the men and to make a decisive stand, and about 100 of the 66th made a final stand in a garden on the southern outskirts of the village, the final eleven survivors dying in a forlorn charge against the encircling enemy masses.[26] Burrows followed the troops through Khig and when he saw that the position was hopeless, ordered them to retire from the village.[27] In the confusion he was probably not aware of the stand being made by the 66th. As he was leaving, he came across Major Iredell of the 30th, whose leg had been broken by a bullet, and gave up his horse to enable Iredell to be taken away. This incident appears to have given rise to reports that Burrows had been killed, but in fact he was finally rescued by the Wordi-Major of the 3rd Sind Horse, who took him up behind him on his horse.*

By 15.00 hours the plain south of Mandabad was covered by a huge column of fugitives fleeing southwards toward Kandahar.† 'The men were panic-struck, and many officers too, and were streaming away as hard as they could. The enemy's cavalry were about twenty yards behind us, pillaging and following us up closely . . . You cannot conceive such a sight as it was, everything confusion and no discipline or order . . .' wrote Slade. The extreme rear of the column was brought up by E/B and by a troop of the Sind Horse under Lieutenant E. V. P. Monteith, together with Quarry's company of the 66th which had been on baggage guard. The Afghan pursuit had begun to diminish as soon as the main ravine had been crossed, the lure of plunder and the stand of the 66th in Khig both playing their part in diverting Afghan attention. But Afghan horsemen continued to follow the column and to cut up stragglers as far as Khushk-i-Nakhud. Much more might have been done to protect the stragglers and the wounded if the cavalry could have been induced to turn about and face the enemy. But although they had recovered their cohesion, the cavalry had forfeited the confidence of Nuttall and their regimental commanders. With the exception of Monteith's troop, the cavalry gave no active assistance during this first, critical phase of the retreat. This gave rise to bitter comment among other survivors and led subsequently to both Currie and Malcolmson being court-martialled.[28]

From the battlefield, the shortest route to Maiwand lay eastwards across the hills and through the Maiwand Pass, but this route had been blocked by the

---

*Whatever Burrows' mistakes as a commander, his personal courage is beyond question. Slade wrote that he was a veritable 'Coeur de Lion'; The Times' Correspondent reported subsequently that he had 'heard it remarked more than once that if Burrows had had the good luck to be a subaltern instead of a General, he would have well-deserved the Victoria Cross'. At this time, Burrows was a man of 53 who had never been on active service and who had spent the previous ten years in sedentary staff jobs.
†Maxwell, op. cit., deduces from the evidence of graves that a major portion of the Grenadiers made a stand. I find his evidence unconvincing, especially when set against the narratives of the survivors.

advance of the Afghan left wing. Forced off this route, the survivors of Burrows' force headed south and east round the edge of the hills. There was thus a possibility that they might be cut off from Kandahar by enemy cavalry taking the shorter route through the Pass. Lieutenant Reid of the 3rd Light Cavalry was dispatched by Nuttall to push ahead, picking up troopers as he went, to prevent the enemy blocking the route of the survivors at Sinjiri. Reid picked up a dozen troopers *en route*, encountered no opposition and reached Kandahar between 05.00 and 06.00 hours the following day.

Burrows himself caught up with the retreating column some three miles south of Mandabad. His subsequent actions suggest that he had lost all real hope of halting the rout. Certainly he could have found little support or encouragement from the morale of the cavalry. Both Malcolmson's and Currie's actions give the strong impression of men who were thoroughly sick of the whole business and anxious only to get their men to Kandahar as quickly as possible. Just beyond Khushk-i-Nakhud, the rearguard was reported to be in trouble and the cavalry, with the exception of Mayne's troop, was ordered back to assist. Burrows himself accompanied by Currie and Mayne, headed south-west towards Ata Karez, five miles away, where he hoped to find water for the horses. The report about the rearguard proved false and, after picking up a number of stragglers on foot, the main body of the cavalry retraced its steps and followed Burrows towards Ata Karez. Malcolmson was leading with the remnants of the 3rd Sind Horse and Nuttall dispatched his Orderly Officer to tell Malcolmson to slow down. The order was repeated by an orderly, to no avail, and finally Nuttall dispatched an order to Malcolmson to halt. Malcolmson sent back a message saying that as he was close to water and his men very thirsty, he would go on as far as Ata Karez and halt there. He arrived at Ata Karez at approximately 20.00 hours and told Burrows that Nuttall, with the rest of the Light Cavalry, was close behind. In fact, Nuttall had lost the route in the gathering dusk and after waiting for an hour, Burrows and Malcolmson moved off at about 21.00 hours, rejoining the route followed by the rest of the force at Hauz-i-Madat, ten miles further on.

Nuttall, with the rest of the cavalry, found water close to Ata Karez and after spending some three-quarters of an hour watering the horses, moved off by compass in the direction of Hauz-i-Madat where they linked up with Burrows and Malcolmson at approximately 01.00 hours on the 28th.

While the cavalry were seeking water at Ata Karez, the remainder of the brigade was continuing its broken flight on Hauz-i-Madat. The men had now been on the move for more than twelve hours in the broiling sun, and water had become their most desperate need. The rum-casks and medical stores had already been broken into and it was clear that unless water could be found, many of the survivors would simply collapse, to be murdered by the local population or by Ayub's troops. Some four miles south of Mandabad, the fugitives had crossed the River Khushk-i-Nakhud where water could have been obtained from the irrigation channels along its banks, but at this stage in the retreat, with the enemy still pressing hard, the men could not be persuaded to halt. Slade's guns and wagons at the rear of the column, already loaded with wounded, had become the last protected point for stragglers. Monteith by showing a bold front had managed to slow down the pursuit, but he could do nothing for those who straggled behind Slade's guns.

Hauz-i-Madat was some fifteen miles beyond Khushk-i-Nakhud. Slade, Leach and the men with them reached it between 23.00 hours and midnight. The well lay some distance away from the road and by the time that Leach and his party had returned to the road, Burrows and Nuttall had arrived with the cavalry. A report now arrived from the rear that the enemy guns had come up and opened fire, and on Burrows' instructions without further ado, the cavalry moved off at a brisk pace. Large numbers of men on foot were still at the well, and stragglers were still coming in. Leach pleaded unsuccessfully with Burrows to allow the cavalry to remain to protect the rear of the column, but Burrows refused, although he allowed Leach to remain with five troopers to round up the men still there. Burrows' own narrative speaks volumes: 'I could not delay longer as I feared a panic among the cavalry and that they might leave me without protection for the guns. Some shots from jezails and matchlocks from surrounding villages were magnified into the enemy's guns pursuing us; every clump of trees on the sides of the road were troops of cavalry threatening our flanks; and all sorts of scares were constantly occurring, originating, I am pained to say, generally with the officers in command of the regiments.' Geoghegan had on Nuttall's instructions now relieved Monteith in charge of the cavalry rearguard and he waited a considerable time at Hauz-i-Madat, directing stragglers, before moving on.

The main body of the cavalry had once again moved on at such a pace as to outstrip the guns, and Burrows dispatched Leach forward to order Nuttall to slow the cavalry down to enable the guns to catch up. The order produced no effect and Leach was again dispatched to call a halt. By this time, Malcolmson at the head of the cavalry, was three miles beyond the guns, approaching Ashu Khan; Nuttall was a mile to the rear, but still two miles ahead of Burrows with the guns. On receipt of the second order, Malcolmson halted and the guns caught up. They then moved on to Ashu Khan, some miles beyond Hauz-i-Madat, which was reached at about 05.00 hours just as dawn was breaking. The artillery horses were now reaching absolute exhaustion. Slade had had to abandon a smoothbore gun at Hauz-i-Madat and he was now compelled to abandon the two smoothbore howitzers. Burrows ordered the cavalry at this point to give up horses to the artillery so that the limbers with their cargoes of wounded could be brought in.

Although pursuit by Ayub's troops had ceased at dusk, the news of the catastrophe to the British had spread rapidly through an expectant countryside. The survivors were continuously sniped and attacked by the peasantry. Between Ashu Khan and Sinjiri, Lieutenant Whitby of the Grenadiers was shot and killed, and Maclaine was made prisoner by villagers as he searched for water. In the darkness and confusion, his disappearance was not noticed. As daylight came, so the attacks redoubled. The cavalry and guns reached the River Argandab, at Sinjiri, at approximately 07.00 hours. The river bed proved heavy going for the guns, and another smoothbore had to be abandoned. While the column was still crossing it was met by a troop of the Poona Horse from Kandahar, the advance guard of a relieving force under Brigadier-General Brooke. The Poona Horse under Captain J. W. Anderson took over the task of protecting the rear of the column.

The first news of the disaster had reached Kandahar at about 02.00 hours, brought by a jemadar of the 3rd Sind Horse who had been dispatched by

Blackwood as soon as he saw the infantry collapse. The jemadar brought Blackwood's field-glasses with him as evidence of the authenticity of his message. Shortly afterwards the Wali himself arrived to confirm the news and at about the same time the first officer – Veterinary Surgeon Major Oliver of E/B – arrived. Oliver immediately saw Primrose who arranged for Brooke to leave at daylight with a small force to assist the survivors in.

Brooke left Kandahar at 05.30 hours with forty sabres of the Poona Horse, 70 men of the 2/7th Fusiliers, 100 of the 28th BoNI and two guns of C/2, RA. He halted at Kokeran, on the Kandahar side of the Argandab, at approximately 09.00 hours, sending Anderson on ahead. His arrival dispersed a large body of tribesmen who had assembled to harass the survivors of Burrows' force.

Brooke started on his own return march at 09.30 hours in order to clear a path for the survivors. At Abbasabad, three miles short of Kandahar, he was forced to deploy and attack to disperse hostile villagers who were blocking the route and killing survivors as they passed. Burrows, with the remnants of his cavalry and E/B, entered Kandahar at approximately 14.00 hours, having been on the move continuously for more than thirty hours. Stragglers continued to trickle in throughout the rest of the day; others were killed in the outskirts of the city. From the time that they had left Khushk-i-Nakhud on the morning of the 27th, they had covered nearly sixty miles.

Burrows' losses amounted to 21 officers and 948 men killed and eight officers and 169 men wounded – 43 per cent of the force engaged. In addition, nearly 800 native followers and drivers were killed, E/B alone losing 111. The very high proportion of killed to wounded and the virtual absence of prisoners is a sobering illustration of the dangers of defeat in this type of warfare. The heaviest losses were among the Grenadiers, who had suffered severely even before the final charge, and who lost just over 64 per cent of their strength. The 66th lost nearly 62 per cent, including twelve out of nineteen officers. The Sappers and Miners lost more than 60 per cent. The cavalry escaped with a loss of only 11 per cent. The relatively small loss in E/B (just under 23 per cent) can fairly be attributed to its splendid discipline and to Slade's leadership; two Victoria Crosses, a CB (Slade) and eight DCMs were a fitting reward.

It is impossible to discover Ayub's losses. Mirza Mohammed Akbar put them at 1,950 for the regular troops and at least 800 killed among the irregulars. One of Ayub's regulars interviewed by Brigadier-General Wilkinson in February 1881 put Ayub's losses at 3,000 killed.[29] Slade, in a letter to his mother shortly afterwards, said that Ayub had admitted to 3,200 killed and 1,800 wounded.[30] Hills says that the ghazis (sic) admitted their losses to be countless ('beshumar') – at least 3,000–4,000 – and that it took them seven days to bury their dead. Primrose in his covering note forwarding Burrows' dispatch put the enemy loss at 5,000. Allowing for natural exaggeration, it seems possible that Ayub's losses were between 2,500 and 3,000, killed and wounded.

Where did the blame for this disastrous affair rest? It lay in the first instance at Simla. Both Army Headquarters and the Government of India were slow to appreciate the threat posed by Ayub. When its seriousness was finally brought home, it was too late to reinforce Kandahar in strength. Writing to Ripon before the disaster had occurred, Haines confessed that 'we are weak because we allowed ourselves to believe that Ayub would not advance on Kandahar. Right to the end, hopes were pinned on Ayub's avoiding Burrows or upon Burrows being able to defeat him.' Ripon was to some extent an exception. As early as 4 July, he had pressed Haines as to whether Primrose had enough British troops to guarantee the safety of Kandahar, but even Ripon was more anxious about Ayub evading Burrows than about Burrows' ability to beat him.[31] There should have been no cause to underestimate Ayub's fighting powers. The near-disaster at Ahmed Khel was only three months old, and what had nearly happened to seasoned Sikh, Gurkha and Punjabi troops could easily happen to others.

Primrose and St John at Kandahar must share a major part of the blame for the optimism and carelessness which infected Simla. Primrose has been criticized – notably by Stewart – for not sending out the whole garrison.[32] No doubt that is what a more aggressive, fighting commander like Roberts might have done. But under an experienced commander like Baker or Macpherson or Roberts himself, Burrows' brigade would never have been beaten.

Burrows himself made serious errors. His position at Khushk-i-Nakhud was well-chosen to intercept Ayub. But its value could be fully realized only by means of an adequate reconnaissance system. The system of daily cavalry patrols was a mistake; it wore out the horses, it invited an ambush (which duly took place) and it left long periods in which the enemy could move without detection. The arrival of Ayub's force at Sangbur on the 26th, shortly after the British patrol had left, illustrates the defects of the system. While accepting the smallness of the available cavalry force, it would surely have been better to have maintained standing patrols at places like Sangbur, Garmab and Band-i-Timur.

Since Burrows could not rely upon receiving speedy, accurate information about Ayub's movements, it was of particular importance that the brigade be ready and able to move quickly. This pointed to the need to reduce the size of the unwieldy baggage train. Burrows had told Primrose that he intended to reduce this baggage so that he could if necessary pursue Ayub if he made for Ghazni, but nothing had been done by the 27th. The brigade was thus seriously delayed on the morning of the 27th by the difficulty in assembling the baggage. Moreover once it started, it moved extremely slowly because of the baggage. The delays were, as it turned out, critical.

Once Burrows had decided to move on Maiwand, there was great deal to be said for moving either the whole or part of his force the same night, as Leach and others had suggested. By leaving it until the morning of the 27th, he was consciously leaving a very narrow margin for forestalling Ayub. Moreover it is not clear why departure on the 27th was fixed as late as 06.30 hours. This was a relatively late hour in the prevailing conditions and it would surely have been better either to have moved the bulk of the force at, say, 04.30 hours, leaving the baggage to follow under strong guard, or at least to have moved the cavalry and guns to occupy Maiwand at the earliest moment to hold it until the infantry could come up. All Burrows' movements from the late afternoon of the 26th onwards were very sluggish. That he thought he had plenty of time in hand is apparent even from the formation adopted for the march, with the cavalry and horse artillery broken up into detachments along the length of the column.

When the enemy was sighted, Burrows had three alternatives – to attack, to retreat or to fight defensively. Ayub claimed that he was not anxious to fight the British and it is possible that if Burrows had decided to retreat, he might have done so with comparative impunity although it would have roused the country-side.[33] Such a course would have been contrary to the tenor of Burrows' instructions and there is no evidence that he ever contemplated it. Hogg thought that retreat would have been impossible.

All experience from Plassey onwards suggested that attack offered the best chance of success. Ayub had been caught, strung out, on the march and the fact that his artillery did not open fire until half an hour after the British guns emphasizes the advantages which might have accrued through a general British advance. At what stage Burrows abandoned the idea, if indeed he ever had it, is not clear. His despatch gives the impression that it was his intention from the start to fight defensively and to encourage Ayub to attack him.*

To fight defensively was clearly a risky operation in view of Ayub's overwhelming numbers and his superiority in artillery. Presumably what Burrows gambled on was that Ayub's troops would not have the patience or discipline to stand a long engagement and that they would bank everything upon a series of headlong attacks which would be defeated by the disciplined fire of the British brigade. That this was not an entirely unfounded hope is shown by Mirza Mohammed Akbar's admission that several times the Afghan forces were on the point of giving way. Where Burrows was very clearly at fault was in his choice of ground. The defects of the ground on which he chose to fight have already been indicated. If he had to fight a defensive battle, the right place to do so was surely behind the cover of the main ravine, utilizing the buildings and enclosures of Mandabad and Khig. This was certainly Leach's view.

Burrows' disposition of his troops can also fairly be criticized. By dispersing his cavalry in small groups, including a detachment of 96 sabres with the baggage, and by keeping them close up behind the firing-line, he went a long way to ensuring that no effective cavalry force was available at the supreme moment of crisis, when the infantry had given way. Even if it could have been concentrated, a force of under 500 sabres could hardly have retrieved the situation but it might well have enabled Burrows' force to conduct a fighting retreat rather than a rout. The behaviour of the cavalry, and particularly of the two regimental commanders, was in any case unsatisfactory. Nuttall had seen active service during the Mutiny and in the Abyssinian Expedition, but he was not a cavalryman. At the time of his appointment to Kandahar, he was Commandant of the Sind Frontier Force and it is tempting to speculate that the unhelpfulness displayed by Malcolmson on the 27th may have had its origin in earlier relations with Nuttall in that Force. At all events Nuttall's handling of the cavalry brigade had already provoked criticism and resentment.[34] Particularly during the retreat, both regimental commanders gave an impression of men who were fed-up of the whole business and anxious

---

*His report was castigated by the C in C and Viceroy as wholly failing to explain the causes of defeat. It is indeed a remarkably bald document. He complains that Maclaine's action precipitated the battle but admits that he would not have made different plans even if he had been given more time. It is clear that he intended to fight defensively: 'I lost the opportunity of reconnoitring the enemy and selecting the position in which I would give battle.' *Reports and Narratives*, p. 1.

only to get clear of it. Malcolmson and Currie were both charged with cowardice and misconduct during the battle and retreat. They were acquitted on the evidence produced. But they certainly did less than they might have done, particularly during the retreat, and this can only have been due to a loss of confidence in Burrows and Nuttall. The casualties during the retreat would have been greatly reduced if all the cavalry had done their duty.

It was a mistake to have placed Cole's two companies of the 30th on the extreme left wing. To entrust such a vital section of the line to suspect troops, under a solitary British officer who had been with the regiment only a month, was taking a serious and unnecessary risk.*

Much effort was subsequently expended on criticizing the quality of the Bombay troops generally. Roberts was a prominent critic but his views were shared, it would appear, by most of the officers who accompanied him from Kabul. Their opinions obviously gained added weight from the fact that their own Bengal troops defeated Ayub fairly easily. The Bombay Army never fully recovered its name, but it is worth noting the verdict of Hume, a British Service officer, who succeeded Roberts at Kandahar. Having inspected all the Bombay infantry regiments under his command in December 1880, his considered judgement was they were 'physically fit for service, steady on parade and, under the circumstances smart in appearance. The tone of the British officers of these regiments is, I consider, excellent. I am quite satisfied with all the Bombay Infantry Regiments I have seen.'[35]

The margin between victory and defeat was in any case a narrow one. The Afghan regular to whom Wilkinson spoke said that Ayub's regular troops had been dismayed by their losses and were ready to run away when they were saved by the final ghazi charge. If Cole's two companies had been less exposed, and E/B better protected, the brigade might have weathered the storm and Burrows might have had his victory.

---

*Leach said in his narrative 'Want of discipline told its tale. The proportion of recruits was large and many of the men had never been through a course of musketry; the majority certainly had no idea of the range of their weapons. Their Native Officers were bad and appeared to have no influence with the men; and their two officers, who both fell gallantly at their posts, were almost boys and could not have known their men. The composition of the regiment was largely Pathans and Pathans are proverbially difficult to command. After the removal of the smoothbore guns, their flank was exposed, they suffered extremely from thirst and they had lost heavily.'

NOTES

1. Le Mesurier, op. cit., p. 621.
2. *Afghanistan (1880)*, No. 1, p. 53.
3. See, for example, Sir Percy Sykes, *A History of Afghanistan*, vol. II, p. 138.
4. For the detailed description of troops in South Afghanistan in May, 1880, see Appendix XXVII of the *Abridged Official Account of the Second Afghan War*, London, 1908.
5. Governor to Simla, 27 February 1880 – HP, vol. 38, f93.
6. *Afghanistan (1880)*, No. 3, p. 6. This was virtually identical with the information from Teheran and fairly accurate. But it made no allowance for tribal levies joining Ayub.
7. Ripon to Haines/Haines to Ripon, 4 July 1880 – HP, vol. 29.
8. 'The proportion of recruits was large and many of the men had never been through a course of musketry; the majority certainly had no idea of the range of their weapons.' *Reports and Narratives of Officers who were engaged at the Battle of Maiwand – 27 July 1880*. Intelligence Branch, India, 1881, p. 15. Eaton Travers, who saw some of the regiments at Quetta in December 1878, thought that they were the smartest-looking native troops he had seen. Combe, in the aftermath of Maiwand, thought they looked 'awful scrubs' (op. cit., p. 201).
9. Captain Harris, DAQMG – *Reports and Narratives*, p. 19. Curiously enough, this was not mentioned in Hogg's narrative which is in the Library of the Royal Military Academy at Sandhurst (hereafter referred to as Hogg).
10. St John, Writing to Simla on 17 July, said 'During my stay of five days, I crossed it in nine different places with a guide, in a distance of five miles.' *Afghanistan (1880)*, No. 3, p. 27.
11. *Afghanistan (1880)*, No. 3, p. 12.
12. Telegram of 21 July, op. cit., p. 16.
13. Op. cit., p. 95. St John appears to have been among those who thought Ayub would not fight – see Hogg, first part, p. 13.
14. Op. cit., p. 96. Haines' telegram in turn reflected Ripon's own strong view – Ripon to Haines, 21 July 1880 – HP, vol. 29.
15. Op. cit., p. 97.
16. Hills, op. cit., p. 18. The officer may have been Hogg, the Cavalry Brigade Major.
17. Burrows reported that the force was well-entrenched (*Afghanistan (1880)*, No. 3, p. 18), but Major Currie said subsequently that 'the entrenchment consisted of a shelter trench thrown up by the 66th on their front and a line of kitbags in front of the rest.' *Reports and Narratives*, p. 43.

There were persistent rumours of a night attack on the force – see, for example, Sandeman's telegram of 21 July – *Afghanistan (1880)*, No. 3, p. 16.
18. On Leach's map in 'Reports and Narratives', this is spelled 'Garmao'. Elsewhere in the narratives it is referred to as Gurmao. The Official History refers to it as Garmab.
19. On the same day (25th), St John recorded in his diary reports that half of Ayub's force would move via Sangbur and half by the Malmund Pass – *Afghanistan (1880)*, No. 3, p. 148.
20. See Hogg – second part, pp. 1–2.
21. Primrose to Simla, 26 July – *Afghanistan (1880)*, No. 3, p. 21.
22. Burrows put the total at 25,000 although he also quoted a figure of 50,000 – *Reports and Narratives*. Hogg, op. cit., says at least 24,000. *The Abridged Official History* (p. 497) puts the figure at 23,000. The most reliable information is from a pay clerk in Ayub's army, Mirza Mohammed Akbar. He gives the strength on leaving Herat as approximately 6,400, to which was subsequently added 1,500 of the Wali's men. Allowing for wastage, the hard core of the Army at Maiwand was therefore about 7,500. It seems doubtful if the number of irregulars exceeded this figure. See *Abridged Official History*, Appendix XXVIII.
23. Of the Grenadiers, 146 NCOs and sepoys were on baggage guard of various types and ten were sick, leaving 470 men (including bandsmen) for the firing-line – *Reports and Narratives*, p. 64. Of the 66th, 63 men were on baggage guard, 42 were in the smoothbore battery and 32 were sick, leaving 364 men available – *Afghanistan (1880)*, No. 3, p. 156. No precise figures are available for the 30th although one company was on baggage guard. Of the cavalry, 349 were available for the fighting line – *Hogg's narrative* in *Reports and Narratives*.
24. 'The former [Ayub's guns] were admirably served and with the exception of their Armstrong shells, which were generally too high, every shot was amongst us' – *Burrows' narrative*. 'Their artillery was extremely well served . . . their fire was concentrated. We were completely outmatched and . . . our guns seemed quite unable to subdue theirs. Their six Armstrong guns threw heavier shell than ours and their smoothbore guns had great range and accuracy, and caused great damage . . .' – *Narrative of Lieutenant N. P. Fowell*.
25. Hogg manuscript, second part, p. 7.

26. Information provided by the Afghans – Primrose's dispatch of 1 October 1880 – *Afghanistan (1880)*, No. 3, p. 156.

27. Burrows' own narrative merely refers to his having gone 'through the gardens near the village' and some accounts, including Hanna's have interpreted this to refer to Mandabad. It is, however, quite clear from the narratives of Colonel Mainwaring and Major Iredell of the 30th that Burrows followed the infantry in the direction of Khig. His obvious move would be to try to head off the infantry and get them to make a stand, and this is consistent with Leach's narrative which has Burrows cutting across the main ravine between Mandabad and Khig, and emerging on the southern outskirts of Khig. See *Reports and Narratives*.

28. Nuttall's report (*Afghanistan (1880)*, No. 3, p. 103), which claimed some credit for covering the retreat, was critically annotated by Burrows when it passed through his hands. Curiously enough, Malcolmson is the only senior officer whose report is not published either in *Reports and Narratives* or *Afghanistan (1880)*, No. 3.

29. HP, vol. 28, ff. 23–28.

30. See Sir Patrick Cadell – *History of the Bombay Army*, London, 1938, pp. 248–9.

31. Ripon to Haines, 21 July 1880 – HP, vol. 29.

32. '. . . the force was always too small considering the strength of the enemy in artillery. This was well-known, and General Primrose should have taken out his whole force and gone himself in command.' Stewart to his wife, 31 July 1880. Elsmie, op. cit., p. 374.

33. Ayub wrote to Roberts in August: 'I was informed that the English had halted at Kushk-i-Nakhud. On the receipt of this news, I thought it well that my troops should not take the road by Kushk-i-Nakhud but should proceed by that of Maiwand and I hoped that the English might show me friendship. Early in the morning [27 July], in the neighbourhood of Maiwand, the English Army came and began to fight.' *Afghanistan (1880)*, No. 3, pp. 90–91.

34. Cf. Currie's narrative – 'a great many things were done to unsteady cavalry which, of course, General Nuttall, never having served in a cavalry regiment, could not be expected to appreciate.'

35. Hume to Adjutant-General, Simla, 8 December 1880 – HP, vol. 38, ff.217–8.

CHAPTER 13

DISASTER RETRIEVED

With the departure of Burrows' brigade on 5 July, Primrose was left at Kandahar with some 2,300 men, including sick and non-effectives. This was potentially dangerous but reinforcements were on their way. The 4th BoNI had been ordered up from Quetta; the leading companies reached Kandahar on 13 and 14 July, the remainder arriving on the 23rd. On receipt of the news of the mutiny of the Wali's troops at Girishk on 14 July, and with the situation now becoming more ominous, Primrose ordered up the 28th BoNI which was garrisoning posts between Kandahar and Quetta. The first four companies reached Kandahar on 28 July, the remainder two days later.

The garrison continued to occupy the extensive cantonments laid out just over a mile west of the city, although immediately after the news of the mutiny at Girishk, two 40-pounders of 5/11, RA had been sent into the citadel to provide a calming influence on a city seething with rumours and expectations. As the tension increased, petty incursions began to multiply – telegraph wires cut, water supplies interrupted, patrols and guards fired upon.[1] With the arrival of the first survivors from Maiwand, it was immediately obvious that the garrison could not hope to defend the cantonment which covered a wide area, had no independent water supply and was dominated by Picquet and Karez Hills, some 500–600 yards to the west. The citadel inside Kandahar already held commissariat and ordnance stores as well as the detachment of 5/11, but it was dominated by surrounding buildings and possessed only a single well. It was not defensible by itself and Primrose had no option but to try to defend the walls of the city (map 13). Although crumbling in parts, they were made of sun-dried mud, fifteen feet thick in places, with an average height of some thirty feet and covered along the north and east fronts by a ditch eighteen feet wide. Experiments in 1879 had shown that the dried mud had a resistance to shot roughly equal to solid masonry so that they would not easily be breached. The basic problem was their length; to defend some 6,300 yards of wall, Primrose would have 5,000 men including sick and wounded.

The decision to retire into the city having been quickly taken, the rest of 28 July at Kandahar was a period of frantic bustle as stores and equipment were hastily moved from the cantonments into the city and the survivors of Burrows' brigade, lame, thirsty and exhausted, staggered in. No one knew when the vanguard of Ayub's army would appear although it was prudent to assume that it might be only 24 hours' away; the rising tide of hostility among the local population had already shown itself in attacks on the survivors from Maiwand and on Brooke's relieving force. The evacuation of the cantonments was thus conducted in great haste and with predictable confusion and loss.* A good deal of the confusion was due to

---

*Some staff officers wanted to retain the cantonments until the next day and the Commander-in-Chief severely criticised Primrose's decision to abandon them in such haste.

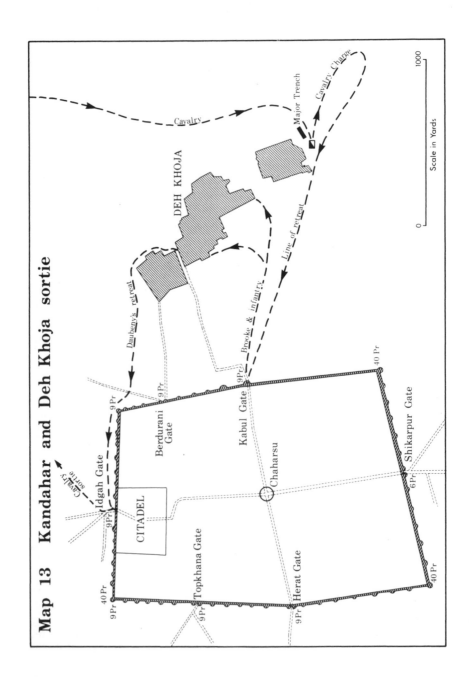

Map 13   Kandahar and Deh Khoja sortie

Brooke's action in closing and barricading all the city gates save the Idgah gate in the northern wall, prior to leaving to bring in Burrows' survivors. Primrose refused to rescind the order despite the changed circumstances, and the long trains of transport animals carrying stores from the cantonments found themselves jostling with the survivors of Burrows' brigade and the hordes of panic-stricken shop-keepers and servants from the cantonments for entry through one narrow passage-way. The officers and men of the 28th BoNI arriving the same day and catching the faint whiff of panic, must have wondered what the fates had let them in for. The most serious loss was the major part of the engineer stores which were left behind when the guard was withdrawn prematurely – in particular, tools and detonators which would have been invaluable subsequently. At nightfall on the 28th the remaining troops were ordered back within the walls and the gates were then barricaded.

When dawn broke the next day, there was no sign of Ayub's troops although looting and destruction was going on around the abandoned cantonments. On Brooke's advice, and against the opposition of the politicals, some 15,000 Afghans were expelled from the city during the next two days in the interest of security and to safeguard food and water supplies. A careful search now revealed a number of wells inside the walls so that water was now no longer likely to be a problem. There was ample food and a month's supply of fodder and grain for the animals. Since the rigid rules of seniority could not in any circumstances be ignored, Burrows was placed in direct command of the garrison, with HQ in the citadel. Excluding 438 sick, the garrison numbered just over 4,600 and was initially distributed as follows:

South and east walls	– 2/7th Fusiliers.
North and west walls	– 28th BoNI, supported by details of 3rd Light Cavalry and 3rd Sind Horse.
Citadel	– the remnants of 1st and 30th BoNI.
Idgah Gate	– remnants of 66th Foot.
General Reserve and internal security	– Poona Horse, 4th and 19th BoNI.[3]

Three of the four 40-pounders and eight available 9-pounders were placed on the walls together with a stray 6-pounder smoothbore. The remaining 40-pounder and the two howitzers of 5/11, RA were placed in the citadel. The gates, the north-west bastion and the square in the centre of the city (the Chaharsu) were linked to HQ in the citadel by telegraph. Finally, a picked body of marksmen was formed from the garrison and distributed round the walls. The garrison then got down to strengthening the defences and clearing away buildings and trees close to the walls to give a clear field of fire. A wire entanglement was run round the foot of the walls as an additional defence, mines were placed in all the gaps in the walls and the main gates were covered with iron sheets.

The tribesmen accompanying Ayub began to appear in the city on 30 July and on the following day a party which had occupied a shrine close to the north-east bastion was attacked and driven out by a troop of the Poona Horse, two companies of the 7th Fusiliers and two companies of the 28th BoNI. Ayub's main body had been delayed by the need to look after the wounded and bury the dead at Maiwand and the vanguard did not appear outside the city until 6 August. Two days later the first of Ayub's guns opened fire from Picquet Hill at a range of 2,000 yards. The siege had begun.

On the same day, three hundred miles to the north, Roberts started his march. One battery and the Central India Horse had not arrived from the Khyber L of C when Roberts's cavalry moved out from Sherpur and Kabul on 8 August, but they had caught up by the following day when the force camped at Saidabad, seventeen miles south of Kabul. The force moved by brigades up the Logar valley to Warsak, and then south-westwards across the Zamburak Pass to strike the main Kabul–Ghazni road just north of Ghazni. From then on it was retracing in reverse the route followed four months earlier by Stewart's force. The march itself was relatively free from incident, the main problem being, as always supplies. In the early stages, when two or more brigades moved together, the prescribed order of march was: first, the main body of fighting troops, then the field hospitals, ordnance and engineer parks and treasure, followed by the baggage and followers, and finally the rearguard. The Force marched each day in the early hours of the morning and halted every hour for ten minutes. Even so there were great difficulties in keeping up a uniform pace. When the Highlanders led the column, the Gurkhas were exhausted trying to keep up; when the Gurkhas led, Highlanders and Sikhs had to slow down, with almost equally tiring results. The main body would halt to make camp at about midday, but the rearguard would not get in till the late afternoon or evening. Private Crane, of the 9th Lancers, has left behind a vivid description of the day's march.

'No one except men who have been on active service and marched with a division could hardly picture to themselves the bustle and shouting of the native followers; the shining glare from the fires that have been lit to show a light to saddle our horses and pack the tents; the neighing of the horses, the dismal moan of the camel as a load is packed on his back; the mules kicking their loads off just as we have packed them on their backs; some mules getting loose and running among the troop horses causing some of them to break loose; . . . the tedious marching along the hot dusty roads, sometimes parched with thirst, water not being procurable in some places; the one continual line of camels, mules, donkeys, the loads on their backs almost bearing them down; the shouting of the native drivers, most of whom get on top of a load, and pretty near breaking the poor animals' backs; the long line of infantry tramping along the hot, dusty road, with the sun peeling the skin off our faces – all tramping on to the next camping ground.'[3]

Thirty days' supply of tea, rum, sugar, salt and dal as well as a few days' supply of mutton on the hoof was taken, but generally each regiment was responsible for its own food supplies *en route*. Wood for baking bread was always a problem, but the Afghan villagers proved remarkably willing to sell their houses for firewood. Shortage of water was a fairly constant problem, aggravated by the high daytime temperatures and the thick, choking dust which the marching columns threw up. The heat of the day, sometimes reaching well over 100° Fahrenheit in the tents contrasted with cold nights approaching freezing point. Tents were taken for every fighting man, but otherwise baggage was ruthlessly pared down – the native infantry, for example, being allowed only twenty pounds per man, including tents. Even so, the many items of equipment which a self-contained force needed to take with it meant a baggage train of about 8,000 animals, with some 8,000 followers.

The march was by no means the smooth, efficient progress that it has sometimes been made to appear. The large number of baggage animals and followers and the very early starts resulted in a good deal of confusion, with the baggage trains of the different brigades getting entangled on the march and causing numerous delays while the traffic jams were sorted out. At one point, MacGregor was so infuriated by the cavalry baggage becoming entangled with his own that he sought to put the cavalry officer concerned under close arrest but could not find him.* On top of this, Roberts set a cracking pace. As far as Ghazni, the force averaged nearly thirteen miles a day, a very high average in the heat.

By the time the force reached Ghazni on 15 August the baggage animals were showing signs of exhaustion and malnutrition. Still Roberts pressed on, marching as much as 21 miles a day. Two days beyond Ghazni, he received a letter from Colonel Tanner, commanding the garrison at Kalat-i-Ghilzai. He reported the countryside there quiet, but Kandahar closely invested. Reaching Shahjui on the 21st Roberts was able to communicate directly with Tanner by heliograph. Tanner was able to tell him that despite a disastrous sortie the garrison at Kandahar was not in serious difficulty. The Kabul force reached Kalat-i-Ghilzai on 23 August, having covered 136 miles in eight days since leaving Ghazni. The troops and animals were now considerably worn down by the continuous marching. So far Roberts had lost only nine soldiers and eleven followers killed or missing, the latter almost certainly murdered by tribesmen prowling round the camps at night. But he had a daily sick list which averaged some 550 soldiers and up to 200 followers – mainly diarrhoea from the poor food, blistered feet,[4] heat-stroke and exhaustion. And the force was beginning to run into serious logistic problems, with heavy wastage and exhaustion among the transport animals and fatigue and malnutrition among the large army of followers on whom the fighting men depended. The rearguard had the unhappy duty of rounding-up and driving along the exhausted followers – Hensman likened the work to that of beaters during a tiger shoot.

MacGregor thought that it all looked more like the disorganized retreat of a beaten army; he suspected that Roberts was driving his force on in order to beat Phayre. Roberts was now only some 88 miles from Kandahar – less than a week's march at his earlier rate of progress – and Tanner was able to show him a letter dated 17 August from Major Adam, Primrose's chief of staff. 'We are very secure,' wrote Adam. 'The buildings round the walls have been mostly cleared away; abattis of trees, wire entanglements, *chevaux de frise*, traverses, flank defences, blue lights, shells, small mines and drains – all have been got ready; and if they do attack, it will be at a great loss of life to them.' Despite the disastrous outcome of the sortie, the garrison was in good health and spirits and there was no serious shortage of supplies.[5]

With the immediate anxiety about Kandahar removed, Roberts was able to give his force a day's rest at Kalat-i-Ghilzai where there was ample forage and water. When he moved on he took with him the 966 men of Tanner's garrison. The garrison served no useful purpose now that Kabul was being evacuated and the troops were a useful accretion to his force. The city was handed back to the Ghilzai chief who had been its Governor before the British occupation in January 1879.

---

*Lieutenant Travers of the 2nd Gurkhas was equally scathing in his diary about the defective staff work – see JSAHR, vol. LIX (1981), pp. 208–28.

Two days later on 27 August, Roberts got news that Ayub had raised the siege of Kandahar and withdrawn to a position on the east bank of the River Argandab. It was vital for Roberts to know what his quarry was up to and Gough was ordered to force march with the 3rd Bengal Cavalry and the 3rd Punjab Cavalry to Robat, twenty miles from Kandahar, where he could signal by heliograph direct to Primrose.

Roberts feared that Ayub might be planning to move north-eastwards through the Argandab valley on Ghazni. Pending firm news from Kandahar, Roberts planned to send his sick and baggage on to Robat under escort, and with the remainder of his force to cut westward through the hills into the upper Argandab valley to block Ayub's possible advance. This potentially hazardous splitting up of his force was abandoned when Gough was able to tell him that Ayub was firmly entrenched west of Kandahar and showing no sign of moving. On 28 August the force moved on to Robat and halted for a day to allow the rearguard escorting the large force of sick to come up.[6] At Robat Roberts was able to discuss the situation with St John, Adam and Leach who had ridden out from Kandahar. Adam in particular advised against any attempt to move westwards into the Argandab valley. In his view, the absence of roads made it impracticable; the right way to tackle Ayub in his present position was from Kandahar, cutting him off from his line of retreat to Herat. Roberts accepted this advice and Leach was commissioned to prepare immediately a detailed map of the country between Kandahar and the Argandab.[7]

On the same day (29 August), a letter arrived from Ayub himself. He claimed that it was the British who had forced a fight on him at Maiwand and asked Roberts to advise him on how matters could best be arranged between him and the British with whom he wished to be on friendly terms. Ayub clearly hoped for British support for his taking over Kandahar. But he did not grasp the British position. Having handed over Kabul to Abdurrahman, the British intended to retain control of Kandahar through Sher Ali and a British garrison. There was no place in their scheme of things for Ayub. For him the only options were to surrender or to fight. Roberts contented himself with a bleak message recommending Ayub to send in his prisoners and surrender himself unconditionally.

At Robat, Roberts learned that Phayre's troops advancing from Quetta could not reach the city for a week at least. What had been irreverently christened 'The Race for the Peerage' had ended in Roberts's favour. If Ayub was to be attacked before he could commence his retreat, the job would have to be done by the Kabul force. The force came in sight of Kandahar early on the morning of 31 August. As the troops with their baggage and a long train of sick crowded into the narrow streets of the city the confusion was indescribable. Adam, however, was struck by the magnificent appearance of the Bengal troops, hardened by three weeks of fierce marching. By 10.00 hours Picquet and Karez Hills had been occupied by troops from the 1st and 2nd Brigades and preparations were in hand for a detailed reconnaissance of Ayub's position, with the object of attacking him as soon as possible.

The circumstances surrounding the dispatch of Roberts's force, the drama of its reappearance at Kandahar after a virtual absence of news for three weeks, the crowning victory outside Kandahar within twenty-four hours of its arrival and the charisma of Roberts himself, all combined to catch the public imagination and to make the march from Kabul to Kandahar still the best-known episode of the war. The reality was something less than the legend. Certainly, to march a force of 10,000 men over 300 miles of difficult country in three weeks was a considerable feat. But it was in some ways an easier march than Stewart's in the reverse direction. Stewart had taken a week or so longer, but he had had to fight one major pitched battle and one lesser engagement *en route* and he had arrived with his force in considerably better shape than Roberts.*[8]

His rival in the race for the peerage, Phayre, had had a much more difficult time. He had received the news of Maiwand early on the morning of 28 July at Quetta, together with the information that Primrose had ordered the garrisons of posts between Abdur Rahman and Chaman to fall back on Chaman. The telegraph line to Kandahar was cut later that day. Between Sibi and Chaman, Phayre had roughly seven battalions of native infantry and three and one half regiments of native cavalry but, apart from artillery, no European troops although the 2/11th Foot was on its way up from Sind. Phayre and Sandeman had no doubts as to what needed to be done. The troops along the projected railway line must be withdrawn and concentrated at the opposite ends of the line, at Sibi and in Pishin, and a strike force assembled to relieve Kandahar. Phayre calculated that he could concentrate four of his seven native infantry battalions and three of his native cavalry regiments. With the 2/11th Foot and one more European infantry regiment to be sent up to him, he would have enough to advance. Assembly of the necessary transport and concentration of the troops would take at least fifteen days but, all things being well, he planned to start his advance on Kandahar about the middle of August. These arrangements were approved by the Government the same day. The garrisons between Abdur Rahman and Chaman were concentrated at Chaman on the evening of the 29th, after being menaced and sniped at all the way by tribesmen among whom the news of the British disaster spread like a brushfire.

Phayre's plans were to· be frustrated by two factors – transport and tribal hostility. The news from Kandahar arrived at the climax of the hot season and followed on two years of drought in most of Baluchistan. Forage was in very short supply and, not expecting to have to campaign until the autumn, the transport authorities had dispersed the transport animals to distant grazing grounds and put the carts and equipment into the workshops for repair. It would take at least two weeks to assemble an adequate amount of transport for an advance in force. To compound the problems the railway from Sukhur to Sibi had been severely damaged by floods which had swept away miles of track. Into this situation, large numbers of fresh troops began to descend. Even before Burrows' departure from Kandahar, part of the Bombay Reserve Division had been moved up on to the Lines of Communication. The remainder of the Reserve Division was now ordered forward and from the Bengal Army the 8th Bengal Cavalry, the 63rd Foot and the 4th BNI were ordered to join Phayre with all haste. As tribal uprisings spread, so Phayre's demands for troops increased and in the middle of August the 38th BNI from Meerut and the 3rd Cavalry Hyderabad Contingent were ordered to proceed to Sibi immediately.[9]

---

*cf. MacGregor's comment 'The march of this force [Roberts's] is that of a disorganized rabble. An Afghan, seeing it, said we were like an Afghan army whereas Stewart's was like a European.' Diary, 25 August 1880.

The single-line railway had never been designed to cope with this. At Sibi, where trains soon began to disgorge large bodies of troops and mountains of supplies, confusion was almost total. To add to the difficulties, temperatures frequently reached 120° Fahrenheit in the sun. 'Amidst the general hurry and confusion prevailing, the Sibi depot was . . . a chaos of military stores, commissariat supplies, transport animals, etc., and the unfortunate officers and men had to hunt for all their requirements in an atmosphere in which, under any other circumstances, a European would have thought he was risking his life by merely exposing himself to the sun . . .'[10] From the railhead near Sibi, eighteen miles of burning desert had to be crossed to reach Dadar at the foot of the Bolan Pass. In the interests of speed and to avoid over-exposure to the deadly Sind sun, arrangements had been made to convey the European troops by cart in batches of 100 to Mach, in the upper Bolan Pass, a distance of some 55 miles. But these arrangements broke down as the animals became exhausted. The troops, forced to march most of the way, abandoned equipment and stores until, as Biddulph remarked 'the impediments of the troops consisted of barely more than the clothes they had on and the cartridges in their pouches.'[11] When the troops finally reached Quetta they found that supplies there were inadequate to provide more than half-rations.

Despite these appalling problems, it was not transport alone which put the brake on Phayre's attempts to advance, but the widespread uprising of the tribes as a result of the news of Maiwand. Tribal hostility and opportunism, never far below the surface, erupted along the whole length of the line of communications as soon as the rumours spread that the British had been beaten. The Achakzais promptly occupied the Khojak Pass on 28 July and were ejected only after two days' fighting by columns from Chaman and the Khojak cantonment. But they continued to hover in the area, exercising a continual threat to the road. At the opposite end of the line, the railway posts between Sukkhur and Sibi were continuously harrassed by prowling bands of marauders. More serious, because they had kept the peace for sixteen years, was the uprising of the Marris. With the Kakars, the Marris proceeded to pillage and destroy the evacuated posts and works along the unfinished Sibi-Pishin railway line. Followers were cut off and murdered and convoys attacked. On 8 August, a party of troops retiring on Sibi were severely handled by the Marris, the party losing sixteen men killed, five wounded, and the whole of the baggage and treasure that it was escorting. Just over a week later, 2,000 Kakars attacked the post at Kach in Pishin, 28 miles north-east of Quetta, which was crowded with some 350 sick evacuated from the posts along the Sibi-Pishin railway. The post was garrisoned by 300 men of the 16th BoNI under Colonel T. W. W. Pierce, who had strengthened his defences and was on the alert when the attack was launched at dawn. After three hours of fierce fighting, the attackers were repulsed and pursued for nearly ten miles. Pierce's losses were two killed and nine wounded, with 31 followers killed and wounded; the enemy left 48 bodies near the post and was estimated to have lost overall at least 200 killed and wounded. Undaunted, the Kakars re-assembled and occupied the surrounding heights, effectively preventing the evacuation of the sick and the replenishment of supplies. Phayre was forced to send a flying column of two guns, three troops of cavalry and a regiment of infantry to disperse the tribesmen and to pass the sick through to Quetta.

These diversions and the consequent need to strengthen the whole lines of communication inevitably delayed the build-up of Phayre's striking force. He had originally expected to start his move forward about the middle of August. In fact he was not able to leave Quetta himself until the 21st, arriving at Chaman, the jumping-off point for the advance, on the 26th. He arrived to find yet another diversionary problem facing him – a thousand of the Khan of Kalat's troops had mutinied and gone off to join Ayub. Four hundred of the 78th Highlanders on their way up from Sibi were diverted to Kalat to restore confidence. As a precaution the posts at Gulistan and Kila Abdullah were strengthened against the possibility of attack by the Baraichis of Shorawak.

On 26 August columns were dispatched to prepare the water supply at Gatai and collect forage and grain. The latter task proved the more difficult and the towers of recalcitrant chiefs had to be blown up before supplies began to flow into Gatai and Dabrai. The advance of the main force across the Khojak Pass began on the 30th, the advance guard reaching Gatai on 1 September, but the rest of the column not clearing the Pass until 5 September. Before the force began its advance, its *raison d'être* had disappeared. On the 24th, Phayre had written to Roberts telling him that the Quetta force hoped to reach Kandahar by 8 September. Three days later, Phayre learned from a letter from Tanner at Kalat-i-Ghilzai that Roberts expected to be at Kandahar on the 29th. It was clear that Roberts had won the race and Phayre had to decide whether there was any point in going on. News received on the 30th from Primrose that the countryside between Chaman and Kandahar, and for fifteen–twenty miles round the latter place, had been denuded of supplies, strengthened Phayre's doubts and on the same day he signalled Simla suggesting that he should push forward only enough troops (roughly a brigade of all arms) to garrison the line of posts between Chaman and Kandahar, to re-erect the telegraph line and to clear away the tribal gatherings which were reported about the Takht-i-Pul Kotal. In this way he hoped to economize in men and food, and to help with the supply of the large force now at Kandahar. In the meantime, his advance guard pushed on and occupied Abdur Rahman only 26 miles from Kandahar on 3 September. There Phayre received Roberts's dispatches announcing his decisive victory over Ayub two days earlier.

It was a hard blow. Although nothing could make up for having been robbed of a share in the final victory, Phayre's men had made a great effort and endured great hardship and their commander was justified in bringing to the attention of the Commander-in-Chief and Viceroy 'the indefatigable energy and zeal with which the officers and men of the whole force met and overcame the natural difficulties of our position . . . all showed by their conduct that they meant to succeed in thoroughly accomplishing the honourable duty which they were called on to perform.'[12] Some idea of the effort involved is given by the fact that at the end of August Phayre had under his command between Sukkhur and Chaman eight batteries of artillery, eight regiments of cavalry and nineteen regiments of infantry, in all about 15,000 men, in addition to the countless numbers of civilians and transport animals.

For nearly a fortnight after Ayub's army had appeared outside Kandahar its activity was limited to desultory shelling by two Armstrong guns and spasmodic sniping, but the villages close to and around the city were steadily being occupied by the Afghans. On 12 August a sortie by a small party of 7th Fusiliers and 19th BoNI demolished an enclosure just outside the western wall and killed a number of the enemy, including the Governor of Farah, at a cost of one killed and nine wounded. The following day Ayub's regular troops occupied the villages of Khairabad and Deh Khoja (to the east of the city) as well as re-occupying the shrine from which the tribesmen had been driven on 31 July. Information reached Primrose the same day that Ayub was planning to assault the city, at a point directly opposite Deh Khoja, where the walls were only fourteen–fifteen feet high and in a dilapidated state.

So far Primrose had managed to keep clear the Idgah Gate and the northern face of the city, giving himself an exit through which a sortie could be mounted. But guns mounted in Khairabad could sweep the north face and deny Primrose this facility. On 14 August the Chief Engineer (Colonel Hills) put a plan before Primrose for a sortie against the enemy forces east of the city, designed to forestall any enemy plans for an attack from this side.* The essence of this plan was that a strong force of cavalry should slip out of the Idgah Gate before dawn and swing in a wide circle east and south round Khairabad and Deh Khoja to take up a final position south of Deh Khoja to block reinforcements of the defenders. At daybreak, three infantry regiments and two guns would leave the Idgah Gate, occupy Kahirabad and then push south into Deh Khoja, exiting through its western face and re-entering Kandahar by the Kabul Gate. In the meantime, artillery from a position between the two villages would sweep the western face of Deh Khoja thus trapping the defenders inside the village. It was a simple, workmanlike scheme which stood an excellent chance of success. But Brooke insisted on it being radically recast and Hills was not even invited to be present at the council of war on the 15th which settled the final plan.† This kept the cavalry part of Hills' plan but totally altered the size and direction of the infantry attack. Only the equivalent of one regiment was to be used, divided into three columns. The First Column (consisting of two companies each of 7th Fusiliers 19th BoNI, under Lieutenant-Colonel Daubeny) and the Second Column (two companies of 7th and three of 28th BoNI, under Lieutenant-Colonel Nimmo) were to exit from the Kabul Gate and head for the southern end of the village. From there, they were to sweep northwards, their final line of retreat being left for decision at the time. The Third Column (one company of 7th, two companies of 19th and one company of 28th, under Colonel Heathcote) was to act as a general reserve, with the potential task of occupying the western entrance of the village where the enemy gun was sited. Brooke now insisted on a preliminary bombardment as well. Adam and Burnett (the AAG) were opposed to the plan and particularly the bombardment, but neither Primrose nor his other two Brigadiers (Burrows and Nuttall) saw any reason to object. So it was settled.

At 04.30 hours on 16 August two squadrons of cavalry under Nuttall left the Idgah Gate and despite a few shots managed to reach their allotted position south of the Deh Khoja. At 04.45, the 40-pounder and the two howitzers in the citadel,

---

*The north and west faces of Kandahar looked on to open ground; the south and east faces had numerous villages and walled enclosures close to the walls, making them the most likely sectors of attack.
†The Official History (vol. V, p. 375) claims that Hills' plan would have involved using too many troops and that Hills 'concurred' in the final plan, which Hills denied in his book.

plus two 9-pounders on the walls, opened fire.* A quarter of an hour later Daubeny's and Nimmo's columns, accompanied by Brooke in overall command, left the Kabul Gate and made their way, under heavy fire, across the thousand yards of open ground to the south end of Deh Khoja. From there they proceeded to sweep northwards through the village. In the meantime, the original bombard-ment having sounded the alarm, parties of tribesmen had been trying to reinforce Deh Khoja from Bala Karez and other villages to the south. They were charged and driven back by a troop of the 3rd Bombay Light Cavalry, under Lieutenant Geoghegan (a survivor of Maiwand). Renewed efforts were defeated by some well-timed volleys from two companies of the 19th BoNI under Major Trench, who had been sent forward from Heathcote's reserve column, and Nuttall seized his opportunity to charge with both squadrons and disperse the attackers again.

By 07.00 hours, Brooke had reached the northern edge of Deh Khoja with Nimmo's and Daubeny's men, but he was short of ammunition, his original force had become thinned out by the demands of street fighting and he faced opposition from the tribesmen occupying Khairabad to the north. The cavalry, supported by Trench's men, were holding their position south of the village. The remainder of Heathcote's column had moved out from the city and was in position just west of Deh Khoja under fierce fire from the village. The defects in the plan were now manifesting themselves. Brooke sent his Brigade Major back to Primrose to get more ammunition and to report that the position was untenable. Primrose had two alternatives: he could either send out fresh troops to assist and cover Brooke's retreat or he could simply order Brooke to retire as best he could. Hills pleaded with Primrose to reinforce Brooke but, overwhelmed by the events, Primrose ordered the recall to be sounded from the city. Brooke thereupon directed Daubeny and Nimmo to fight their way through to the Idgah Gate and ordered Nuttall to retire on the Kabul Gate, covering the retreat of any infantry left south of the village. Brooke himself with a small party moved back through Deh Khoja to retrieve any troops still left in the village.

Daubeny and Nimmo made good their retreat despite heavy fire from Khairabad. But as soon as Nuttall and Trench evacuated their position south of the village, the way was clear for large numbers of tribesmen to reinforce Deh Khoja, adding their fire to that of the original defenders. Retreating across open ground, Nuttall's, Trench's and Heathcote's men suffered heavily before the remnants reached the Kabul Gate. Brooke, reaching the south end of the village with some 200 men, ran into a large group of the enemy, but charged through it with the bayonet and finally emerged into open country where he paused to wait for Captain Cruickshank of the Royal Engineers, who had been seriously wounded, to be brought up. When Brooke and his men rose to make their final dash for the Kabul Gate they faced a fusillade of fire and repeated attacks by swordsmen. Brooke was killed and the wounded and dead had to be left where they fell: only a handful got back to the shelter of the city. The British casualties in this disastrous affair were 99 killed and 109 wounded. Brooke, Cruikshank, Trench, Colonel Newport of the 28th BoNI and the Reverend G. M. Gordon were among

---

*The defenders of Deh Khoja sought shelter in their extensive cellars and it is doubtful whether the shelling did any real damage.

those killed; Nimmo, Shewell (the Deputy Commissary General, who later died of his wounds) and Malcolmson of the 3rd Sind Horse were among the wounded. Lieutenant Chase of the 28th and Private Ashford of the 7th Fusiliers earned the Victoria Cross for rescuing a wounded man under fire.

It had been a bad plan, disastrously mishandled by Primrose, and the heavy casualties had a temporarily disheartening effect on the garrison. But it had a significant effect on the Afghans who evacuated Khairabad for fear of another attack. Many tribesmen, sobered by the encounter, returned home and even Ayub's regular troops clamoured to be removed from Deh Khoja where they felt that they had not been properly supported. For two days after the sortie, the whole of Ayub's army stood to arms expecting a general attack and Ayub began to contemplate a retreat to the Helmund. From the British point of view, although they did not yet know it, the crisis of the siege had passed.

The garrison at Kandahar had been in communication with Tanner at Kalat-i-Ghilzai until 12 August. Letters which arrived from Phayre on 11 August gave the news that a relief force of two brigades was assembling in the Pishin valley and that Roberts was leaving Kabul with a strong division. On 23 August it became clear that Ayub was evacuating his positions east and south of the city and on the 24th he abandoned the investment of the city altogether, taking up instead a strong position on the east bank of the Argandab, protected by a high range of hills between him and the city. Primrose took the opportunity to send out a party to bury the British dead left in and around Deh Khoja and to reconnoitre the abandoned cantonments. On the morning of the 27th the flash of a heliograph from Robat announced Gough's arrival there with two regiments of cavalry, the advance guard of Roberts's relieving force. Ayub had of course picked up the news of the arrival of the relief force at Kalat-i-Ghilzai four days before.

It may be as well to deal at this point with the question of the morale of the garrison. In his memoirs, published some twenty years later, Roberts was scathing about this and his criticism had been largely accepted unchallenged ever since.[13] Roberts, with his prejudice against Bombay troops intensified by the defeat at Maiwand, was perhaps predisposed to find grounds for criticism. Hills, who was no doubt predisposed the other way, admits that Primrose and Burrows were dejected and despondent when they met Roberts. It is also true that, on Primrose's orders, the garrison remained at their posts and did not turn out to welcome the Kabul force as might have been expected.[14] Adam believed that the confusion which attended the arrival in the city of Roberts's men helped to create an unfavourable impression. On the other hand, the siege had been effectively lifted eight days before, and the garrison throughout had undergone no real hardship or deprivation beyond that incidental to any siege. The sortie against Deh Khoja, although apparently unsuccessful and costly, had shown no lack of fighting spirit among the troops.[15] Roberts himself records that the letter he received from Tanner on 23 August reported the garrison to be in good health and spirits and in no straits. Phayre reported to Simla on 30 August that he had just received a letter from Kandahar reporting Ayub's withdrawal and that all was well with the garrison. The sick list, often a good indicator of morale, when Roberts arrived was just over 520 or about 10 per cent of the garrison – by no means a high proportion in the circumstances and virtually the same as that in Roberts's own force.*

Excluding the Deh Khoja affair, casualties during the siege numbered only eight killed and 36 wounded. The accusations of poor morale would therefore seem at the very least exaggerated. It may be that subconsciously Roberts and his troops were doing so in order to emphasize their own quality and achievements.[16] Certainly those who accompanied Roberts were critical of the Bombay troops they saw; Hensman described them as 'weedy, under-grown' and 'sorry apologies for sepoys', while Combe's view was that 'The Beloochis are fine men but the other Bombay troops do not compare well with the up-country Sepoys, Sikhs, Goorkhas, etc.' But it is worth contrasting this with Hume's very careful observation a few weeks later.[17]

Roberts was senior to Primrose by some four months so he immediately assumed command at Kandahar. It was not in his nature to delay unnecessarily. From information which Adam and Leach had been able to give him at Robat, he had already a good general idea of the situation. The same afternoon, Hugh Gough with the 3rd Bengal Cavalry, 15th BNI and two guns, accompanied by Roberts's Chief of Staff (Colonel Chapman), conducted a close reconnaissance of the Afghan position. Gough was heavily pressed when he commenced his retirement and the withdrawal was safely completed only after the whole of Roberts's force had been put under arms and two brigades deployed. In retrospect the fierceness of the Afghan reaction would seem to have fully justified Primrose's refusal to accede to Roberts's demand a week or so earlier to re-occupy the water supplies near the old cantonment. Despite a fairly anxious time, Gough had achieved his object and Roberts now had a full picture of Ayub's position and dispositions. He summoned all senior officers to meet him at 06.00 hours next morning to hear the plan of attack which he intended to carry out that day.

Some two and a half to three miles west of Kandahar, a long range of hills runs north-east and south-west at an average height of some 2,000 feet above the surrounding plains (map 14). Beyond this range and parallel to it flows the River Argandab. The south-western end of the range terminates near the village of Pir Paimal, due east of Kandahar. Two passes (the Baba Wali, two and half miles north-west of the city, and the Murcha, due north of the city) provide routes through the range to the river. The Murcha was considered impassable for guns, but the Baba Wali was practicable for all arms and in consequence had been heavily fortified with artillery by Ayub. His main camp lay near the western exit on a flat space between the hills and the river. Roberts had decided that the Baba Wali was too formidable to attack; the Murcha was suitable only for a diversion. He planned therefore to make a feint against the Baba Wali and to launch his attack round the southern end of the range; then swing northwards along its western slopes to attack Ayub's camp, cutting him off from his direct line of retreat in the process. Despite the difficulties caused by the presence of numerous villages, enclosures, orchards and water courses, this was the direction of attack which Adam had recommended at Robat. Ayub's strength was estimated at 4,800 regulars, with 32 guns and some 8,000 irregulars and tribesmen. Roberts, with his

---

*The state of Roberts's own force was a surprise to some onlookers in Kandahar: 'These [the sick] were slowly driven in (I can use no other word) by the Baluchi Regiment, thus closing the march of the Bengal Division. They certainly numbered five hundred wretched cripples and creatures, mounted on refuse transport or in dandies and doolies, for whom it was difficult to find room.'

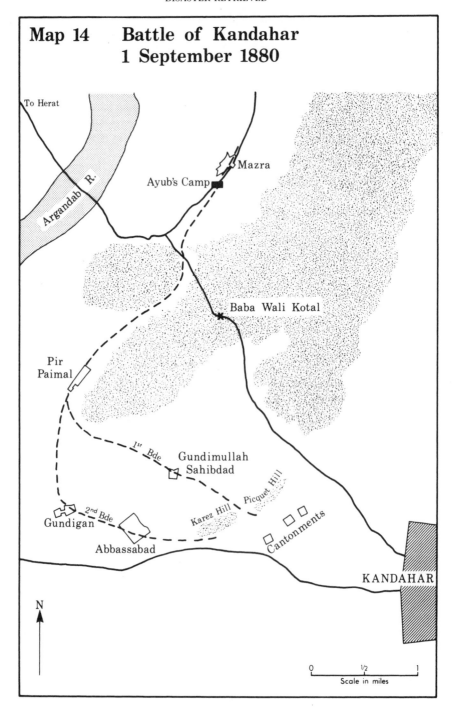

Map 14   Battle of Kandahar
1 September 1880

To Herat

Argandab R.

Mazra

Ayub's Camp

Baba Wali Kotal

Pir
Paimal

1ˢᵗ Bde

Gundimullah
Sahibdad

2nd Bde

Gundigan

Picquet Hill

Karez Hill

Abbassabad

Cantonments

KANDAHAR

N

0   ½   1
Scale in miles

own troops and those of the garrison, had about 12,500, but he would have to leave a garrison in Kandahar to protect his supplies, baggage and sick. It would be necessary to employ every available man.

Not surprisingly, Roberts preferred to use the troops he had brought with him from Kabul for the main operation, leaving Primrose's troops in the supporting role. Nuttall's Bombay cavalry brigade from a position a mile north of Kandahar was to watch the Murcha Pass and protect the British right flank. Burrows with four companies of the 7th Fusiliers, the 4th and 19th BoNI and the four 40-pounders of 5/11, RA, was to threaten the Baba Wali Pass from a position just north of the old cantonments, while Daubeny, with the remnants of the 66th Foot and Grenadiers and two companies of the 28th BoNI was to hold the line of pickets along Picquet and Karez Hills as far as the village of Chihilzina – in effect the baseline from which the main operations were to start. Macpherson's 1st Brigade was to seize the village of Gundi Mullah Sahibdad due west of Picquet Hill and then continue westward to seize Pir Paimal. Baker's 2nd Brigade was to advance in parallel on Macpherson's left and seize the village of Gundigan. The two brigades would then swing northwards round the southern end of the hills to attack Ayub's camp. MacGregor's 3rd Brigade, from its position near the village of Abbasabad just south of Karez Hill, was to act in support. Gough with his cavalry brigade augmented by E/B, RHA and with four companies of the 7th Fusiliers, and four companies of the 28th BoNI in support, was to cross the River Argandab and threaten Ayub's lines of retreat via Kakrez or the main road to Sinjiri and the Helmund. Roberts proposed to use in all nearly 11,000 men and 32 guns.

Whether Ayub had divined Roberts's intentions as a result of observing Gough's reconnaissance on the afternoon of the 31st, or whether he had quite independently decided to attack is not clear, but during the night of the 31 September, the villages of Gundi Mullah Sahibdad and Gundigan which lay across the axes of advance of the British main attack were strongly reinforced by the Afghans.

The British troops were in position and had breakfasted, by 09.00 hours and Roberts took up his own position on Karez Hill. Ayub's forces had already opened fire from their position on the Baba Wali Kotal and from Gundi Mullah Sahibdad and Gundigan. On the British side the ball was opened just before 09.30 hours when the 40-pounders began to shell the Baba Wali. Shortly afterwards, C/2, RA and 6/8, RA opened fire on Gundi Mullah Sahibdad and the leading regiments of the 1st Brigade (92nd Highlanders and 2nd Gurkhas) advanced to attack the village, supported by the 23rd and 24th BNI. Gundi Mullah Sahibdad was cleared in fierce hand-to-hand fighting by 10.30 hours and by 11.15 the brigade was approaching Pir Paimal. On its left the 2nd Brigade, led by the 72nd Highlanders and the 2nd Sikh Infantry, had cleared the dense network of walled enclosures and orchards around Gundigan although the 72nd lost their Colonel, Brownlow, in the process; by 11.15 hours it too was approaching Pir Paimal although slightly behind the 1st Brigade. Fighting fiercely, the Afghans were steadily pushed back and by 12.15 hours the 1st and 2nd Brigades had rounded the southern end of the hills, seized Pir Paimal and were ready for the final advance on Ayub's camp. The 3rd Brigade was now ordered forward to give added weight to the attack. Ayub's troops on the Baba Wali had so far been helpless spectators – an attempt to seize the guns of 5/11 had been still-born in face of Burrows' troops.

259

As Roberts had foreseen, the Afghans were sensitive to any threat of encircle-
ment and as soon as the British troops were in possession of Pir Paimal, Ayub's
regular troops began to abandon their positions and make off through the
orchards and gardens which fringed the east bank of the Argandab, intent only on
securing their retreat to the Helmund. Macpherson and Baker now came up
against the main Afghan defences commanding the open piece of ground about a
mile south of Ayub's camp. The enemy line ran from the western slopes of the Pir
Paimal across the shallow depression to the eastern slopes of Khoroti Hill. In the
centre, a deep water cut, with loopholed banks two–three feet high, formed the
main defence. It was supported at one end by three guns on the slope of Khoroti
Hill and by another two guns in the middle. The guns on the Bala Wali Kotal were
also swung round to bear on the advancing British troops. It was the moment for a
final, supreme effort and, fittingly, George White of the 92nd now made his final
decisive appearance on the stage of the Second Afghan War. Led by White, the
Afghan defences were attacked and taken at the point of the bayonet by the men of
the 92nd, 2nd Gurkhas and 23rd BNI.* The last resistance on the Afghan right
round the three guns of Ayub's famous artillery was overcome by a charge by the
3rd Sikh Infantry of the 2nd Brigade, under another officer who had frequently
played a distinguished part during the war – Lieutenant-Colonel Money.

Ross, who was in overall command of the infantry, now ordered the brigades to
halt to reform and replenish ammunition in preparation for the further fighting he
expected. In fact the way ahead was clear, the Afghans being in full retreat.
Pushing on, Ross found himself shortly after 13.00 hours in possession of Ayub's
camp and artillery which had been abandoned virtually intact.

This was clearly the point at which Gough's cavalry should have been exercising
maximum effect in pursuing and dispersing the remnants of Ayub's army. But
they had had a frustrating and unsuccessful morning. As soon as Gundigan had
been cleared by the 2nd Brigade, Gough had dropped off E/B, RHA with its escort
of 7th Fusiliers and 28th BoNI near the village, and with the remainder of the
brigade he cantered off along the main Herat road towards Kokeran and the
Argandab. But Roberts's orders had instructed Gough to operate on the east bank
of the river and pursuant to these orders the brigade swung northwards beyond
Gundigan, keeping on the outer flank of the 2nd Brigade. Near Mianjui, Gough
received orders to make for Kokeran (now three miles in his rear), cross the river
and operate northwards along the west bank to try to cut off the retreating
Afghans. But the brigade had to pick its way slowly through orchards and gardens
and across deep irrigation channels.[19] By the time it finally reached the west bank
the bulk of the enemy was gone and the brigade's horses were exhausted. In the
distance, a cloud of dust marked the retreat of Ayub and his escort. Apart from
killing a few stragglers, Gough's brigade achieved nothing and towards the
evening it recrossed the river opposite Ayub's camp site and made its way back via
the Baba Wali Pass to Kandahar.[20] In retrospect it is clear that the brigade's
original orders should have been to cross the river at Kokeran and operate along
the west bank. It would then almost certainly have destroyed a large part of Ayub's
army and perhaps prevented a great deal of later trouble.

---

*White himself was the first to reach the enemy guns, but he was closely followed by Sepoy Inderbir Lama
who claimed one of the guns for his regiment, the 2nd Gurkhas, by putting his cap over the muzzle.

In the early afternoon the Bombay cavalry under Nuttall were ordered to advance through the Baba Wali Pass and pursue those remnants of Ayub's army who were retreating up the Argandab valley. Nuttall pursued for some fifteen miles, killing upwards of 100 of the enemy and abandoning the pursuit only as darkness fell. It reached Kandahar at about 22.00 hours, having played a rather more useful part than Gough's regiments.

The failure to use Gough's brigade effectively marred what had otherwise been a very complete victory. Among the spoils was virtually the whole of Ayub's artillery, including the two guns lost by E/B, RHA at Maiwand.* British casualties numbered 35 killed and 213 wounded, the largest loss falling on the 92nd. At least 600 Afghan bodies were actually counted on the ground and the total killed was probably double that; wounded may have doubled that again. Ayub's army had been totally dispersed, the regulars making for Herat and the tribesmen dispersing to their homes. But the victory was clouded by the discovery in Ayub's camp of the still warm body of Maclaine. According to the story of five sepoys who were found alive in the camp after being captured at Maiwand, Ayub had left instructions before he fled that the prisoners were not to be killed. Despite this, the guards had shot one sepoy and cut Maclaine's throat just as Ross's troops were entering the camp.[21]

The same evening the bulk of the troops marched back to Kandahar leaving Macpherson's brigade to occupy Ayub's camp and guard the booty. They were relieved by some of Primrose's troops the next day. The medical arrangements seem to have left something to be desired since Travers on the day after the battle found some of his men lying where they had been hit 24 hours earlier.

The fighting over, Roberts faced the inevitable problem of supplies. To ease the problem, the Bengal cavalry brigade with E/B, RHA and a large number of sick was located at Kokeran. Phayre's force was halted at Karez-i-Zarak, twelve miles east of Kandahar, the 3rd Bombay Light Cavalry and the 19th BoNI being dispatched from the city to restore the telegraph and link up with Phayre's advance guard. Phayre himself arrived in Kandahar on the 6th. Two days later MacGregor's 3rd Brigade left Kandahar for Chaman and Pishin, as the first stage in its return to India. With it went Roberts, worn down by the mental and physical strains to which he had been subjected over the last twelve months. A medical board had recommended his immediate return to England, but he was reluctant to leave until the question of the occupation and administration of Southern Afghanistan had been settled. He remained at or near Quetta in close touch with Sandeman, but requested that he might be relieved in October. The troops were now divided into three divisions, the 1st under Primrose, the 2nd under Phayre and the 3rd (the original Kabul Field Force) under Ross.

Eight days after the battle, Daubeny, with a column consisting of the 3rd Sind Horse, half of the Poona Horse, C/2, RA, the 2/7th, the 4th BoNI and representative detachments of the 66th, 1st and 30th BoNI and the Bombay Sappers and Miners, left for Maiwand to examine the battlefield and to give decent burial to the British dead. Retracing the route followed by the survivors after the battle, Daubeny found and buried 128 bodies between Kandahar and Maiwand; a lance-

---

*These were presented by the Government to Roberts.

naik of the Grenadiers, a lance-naik of Jacob's Rifles and four followers who had been in hiding were located and sent back to Kandahar. At Maiwand, some 400 bodies were found and re-buried; among the officers, the bodies of Blackwood, Henn, Galbraith, McMath, Rayner, Chute, Olivey and Smith were identified. Ayub's dead had been buried in some 300 graves each of which, according to the local villagers held two or three bodies. Lieutenant Talbot, of the Royal Engineers, took the opportunity to make a detailed drawing of the battlefield, plotting the positions of Burrows' troops by the quantities of spent cartridge cases.

A number of loose ends remained to be tidied up. There was the awkward problem of what to do with Primrose and Burrows. On receiving Roberts's report of conditions at Kandahar, Simla ordered Primrose, Burrows and Nuttall to report immediately to the Commander-in-Chief Bombay. Before they left, Burrows and Nuttall made serious accusations against Currie and Malcolmson which had been investigated by a Court of Inquiry under Phayre. In consequence, Currie and Malcolmson were placed under arrest by Roberts and dispatched to Bombay where they appeared before a Court Martial some months later. The troops of Roberts's original Kabul force needed to be withdrawn to India and replaced by Bombay troops. The abandoned railway had to be reoccupied. It was desirable for a column to visit Shorawak, and the Achakzais and Marris had to be punished for their activities after Maiwand. The lines of communication were busy throughout September and October as fresh troops moved up towards Kandahar and the Kabul troops moved down towards India. Roberts's original intention had been to divide MacGregor's 3rd Brigade into two columns to march respectively through Shorawak and via Kawas and to reunite at Quetta before proceeding down to India. Under the modified plan adopted, a small column under Colonel Rowcroft moved via Kach and Kawas while the remainder of the brigade accompanied by the 23rd Pioneers and the Central India Horse, marched straight on to Quetta where it arrived on 18 September. Baker's 2nd Brigade left Kandahar on 15 September, taking with it the sick and wounded, and halted temporarily at Chaman. For both MacGregor's and Baker's men there was more work to be done before they could say goodbye to Afghanistan, but for Macpherson's 1st Brigade there was nothing to interrupt their march down the Bolan to the plains of India and thence to their future peacetime stations.

To Baker fell the task of punishing the Achakzais. He left Chaman on 21 September with a reduced brigade* and moved eastwards along the edge of the Khwaja Amran range to the Bogra Pass. From there he swung south-eastwards back to Kila Abdullah and Quetta where he arrived on the 28th. The Achakzais had prudently evacuated the area and there was virtually no opposition. The tribe was fined a nominal sum and some 2,500 animals were seized while houses and crops near the scene of the murder of a sepoy of the 2nd Sikh Infantry were burned. The brigade reached Sibi en route for India on 7 October.

MacGregor's first task was to re-open the road and to re-establish the posts along the abandoned railway line between Kach and Sibi. He left Quetta on 24 September,† reached Kach on the following day and then proceeded southwards

---

*1 squadron 3rd Bengal Cavalry, 72nd Highlanders, 2nd Sikh Infantry, 5th Gurkhas, No. 2 Mountain Battery.
†1 squadron CIH, 15th and 25th BNI, 1 Coy 2/60th Rifles, 11/9 RA, 4th Gurkhas.

along the line, re-establishing posts and restoring the road as he went. He reached Sibi on 8 October.

His next task was to punish the Marris. The force detailed for the task consisted of the 2/60th and 4th Gurkhas from his old brigade, plus the 2nd and 3rd Sikh Infantry and 5th Gurkhas from Baker's old brigade. The 3rd Punjab Cavalry from Gough's original Cavalry Brigade and 11/9, RA were attached. A column of Bombay troops under Colonel Morris was to co-operate, moving from Kach via the Harnai valley to link up with MacGregor at Spin Kach north-east of Sibi and thence to Thal-Chotiali which it was to garrison. The expedition was highly successful. Between 14 October and 12 November, MacGregor quartered the Marri country, encountering little opposition and eventually forcing the submission of the main body of the Marris who were fined 260,000 rupees and made to give hostages. The force reached Drigri, in British territory some 55 miles southwest of Dera Ghazi Khan, in the middle of November, where it was broken up and the regiments dispersed to their peacetime stations.[22] For some, like the 2nd Sikh Infantry and the 4th and 5th Gurkhas it was the end of two years' active service. They were the last of the original Kabul Field force engaged in active operations beyond the frontier. By the end of December 1880 the entire force was back in India except for 6/8, RA which stayed on at Kandahar until the final evacuation in the spring of 1881.

Long before the last of the original Kabul Field Force had left Afghanistan, their commander had gone. On 15 October, Roberts handed over command in Southern Afghanistan to Phayre and left for Simla and thence for England. Phayre held temporary command for under a month, being superseded on 10 November by Major-General Hume; Phayre then reverted to command of the Lines of Communication. It was not perhaps a very gracious way of rewarding Phayre for his efforts, but he had acquired a reputation for being hot-tempered and difficult to get on with. The last active operations of 1880 featured a march through Shorawak by a small column, consisting of a squadron of the 1st Madras Light Cavalry, the 4th BNI and two guns of No. 2 Bombay Mountain Battery, which left Gulistan Karez on 9 October. Its purpose was to open up fresh sources of supplies. No opposition was encountered and the force ultimately encamped at Mandozai, 35 miles north of Mushki, in the territory of the Khan of Kalat, where it remained, sending in grain and forage to Quetta to relieve the supply problem there.

At the end of October 1880, the military situation in Southern Afghanistan had stabilized. The forces, although largely provided from the Bombay Army, came under the direct operational control of Army Headquarters at Simla. The garrison at Kandahar was fixed for the moment at a brigade of cavalry, three brigades of infantry (each of four British and six native regiments) and five batteries of artillery. Quetta and its immediate posts were to be garrisoned by three regiments of infantry, two batteries and a section of artillery and a troop of cavalry. The Harnai valley railway line absorbed some three regiments of infantry, and spread along the rest of the L of C from Sibi to Kandahar were a further five or six battalions (including one in Shorawak and one in the Marri country, at Thal-Chotiali), five regiments of cavalry and three and one-half batteries of artillery – nearly 20,000 men in all.

As always, transport and supplies presented severe problems. By dispersing the regiments as widely as possible to tap fresh areas of supplies the transport problem could be eased although it remained formidable. From the Indus to Sibi the railway reigned supreme.* From Sibi a twice-weekly convoy of Government carts ran through the Bolan to Quetta and Chaman. This was supplemented by a twice-weekly train of fifty carts from Quetta to Kila Abdullah. In addition, a pack train worked to and fro across the Khojak Pass, and Sandeman had arranged a contract with the Brahuis to carry 1,000 pounds of supplies a day to Chaman until the end of November 1880.

This continuing massive military involvement reflected the policy decision taken some months before to maintain a permanent force in or around Kandahar. But Maiwand had revived in acute form the whole question of the viability of an independent Kandahar under Sher Ali and the basis of the continuing British presence. In accepting the separation of Kandahar from Kabul, Ripon and Hartington had felt constrained to honour agreements already entered into with the Wali. Conceptually they were both in favour of a united Afghanistan. If Sher Ali was unable to maintain his independence save with the aid of British bayonets, it was necessary to look at the military and financial burden involved. Superficially the problem appeared a military one; could a Russian advance on India via Herat and Kandahar be met by forces based upon Quetta or was it essential to meet it farther forward by basing troops at Kandahar? But this question concealed a number of more basic issues. How likely was it that the Russians would ever contemplate an invasion of India? How easy was the Herat-Kandahar route? Was it possible without construction of railways and, if not, would not the act of construction give the British authorities ample time to re-occupy Kandahar and advance to the Helmund? Would Afghan resistance to the Russians be strengthened or weakened by a permanent British presence at Kandahar? In the light of previous events, was there a foreseeable Afghan threat to India and, if not, was there any longer a case against uniting the country? Could India sustain the continuing financial burden of a continuing garrison in Kandahar? What were the likely consequences for the Indian Army?

All these questions were vigorously debated in Simla and Whitehall in the closing months of 1880. Among the military men, opinion was sharply divided – Wolseley and Stewart (who thought little of the strategic value of Kandahar) supported retirement from Kandahar while the Commander-in-Chief in India, the Commander-in-Chief at Home (the Duke of Cambridge) and Field Marshal Lord Napier of Magdala were opposed; Roberts, originally strongly opposed to retirement, was now tending to hedge his bets. Among the civilians the strongest voice against retirement was predictably that of Sir Henry Rawlinson. On the Viceroy's Council his views were echoed by Stokes and Rivers Thompson, and on the Secretary of State's Council by Sir William Merewether (a former Commissioner of Sind). But retirement was strongly advocated by Sandeman, Sir Robert Montgomery, Sir Henry Norman, Evelyn Baring and Sir Edward Perry. There were numerous differences of view even within the opposing camps. Norman, Baring, Perry and Montgomery wanted to withdraw even from Quetta and to stand on the

---

*The railhead was actually at Pir Choki, some twenty miles west of Sibi.

so-called 'natural' frontier which was roughly the line of the hills immediately west of the Indus; Wolseley and Sandeman favoured retaining Pishin, Quetta and Sibi. Among the advocates of the forward policy, Haines, Napier and Merewether wanted to annex Kandahar outright while Rawlinson favoured handing it over to Abdurrahman; Stokes, as perhaps benefited the Legal Member, was in favour of restoring the whole of Afghanistan to the ex-Amir Yakub Khan in whose innocence he firmly believed. Much attention was given to estimating the net cost of annexation – Baring and Norman predicting that it would exceed £1,000,000 a year, Merewether claiming that it would virtually pay for itself. In retrospect, the balance of intellectual authority was clearly in favour of retirement. It would have required evidence of a kind which was simply not available to persuade the Liberal Administration to abandon its basic beliefs and acquiesce in a continuing British protectorate over Kandahar. The destruction of the expectations and prophecies of Lytton and the 'Forward School' as a result of the murder of Cavagnari served only to confirm in the minds of Gladstone and his colleagues the essential rightness of those principles of foreign policy to which they had long been attached.

The debate – or rather the fusillade of opinions and counter-opinions – continued vigorously for some months. Essentially the die was cast early in November 1880 when Hartington notified Ripon that the Government had rejected the arguments of the 'forward school' and had decided that the best way of defeating any Russian threat against India was by acting as the defenders, not the destroyers, of Afghan independence. Ripon was directed to arrange for the evacuation of Kandahar as soon as reasonably practicable. He was given full discretion as to the nature of the regime he left behind, the only proviso being that the future ruler must be absolutely clear that he would have to rely entirely upon his own resources and not upon the prospect of British support.[23] One thing was clear – the Wali Sher Ali was not the man to hold Kandahar. Lyall was sent to Kandahar to persuade him to abdicate; it took him five days. His intention was announced on 30 November and he left for India on 16 December. He had played his part throughout with dignity; his misfortune was to find himself faced with a situation for which he had neither the prestige nor the personality to cope.

With the Wali out of the way, the two possible contenders for Kandahar were Ayub and Abdurrahman. Gladstone himself toyed with the idea of Ayub, but an Afghanistan divided between Ayub and Abdurrahman would have remained permanently unstable and a source of perpetual anxiety to the British. The decision was made in favour of the latter even though there remained considerable doubts on the British side as to his chances of consolidating his hold on Afghanistan. For Abdurrahman, the timing was unfortunate. He had not yet had time to establish himself firmly in Kabul and he lacked resources both to take over Kandahar and to tackle the destruction and poverty which surrounded him as a result of the war. Nevertheless he regarded the kingdom of Kabul without Kandahar as like a fort without a gate and he could not allow it to fall into other hands. To occupy and hold Kandahar against Ayub he needed arms and ammunition and he appealed to the British Government to provide them.[24] In the meantime he made his plans to take over when the British left.

What is notable is the almost total lack of attention paid to the future of Herat. It is the more notable because of the almost exaggerated anxiety devoted by British Governments to Herat prior to 1878 even to the extent of going to war with Persia over it in 1856. The failure of the negotiations with Persia in 1879–80 had left the future of Herat floating in the air – and Maiwand had revealed how dangerous that situation could be. Ayub was back in Herat licking his wounds but still dangerous. Yet here was a British Government preparing to evacuate Afghanistan without any arrangement at all on Herat. In part, of course, the argument of the forward school for retaining Kandahar rested upon the assumption that, with Kandahar firmly held, Herat automatically became of less importance.[25] The Cabinet view clearly rested upon a different assumption, namely, that Abdurrahman would take over Kandahar and would then be in a position to deal with any trouble from Herat. But unless Abdurrahman actually took over Herat physically, there could be no guarantee that Ayub would not flirt with Persia or Russia and that Herat would not continue to be an element of instability and danger. In due course, the Cabinet's calculation proved correct.

For the British troops left in Afghanistan, the remaining months of the occupation were a trial to be endured. Hartington had left it to Ripon to decide upon the timing of the evacuation and it was not until the third week in January 1881 that Hume was asked by Army Headquarters in Calcutta to submit a detailed evacuation plan. As far as the troops were concerned the strain that they had all undergone in August, the difficulties of obtaining adequate food supplies, the problem of overcrowded camp sites round Kandahar and the onset of winter brought an inevitable toll in the way of sickness, principally dysentery. By 16 December, the 2/11th Foot alone had 138 men in hospital out of a total strength of 556. Inevitably, too, some of the Indian regiments had begun to show signs of strain after nearly two years of campaigning away from their homes and families. Roberts had already drawn the attention of the authorities to this matter some months earlier.

> 'I cannot too strongly urge upon the consideration of the Government of India the desirability of not leaving the Native portion of the army in the field after the ensuring autumn. Many of the regiments will then have been on service since October 1878; they have done admirably – indeed, I doubt if at any former period the Native army has ever behaved more loyally or gallantly; all ranks are in good heart and will cheerfully carry out any work which they may be called upon to perform. There is however a limit beyond which it would be impolitic to require them to remain away from India. This limit I place at two years.'[26]

Throughout the winter of 1880–81, the strength of the force on the lines of communications and at Kandahar averaged seven regiments of cavalry, fifteen regiments of infantry, seven batteries of artillery and four companies of sappers and miners. Particularly at Kandahar, where there was the equivalent of a full division of all arms, this caused constant anxieties over the supply of food and forage. Snow in the passes back to India meant that the only reliable sources of grain lay to the west towards the Helmund and Zamindawar. This was precisely the area which continued to be unsettled by renewed rumours about Ayub's further intentions as well as by the more general rumours about a British withdrawal.

With most of his regular troops, Ayub had made good his retreat to Herat where he busied himself building up his army again. He was rumoured to be planning a raid on Khuskh-i-Nakhud where it was popularly believed the British had accumulated grain and money; normal supplies to Kandahar appeared to be being interfered with; and generally reports from Tehran as well as from Herat itself suggested some vague impending activity from the direction of Herat. St John, who had survived in a double sense the Maiwand débâcle and was still Resident at Kandahar, suggested the dispatch of a small, largely cavalry force to the area of Maiwand to help calm the situation and to ensure the free flow of supplies into Kandahar. It would also help in a small way to ease the supply position around the city by tapping fresh sources of supplies in the Maiwand area.

St John believed that the Kandaharis greatly preferred Ayub to Abdurrahman and that if the British left there would be a general uprising in favour of Ayub. With the approval of Army Headquarters, a small force under Brigadier-General Wilkinson* concentrated at Sinjiri on 20 January, preparatory to moving to a position close to Maiwand whence it would be linked by heliograph and by posts at Karez-i-Salim and Sinjiri to Kandahar 38 miles away. An immediate reserve consisting of the 63rd Foot and D/B, RHA was held in readiness at Kokeran. Wilkinson's force reached Maiwand on 22 January and remained there for just over a fortnight. It achieved its objects but its stay was cut short by the receipt of instructions at Kandahar to prepare for the early evacuation of Southern Afghanistan. It arrived back at Kokeran on 11 February. Abdurrahman was formally invited by Ripon at the end of January to take over Kandahar and it was clear that he would accept. The way was effectively clear to plan the evacuation.†

Hume submitted his detailed plans on 8 February and they were formally approved on the 24th, but he had already begun to concentrate transport. He had been told that only existing transport was to be used, but at Kandahar he had in hand only about half of the transport estimated to be required. To supplement this, four divisions (about 1,800 carts) of the cart train which had run between Sibi and Chaman were ordered up to Kandahar, together with extra bullocks for the spare wagons already there. Substantial purchases or hire of animals would be necessary in addition. The need to concentrate transport, coupled with the expectation of snow and wintry weather in the passes, indicated 15 March as the earliest date on which the main evacuation could begin. But a good deal of preliminary work could go on before then; camping grounds and rest camps had to be provided along the route, repairs made to the road, supplies accumulated *en route*, and officers and doctors appointed to superintend the various sections of the L of C. By setting up permanent camp sites between Quetta and Sibi, Hume was able to arrange for the returning regiments to dump their camp equipment, along with reserve ammunition, tools, etc., in the arsenal at Quetta; this speeded up the passage of the troops between Quetta and Sibi and greatly reduced the amount of rail transport required. Two convoys of ordnance stores left Kandahar on 9 and 17

---

*13th Hussars, Poona Horse, 27th BoNI, 6/8 RA and half of No. 3 Company Bombay Sappers and Miners – in all, about 1,400 men.

†Two envoys from Ayub arrived unexpectedly in Kandahar at the end of February to press their Master's case for taking over the province. They were kept hanging about for a month and then summarily dismissed. The excitement that their arrival caused made it very clear that Abdurrahman would have a hard fight to retain Kandahar.

February and these were followed, despite the weather, by a steady stream of convoys carrying down stores, surplus equipment and invalids. By 21 March Hume's arrangements at Kandahar were complete, but the date of the final evacuation was not settled until the 27th when he received orders to withdraw on or about 10 April when the Amir Abdurrahman's troops should arrive to take over the city.

On 1 April, the last convoys of stores, invalids and spare personnel left Kandahar and the first of the Amir's officials arrived. Rumours of the approach of the Amir's forces and of the activities of Ayub at Herat, coupled with the news of the British retirement, had created high excitement and tension in the city and this was spreading in the countryside, notably among the Achakzais inhabiting the Toba plateau east of the Khojak Pass. Hume strengthened his post at Kushdil Khan, but there was every prospect that evacuation might prove a difficult and hazardous affair.

By 5 April, the advance guard of the Amir's occupation force was at Robat. Four days later, Hume was instructed to begin the final evacuation as soon as possible; Quetta was to be held by a brigade of cavalry, five battalions of infantry and three batteries of artillery and this force would man the outposts between Quetta and Chaman. The line of the Harnai valley railway would be garrisoned by a further four battalions of infantry, together with a regiment of cavalry and a mountain battery; this force would also garrison Thal-Chotiali.

The final evacuation began on 15 April when the 2/11th Foot, 14/9 RA and the remaining sick of the garrison left Kandahar. On the following day, the Amir's appointed Governor (Mohammed Hashin Khan) entered the city and discussed the detailed handover arrangements with St John. On 17 and 18 April, the 3rd Brigade under Brigadier-General Henderson marched for Quetta and Sibi, followed by the 2nd Brigade under Brigadier-General Penton on the 20th. Finally, on the 21st, the city, together with a quantity of guns, muskets, ammunition and money, were formally handed over to the Governor and the remaining British troops comprising the 1st and the Cavalry Brigades went into camp outside the city. They marched early on the 22nd, accompanied by Hume and St John, and the new frontier at Chaman was crossed on the 27th. Dropping off those troops that were to man Chaman and the other posts, the two brigades reached Quetta on 4 and 5 May. By now, the 2/11th were approaching the railhead at Pir Choki where it entrained on 8 May for its new peacetime station at Jullundur in the Punjab. It was followed by a steady stream of regiments bound for India. On 23 May, Hume reported to Army Headquarters in Calcutta that the last regiment for India had left Pir Choki. The troops left at Quetta and elsewhere under Hume were now formally designated the Quetta Division.

The Second Afghan War was at an end. It had lasted two and a half years.

NOTES

1. See Primrose's report of 10 September 1880, reproduced in *Papers connected with operations in Southern Afghanistan, Part III.* Office of Quartermaster-General in India, Calcutta 1881, p. 78. Primrose claimed that this had prevented him sending on some of the 4th BoNI to reinforce Burrows.
2. Detailed figures in Primrose's dispatch, printed in C-2736 *Papers relating to the Advance of Ayub Khan on Kandahar*, p. 115.
3. Private B. P. Crane, *The Ninth Lancers in Afghanistan, 1878–1879–1880*, London, n.d., pp. 61–2.
4. The Principal Medical Officer was scathing about the force's footwear: 'Probably a worse-shod army never took the field.' The standard ammunition boot was badly made of poor material and lost its shape after a few days marching. The native troops wore chaplis (open-toed sandals) 'ingeniously contrived to cripple and blister'. Report by Deputy Surgeon-General J. Hanbury.
5. Quoted in Roberts's Dispatch No. 88 dated 26 September 1880, from Quetta. Adam's letter is significant in the light of later allegations that the garrison's morale was poor.
6. Roberts himself was ill and Hanbury put the total sick at roughly a thousand. 'After Khelat-i-Ghilzai everyone suffered much from diarrhoea. This, added to the poor food, reduced the men so that I do not think the Force could have reached much further than it did' – an officer, quoted in Duke, op. cit., p. 265.
7. MacGregor continued to believe that the right course was to move westwards into the Argandab valley – *Diary*, p. 237.
8. Of the 9,000 animals (including cavalry and artillery but excluding camels) which accompanied the Kabul Field Force, 1,050 died and 2,160 were sick and ineffective on arrival at Kandahar. Just under a thousand soldiers and followers were sick. *Abridged Official History*, Appendix XXXX.
9. As a measure of the impact of the war, Phayre's troops ultimately included Bengal, Bombay, Madras and Hyderabad Contingent regiments.
10. C. E. Biddulph (an Assistant Political Officer) 'The March to Quetta in August 1880' *United Service Magazine*, July 1894.
11. Biddulph, ibid.
12. Dispatch quoted in Official History, vol. VI, p. 75. The Secretary of State for India subsequently conveyed his thanks to all members of Phayre's force for their efforts. It may nevertheless have been a blessing

that Roberts's troops were left to tackle Ayub Khan rather than Phayre's relatively untested regiments.
13. See *Afghanistan (1880)*, No. 3 (C-2736), p. 53. A rumour that Stewart (sic) was marching from Kabul to Kandahar reached the garrison via Kalat-i-Ghilzai on 7 August – that is to say, *before* the Kabul force had begun its march! See also Hamilton, op. cit., pp. 80–81.
14. See *Forty-One Years in India*, pp. 484–5. Hensman, who accompanied the Kabul force, echoed Roberts.
15. Hills, op. cit., p. 54.
16. Primrose claimed that it had actually raised the morale of his force – see Official History, vol. V, p. 386.
17. Roberts was equally critical of Phayre's troops, describing them to Lyall as having 'the appearance of troops retreating, not advancing; they were all over the country and there was a want of cohesion and arrangements which could never be with troops commanded by men who know what they are about'. RP 7101-23-101, p. 561.
18. See Chapter 12, n. 51.
19. Travers, in his diary, wrote that Ayub, deceived by Gough's withdrawal the previous afternoon, had assembled his regular troops and guns behind the Bala Wali Kotal in readiness for an attack on Kandahar – see JSAHR vol. LX, No. 241, p. 37.
20. 'Hampered as the cavalry were by narrow lanes and unbridged water-channels, our progress to the Argandab river was but slow, and a lot of precious time was needlessly wasted, especially in crossing the canals' – diary of Major Gerard, Central India Horse.
21. Lieutenant Hunter of the 9th Lancers wrote ironically: 'We arrive as usual just an hour too late. However, we did a great advance across the plain in echelon of squadrons against what turned out to be a party consisting of women and children, donkeys, cows and camels, which presented a most formidable appearance at a distance.' Major E. W. Sheppard. *The Ninth Queen's Royal Lancers 1715–1936*. London, 1939, p. 175.
22. 'I dismounted and examined the body. He had a clean, incised wound on the neck, which all but severed the head from the body. His death could not have taken place more than half an hour before I saw him.' – Hanbury's diary. In addition to the five sepoys mentioned here, another 24 native soldiers had reached Kandahar. Others were

still in hiding in villages near the city.
23. For a detailed account of the operations see *Frontier and Overseas Expeditions from India*, vol. III, pp. 142–8.
24. Secretary of State to Viceroy, 11 November 1880. *Afghanistan (1881)*, No. 1, pp. 89–93. Some members of the Cabinet, notably Northbrook, were equally strongly against the retention of Pishin and Sibi. The Cabinet would not agree to annexation of these districts but it did not insist upon evacuation. Ripon on his own responsibility decided to stay.
25. Abdurrahman to Viceroy, 10 February 1881 – *Afghanistan (1881)*, No. 5, p. 68.
26. That was certainly Lytton's view; see his speech on the Address in the House of Lords in January 1881.
27. Memorandum to Government of India, 12 May 1880 – *Afghanistan (1880)*, No. 1, p. 71.

CHAPTER 14

RESULTS AND REFLECTIONS

'Our retirement without having established a settled government, or left a strong and friendly ruler at Kabul, would be treated by all opponents of our policy as a confession of failure. That it would not be an altogether satisfactory termination, I agree. But while critics of the present judge generally by what has not been done, future critics will judge more fairly by what has been done. In 1876, the two great passes of the Bolan and the Khyber, as well as the minor one of Kohat, were closed to us. At a time of nominal peace, no European's life was safe a mile beyond our border . . . and immediately opposite us was growing up a great hostile military power, daily drawing further from us and nearer Russia. Now the passes are open . . ., our officers move freely over most parts of the border, and that great threatening military power on our northern border is utterly broken up and dispersed.'

Lytton to his Council, 2 April 1880

'Thus it appears that as a result of two successful campaigns, of the employment of an enormous force, and of the expenditure of large sums of money, all that has yet been accomplished has been the disintegration of the State which it was desired to see strong, friendly and independent, the assumption of fresh and unwelcome liabilities in regard to one of its provinces, and a condition of anarchy throughout the remainder of the country.'

Hartington to Ripon, 21 May 1880

In Afghanistan the aftermath of the war rumbled on.

Abdurrahman was not master of the whole country and the irrepressible Ayub Khan was not yet prepared to abandon the prize of Kandahar and the chance of disputing for the throne of Kabul. A year after his first disastrous attempt, Ayub crossed the Helmund with another army, defeated the Amir's troops and seized Kandahar again at the end of July 1881. His triumph was short-lived. Abdurrahman was too shrewd a statesman not to see that if Ayub remained in possession of Kandahar his own rule at Kabul could never be secure. At the end of August 1881, he took the field himself and reached Kandahar with some 12,000 troops and a strong body of loyal tribesmen. The ensuing battle on 22 September was hard-fought and the result in doubt until it was decided in the Amir's favour by the desertion of some of Ayub's troops. This time there was to be no refuge in Herat because that city had been seized in Ayub's absence by the Governor of Afghan Turkestan on Abdurrahman's orders. Ayub fled to Persia where he continued to be a source of trouble until 1888 when he finally gave up the contest and accepted asylum in British India, ending his days, ironically, as a British pensioner. He died at Lahore in April 1914. Abdurrahman could at last concentrate on the long process of taming his turbulent subjects and recreating a centralized state of Afghanistan, revealing in the process that sardonic gallows humour which so fascinated Kipling.*

On the British side the conclusion of the war brought mixed fortunes for the participants. George White of the 92nd finally got his Victoria Cross for his part in the attack on Ayub's camp. He was appointed Military Secretary to Ripon and rose rapidly, succeeding Roberts as Commander-in-Chief, India in 1893. He proved an inept general in Natal in 1899, allowing himself and his troops to be shut up in Ladysmith and displaying a good deal of pessimism in the process; nevertheless he ended up as a Field Marshal. Macpherson, Baker and MacGregor received KCBs for their part in the final victory. Macpherson went on to command the Indian contingent in the Egyptian Campaign in 1882 and to become Commander-in-Chief of the Madras Army; he died in 1885 *en route* to take over command in the Third Burmese War, the Madras Army's last campaign. Baker died in office in 1893 as Quartermaster-General of the British Army. MacGregor died in 1887 as Quartermaster-General in India; his reputation had suffered a set-back in later years and it seems doubtful if he would have got to the top. Colour-Sergeant Hector Macdonald of the 92nd, who had distinguished himself in the Karatiga defile in September 1879, at Charasiab and on the Sher Darwaza Heights in December 1879, was commissioned in the field and had a meteoric rise to fame. As a brigade commander at the battle of Omdurman in 1899, he played a critical and decisive role which made his a household name. His career ended tragically in 1903 when he shot himself in Paris as a result of allegations of homosexual conduct while GOC, Ceylon. Lytton's military *éminence grise*, George Colley, is now best remembered as the commander responsible for the disaster on Majuba Hill in 1881 where he was killed. A survivor of that melancholy affair was Ian Hamilton, the future commander of the assault on Gallipoli, who had served with the 92nd in Afghanistan. O'Moore Creagh, the hero of Kam Dakka, ended up as Commander-in-Chief, India, retiring in 1914. A predecessor as Commander-in-Chief was A. P. Palmer who had led the tribal levies at the Peiwar Kotal. Ripon went on to hold a series of important Ministerial posts, finally retiring from office in 1908 and dying the following year. Lepel Griffin was knighted and got the plum job of Agent to the Governor-General in Central India, but he retired prematurely at the age of 50, disappointed of his ambition to become Lieutenant-Governor of his old province, the Punjab. St John, after what now seems an ambiguous record in the war, went on to hold a series of important political appointments in India, culminating in the prize of the Residency at Mysore. Burrows, perhaps the most tragic figure of the whole war, was never employed again; he died a long-forgotten figure, in 1917 in the midst of a war where British casualties on a quiet day exceeded the total at Maiwand. Primrose too was never employed again. But Nuttall, whose performance at Maiwand was, to say the least, undistinguished, rose to be a Lieutenant-General and to be knighted. Several others among the survivors, including Leach,

---

*See, for example, the story 'The Amir's Homily' and the poems *The Ballad of the King's Jest* and *The Ballad of the King's Mercy*. Kipling saw Abdurrahman when the latter paid a formal visit to the Viceroy, Lord Dufferin, at Rawalpindi in 1885.

Slade and Anderson, retired as full Generals. Phayre was knighted, rose to be a full General and retired in 1889. Lytton never held Ministerial office, but was a highly successful Ambassador in Paris, dying of a heart attack there in 1891.

On the Afghan side, Abdurrahman ruled Afghanistan with an iron hand until 1901. He took care to remain on good terms with the British, a policy carried on by his son, Habibullah. But the latter's death ushered in a period of dynastic instability which led directly to the Third Afghan War in 1919. Yakub Khan died at Mussourie in 1923; he had reigned for less than a year and lived as a British pensioner for forty-four.

The outstanding personality, and, in more ways than one, the victor of the Second Afghan War was Roberts. The war had established him as a rival to that other late-Victorian star, Wolseley, a rivalry which was to last for the next twenty years. A period as Commander-in-Chief, Madras brought him to the post of Commander-in-Chief, India in 1885 in succession to Stewart. He held that post for the unusually long period of eight years and as a result was able to put a lasting stamp on the Indian Army. Technically he had been a British Army officer since the Bengal Artillery was abolished in 1861. He was therefore eligible for the higher appointments in the British Army and on leaving India he succeeded Wolseley as Commander-in-Chief in Ireland. By now Wolseley's powers and reputation were in decline and when someone was needed to retrieve the situation in South Africa in 1899 Roberts was the inevitable choice. He went on to succeed Wolseley as the last Commander-in-Chief of the British Army. Fittingly, he died while visiting the Indian contingent in France in 1915, leaving an immortal image as 'Bobs', the little fighting general.

He was by no means the simple *chevalier pur et sans reproche* which biographers have sought to portray. In his activities in Afghanistan, he showed a keen political instinct and considerable agility in creating and maintaining good relations with both Lytton and Ripon. It would be unfair to regard him as a 'trimmer' but he was quick to adapt to the changing political situation – for example, in his views on the relative importance of the Kurram and Khyber routes, on the restoration of Yakub and on the retention of Kandahar. Unusually at this period, he had also a clear perception of the importance of the Press – his careful treatment of Hensman as the only journalist to accompany him to Kabul, his handling of the other correspondents in Kabul and his expulsion of Macpherson, the *Standard* correspondent who had written critically of the Khost expedition, illustrate different aspects of this perception.* Above all, there was in Roberts's character an element of harshness which is not apparent in the popular image. I have speculated elsewhere that this aspect of his character may have been moulded by the grim experience of the Mutiny. The executions at Kabul caught the public attention, but elsewhere executions and floggings were an element of both Roberts's first and second campaigns.† Of his great qualities as a commander there can be no doubt. Quick

---

*Combe made an interesting comment in January 1880: 'It is very lucky we have no *independent* [author's italics] Special Correspondents to publish full and true accounts of all that has been done, or left undone, up here.' (op. cit., p. 131).
†In fairness to Roberts, he was not alone in meting out swift, stern justice. At different times, Bright, Stewart, Tytler and Charles Gough, among others, were responsible for summarily shooting tribesmen guilty of attacks on the British forces.

to assess a situation, prompt to decide on a course of action, never flustered or disheartened, always keen to seize the initiative and always confident of his own abilities, he was a consummate field commander. If he was prone to take risks, especially in logistics and to underestimate his enemy, nevertheless his marvellous tactical sense and his ability to inspire his own troops made him probably the ablest British commander in the field since Wellington. Among modern generals, one is irresistibly reminded of Rommel. It has sometimes been argued that Roberts would not have measured up to the greater demands of European war. That is a point which can never be settled, but his success in South Africa, at an age when modern Generals are long past retirement, offers material at least for debate.*

The Second Afghan War was not a war of significant technological progress. The Gatling gun made a small and inauspicious appearance, the electric telegraph played a major role in communications and the railways had proved their enormous strategic value – but all of these had appeared earlier in other wars. It was the first major campaign in which the Indian Armies had gone to war equipped with breech-loaders and dressed in khaki, but the only real technological advance was in the use of the heliograph. By the end of the war ranges of up to 50 miles were being achieved with it. Because it was critically dependent upon the weather it could never be a substitute for the later radio, but until the latter became a practical proposition the heliograph continued to meet an essential tactical need and it was widely adopted in other armies.

In its operational aspects the Second Afghan war was essentially an old-fashioned war in which Wellington or Charles Napier or Colin Campbell would have found themselves readily at home. Against largely undisciplined and relatively poorly armed opponents the Indian armies had acquitted themselves well. But certain perennial weaknesses, such as transport, under-officering and difficulties in replacing equipment and casualties, had shown up once again, and the war had undeniably been expensive. At the end of the first campaign, Lytton had appointed a commission under Sir Ashley Eden, the Lieutenant-Governor of Bengal, to examine the whole organization of the Indian armies, primarily to see how their efficiency could be improved and their cost reduced. Apart from Eden, the members of the Commission included the Adjutant-General (Lumsden), Phayre, Roberts, Macpherson, Baker and MacGregor. Despite the departure of the last four to take part in the second campaign, the Commission completed its report on 15 November 1879.[1] It contained well over 500 detailed recommendations covering every aspect of organization and administration and proposing savings of some 12½ million rupees a year. The four thick volumes of appendices contain a storehouse of detailed information about the army in India at that period, as well as a good deal of useful information about the campaign just concluded. Basic to the whole report was the proposal that the three Presidency armies should be replaced by four army corps (Bengal, Punjab, Madras and Bombay) and the existing geographical division and brigade organization by a system of 1st and 2nd class districts, with the primary object of being able to place

*I do not accept the very critical view in Thomas Pakenham's The Boer War (London, 1979), for reasons which it is not possible to go into here. MacGregor paints a savagely critical portrait of Roberts, both as a man and as a commander, in his diary but much of this, although not all, can be ascribed to MacGregor's jealousy and envy.

in the field in emergency a balanced force of some 75,000 men with 240 guns.* From this flowed a series of proposals for a unified War Department, the creation of a General Staff including an Intelligence Department and a new post of Chief of Staff to the Commander-in-Chief, the strengthening of the commissariat and transport services and the placing of the Punjab Frontier Force directly under Army Headquarters. Further proposals covered increases in the size of British and Native regiments (and an increase in the number of British officers for the latter), the abolition of the Staff Corps system and the formation of a General List, and the creation of a system of regimental depots and reserves for the native regiments. Much the most controversial of its proposals was that the Commander-in-Chief should no longer be a member of the Viceroy's Council; of more direct importance for the future size and shape of the Indian Army were the proposals that the Bengal regiments should be recruited mainly on a class-company basis and that the Bombay and Madras regiments should be restricted henceforth to recruiting from their own areas. There was naturally a direct price to be paid for all this and that price was to be a large reduction in the number of native regiments – seventeen Madras, six Bombay and seventeen Bengal and PFF.

It was not to be expected that the implementation of the proposed reforms could be speedy or comprehensive; there were too many traditional beliefs and vested interests to overcome. But it is true to say that the Eden Commission report provided the basic blueprint for Indian Army reform for the rest of the century. Predictably, the basic proposal for the abolition of the separate Presidency armies and the creation of a system of army corps took the longest to achieve. The Presidency armies were not finally abolished until 1895 when they were replaced by four 'Corps' recommended by the Commission. But there was steady progress in other directions. The separate Ordnance Departments were unified in 1884, followed between 1887 and 1891 by the unification of the clothing, legal, commissariat and transport departments. In 1886, the Punjab Frontier Force was brought under the direct control of the Commander-in-Chief, India, and three years later the divisional and brigade system was replaced by a district system. A system of reserves for the native regiments was brought into being in 1886. Reform of the Staff Corps system was taken in hand in 1882 and brought to completion in 1891 when the three Presidency Staff Corps were amalgamated to form in effect a General List. Twelve years later, the title 'Staff Corps' was abolished altogether and henceforth all officers joined 'the Indian Army'.

It was in the field of transport that the Eden Commission was least forward-looking. Conscious of the defects revealed in the first campaign of the Second Afghan War, it nevertheless recommended little more than a reorganization of the regimental and station transport already in existence while still envisaging reliance in emergency on large-scale hiring and requisitioning. It was not until 1899 that the correct solution – the creation of specialist army transport units – began to be put into effect.

One other weakness – medical care – survived to create a major scandal in Mesopotamia in 1915. The incidence of disease in Afghanistan had been high and

---

*Roberts claimed (*Forty-One Years in India*, p. 382) that he was responsible for the idea of four Army Corps. If so, it is slightly surprising that more progress was not made with it during his long tenure as C in C, India.

hospital facilities inadequate. There had been no proper training, supervision or care of the native stretcher- or doolie-bearers.[2] There was moreover general agreement that the native troops had been inadequately fed and clothed, so that they succumbed too easily to exhaustion and disease.[3]

Long before then, the most fundamental effect of the Second Afghan War upon the size and composition of the native armies had taken shape. Prejudice against the Madras and Bombay regiments in favour of the regiments recruited from the so-called 'martial races' of the north had been growing since the Mutiny. In part, this was little more than racial prejudice – the larger, paler, Aryan-featured Sikhs, Punjabis and Pathans created a better impression on British officers than the smaller, darker races of Bombay and Madras. Very largely it was due to the fact that the centre of military gravity had been moving steadily to the north since the 1820s. It was in the north, in the Bengal Army and the PFF, that opportunities for action were to be found. The two southern armies were increasingly shut out and the Madras Army in particular had become little more than a police force which the younger, more active officers avoided. The Second Afghan War had strengthened these prejudices. It was the Sikh, Punjab and Gurkha regiments, which had stolen the limelight. The Madras regiments had played little part and had been used mainly to release Bengal regiments from garrison duty for service in Afghanistan. The Bombay regiments had suffered a major blow to their reputation at Maiwand.

Haines, as Commander-in-Chief, had fought hard for the Madras and Bombay regiments, but the battle was largely lost when he retired in 1881. The point was diplomatically put by Sir Henry Norman: 'Doubts too have been expressed as to the suitability of all parts of our Native Army for service in Afghanistan. Loyal, well-disciplined and brave as these troops are, many of our soldiers are physically inferior to the Afghans. A determined attack by fanatical Afghans tries the best troops, and there is an opinion among officers who have recently served that the result of such attacks, if really carried home, may be doubtful unless our forces were in the main British, Sikhs, Pathans and Gurkhas.' In 1882 as an economy measure seven Bengal, five Bombay and eight Madras regiments were abolished, but whereas all seven Bengal regiments and one of the Bombay regiments were subsequently reformed in 1885 and 1887, the loss of Madras regiments was permanent. Even more damaging was the apparent inability of the Madras and Bombay regiments to recruit adequately from their own local sources. Again the difficulty was more apparent than real because some races, such as the Telegus who had formed a large proportion of the old Coast Army, were deliberately excluded from recruitment. But the temptation to draw further on the apparently inexhaustible recruiting well of the Punjab was irresistible. By 1902 fourteen out of the 28 Madras Infantry regiments were recruited wholly from the Punjab; sixteen out of 26 Bombay regiments contained at least 25 per cent of men from the Punjab.*

---

*The First World War ensured the final disappearance of the Madras Infantry regiments all of whom had disappeared by 1925. By 1939, only the Mahratta Light Infantry, the Indian Grenadiers and the Rajputana Rifles recalled the old Bombay infantry. The Second World War saw the reconstitution of the Madras Regiment however.

The emphasis on financial retrenchment which underlay the work of the Eden Commission was strengthened by the disclosure in Lytton's last four months as Viceroy of a great financial blunder by the Indian Government. At the end of February 1880 the Indian authorities had informed the Secretary of State in London that the net cost of the war to the end of the financial year 1880/1881 was expected to be only some £9.25M, of which £3.75M was in respect of capital expenditure on railways.[5] Within six weeks Lytton was warning Cranbrook that '[the] outgoing from our treasury for the war [is] very alarming, far exceeding estimate'.[6] A month later the Government of India told the Secretary of State that the very heavy drain on the frontier and provincial treasuries which had come to light in March had caused uneasiness about the original estimate; it now appeared on investigation that the cost of the war would be at least £13.25M.[7] Even this was not the end because in October 1880 the estimated net cost was put at £17.5M, including nearly £5M for railways. Supplementary estimates submitted in March 1881 raised the cost to just over £19.5M. What made it the more galling for Lytton and the home Government was the fact that at the beginning of 1880 Gladstone had accused the Conservatives of deliberately falsifying their estimate of the cost of the war by at least £6M. It now appeared that Gladstone's accusation was considerably understated.

The explanation for the enormous increase turned out to be basically simple.[8] In framing its estimates, the Government of India relied upon figures provided by the Military Accounts Department which in turn were based upon properly audited and verified accounts. That system worked well in normal times; in wartime, however, the preparation of audited accounts inevitably ran far behind actual cash expenditure. Transport officers, for example, faced with an urgent need to purchase pack-animals or supplies, would draw on the local provincial treasury for large amounts of cash and it would be months before these bills filtered through to the Military Accounts Departments for checking and clearance. What is incredible is that no one, from Lytton downwards, seems to have queried the very low estimates of the cost of the war which the Military Accounts Department was putting forward, while that Department seems to have made no attempt to cross-check its estimates with the actual cash accounts of the provincial treasuries.

Formal responsibility fell on Sir Edwin Johnson who, as Military Member, was responsible for the Military Accounts Department and he duly resigned along with Sir John Strachey, the Finance Member and close friend of Lytton. Despite Indian protests that the war was the result of imperial, not local, policy the home government ultimately contributed only £5M to the cost. The remaining £15M or so had to be found from Indian revenues. It was a heavy burden for a country already saddled with a commitment to remit large sums annually to the home treasury and where in 1878–79 the surplus of revenue over expenditure was only £2M. Nevertheless the Indian economy was essentially sound and the Indian budget was in surplus within two years.

On the wider political and strategic scene, the conclusion of the Second Afghan War ushered in a period of peace between Britain and Afghanistan which lasted unbroken for 38 years. Nevertheless, there was scarcely a moment up until their final withdrawal from India in 1947 when the British were free from worry about Russian designs on Afghanistan. The end of the Second Afghan War coincided with the final defeat at Gek Tepe of the Turkoman tribes who inhabited the corner of territory between the Caspian and the northern border of Afghanistan. The Russian border for all practical purposes was now contiguous with that of Afghanistan and the Russians proceeded to bind together their territories in Central Asia by strategic railways, the first of which from the Russian base at Krasnovodsk on the Caspian to Kizl Arvat was opened in 1881 and extended to the Amu Darya in 1885 and to Samarkand in 1887. The details of the Pendjeh crisis of 1885 which was essentially a dispute about a relatively minor border demarcation need not concern us here, but the fact that it could bring Russia and Britain to the verge of war illustrates the continuing sensitivity with which the British authorities regarded the inviolability of Afghanistan. Despite frequent invasion scarces (vividly evoked in John Masters' novel *The Lotus and the Wind*, whose opening scenes incidentally are set during the Second Afghan War), there is no real evidence that the Russians ever seriously contemplated any attack on India,[9] but the events of 1876–81 had brought home to them the powerful diplomatic lever which British fears about Afghanistan placed in their hands. Nicholas II put it bluntly, if accurately, in 1899 when he boasted that he could immobilize British policy throughout the world by mobilizing the Russian forces in Turkestan.

Moreover, as time went on, new areas of pressure opened up. The Russian occupation of Kokand in 1876 followed two years later by the fall of the extraordinary kingdom of Yakub Beg at Kashgar opened up the whole area of the Pamirs to Russian exploration. The British now had to contend with a new set of fears about a possible Russian invasion route over the Pamirs direct into Northern India. That situation was not resolved until 1895, when the Anglo-Russian Convention on the Pamirs interposed a 'panhandle' of new Afghan territory between the two great empires. By 1900, Curzon and his colleagues in the Government of India were worrying about yet another potential threat – that of a Russian advance through Persia and Seistan on Quetta. Vast amounts of staff effort were devoted to calculating how fast the Russians could lay a railway towards Quetta and conversely how fast the British railway which had reached Quetta in 1887 could be extended towards Seistan, and what the relative rates of build-up of forces and supplies might then be. The Anglo-Russian Convention of 1907 was itself a direct recognition of the fact that the British could no longer guarantee by themselves the security of their worldwide possessions and that, in particular, the stability of the Raj in India depended upon its being relieved of the fear of a Russian attack.

The occupation of the Khyber, the Kurram and Pishin and Sibi[10] had gone a considerable way to meeting the wishes of the 'forward school' and from a narrow General Staff view had improved the British military position *vis-à-vis* the defence of the North-West Frontier. But there was a heavy price to pay in terms of tribal hostility. In the early 1870s, relations with the tribes on the edge of the British administered zone had appeared to be stabilizing. Given the poverty of the tribal areas and the temptations offered by the settled areas of British India, there was never likely to be complete peace but there was hope that friction could be kept within reasonable bounds. Writing in 1876, Lepel Griffin could claim: 'The frontier tribes are slowly, but surely, losing their suspicion of and dislike to the British Government. The change is gradual; but if we look back twenty, even ten years we see how substantial has been the progress made. They are still savage, fanatical, and ignorant but they have learned to believe in the fairness of our intentions, and so far appreciate our rule that they leave their hills in large numbers, abandon their predatory life, and live quietly in British territory.'[11]

That optimistic note could not credibly be repeated for the next fifty years. The war changed the situation fundamentally. By the time it ended the British had been brought into sharp conflict with all the major tribes between the Khyber and the Bolan – Mohmands, Afridis, Shinwaris, Wazirs, Mahsuds, Kakars, the Zhob valley tribes, Achakzais, Marris. Moreover, the extension of British-occupied territory under the terms of the Treaty of Gandamak involved a continuing process of penetrating tribal territory, of which the penetration of the Zhob valley was a classic example. The tribesmen had no natural ethnic affinity with the British as they had with the Durani rulers of Afghanistan. Durani (and Sikh) rule had been spasmodic and inefficient in its operation and some tribes such as the Afridis of the Tirah and the Wazirs had never lost their effective independence. The British were not just aliens and unbelievers – they were interfering, efficient and heavy-handed. And they had a well-deserved reputation for never letting go of anything they seized. The British were not their own masters in this; they were in the grip of exactly the same forces which had impelled the Russians to extend their sway in Central Asia. In the words which Gortchakoff had used about the Russian dilemma in Central Asia in his circular memorandum of November 1864, the Government of India must either 'abandon the incessant struggle and deliver its frontier over to disorder, which renders property, security and civilianization impossible, or it must plunge into the depths of savage countries, where the difficulties and sacrifices to which it is exposed increase with each step in advance.'

It was, therefore, inevitable that one result of the war would be increased friction between the tribes and the British. So it proved. From 1881, the frequency, as well as the individual size, of major expeditions against the tribes steadily increased culminating in the great tribal explosion of 1897–8. Nor was there any noticeable diminution after 1898. The most critical campaign ever fought on the North-West Frontier was in Waziristan in 1919–20 when for a moment it looked as though the Indian Army could no longer meet the tribesmen on even terms. The last Victoria Cross won on the Frontier was in 1935 when two platoons of the 5th Battalion of the 12th Frontier Force Regiment, lineal descendants of the original Guides Infantry, were overwhelmed and wiped out despite the support of aircraft, tanks and machine-guns. On balance, it is arguable that the military drain caused by this incessant warfare outweighed the strategic advantages gained under the Treaty of Gandamak.

But if the Russian threat remained and if the extension of the frontier had led to an increased military and economic burden, what defence then could be made to Hartington's bitter summary of the war? What *had* the expenditure of some £19.5M and many thousands of casualties achieved? Was it all worthwhile and, if not, had there been a rational alternative?

Much depends upon the perspective. For Lytton, Roberts, Stewart, Rawlinson, Frere, Cranbrook and probably a majority of the military men, there had been no alternative: in their view, Sher Ali, left alone, would have turned more and more to the Russians, a Russian, not a British, envoy would have held sway at Kabul and in

279

the course of time a Russian Army would have appeared on the Indus. The war had toppled Sher Ali, removed the Russians from Kabul, improved the strategic frontier and placed Afghanistan in the hands of a ruler who owed virtually everything to the British.* More intangibly, the British will and power to defend its position in Asia had been demonstrated; the effect in India, as well as in the rest of Asia, could only have been good. It was a view which it was perfectly respectable to hold for a limited period immediately after the conclusion of the war. It became more difficult to hold when the Pendjeh crisis and then the Pamirs confrontation threw doubts upon the disappearance of the Russian menace and when the effect of the war in terms of conflict with the tribes began to be apparent.

Inevitability is a doubtful concept for historians and there was nothing inevitable about the outbreak of the Second Afghan War unless it be in the personality of Lytton himself. Although it is too simplistic to regard him as solely responsible, there can be no doubt that he was the dominant influence, alternatively urging Cranbrook and the Cabinet with all the authority of the man on the spot and then, in the later stages of the crisis, acting decisively to pre-empt decision in London.

How far Sher Ali was alienated from the British and determined to seek a Russian alliance is impossible to determine. What is clear is that by 1876 he had become rightly anxious about the growing Russian presence on his doorstep. Both at Herat and in Afghan Turkestan the Russians were able to exert a direct, geographic threat which was the more serious because less easily countered militarily than that exerted by the British on Kabul and Kandahar. Sher Ali had fought long and hard to consolidate his rule. If he could not obtain British support against Russian pressure, he was bound to consider some accommodation with the Russians. But either way, there is no reason to doubt that his dominant and fixed motive was to maintain the independence and integrity of his kingdom. If so, British policy should have been to give him a clear guarantee of support such as Northbrook had wished to give in 1873 and to refrain from insisting on the stationing of British envoys in Afghanistan. The view that without such envoys the information available to the British would be too inadequate to risk giving Sher Ali the guarantee he sought had been rejected by Northbrook, his Council and the preponderance of experienced official opinion in India. We come back therefore to the central importance of Lytton's perception.

If the war were not inevitable, and if the short-term gains in terms of strategic territory and Russian withdrawal had proved, on balance, somewhat illusory, what had the British achieved in the longer term? The war had, in the first place, defined the stakes for which the Russians were playing. Henceforth, they could be under no illusion that any attempt to supplant the British at Kabul or to take over any substantial part of Afghanistan would mean an Anglo-Russian war. That factor was clearly much in mind during the resolution of the Pendjeh crisis. Secondly, the Afghans themselves were forced to accept that they could have no allies but the British unless they wished to risk a third Anglo-Afghan war. In sum, what the Second Afghan War had done was to establish in practice, if not exactly in the form originally desired, that buffer zone which Clarendon had pursued in the 1860s.

---

*Kauffmann continued to correspond at intervals with Abdurrahman, and five Russian officers escorted the latter's family to Kabul in April 1881.

NOTES

1. *Report of the Special Commission appointed by His Excellency the Governor General in Council to enquire into the organization and expenditure of the Army in India.* Government Central Branch Press, Simla 1879 – hereafter referred to as the Eden Commission. For a convenient summary and analysis see Brian Robson *The Eden Commission and the reform of the India Army, 1879–1895.* JSAHR, vol. LX, No. 241, pp. 4–13.
2. Army Medical Department Report for 1880, Annex III, p. 271.
3. Ibid., p. 284. See also the long correspondence in HP, vol. 38, p. 278 *et seq.*
4. *Afghanistan (1881)*, No. 2, C-2811, p. 55.
5. *Correspondence Relating to the Estimates for the War in Afghanistan.* C2560 (1880), p. 68.
6. Telegram, 8 April 1880 – ibid., p. 69.
7. Dispatch No. 143 (Financial) dated 4 May 1880 – ibid., p. 82.
8. *Further Correspondence Relating to the Estimates for the War in Afghanistan.* C-2617 (1880), pp. 4–12.
9. An exception might perhaps be made in respect of the three columns set in motion by Russia at the height of the crisis in May 1878. Even here it is difficult to distinguish bluff from genuine intention.
10. Despite the Treaty of Gandamak, Pishin and Sibi were formally annexed to India in 1887.
11. Quoted in Hanna, op. cit., vol. III, pp. 553–4.

APPENDIX 1

THE AFGHAN RULERS, 1747–1901

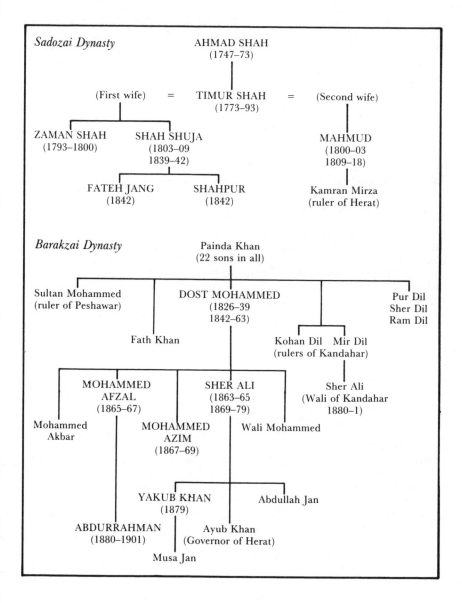

Sadozai Dynasty

AHMAD SHAH
(1747–73)

(First wife) = TIMUR SHAH = (Second wife)
(1773–93)

ZAMAN SHAH   SHAH SHUJA   MAHMUD
(1793–1800)   (1803–09   (1800–03
                    1839–42)   1809–18)

        FATEH JANG   SHAHPUR   Kamran Mirza
        (1842)   (1842)   (ruler of Herat)

Barakzai Dynasty

Painda Khan
(22 sons in all)

Sultan Mohammed   DOST MOHAMMED   Pur Dil
(ruler of Peshawar)   (1826–39   Sher Dil
                        1842–63)   Ram Dil

        Fath Khan   Kohan Dil Mir Dil
                               (rulers of Kandahar)

MOHAMMED   SHER ALI   Sher Ali
AFZAL   (1863–65   (Wali of Kandahar
(1865–67)   1869–79)   1880–1)

Mohammed   MOHAMMED   Wali Mohammed
Akbar   AZIM
                (1867–69)

        YAKUB KHAN   Abdullah Jan
        (1879)

ABDURRAHMAN   Ayub Khan
(1880–1901)   (Governor of Herat)

        Musa Jan

APPENDIX 2

BIOGRAPHICAL NOTES

Baker, Thomas Durand (1837–93). Commissioned 18th Foot 1854. Crimea 1854–6. Mutiny 1857–8. Maori War 1864–6. Ashanti Expedition 1873–4. Adjutant-General, India 1884–6. Third Burmese War 1886–7. Allahabad Division 1887–90. QMG, War Office 1890–3.

Biddulph, Michael Anthony Shrapnel (1823–1904). Commissioned Royal Artillery 1843. Crimea 1854–5. Major-General 1869. Rohilkund Division 1875–8. Rawalpindi Division 1880–6. Lieutenant-General 1881. General 1885. President, Ordnance Committee 1887–90.

Bright, Robert Onesiphorus (1823–96). Commissioned 19th Foot 1843. Crimea 1854–5. Hazara Field Force 1868. Major-General 1868.

Brooke, Henry Francis (1836–80). Commissioned 63rd Foot 1854. Crimea 1855. China 1860. Adjutant-General, Bombay Army 1872–80.

Browne, Samuel James (1824–1901). Commissioned Bengal Army 1840. Second Sikh War 1848–9. Mutiny (VC) 1858. Military Member of Council 1878. Lahore Division 1879. General 1888.

Burrows, George Scott Reynolds (1827–1917). Commissioned Bombay Infantry 1844. No active service. QMG, Bombay Army 1871–79.

Cavagnari, Pierre Louis Napoleon (1841–79). Commissioned Bengal Infantry 1858. Mutiny 1858–9. Political Service 1861. Deputy Commissioner, Kohat 1866–77. Deputy Commissioner, Peshawar 1877–8.

Chamberlain, Neville Bowles (1820–1902). Commissioned Bengal Infantry 1837. First Afghan War 1839–42. Gwalior Campaign 1843. Second Sikh War 1848–9. Punjab Irregular Force 1854–64. Mutiny 1857. Ambeyla Expedition 1863. CinC, Madras Army 1876–81. Field Marshal 1900.

Colley, George Pomeroy (1835–81). Commissioned 2nd Foot 1852. China 1860. Professor at the Staff College. Ashanti 1873–4. Colonel 1874. Zululand 1879. Natal 1881.

Gordon, John James Hood (1832–1908). Commissioned 29th Foot 1849. Mutiny 1857–9. Jowaki Expedition 1877. Major-General 1886. Third Burmese War 1886–7. Assistant Military Secretary, War Office 1891–6. General 1894.

Gordon, Thomas Edward (1832–1914). Commissioned 4th Foot 1849. Mutiny 1857–8. Rohilkund Brigade 1882–7. Major-General 1886. Secretary and Military Attaché, Tehran 1889–93. Lieutenant-General 1890. General 1894.

Gough, Charles John Stanley (1832–1912). Commissioned Bengal Cavalry 1848. Second Sikh War 1848–9. Mutiny 1857–8 (VC). Bhutan Expedition 1864–5. Commanded Hyderabad Contingent 1881–5. Oudh Division 1885–90. General 1891. Father of Sir Hubert Gough, Commanding Fifth Army 1917–18.

Gough, Hugh Henry (1833–1901). Commissioned Bengal Cavalry 1853. Mutiny (VC) 1857–8. Abyssinia 1868. Major-General 1887. Lahore Division 1887–92. General 1894. Brother of Charles Gough (q.v.) and present with 3rd Bengal Cavalry at Meerut on 10 May 1857.

Griffin, Lepel Henry (1838–1908). Bengal Civil Service 1860. Chief Secretary, Punjab 1870. KCSI 1881. Agent to Governor-General in Central India 1881–89. Retired 1889.

Haines, Frederick Paul (1819–1909). Commissioned 4th Foot 1839. First and Second Sikh Wars. Crimea 1854–5. Major-General 1864. Mysore Division 1865–70. CinC, Madras Army 1871–5. CinC, India 1876–81. Field Marshal 1890.

Hills, James (later Hills-Johnes), (1833–1919). Commissioned Bengal Artillery 1853. Mutiny (VC) 1857–8. Abyssinia 1868. Lushai Expedition 1871–2.

Lytton, Edward Robert Bulwer (1831–91), First Earl of Lytton. Diplomatic Service 1849–72. Minister at Lisbon 1872–76. Viceroy of India 1876–80. Ambassador to France 1887–91.

MacGregor, Charles Metcalfe (1840–87). Commissioned Bengal Army 1857. Mutiny 1857–9. China 1860. Bhutan Expedition 1864–5. Abyssinia 1867–8. Major 1876. Lieutenant-Colonel 1882. QMG, India 1881–5.

Macpherson, Herbert Taylor (1827–86). Commissioned Bombay Army 1845. Persian War 1857. Mutiny (VC) 1857–8. Hazara Expedition 1868. Lushai Expedition 1871–2. Jowaki Campaign 1877. Commanded Indian Contingent, Egypt 1882. CinC, Madras Army 1885. Died at Prome in Burma while taking over command in Third Burma War.

Massy, William Godfrey Dunham (1838–1906). Commissioned 1854. Crimea (VC) 1854–6. Lieutenant-Colonel 1871. Rawalpindi Brigade 1879–84. Major-General 1886. GOC, Ceylon 1888–93. Led attack on Redan at Sevastopol September 1855.

Maude, Frederick Francis (1821–97). Commissioned 3rd Foot (Buffs) 1840. Gwalior Campaign 1843. Crimea (VC) 1855. Adjutant-General, Gibraltar 1861–66. Major-General 1868. Rawalpindi Division 1875–80. Father of Sir Stanley Maude, CinC, Mesopotamia 1916–17.

Nuttall, Thomas (1828–90). Commissioned Bombay Infantry 1845. Persian Expedition 1857. Mutiny 1857. Abyssinia 1868. Sind Frontier Force 1876–6. Major-General 1885. Lieutenant-General 1887.

Phayre, Robert (1820–97). Commissioned Bombay Infantry 1839. First Afghan War 1839–42. Sind Campaign 1844. Persian War 1856. Mutiny 1857–8. Abyssinia 1867–8. Major-General 1879. Mhow Division 1881–86. General 1889.

Primrose, James Maurice (1819–92). Commissioned 43rd Foot 1837. South Africa 1851–3. Mutiny 1858. Major-General 1868. Poona Division 1878–80.

Ripon, First Marquis of (George Frederick Samuel Robinson) (1827–1909). MP 1852–9. Under-Secretary of War 1859–61. Under-Secretary, India Office 1861. War Office 1861–66. India Office 1866–68. Lord President 1868–73. First Lord of Admiralty 1886. Colonial Officer 1894–5. Lord Privy Seal 1905–8.

Roberts, Frederick Sleigh (1832–1914). Commissioned Bengal Artillery 1851. Mutiny (VC) 1857–8. Ambeyla Expedition 1863. Abyssinia 1868. Lushai Expedition 1871. Major-General 1875. QMG, India 1875–8. Commanded Punjab Frontier Force 1878. CinC, Madras 1881–5. CinC, India 1885–93. Field Marshal 1895. CinC, South Africa 1899–1900. CinC, British Army 1901–4. Son of General Sir Abraham Roberts who commanded a brigade at Kabul in First Afghan War.

Ross, John (1829–1905). Commissioned Rifle Brigade 1846. Crimea 1854–55. Mutiny 1857–59. Perak Expedition 1875–6. Commanded troops in Malta 1878. Poona Division 1881–86. CinC, Canada 1888–93. General 1891.

Stewart, Donald Martin (1824–1900). Commissioned Bengal Infantry 1840. Major 1858. Mutiny 1857–8. Abyssinian Expedition 1868. Chief Commissioner,

Andaman Islands 1871–5. Lahore Division 1875–8. CinC, India 1881–5. Field Marshal 1894.

St John, Oliver Beauchamp Coventry (1837–91). Commissioned Bengal Engineers 1856. Employed on telegraph line through Persia 1863–7. Abyssinian Expedition 1868. Principal, Mayo College, Ajmer 1875–78. Subsequently, Resident in Kashmir and Baroda and Agent to Governor-General in Baluchistan.

Tytler, John Adam (1825–80). Commissioned Bengal Infantry 1844. Mutiny (VC) 1858. Ambeyla Expedition 1863. Hazara Expedition 1868. Lushai Expedition 1871–2. Died of illness at Thal, in the Kurram, February 1880.

Watson, John (1829–1919). Commissioned Bombay Infantry 1848. Second Sikh War 1848–9. Mutiny (VC) 1857–8. Malta 1878. Resident, Gwalior 1881–2. Major-General 1881. Resident, Baroda 1882–88. Lieutenant-General 1887. General 1891.

White, George Stewart (1835–1912). Commissioned 27th Foot 1853. Mutiny, 1857–9. Major 1873. Lieutenant-Colonel 1881. Nile Expedition 1884–5. Third Burmese War 1885–9. Major-General 1887. Zhob Expedition 1890. CinC, India 1893–97. QMG, War Office 1897–99. Natal 1899–1900. Governor of Gibraltar 1901. Field Marshal 1903.

UNITS THAT SERVED IN THE WAR

Unit		Pre-war station	Period of war service
BRITISH CAVALRY			
6th Dragoon Guards		Ambala	Oct 1879–Aug 1880
8th Hussars		UK	Dec 1879–May 1880
9th Lancers		Sialkot	Mar 1879–Dec 1880
10th Hussars		Rawalpindi	Nov 1878–June 1879
13th Hussars		Lucknow	Nov 1880–April 1881
15th Hussars		Meerut	Nov 1878–April 1879
			Aug 1880–Sept 1880
ROYAL ARTILLERY			
D Battery		Meerut	Nov 1878–June 1879
E Battery	A Brigade, RHA	Ambala	Jan 1880–Aug 1880
F Battery		Campbellpore	Nov 1878–May 1880
I Battery		Rawalpindi	Nov 1878–June 1879
			Sept 1879–June 1880
A Battery		Mian Mir	Nov 1878–Aug 1880
D Battery	B Brigade, RHA	Bombay	Jan 1880–April 1881
E Battery		Mhow	Jan 1880–Dec 1880
H Battery	C Brigade, RHA	Sialkot	Dec 1878–May 1879
I Battery		Peshawar	Nov 1878–June 1879
			Dec 1879–Feb 1880
H Battery	1st Brigade, RA	Secunderabad	Nov 1878–April 1881
I Battery		Hyderabad	Dec 1878–March 1879
C Battery		Belgaum	Feb 1880–Oct 1880
D Battery	2nd Brigade, RA	Karachi	Nov 1878–Sept 1879
F Battery		Kirkee/	
		Ahmedabad	Jan 1880–April 1881
C Battery		Jullundur	Nov 1878–June 1879
			Sept 1879–Aug 1880
E Battery	3rd Brigade, RA	Peshawar	Nov 1878–June 1879
			Sept 1879–Oct 1880
G Battery		Rawalpindi	Nov 1878–Aug 1880
A Battery		Agra	Aug 1880–Oct 1880
C Battery		Meerut	Nov 1878–Oct 1880
D Battery	4th Brigade, RA	Benares	Dec 1879–May 1880
E Battery		Multan	Nov 1878–March 1879
G Battery		Mian Mir	Nov 1878–Aug 1880
L Battery	5th Brigade, RA	Meerut	Dec 1879–Aug 1880
1 Battery (Mountain)		Rawalpindi	Oct 1879–Oct 1880
5 Battery (Mountain)		Bombay	Aug 1880–Dec 1880

Unit		Pre-war station	Period of war service
6 Battery (Mountain)	8th Brigade, RA	Lucknow	March 1880–April 1881
13 Battery (Heavy)		Cannanore	Nov 1878–July 1879
16 Battery (Heavy)		Colaba/Toungoo	Nov 1878–July 1879
11 Battery (Mountain)		Rawalpindi	Nov 1878–March 1881
12 Battery (Heavy)		Attock	March 1880–Aug 1880
13 Battery (Heavy)	9th Brigade, RA	Peshawar	Nov 1878–June 1879
14 Battery (Heavy)		Ferozepore	March 1880–April 1881
15 Battery (Garrison)		Mian Mir	Aug 1880–April 1881
5 Battery (Heavy)		Morar	Nov 1879–Nov 1880
6 Battery (Heavy)		Gwalior	Nov 1878–Aug 1880
8 Battery (Heavy)	11th Brigade, RA	Lucknow	Dec 1878–July 1879
10 Battery (Heavy)		Delhi	March 1880–May 1880
11 Battery (Mountain)		Jutogh	Nov 1878–Sept 1880

INDIAN MOUNTAIN ARTILLERY

Unit		Pre-war station	Period of war service
No. 1 (Kohat)		Kohat	Nov 1878–Aug 1880
No. 2 (Derajat)		Abbottabad	Nov 1878–April 1881
No. 3 (Peshawar)		Quetta	Nov 1878–March 1879
No. 4 (Hazara)		Abbottabad	Nov 1878–Aug 1880
No. 5 (Garrison)		Kohat	Nov 1878–Oct 1880
No. 1 Bombay		Rajkot	Aug 1880–Oct 1880
No. 2 Bombay		Jacobabad	Nov 1878–April 1881

INDIAN SAPPERS AND MINERS

Unit		Pre-war station	Period of war service
No. 2 Company		Peshawar	Nov 1878–June 1879
			Sept 1879–Aug 1880
No. 3 Company		Peshawar	Nov 1878–June 1879
			Sept 1879–Aug 1880
No. 4 Company		Roorkee	Nov 1878–Aug 1880
No. 5 Company		Quetta	Nov 1878–June 1879
	Bengal Sappers		Dec 1879–Aug 1880
No. 6 Company	and Miners	Roorkee	Nov 1878–June 1879
			Sept 1879–Aug 1880
No. 7 Company		Rawalpindi	Nov 1878–Aug 1880
No. 8 Company		Roorkee	Nov 1878–June 1879
No. 9 Company		Roorkee	Nov 1878–March 1879
No. 10 Company		Roorkee	Nov 1878–Aug 1880
A Company		Secunderabad	Nov 1879–Aug 1880
B Company		Bangalore	Jan 1879–July 1879
C Company	Madras Sappers and Miners	Rangoon	Dec 1879–Aug 1880
E Company		Bangalore	Jan 1879–July 1879
I Company		Secunderabad	Nov 1879–Aug 1880
K Company		Bangalore	Jan 1879–July 1879
No. 2 Company		Kirkee	Dec 1878–Nov 1880
No. 3 Company	Bombay Sappers	Kirkee/Malta	Jan 1879–April 1881
No. 4 Company	and Miners	Kirkee/Malta	Jan 1879–April 1881
No. 5 Company		Kirkee/Malta	Jan 1879–April 1881

BRITISH INFANTRY

Unit	Pre-war station	Period of war service
1/5th Fusiliers	Chakrata	Nov 1878–June 1879
		Oct 1879–Aug 1880
2/7th Fusiliers	Bombay/ Ahmadnagar	Feb 1880–April 1881

Unit	Pre-war station	Period of war service
2/8th (King's)	Rawalpindi	Nov 1878–Oct 1880
2/9th (East Norfolk)	Peshawar	Nov 1878–May 1879
		Sept 1879–Sept 1880
2/11th (North Devonshire)	Poona	July 1880–April 1881
1/12th (East Suffolk)	Ambala	April 1879–May 1880
2/14th (Prince of Wales's Own)	Raniket	Dec 1879–Aug 1880
2/15th (Yorkshire East Riding)	Deesa	Aug 1880–Nov 1880
1/17th (Leicestershire)	Murree	Nov 1878–Aug 1879
1/18th (Royal Irish)	Ferozepore	Jan 1880–Aug 1880
1/25th (King's Own Borderers)	Faizabad	Nov 1878–May 1879
51st (King's Own Light Infantry)	Subathoo	Nov 1878–June 1879
		Oct 1879–Aug 1880
59th (2nd Nottinghamshire)	Dagshai	Nov 1878–Aug 1880
2/60th (KRRC)	Meerut	Nov 1878–Nov 1880
63rd (West Suffolk)	Ambala	Aug 1880–April 1881
66th (Berkshire)	Colaba/	
	Ahmadnagar	Dec 1878–Oct 1880
67th	Bangalore	Dec 1878–Aug 1880
70th	Multan	Nov 1878–April 1879
72nd Highlanders	Sialkot	Nov 1878–Oct 1880
78th Highlanders	Poona	Aug 1880–April 1881
81st	Peshawar	Nov 1878–Dec 1878
85th (King's Light Infantry)	Lucknow	Sept 1879–Jan 1881
92nd (Gordon) Highlanders	Sitapore/	
	Benares	Dec 1878–Oct 1880
4th Battalion, Rifle Brigade	Peshawar	Nov 1878–Sept 1880

BENGAL CAVALRY

1st	Sialkot	Nov 1878–Sept 1880
3rd	Lucknow	Sept 1879–Oct 1880
4th	Deoli	March 1880–Aug 1880
5th	Nowgong	Jan 1880–April 1881
8th	Multan	Nov 1878–April 1879
		Aug 1880–April 1881
7th	Morar and Sipri	Jan 1881–April 1881
10th (Lancers)	Ambala	Nov 1878–Feb 1880
11th (Lancers)	Nowshera	Nov 1878–May 1879
12th	Jhelum	Nov 1878–Jan 1880
13th (Lancers)	Rawalpindi	Nov 1878–June 1879
		Sept 1879–Oct 1880
14th (Lancers)	Peshawar	Jan 1879–Jan 1880
15th	Cawnpore	Feb 1879–Dec 1879
17th	Peshawar	Sept 1879–Aug 1880
18th	Bareilly	Sept 1879–Oct 1880
19th (Lancers)	Mian Mir	Nov 1878–Aug 1880

BENGAL INFANTRY

1st	Benares	Nov 1878–Aug 1880
2nd	Faizabad	
3rd	Dinapore	Aug 1880–April 1881
4th	Lucknow	Aug 1880–April 1881
5th	Bhagalpore	Nov 1879–Nov 1880
6th	Lucknow	Nov 1878–Aug 1880
8th	Rawalpindi	Aug 1879–Aug 1880
9th	Mian Mir	Jan 1880–Aug 1880

Unit	Pre-war station	Period of war service
11th	Rawalpindi	Jan 1879–June 1880
12th	Jullundur	Nov 1878–March 1879
13th	Agra	Sept 1879–Oct 1881
14th (Sikh)	Peshawar	Nov 1878–Dec 1878
15th (Sikh)	Sialkot	Nov 1878–Dec 1880
16th	Calcutta	Feb 1880–Aug 1880
17th	Morar	Aug 1880–April 1881
19th (Punjab)	Multan	Nov 1878–Aug 1880
20th (Punjab)	Peshawar	Nov 1878–June 1879
21st (Punjab)	Rawalpindi	Nov 1878–Oct 1880
22nd (Punjab)	Peshawar	Sept 1879–Aug 1880
23rd (Punjab) (Pioneers)	Mian Mir	Nov 1878–Sept 1880
24th (Punjab)	Jhansi	Nov 1878–Sept 1880
25th (Punjab)	Cawnpore	Nov 1878–Oct 1880
26th (Punjab)	Mian Mir	Nov 1878–March 1879
27th (Punjab)	Nowshera	Nov 1878–Aug 1880
28th (Punjab)	Moradabad	Dec 1878–Aug 1880
29th (Punjab)	Talagaon	Nov 1878–Oct 1880
30th (Punjab)	Ferozepore	Sept 1879–Aug 1880
31st (Punjab)	Rawalpindi	Sept 1879–Aug 1880
32nd (Punjab) (Pioneers)	Quetta	Nov 1878–April 1879
39th	Meerut	March 1879–Nov 1879
41st	Morar	Jan 1880–Aug 1880
45th (Sikh)	Alipore	Nov 1878–Aug 1880
1st Gurkha (Light Infantry)	Dharamsala	Nov 1878–April 1879
		Dec 1879–Aug 1880
2nd Gurkha (Prince of Wales's Own)	Cyprus	Dec 1878–June 1879
		Sept 1879–Sept 1880
3rd Gurkha	Almora	Nov 1878–Sept 1880
4th Gurkha	Bakloh	Nov 1878–June 1879
		Sept 1879–Nov 1880
5th Gurkha	Abbottabad	Nov 1878–Nov 1880
PUNJAB FRONTIER FORCE		
1st Punjab Cavalry	Dera Ghazi Khan	Nov 1878–Aug 1880
2nd Punjab Cavalry	Rajanpore	Nov 1878–Aug 1880
3rd Punjab Cavalry	Edwardesbad	March 1880–Dec 1880
5th Punjab Cavalry	Kohat	Nov 1878–March 1880
Guides (Cavalry and Infantry)	Mardan	Nov 1878–June 1879
		Sept 1879–Aug 1880
1st Sikh Infantry	Kohat	Nov 1878–June 1879
2nd Sikh Infantry	Dera Ghazi Khan	Nov 1878–Dec 1880
3rd Sikh Infantry	Dera Ismail Khan	Sept 1879–Nov 1880
1st Punjab Infantry	Quetta	Nov 1878–March 1879
2nd Punjab Infantry	Kohat	Nov 1878–April 1879
4th Punjab Infantry	Edwardesbad	Oct 1879–Dec 1879
5th Punjab Infantry	Kohat	Nov 1878–Aug 1880
MADRAS CAVALRY		
1st Light Cavalry	Secunderabad	April 1880–March 1881
MADRAS INFANTRY		
1st	Secunderabad	Oct 1879–Aug 1880

Unit	Pre-war station	Period of war service
4th	Bangalore	Oct 1879–Aug 1880
15th	Bangalore	Oct 1879–Aug 1880
21st	Bellary	Dec 1878–Dec 1879
30th	French Rocks	Jan 1879–Nov 1880
36th	Bangalore	Jan 1879–June 1879
BOMBAY CAVALRY		
2nd Light Cavalry	Deesa/Rajkot	Feb 1880–April 1881
3rd Light Cavalry	Nimach/	
	Nasirabad	Feb 1880–April 1881
Poona Horse	Sirur	Jan 1880–April 1881
1st Sind Horse	Jacobabad	Jan 1881–April 1881
2nd Sind Horse	Jacobabad	Nov 1878–April 1879
		Feb 1880–April 1881
3rd Sind Horse	Jacobabad	Nov 1878–Oct 1880
BOMBAY INFANTRY		
1st (Grenadiers)	Ahmedabad	Dec 1878–Oct 1880
4th	Sattara/Bombay	Feb 1880–April 1881
5th	Poona	Jan 1880–April 1881
8th	Poona	Aug 1880–April 1881
9th	Malta	Jan 1880–April 1881
10th	Nimach	Feb 1880–April 1881
13th	Mhow	Aug 1880–April 1881
15th	Ahmednagar	Aug 1880–April 1881
16th	Malegaon	Jan 1880–April 1881
19th	Karachi	Dec 1878–March 1881
23rd	Mhow	March 1880–April 1881
24th	Mehidpore/Agar	Feb 1880–April 1881
27th (Belooch)	Hyderabad/Sind	Nov 1878–April 1881
28th	Rajkot	Jan 1880–April 1881
29th (Belooch)	Dera Ghazi	
	Khan/	
	Rajanpore	Nov 1878–March 1881
30th (Jacob's Rifles)	Jacobabad	Nov 1878–Oct 1880
HYDERABAD CONTINGENT		
3rd Cavalry	Aurangabad	July 1880–Sept 1880
LOCAL CORPS		
Central India Horse	Gunah/Agar	Dec 1879–Oct 1880
Bhopal Battalion	Sehore	Nov 1878–June 1879
Mhairwarra Battalion	Ajmer	Nov 1878–June 1879
Deoli Battalion	Deoli	Feb 1880–Aug 1880

TOTAL   35 Cavalry Regiments
            95 Infantry Battalions
            45 Batteries of Artillery
            19 Companies of Sappers and Miners

APPENDIX 4

NOTES ON UNIFORMS

The use of mud-coloured clothing for active service had been pioneered in India by Lumsden when he formed the Guides in 1849. Its use became widespread during the Mutiny. Although the term 'khaki' (from the Urdu word for dust) was subsequently used generically for this type of clothing, the colour was not standard and reflected the different methods of dyeing – coffee-grounds, curry powder, cold tea, bazaar dyes of various kinds. By 1878, khaki was in general use in India for hot-weather campaigning, but colour, type of cloth and design continued to vary widely. Eaton Travers recorded in his diary that the Bengal Sappers and Miners had 'gone in for khakhie, but of a most curious colour, a sort of very green olive. I think we have very nearly every imaginable shade represented here now.'[1]

British Troops

Infantry regiments of the line appear to have started the campaign in their cold-weather undress serge (red, blue or green as appropriate) uniforms. A khaki cloth or tweed jacket was often worn over the serge, supplemented as necessary by greatcoats and Afghan sheepskin coats (poshteen). In the depths of winter, jerseys and jerkins of various kinds were added as well. In hot weather, the serge uniforms were replaced by light-weight khaki obtained in the first instance by dyeing the white hot-weather clothing issued in peacetime India.

The 92nd Highlanders wore the kilt throughout and the 72nd wore tartan trews, both with khaki jackets. Sir Ian Hamilton, of the 92nd, noted that '[we] dyed our white summer drill coats . . . by boiling them up with tea leaves. We wore these in winter over our red serges. Towards the close of the campaign in 1880 we were issued with Khaki cloth or drill.'

A scarlet tunic in the Regimental Museum of the King's Regiment is catalogued as having been worn by Sergeant T. Howard of 2nd Battalion, 8th Foot at the storming of the Peiwar Kotal.[2] This was probably worn under a khaki jacket because I have found no evidence of scarlet being worn uncovered in action.

Cavalry and artillery wore their normal Indian cold-weather blue serge uniforms at the start of the campaign and during the subsequent winters, supplemented by greatcoats, poshteen, jerkins and jerseys.[3] In the warm weather, the cavalry and horsed artillery wore khaki tunics over blue or, later, khaki breeches.[4]

The normal service headdress was the white or khaki tropical helmet. This consisted of a wickerwork frame covered in cloth. It was frequently criticized as being a 'bug trap'. The 'pillbox' hat was often worn off duty or on sentry duty in cold weather.

Officers appear broadly to have followed other ranks, but with a great deal of diversity as to pattern. Major Kinloch, DAQMG of the Peshawar Valley Field Force, in a paper to the Eden Commission, commented 'The first thing that nearly every officer who was ordered on service for the late Afghan campaign proceeded to do was to discard nearly the whole of his uniform and adopt some other dress and a new equipment varying according to individual tastes. The result was that everyone wore 'fancy dress' and it was quite impossible to tell the rank of an officer or even what branch of the service he belonged to.' Le Mesurier, making much the same point, reveals that he himself had ordered two sets of uniform to his own design! One item however which rapidly became universal was the famous belt invented by Sam Browne himself.[5]

Other ranks wore ammunition boots with puttees or gaiters, except that cavalry troopers and artillery drivers often wore knee-boots. Officers tended to follow suit.

Some regiments, but not necessarily all, took their full dress with them or subsequently had it sent up to them. These included the 67th, 92nd, 2/60th, 9th Lancers and Royal Horse Artillery. Combe recorded, apropos the review at Kabul on 8 December 1879, that 'the Royal Horse Artillery, 9th Lancers and 92nd Highlanders have all their Full Dress and turn out as they would at home, and they looked splendid this morning.'

Indian Troops

The native infantry, except Gurkhas, wore khaki drill in hot weather and a heavier-weight khaki uniform in winter, supplemented by greatcoat and poshteen. (In evidence to the Eden Commission, Major Ross of 1st Sikh Infantry reported that on crossing the frontier on 20 November 1878 the men wore khaki drill coat and knickerbockers and carried a cloth coat, greatcoat and poshteen.)[6] In winter, they wore the cloth coat with khaki drill knickerbockers, plus jersey, poshteen and greatcoat. Some regiments may have taken their full-dress scarlet coats for ceremonial purposes. The Gurkhas appear to have worn their dark-green cloth uniforms in winter, changing to khaki as the war progressed.

Gaiters or puttees were worn with native shoes or sandals of Indian pattern, which proved quite useless in the stony wastes of Afghanistan. Ammunition boots were issued on payment to some regiments particularly Gurkhas, and Roberts found that a shoe of Kabuli design was very serviceable and recommended its general adoption. Regiments wore their regimental pattern of turban except the Gurkhas who wore their own special pillbox.

Native cavalry normally wore khaki *kurtas* or *alkalaks* (knee-length blouse-coats), with pyjamas and long boots, in the summer and blue serge *kurtas/alkalaks* in winter. Le Mesurier records the 19th Bengal Lancers at Kandahar in February 1879 as wearing blue serge *kurtas*, loose yellow pyjamas with long boots and blue *pagris* (turbans) over a red *kulla* (pointed cap).[7] Combe, at Kandahar in September 1880, noted that the men of the 3rd Bombay Light Cavalry wore large turbans of blue and red, loose short blouses, pants and knee-boots.[8] No. 2 Mountain Battery at Kabul in the spring of 1880 is recorded as wearing blue serge; it had crossed the frontier in November 1878 in khaki drill.[9] Photographs taken at Sherpur in December 1879 show the Bengal Sappers and Miners wearing blue serge.

General Comment

It is clear from the wide variations and improvisations and subsequent comment that the uniform situation was not satisfactory. The Eden Commission reported acidly that: 'It is undeniable that during the recent campaigns officers and men, as far as they could, left off their uniform and took to improvised service clothing. A majority of officers are agreed that this system is bad and that some part at any rate of Her Majesty's uniform ought to be fit for use as a serviceable clothing in the field; we feel that this view is undoubtedly correct.'[10] What was wanted was a suitable pattern of khaki drill uniform for summer and khaki serge for winter campaigning, and for the native infantry to wear proper boots rather than native shoes or sandals. By 1914 that was how service dress had broadly evolved.

NOTES

1. Travers, Diary, 24 October 1878 (at Multan).

2. See JSAHR, Museums Supplement No. 14 (1952), p. XXX.

3. Le Mesurier records the 15th Hussars at Kandahar in February 1879 as wearing blue cloth with yellow facings, black knee-length boots and khaki helmets. Op. cit., p. 127.

4. Combe noted in October 1878 that 'our new Khakhie equipment (blouses and helmet covers) looks very serviceable and workmanlike, and is very comfortable'. Combe, op. cit., p. 8.

5. 'We have all discarded our uniform sword-belts and taken to the "Sam Browne Belt", which is now worn by almost every officer in the force.'

6. Travers described the 30th Bombay Native Infantry in December 1878 as wearing short, tight-fitting khaki jackets with trousers of the same material, and brown leather gaiters and boots, with turban. Travers, Diary, 24 December 1878.

7. Le Mesurier, op. cit., pp. 128–9.

8. Combe, op. cit., p. 198.

9. Brigadier-General R. A. L. Graham *A History of the Indian Mountain Artillery* (Aldershot, 1957), p. 47n.

10. Cf. also, Combe's comment 'It is perfectly absurd the way everything "Regulation" is discarded directly a regiment takes the field, showing that our uniform is certainly not a practical one.' (Op. cit., p. 145.)

VCs AND CAMPAIGN MEDALS

Sixteen VCs were awarded during the war, all to Europeans since native soldiers were not at this time eligible. The recipients were:

Name	Unit	Action
Reverend J. W. Adams	Bengal Ecclesiastical Department	Saving men at Kila Kazi outside Kabul, 11 December 1879.
Private J. Ashford	7th Foot (Royal Fusiliers) }	Rescuing a wounded soldier at Deh Khoja, 16 August 1880.
Lieutenant W. L. Chase	28th Bombay NI	
Gunner J. Collis	Royal Horse Artillery	Bravery under fire during retreat from Maiwand, 27 July 1880.
Captain J. Cook	5th Gurkhas	Gallantry in leading attack at the Peiwar Kotal, 12 December 1878.
Captain O'Moore Creagh	Mhairwarra Battalion	Defence of Kam Dakka, 22 April 1879.
Lieutenant W. H. Dick Cunyngham	92nd Highlanders	Gallantry in leading assault on Takht-i-Shah, 13 December 1879.
Lieutenant W. P. Hamilton	Guides Cavalry	Gallantry in leading charge at Fatehbad, 2 April 1879.
Captain A. G. Hammond	Guides Infantry	Gallantry in covering retreat from Asmai Heights, 14 December 1879.
Lieutenant R. C. Hart	Royal Engineers	Rescuing a wounded soldier, 31 January 1879.
Captain E. P. Leach	Royal Engineers	Gallantry in the action at Maidanak, 17 March 1879.
Sergeant P. Mullane	Royal Horse Artillery	Rescuing a wounded soldier at Maiwand, 27 July 1880.
Captain E. H. Sartorius	59th Foot	Gallantry in leading attack at Shahjui, 24 October 1879.
Lance-Corporal G. Sellar	72nd Highlanders	Gallantry in attack on Asmai Heights, 14 December 1879.
Captain W. J. Vousden	5th Punjab Cavalry	Gallantry in leading cavalry charge at Kabul, 14 December 1879.
Major G. S. White	92nd Highlanders	For gallant leadership at Charasiab, 6 October 1879 and Kandahar, 1 September 1880.

Two campaign awards were made. The campaign medal proper was issued to all who served beyond the boundaries of India between 21 November 1878 and 1 September 1880. It is of silver (although some rare specimens in bronze are apparently known); on the obverse is the head of Queen Victoria; on the reverse is a scene of marching soldiers with an elephant carrying a gun in the foreground and the date '1878–79–80'. The ribbon is green with a red bar at each end.

Six bars were awarded: 'ALI MASJID', 'PEIWAR KOTAL', 'CHARASIA', 'AHMED KHEL', 'KABUL' (for the period 10–23 December 1879) and

'KANDAHAR' (for the reconnaissance of 30 August 1880 and the battle on 1 September 1880).

Those who took part in the march from Kabul to Kandahar in August 1880 received the Kabul-Kandahar Star. It was cast in bronze with the recipient's name on the back. The ribbon is the rainbow-pattern used previously for some of the First Afghan War medals such as the Jellalabad Medal (1842) – red shading into white shading into yellow shading into white shading into blue; it is supposed to represent the colours of the Indian sunrise.

APPENDIX 6

CASUALTIES

Hanna put the overall total at 40,000 but did not say what that included or how it had been arrived at. I have found no detailed official record of casualties on the British side.

In the six major actions (Ali Masjid, Peiwar Kotal, Charasiab, Ahmed Khel, Maiwand and Kandahar) casualties totalled 1,075 dead and 682 wounded. In the various lesser actions and skirmishes of the war, they totalled some 420 dead and 730 wounded. A proportion of the wounded – perhaps 25 per cent – died subsequently of their wounds, giving a grand total of some 1,850 killed in action or died of wounds.

Very much larger numbers of men died of disease, either in Afghanistan or subsequently as a result of disease contracted on active service. Of the 135 officers who died as a result of the war, 67 were, in effect, battle casualties, 64 died from disease and four were killed accidentally. If one were to apply the same proportions overall to all troops, one would arrive at a figure of some 1,800 deaths from disease. But the figure is clearly much too low. Even in peacetime, the average number of deaths from disease among Europeans of the Bengal Army was 1,100 a year between 1870 and 1879. On the native side, 1,282 soldiers died in hospital in 1879. Some regiments in Afghanistan clearly suffered heavily – for example, the 2/11th Foot lost at least 120 men during the relatively short period it was on active service and the 1st Punjab Infantry lost 67 men in the six months from November 1878 to May 1879. If one were to assume that each cavalry and infantry regiment lost 60 men on average, and artillery and engineers the same in proportion, one arrives at a theoretical total of nearly 8,000 deaths from disease. Spread over the 2½ years of the war, this represents some 3,200 deaths a year which is about a third more than the normal loss of the Bengal Army in peacetime. It would mean that with battle casualties, the British lost nearly 10,000 men dead.

Non-fatal cases of sickness clearly vastly out-numbered fatalities. Many cases probably never even reached the hospitals. Some instances of regiments badly hit by sickness are recorded in various chapters of this book, but an overall calculation is not worth attempting. If Hanna's figures referred to deaths, it is too high. But it may not be too far adrift if it allows for cases of sickness – if anything, it may then be too low.

There is no possibility of assessing Afghan losses with any degree of precision. Their battle casualties were clearly much higher. In the six major actions alone, plus the attack on Sherpur, they probably lost upwards of 5,000 dead, and deaths from wounds are also likely to have been proportionately much higher than on the British side. Deaths from disease may well have been lower because of acclimatization. It would in any case be impossible to distinguish deaths from disease caused by participation in the war from those due to the normal incidence of disease among the population. Equally impossible to disentangle is the incidence of death, particularly among women and children, caused by starvation and the other side-effects of war. Clearly the war was not cheap in terms of human life or suffering.

SELECT BIBLIOGRAPHY

Manuscript Sources

Lytton Papers (India Office Library) MSS Eur E218
- 516 Letters from the Secretary of State
- 517 Letters from England
- 518 Letters dispatched
- 519 Correspondence in India
- 521 Miscellaneous papers on Afghanistan

Roberts Papers (National Army Museum)
7101-23-101 Correspondence with India and England, 1878–80
     -139 Scrapbooks of Press cuttings
     -147 Miscellaneous letters and telegrams, 1879–80
     -148 Confidential Reports on officers of the Kurram Force
     -149 Notes by Colonel Sir Neville Chamberlain
     -152 Miscellaneous financial papers
     -153 Criticisms of Hanna's *History* by Colonel Sir Neville Chamberlain
     -154 Miscellaneous papers
7101-24-92-18 Diary for 1878
     -19 Diary for 1879

Haines Papers (National Army Museum) Accession No. 8108-9 47 Volumes
Hogg Papers (Royal Military College Collections, Sandhurst)
Slade, Captain J. R. Manuscript letters, 1880 (Royal United Services Institute)
Travers, Lieutenant Eaton. Diary, 1878–80 (Gurkha Museum, Church Crookham)
Courts Martial proceedings on Major Currie and Colonel Malcolmson 1881. India
  Office Library L/Mil/3/915

Parliamentary Papers

C2190 - Correspondence Respecting the Relations between the British Govern-
  ment and that of Afghanistan since the Accession of the Ameer Shere Ali Khan.
  HMSO, 1878
C2401 - Further Correspondence. HMSO, 1879
C2402, C2190, C2250 - Further Papers Relating to the Affairs of Afghanistan.
  HMSO, 1878–9
C2736 - Papers Relating to the Advance of Ayub Khan on Kandahar. HMSO, 1880
C2811 - Papers Relating to the Occupation of Kandahar. HMSO, 1881
C2457 - Correspondence Relative to the Affairs of Afghanistan. HMSO, 1880
C2560 - Correspondence Relating to the Estimates for the War in Afghanistan.
  HMSO, 1880
C2617 - Further Correspondence Relating to the Estimates for the War in
  Afghanistan. HMSO, 1880
C2772 - Further Correspondence Relating to the Estimates for the War in
  Afghanistan. HMSO, 1881

C2776 - Further Correspondence Relating to the Affairs of Afghanistan. HMSO, 1881

C2523 - Dispatch from the Government of India (with report of Lieutenant-General F. S. Roberts). HMSO, 1880

Other Printed Papers

The Second Afghan War, 1878–80. Abridged Official Account. London, 1908

Report of the Special Commission to inquire into the Organization and Expenditure of the Army in India. Government Central Press, Simla, 1879

Army Medical Department Report for 1880 (Appendix 3 – Special Report on wars in Afghanistan). HMSO, 1882

The Second Afghan War (6 vols.). Government Central Press, Simla, 1885

Papers Connected with the Return of the Northern Afghanistan Field Force to India from 7 June 1880 to 31 August 1880. (QMG India's Department). Calcutta, 1881

The Anglo-Afghan War, 1878–79 (Compiled by Captain A. R. Savile and Captain F. H. W. Milner). Simla, 1878–79

Summary of the Preparations preceding . . . war with Afghanistan . . . and or operations during 1878–79. Simla, 1879

Reports and Narratives of officers . . . engaged at Battle of Maiwand. Simla, 1881

Papers connected with Operations in Southern Afghanistan. Calcutta, 1881

Diary of the Third Afghan War (C. M. MacGregor) (Royal Society for Asian Affairs Library, reference no. 59 HC)

General Background

Alder, G. J. *British India's Northern Frontier, 1865–1895.* London, 1963

Bellew, H. W. *The North West Frontier and Afghanistan.* Lahore, 1879

Caroe, Sir Olaf. *The Pathans.* London

Cecil, Lady Gwendolen. *Life of Robert, Marquis of Salisbury, 1830–1902* (4 vols.) London, 1921–32

Cheshire, H. T. 'The Expansion of Imperial Russia to the Indian Border'. *Slavonic Review*, XIII, 1934–5

Dallin, D. J. *The Rise of Russia in Asia.* London, 1950

Davies, C. C. *The Problem of the North-West Frontier, 1890–1908.* Cambridge, 1932

Dilks, David. *Curzon in India*: vol. 2 – *Frustration.* London, 1970

Duthie, J. L. 'Some further insights into the working of mid-Victorian Imperialism; Lord Salisbury and Anglo-Afghan relations 1874–1876.' *Journal of Imperial and Commonwealth History*, vol. VIII, 1979–80

Elliott, Major-General J. G. *The Frontier, 1839–1947.* London, 1968

Fraser-Tytler, Sir W. *Afghanistan: a study of political developments in Central Asia.* Oxford, 2nd edn., 1953

Gimlette, Lieutenant-Colonel G. H. D. *A Postscript to the Records of the Indian Mutiny.* London, 1927

Holdich, Sir T. H. *The Indian Borderland, 1880–1900.* London, 1901

Holdich, Sir T. H. *India.* London, 1906

Ingram, Edward. *In Defence of British India.* London, 1984

Ingram, Edward. *The Beginning of the Great Game in Asia, 1828–1834.* Oxford, 1979

Ingram, Edward. 'The Defence of British India'. *Journal of Indian History*, XLVIII (1970), XLIX (1971), Golden Jubilee Volume (1973)

Klein, Ira. 'The Anglo-Russian Convention and the Problems of Central Asia, 1907–1914'. *Journal of British Studies*, XI (1971)

Lutyens, Mary. *The Lyttons in India*. London, 1979
Malleson, Colonel G. B. *A History of Afghanistan*. London, 1878
Martineau, J. *The Life and Correspondence of the Right Hon. Sir Bartle Frere* (2 vols.). London, 1895
Moneypenny, W. F. and Buckle, G. E. *Life of Disraeli* (6 vols.). London, 1920
Phillips, C. H. *The East India Company, 1784–1834*.
Pierce, R. A. *Russian Central Asia, 1857–1917*. Berkeley, 1960
Sykes, Sir P. *A History of Afghanistan* (2 vols.). London, 1900
Walsh, W. B. 'The Imperial Russian General Staff and India: a footnote to diplomatic history', *Russian Review*, XVI (1957)
Wheeler, Geoffrey. *The Modern History of Soviet Central Asia*. London, 1964
Williams, B. J. 'The Strategic Background to the Anglo-Russian Entente of August 1907', *Historical Journal*, IX
Yapp, M. E. *Strategies of British India*. Oxford, 1980

Anglo-Afghan Relations

Alder, G. J. 'The Key to India?: Britain and the Herat Problem 1830–1863', *Middle Eastern Studies*, X (1974)
Alder, G. J. 'Britain and the Defence of India – the origins of the problem, 1798–1815', *Journal of Asian History*, VI (1972)
Afghan Committee. *The Causes of the Afghan War*. London, 1879
Argyll, 8th Duke of. *The Afghan Question from 1841 to 1878*. London, 1879
Balfour, Countess of. *The History of Lord Lytton's Indian Administration 1876–1880*. London, 1899
Balfour, Countess of (ed). *Personal and Literary Letters of Robert, First Earl of Lytton* (2 vols.). London, 1906
Chakravarty, S. *From Khyber to Oxus: A Study in Imperial Expansion*. New Delhi, 1976
Cowling, Maurice. 'Lytton, The Cabinet and the Russians, August to November 1878', *English Historical Review*, LXXVI (1961)
Durand, Sir H. *The Amir Abdur Rahman Khan*. London, 1907
Edwards, H. S. *Russian Projects against India, from the Czar Peter to General Skoboleff*. London, 1885
Evans, de Lacey. *On the Practicability of an Invasion of British India*. London, 1829
Elphinstone, Mountstuart. *An Account of the Kingdom of Caubul*. London, 1815
Forrest, G. W. *Life of Sir Neville Chamberlain*. London, 1909
Ghose, D. K. *England and Afghanistan*. Calcutta, 1960
Gopal, S. *British Policy in India, 1858–1905*. Oxford, 1965
Gopal, S. *The Viceroyalty of Lord Ripon, 1880–1884*. London, 1953
Greaves, R. L. *Persia and the Defence of India, 1884–92*. London, 1959
Habberton, W. 'Anglo-Russian relations concerning Afghanistan, 1837–1907', *University of Illinois Studies in the Social Sciences*, XXI (1937)
Hambly, G. R. G. 'Unrest in Northern India during the Viceroyalty of Lord Mayo: the background to Lord Northbrook's policy of inactivity', *Journal of the Royal Central Asian Society*, XLVII (1961)
Klein, Ira. 'Who made the Second Afghan War?', *Journal of Asian History*, vol. 8, No. 2 (1974)
Kundu, N. 'The Afghan Policy of Lord Lawrence, 1864–69', *Unpublished MA thesis*, London University
Huttenback, R. A. *British Relations with Sind, 1799–1843*. Berkeley, 1962
Lambrick, H. T. *Sir Charles Napier and Sind*. Oxford, 1952
McNeill, J. *The Progress and Present Position of Russia in the East*. London, 1836

Moulton, E. C. *Lord Northbrook's Indian Administration, 1872–1876*. London, 1968
Norris, J. A. *The First Afghan War, 1838–1842*. Cambridge, 1967
Pal, D. *The Administration of Sir John Lawrence in India, 1864–69*. Simla, 1952
Rawlinson, Sir H. *England and Russia in the East*. London, 1875
Singhal, D. P. *India and Afghanistan, 1876–1907*. Queensland, 1963
Thornton, J. *Life of Sir Robert Sandeman*
Thornton, A. P. 'Afghanistan in Anglo-Russia Diplomacy 1869–73', *Cambridge Historical Journal*, XI (1953–55)
Thornton, A. P. 'The Re-opening of the Central Asian Question, 1864–9', *History*, XLI (1956)
Thornton, A. P. 'British Policy in Persia 1858–90', *English Historical Review*, LXIX (1954–5)

Operations, 1878–81

Berridge, P. S. A. *Couplings to the Khyber*. Newton Abbott, 1969
Cadell, Sir P. *The History of the Bombay Army*. London, 1938
Colquhoun, Major J. A. S. *With the Kurram Field Force, 1878–79*. London, 1881
Combe, Captain B. A. *Letters from Afghanistan, 1879–80*. Privately printed, London, 1880
Cooper, Private H. *What the Fusiliers did*. Lahore, 1880
Crane, Private B. P. *The Ninth Lancers in Afghanistan, 1878–80*. London, 2nd edn., N.D.
Duke, J. *Recollections of the Cabul Campaign, 1879 and 1880*. London, 1883
Elsmie, G. R. *Life of Field Marshal Sir Donald Stewart*. London, 1903
Gough, General Sir Hugh, VC. 'Old Memories: Afghanistan 1878–80', *Pall Mall Gazette*, 1898–99
Hamilton, Lieutenants P. F. B. and E. O. F. *Letters from Afghanistan 1878–80*. Privately printed. Dublin, 1881
Hanna, Colonel H. B. *The Second Afghan War, 1878–79–80*, (3 vols.). London, 1899–1910
Harrison, Frederick. *Martial Law in Kabul*. London, 1880
Heathcote, T. A. *The Afghan Wars, 1839–1919*. London, 1980
Hensman, Howard. *The Afghan War of 1879–80*. 2nd edn., London, 1882
Hills, Major-General Sir J. *The Bombay Field Force, 1880*. 1900
James, David. *Lord Roberts*. London, 1954
Khan, Sultan M. *The Life of Abdur Rahman* (2 vols.). London, 1900
Le Mesurier, Major A. *Kandahar in 1879*. London, 1880
Male, Revd. Arthur. *Scenes Through the Battlesmoke*. London, 1891
MacGregor, Major-General Sir C. M. *The Life and Opinions of Major-General Sir C. M. MacGregor* (2 vols.). London, 1888
—— *War in Afghanistan 1879–80: the personal diary of Major-General Sir Charles Metcalfe MacGregor* Ed. William Trousdale. Wayne State University Press, Detroit 1985
Maxwell, Leigh. *My God! Maiwand*. London, 1979
Mitford, Major R. C. W. *To Cabul with the Cavalry Brigade*. London, 1881
Petre, F. Lorraine. *The Royal Berkshire Regiment*. vol. I, Reading, 1925
Roberts, Field Marshal Lord, VC. *Forty-One Years in India*. (2 vols.). London, 1897
Robertson, Lieutenant C. G. *Kurum, Kabul and Kandahar*. Edinburgh, 1881
Robson, Brian. 'Maiwand, 27th July 1880', *Journal of the Society for Army Historical Research*, 1973
Shadbolt, S. H. *The Afghan Campaigns of 1878–80*. (2 vols.). London, 1882
Shepherd, Major E. W. *The Ninth Queen's Royal Lancers, 1715–1936*. London, 1939

Sobolev, Major-General L. *The Anglo-Afghan Struggle* (translated and condensed). Calcutta, 1885

Trousdale, William (ed). *The Gordon Creeds in Afghanistan*. London, 1984

Swinnerton, Revd. C. *The Afghan War: Gough's action at Futtehbad*. London, 1880

INDEX

(Note: ranks are those held during the war)